MASTERING

CATE~~RING~~

D1424288

MACMILLAN MASTER SERIES

Accounting
Advanced English Language
Advanced Pure Mathematics
Arabic
Banking
Basic Management
Biology
British Politics
Business Administration
Business Communication
Business Law
Business Microcomputing
C Programming
Chemistry
COBOL Programming
Commerce
Communication
Computers
Databases
Economic and Social History
Economics
Electrical Engineering
Electronic and Electrical Calculations
Electronics
English as a Foreign Language
English Grammar
English Language
English Literature
English Spelling
French

French 2
German
German 2
Human Biology
Italian
Italian 2
Japanese
Manufacturing
Marketing
Mathematics
Mathematics for Electrical and
    Electronic Engineering
Modern British History
Modern European History
Modern World History
Pascal Programming
Philosophy
Photography
Physics
Psychology
Science
Social Welfare
Sociology
Spanish
Spanish 2
Spreadsheets
Statistics
Study Skills
Word Processing

MASTERING

CATERING

THEORY

EUNICE TAYLOR
BSc(Hons), MIFST, MCFA, CertEd

and

JERRY TAYLOR
BA, MEd, FCHIMA, FCFA, LCG

MACMILLAN

First published 1990 by
MACMILLAN PRESS LTD
Houndmills, Basingstoke, Hampshire RG21 6XS
and London
Companies and representatives
throughout the world

ISBN 0–333–47190–3 hardcover
ISBN 0–333–47191–1 paperback
ISBN 0–333–47192–X paperback export

A catalogue record for this book is available
from the British Library.

10   9   8   7   6   5   4   3
03   02   01   00   99   98   97   96

Printed in Malaysia

To our daughters, Joanne and Shelley

CONTENTS

CONTENTS

CONTENTS

LIST OF PLATES

LIST OF FIGURES

LIST OF FIGURES

LIST OF TABLES

LIST OF TABLES

ACKNOWLEDGEMENTS

The authors would like to thank the following:

Martin Brito LCG, ACF, CertEd
Dillip Banerjee MBBS, PhD, MD, FRCPath
Kamlesh Banerjee BSc, MSc, PhD, CertEd
Harry L Cracknell FHCIMA, FCFA, ARSH
Mostyn Davey BA(Oxon), MSc, PhD, CertEd
Tony Deag BSc(Hons), DMS, MIEHO
Rev Dr Peter C Graves ThM, CEd
Terry Pugh MHCIMA, MCFA
Ken Melsom JP, FHCIMA, MBIM, MRIPHH
Linda Redding BSc(Hons)
Ann Walker BSc, PhD, DipTropAgr, AIFST
B. S. Ward FHCIMA, MCFA
Ian Woods CertEd
Mary Withall BSc, MIBiol, AMHCIMA, MRSH, MAHE
Ken Woodward LHCIMA, MRIPHH, ACF

The author and publishers wish to acknowledge the following photographic sources: The Anthony Blake Photo Library; Mary Evans Picture Library. And grateful thanks go to Compeat Nutritional Analysis System Life Line Services Ltd, London, for permission to use copyright material.

THE CATERING INDUSTRY

1.1 THE HISTORY AND DEVELOPMENT OF CATERING

Introduction

The provision of shelter, food and drink for travellers has been a feature of civilised societies at least since ancient Greek and Roman times. This section briefly traces the history of catering in Britain through recent times to highlight the nature of the catering business and some of the principles that are characteristic of all catering operations.

Eleventh to fifteenth century

During the Middle Ages the number of travellers, despite being limited by poor roads and dangerous routes, increased. They were concerned with religious pilgrimages or trade and stayed in monasteries or private houses. The private houses became the first inns and offered typically a simple meal eaten in a hall which was later used for sleeping. At this period taverns emerged as a rendezvous for the local community offering food, wine and entertainment alongside the long-established ale houses serving only beer.

Sixteenth to eighteenth century

The period after the Middle Ages saw the emergence of the stagecoach creating a further demand for travellers' accommodation. Facilities at the larger commercial inns were improved particularly as a result of the increased wealth of their clientèle, brought about by the Industrial Revolution. The seventeenth century saw the introduction of coffee and then chocolate into Europe. Despite condemnation from King and Bishops against the *evil and dangerous effects*, a taste for these *exotic* beverages swept the country. They were served in coffee and chocolate houses which became popular meeting-places for artists, poets, lawyers, etc. and were very exclusive. This led directly to the exclusive (members only) British institution, *the club*.

Nineteenth century

The early nineteenth century saw the emergence of the railways, with a further demand for hospitality away from home, giving rise to the large Railway Hotels. The railway, and the newly developed motor-car, vastly increased the number of people who could experience the health-giving properties of the sea. Seaside hotels and boarding houses sprang up at every suitable resort. By the end of the nineteenth century clubs, large hotels and some independent restaurants were offering dining-out facilities. Such establishments were high-class, sophisticated, expensive, and becoming very popular. This expansion of eating out was a very significant development for the catering industry as the expertise required to organise and run it was imported from the continent.

Escoffier (see Plate 1.1), who had established a reputation as a first-class chef in France, came to England in 1889, initially to join César Ritz at the Savoy Hotel. As a team, they went on to the Ritz and later Escoffier worked at the Carlton Hotel. Escoffier was responsible for

Plate 1.1 *Auguste Escoffier*

establishing a model of excellence in cuisine that is still the greatest influence for cooks 100 years later.

A further development at this time was a demand for less expensive eating places for people who could not afford these restaurants. This led to the creation of cafés and tea shops and eventually to the less exclusive, cheaper commercial restaurants.

Twentieth century

The First (1914–1918) and Second (1939–1945) World Wars brought about an increase in the number of industrial canteens. During the Second World War communal feeding emerged on a very large scale so that maximum use could be made of the limited food available. Hotels and boarding houses were requisitioned for the troops and for various government departments and the industry suffered a temporary set-back. Between the wars there was a large increase in travel both inland and abroad. The introduction of holidays *with pay* increased still further the need for accommodation away from home, and holiday camps emerged. These catered for a large section of the population, providing one of the first *package holidays*. At this time the availability and popularity of fresh milk and ice-cream increased and the first of many 'milk bars' were opened in Fleet Street in 1935.

Since the end of the Second World War, there have been a large number of developments in the industry, such as mass catering, fast food and speciality operations. Table 1.1, whilst not exhaustive, identifies some of these innovations, as well as some of their forerunners. It is important to realise that the industry is made up of many different kinds of operations providing very different jobs and career opportunities.

Table 1.1 *Overview of some developments in Britain relevant to catering*

1183	Public cook-houses in London
1551	Inns and taverns defined by law
1555	Stage coaches
1630	Coffee houses (cafés)
1657	Chocolate houses
1760	Word 'hotel' introduced in London
1784	Royal Mail stagecoach routes
1826	Railroads started
1838	First railway hotel
1838	Steamships
1848	Simpson's Tavern in the Strand opened
1869	Early Italian restaurant

1879	Railway-car catering
1880	Railway refreshment rooms
1884	ABC tea rooms
1887	J. Lyons's first catering operation
1894	First Lyons tea shop
1895	First automobile made
1899	Department-store tea-rooms
1906	Holiday camps (under canvas)
1906	School meals (limited start)
1908	Earliest Chinese restaurant
1909	First Lyons Corner House
1915	Industrial canteens
1919	In-flight catering
1920	Continental coach tours
1920	Tea dances
1923	First restaurant orchestra radio broadcast
1928	Early Hungarian restaurant
1930	Youth hostels
1934	Vegetarian restaurants
1935	Holiday camps (in permanent buildings)
1935	Milk bars
1940	Local authority British Restaurants
1941	Army Catering Corps
1949	Chicken Inns
1953	Spaghetti Houses
1953	Motels
1954	Wimpy Bars
1959	Motorway catering
1959	First jet plane flight
1959	City Youth Hostels
1961	Steak houses
1961	Cranks' vegetarian restaurant
1965	Pizza Express
1973 .	Happy Eater
1974	MacDonalds

1.2 THE STRUCTURE OF THE CATERING INDUSTRY

The word '*catering*' means 'providing food as one's business'. The term is widely used to refer to all establishments that are concerned with one or more of the following services:

1. provision of *food*;
2. provision of *drink*;
3. provision of *accommodation*

In addition to one or more of the above, other services such as conference facilities or entertainment may be provided.

The word *'hospitality'* is defined as: 'friendly and liberal reception of guests or strangers'. The term is used in relation to various types of catering operation, in particular, hotels.

The scope of the catering industry

The catering industry is one of the largest employers of labour in Britain. The total number of people employed by it in 1985 was 2 195 200 men and women (British Hotels, Restaurants and Caterers Association). To many people, the first thing that comes to mind when the word *catering* is mentioned, is an *hotel*. Whether this is the case or not, the fact remains that few people realise the vast extent of different types of catering operations that exist. Figure 1.1 shows the wide range of the different sectors of the catering industry.

Figure 1.1 *Sectors of the catering industry*

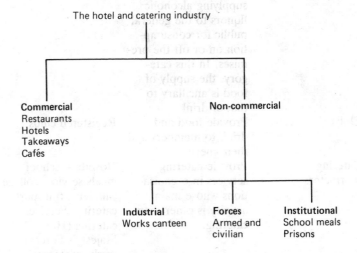

Classification of the catering industry

The industry is made up of many different types of operation. Clear-cut classifications are difficult because of the overlap between the various operations which have so many features in common. Two useful classifications are defined below:

1. The *Standard Industrial Classification* (1968) – used for government statistical reports which analyse and compare different industries – divides the industry into five categories as shown in Table 1.2.

6

Table 1.2 *The Standard Industrial Classification*

Types of establishment	Designation	Examples
1. Hotels and other residential establishments	Provides furnished accommodation with food and drink on demand for travellers and temporary residents, for reward	Hotels, motels, holiday camps, guest-houses, boarding-houses, hostels
2. Restaurants, cafes and snack bars	Non-residential establishments which supply food for consumption on the premises with or without drink	Restaurants, cafés, refreshment rooms, tea-rooms, tea-shops, snack bars, coffee bars, milk bars, fried–fish shops, function rooms, motorway service stations
3. Public houses	Mainly engaged in supplying alcoholic liquors to the general public for consumption on or off the premises. In this category, the supply of food is ancillary to that of drink	Public houses
4. Clubs	Provide food and drink to members and their guests	Registered clubs
5. Catering contractors	Provide catering services in organisations whose main activity is other than catering.	Hospitals, school meals service, college canteens, transport catering, Services catering (Her Majesty's Forces), works canteens

Source: Department of Employment (1968).

2. An alternative classification into eight sectors is shown in Table 1.3. In this illustration the sector sizes are expressed as percentages.

Tourism

Britain has been visited by tourists since Victorian times but it was only after the Second World War that the government began to recognise the

Table 1.3 *Analysis of hotel and catering industry (1986)*

Type of establishment	% of whole industry
Public houses	23
Restaurants and cafés	22
Educational catering	14
Clubs	13
Hotels and other tourist accommodation	12
Industrial and office catering	8
Medical and other health service catering	5
Contract catering	3

Source: British Hotels, Restaurants and Caterers' Association *Annual Report* (1987)

part tourism contributed to the balance of payments. In 1986 this amounted to a turnover of over £15m. The relationship between *catering* and *tourism* is best illustrated by Figure 1.2 based on data from the BHRCA *Annual Report* 1986.

Figure 1.2 *Relationship between catering and other aspects of the UK tourist industry (1986)*

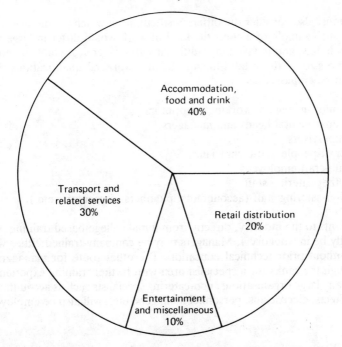

1.3 BRANCHES OF THE CATERING INDUSTRY

Specialist areas of work

Having looked briefly at the history and structure of the industry, we turn to the kinds of work which catering employees do. Within the catering industry are many specialist areas of work, each involving various levels of skill. Table 1.4 summarises the scope of specialist areas of work. There are levels of *progression* within each of these specialisations which could ultimately lead to supervisory or management jobs.

Table 1.4 *Specialist areas of work*

Specialist area	Kinds of jobs
Food preparation	Chef, chef/manager
Food service	Restaurant manager, waiter
Accommodation operations	Housekeeper, linenkeeper, chambermaid
Front office reception	Receptionist, control clerk, hall porter
Beverage service	Wine waiter, barperson

Levels of work (Hotel and Catering Training Board Classification)

We must also consider the different situations in which people work. To take the example of a chef, the kind of work would differ in large and small hotels; and in fast and traditional styles of service, etc. Depending on the size of the establishment and the workers' qualifications they might be employed as:

1. Senior managers, working proprietors
2. Departmental heads and managers
3. Supervisors
4. Craftspeople and technicians
5. Sub-craft employees
6. Other catering staff
7. Non-catering staff (accountants, plumbers, carpenters, etc.).

Entrants to the industry, directly from initial college-based training, will mostly be in category 4. Managers may be company-trained either with or without prior technical education. The other route for managers is through the ranks for a specialist area with further training experience. In many large organisations, non-catering specialists such as accountants, architects, electricians, personnel managers, etc., will also be employed.

1.4   CAREER STRUCTURE AND VOCATION

Flexibility

This section is closely related to the preceding one but will consider other aspects of jobs and careers.

Career routes in the catering industry are not so easily definable today as they might have been twenty to thirty years ago. In this industry, which is based on the provision of services, career progression is dependent not only upon technical qualifications but also upon a range of other personal qualities as well. It follows quite naturally that flexibility in career routes is quite common, for example, an initial training and experience in craft, could if desired, be developed in a number of directions such as advanced craft, supervisory positions or management. This career-flexibility may also span a number of industrial sectors where the kinds of responsibilities and the working environment will differ.

Many people start their careers in the catering industry with a course of technical education and training. There is a wide range of courses for crafts, supervisory and management jobs with progression routes existing between these courses, subject to conditions laid down by the examining bodies.

Options

The options available for starting and progressing within a career in catering include:

1. Full-time course in further education (Technical Colleges) or higher education (Polytechnics, Universities). These may be of one, two or three years duration, leading to one or more of the following qualifications: City and Guilds (CGLI), Business and Technician Education Council (BTEC), Council for National Academic Awards (CNAA).
2. Full-time courses at school and college linked, most usually from the age of 14 to 18. These may be of four years' (in some cases less) duration on a Technical Vocational Extended Education scheme (TVEE) which involves attending college and work placements. The subjects studied will include GCSE and City and Guilds courses and examinations.
3. Full-time work with part-time study. This may be in permanent employment with release to college by a variety of arrangements. One example is the Youth Training Scheme for one or two years, according to age. This provides work with job-based assessment and college-based certification.
4. Full-time work, where training is given while the trainee is in permanent employment and following a job-based assessment and

accreditation scheme such as CATERBASE controlled by the Hotel Catering Training Board.

Qualifications

Information on current catering qualifications and courses is available at educational institutions, public libraries, careers offices and so on. To gain an awareness of the full range of courses on offer in order to make the most appropriate choice is not an easy task. Help and guidance will usually be necessary and points to consider include (1) whether the course is aimed at operative, craft, supervisory or management; (2) whether the courses are specialist or general; (3) the progression routes available for industry and further study; (4) availability of courses as full-time, part-time, distance learning, industry-based and so on; (5) the different entry requirements for any one course; (6) NVQ accreditation level.

Staff turnover

One factor that may contribute to promotion and/or indicate job satisfaction is the rate of turnover among staff. The catering industry is very fortunate in being one of the largest employers, and well-qualified and experienced staff are able to pick and choose. In a recent survey sponsored by the *Caterer and Hotelkeeper* in 1987, statistics were obtained for various industrial sectors. These are reproduced in Table 1.5 and will provide an indication of this aspect of employment conditions.

Table 1.5   *Staff turnover: kitchen*

Sector of the catering industry	under 3 mths %	4–6 mths %	7–9 mths %	10–12 mths %	over 1 yr %
Pub counter service	6	4	2	13	39
Pub restaurant/steakhouse	12	18	5	9	54
Fish and chip shop	4	17	2	2	60
Pizza restaurant	24	8	8	14	35
Chicken/burger fast food	19	18	8	6	36
Café/in-store restaurant	5	9	5	16	55
English restaurant	12	14	7	7	49
Continental restaurant	13	13	0	6	64
Hotel	11	27	8	13	34
Chinese/Indian restaurant	4	13	0	11	62
Theme/US-style restaurant	45	14	7	3	31
Wine bar	13	17	4	13	42

Several factors account for the turnover of staff:

1. staff working for the season only;
2. staff moving around to gain experience which was not possible in the days of apprenticeships;
3. fairly rapid promotion;
4. high demand for well-qualified staff.

By studying the figures all sorts of further analysis may be done. For example, looking at the sectors whose staff leave before the end of one year, kitchen-staff turnover is lowest in the multi-ethnic sector and highest in new fast-food sector. Hotels are also high on staff-turnover in the kitchen.

1.5 WORKING CONDITIONS AND PAY

Working conditions

During the first half of this century, the catering industry earned a reputation for poor working conditions – in particular, long and unsociable hours, low pay, subservience, dependence and generally, a poorly educated workforce. Conditions, however, have improved radically in more recent years and a number of factors continue to influence this change including:

1. improved education in both schools and colleges;
2. competition with other industries in workforce recruitment;

Table 1.6 *Employment patterns: Employees in employment by catering sector December 1987: Analysis of male and female by catering sector (000's)*

	Male		Female		All
Divisions	All	P/T	All	P/T	
Restaurants, snack bars, cafés, etc.	90.5	33.8	139.5	95.6	230.0
Public houses and bars	78.5	46.6	207.6	171.2	286.1
Night clubs and licensed clubs	57.0	36.6	98.0	82.6	155.0
Canteens and messes	33.2	5.0	102.6	50.0	135.8
Hotel trade	93.2	26.0	163.7	82.0	257.0
TOTAL					
Hotel and catering	360.3	150.0	716.6	484.2	1076.9

Source: *Department of Employment Gazette*, April 1988, p. 512.

3. steady growth of the industry;
4. more enlightened management recruited on the basis of experience and qualifications;
5. some government legislation securing minimum conditions;
6. some trade union influence;
7. much more choice of job situations, in a more diverse industry, i.e. from haute cuisine to fast foods;
8. breakdown of traditional barriers resulting, for example, in having more women in trade kitchens and more British restaurant managers.

Pay

At present minimum rates of pay, holidays and hours of work, are laid down each year by Wages Councils, which review minimum conditions in each industry and industrial sector. These conditions are *minimum* requirements, although in practice employers in the commercial sector pay more than this minimum to attract more highly skilled staff. It must be pointed out that total job-satisfaction derives from more factors than minimum statutory conditions.

Because of the many different sectors and job titles in the catering industry, a clear picture of pay related to jobs is difficult to produce. However, statistics on pay increase are provided by the *Department of Employment Gazette*, published monthly. In the index for average earnings, the figures for the hotel and catering industry indicated pay increases of 81.9 per cent for the period January 1980–December 1986. (See Table 1.6 on p. 11 for a review of 1987 employment patterns.)

1.6 HISTORY AND DEVELOPMENT OF COOKERY

Introduction

Cookery started with the introduction of fire more than one million years ago. Early man discovered that the meat of an animal cooked by fire, not only tasted good, but required less effort to chew. These factors increased the range of food supply helping early man to transform from a hitherto solely vegetarian diet. Cooking with fire revolutionised early man's life, as the protein and fat of meat provided more energy in a compact form than did vegetarian food. Weaker and older members of the tribe could now survive longer with the new foods. Following the invention of cookery, man's appearance changed, his teeth, jaws and face becoming smaller.

Early history

The evolution of cookery has been moulded by the development of cooking methods, the invention of different means to cook food, the availability of food commodities, herbs and spices, and influences from abroad in terms of fashions and imported foodstuffs. By 4000 BC in Britain all the basic cookery methods – boiling, stewing, braising, baking, roasting and grilling – were being used. Crops were grown, animals bred, and stone pots were used for cooking and storage. The types of food available at this time were wheat, barley, milk, meat, bread, porridge, cheese and butter.

Later, around 700 BC the Romans developed cookery to a high level and enjoyed a sophisticated range of foods and dishes. The great banquets involved complex preparations cooked on charcoal stoves and the cooks were well paid. This style of cookery left Britain with the retreat and fall of the Roman Empire.

Eleventh to sixteenth centuries

In medieval and Tudor times the food of the wealthy was varied and substantial, main meals consisting of several courses including beef, pork, mutton, poultry and game.

In the typical kitchen the stores of fowl and vegetables would be lying around on the floor. It would be very smoky with pots in which most of the cooking took place, hanging over the fire. Also, there was a spit for roasting meat and fowl. The fire was kept going day and night and this acted as a source of ignition for the rest of the household. Food was prepared on large heavy oak tables, with the cooking done in pots made from heavy iron, copper and brass. In very large households there would be plenty of scullions, cooks and serving maids.

The ordinary people's diet, however, consisted of coarse black bread made of barley, rye or bean flour or a mixture known as maslin; cheese; bread; butter; eggs, ale and occasionally meat.

Imports of spices were brought about by the increased trade between the eastern Mediterranean and Europe during the Crusades in the eleventh, twelfth and thirteenth centuries. The major items introduced into British cookery at this time were pepper, ginger, cinnamon, cloves, galingale and mace. Other commodities in use at this time were parsley, sage and marjoram which were grown in Britain.

Seventeenth to nineteenth centuries

Kitchen design changed during the later centuries, reflecting the wealth derived from the new colonies. The seventeenth century saw the replacement of wood by coal, and the development of the stove in kitchens of the wealthy. A fuller range of cutlery was also introduced from abroad and the knife, fork and spoon were used together for the first time.

The nineteenth century was the time of the Industrial Revolution and many more labour-saving devices were introduced into kitchens. The closed-top cooking range came into use and many different makers' versions were available by the end of the century. Refrigerators started to appear in some of the larger households in the 1880s. By the end of the nineteenth century gas cookers came into use, although these were mistrusted at first largely because of fear of explosion. The introduction of electricity gave rise to a number of electrical appliances including the electric stove, but these were not widely used until the twentieth century.

Twentieth century

The first half of the century was a period of rapid change in the life styles of all social classes largely because of the two world wars. Because of the shortage of servants, many of the large households were no longer able to cater in the style to which they had been accustomed, and consequently there were fewer large household kitchens. After the depression of the 1930s there was a huge increase in the manufacture of kitchen furniture and appliances. The initial factors that supported this market were the need for labour-saving devices, because of the shortage of servants, and also, for less wealthy families, the availability of hire purchase.

Kitchen planning as a science was introduced from America. It was based on the principles of time and motion study (ergonomics). By the 1950s and 1960s the fitted domestic kitchen and mechanisation in the form of kitchen machines were well established.

Apart from cooking and directly related tasks such as buying, storing, serving and washing-up, the domestic kitchen is also the centre of many other household activities such as laundering, maintenance and cleaning. It follows, therefore, that with most people's familiarity with the domestic kitchen from early childhood, it is natural to regard a kitchen as a centre of activity and a significant part of the household. It was noted earlier that the commercial hotel as we know it today, owes its origins to domestic hospitality, so the parallels between trade and domestic kitchens exist in history.

1.7 PORTRAIT OF THE CHEF

The first restaurants and French cooking

In the latter part of the nineteenth century high-class dining-out facilities were developing. These were modelled on the establishments that had opened in France, about 120 years earlier, and the French term *restaurant* was used to describe them. The term *cuisine* was used to describe the style of cooking.

European expertise was imported into Britain to run these restaurants and this led to the domination of the French style of food preparation, kitchen organisation, uniform and language. The French Revolution of 1789 had caused some earlier immigration of French chefs which was a supportive influence to these developments.

Chef – cook

Despite the fact that the term *cook* had been in use since Anglo-Saxon times, the 1860s saw the introduction of the hotel with its French cuisine and the term chef (literal translation, *chief*) in use. Meanwhile, the term 'cook' was relegated to boarding-houses.

In the 1980s the term chef is in more general use and can be applied to both male and female cooks in a variety of catering situations. Traditional barriers of gender demarcation have been blurred and more females are now working in hotel and restaurant kitchens with men found in institutional catering.

Uniform requirements

Because of the prestige still attached to the French kitchen, the uniform of the French chef has been adopted in most catering outlets today. It denotes, symbolically, the status of a skilled craftsperson.

Although in the past there have been differences between the uniform worn by males and females, the French uniforms are increasingly worn by both sexes. However, there have been some modifications to the norm outlined below, as for example, with the range of hats designed for women.

The French chef's uniform (see Figure 1.3) consists of the following:

1. *Hat*: this is tall in shape and white. It can be made from either disposable paper, starched linen, or light weight reinforced material. Linen is regarded as the most professional. Hats are rarely worn to their fullest height.
2. *Jacket*: this is white, double-breasted, and may have removable plastic buttons.
3. *Neckerchief*: this is usually white and often a table napkin is used instead of the tailored neckerchief.
4. *Apron*: this is thick white linen with removable tapes. It should be worn to knee length.
5. *Trousers*: these are made of light cotton material, in blue and white checks.
6. *Shoes*: suitable footwear is as important as any other part of the uniform. Safety shoes are strongly recommended, but where alternatives are used they should have strong uppers.

Laundering

Chefs' whites are usually sent to a commercial laundry. The process of ensuring a clean white finish will entail the use of high temperatures and chemicals which will reduce the wearing properties in time. Other damage may be reduced by the use of removable buttons and apron tapes.

Figure 1.3 *Chefs' uniforms*

Personal qualities

The demands placed upon a person described as a chef will vary according to the precise work situation. Table 1.7 sets out some of the qualities that all chefs should possess to some degree, with some reason given for the choice.

Table 1.7 *Personal qualities of the chef*

Qualities	Demands of the job
Reliability	High level of team-work
Commitment	Unsociable hours (such as meal-times)
Communication	High level of team-work
Self-control	Continuous pressure to meet deadlines
Artistic flair	Need to make food look attractive
Sobriety	Pressure; availability of alcohol
Meticulousness	Considerable amount of detail
Self-organisation	Need to organise others
Honesty	Supervision of security

1.8 GASTRONOMY

By definition gastronomy is the study of the art and science of good food and wine. As a subject it emerged during the sixteenth century out of a concern for preserving health by those who enjoyed the richest tables. As with other subjects, the establishment of the printing press developed the literature and, hence, study of gastronomy considerably.

Gastronomy today is a vast subject, but not all alleged experts know as much as might at first appear. For the caterer, however, a reasonable degree of knowledge of gastronomy is a useful asset as customers may like to discuss aspects of food and wine. Furthermore, there might be business-promotion potential involved, as well as other advantages such as:

1. prestige and publicity for the catering concern;
2. special functions, e.g. local societies;
3. raised standards;
4. increase in job-satisfaction.

Considering these points, it is interesting to note the involvement of a wide variety of catering sectors in such events as the Salon Culinaire at Hotelympia, which is one of many food exhibitions and festivals held in many parts of the country at various times.

CATERING OPERATIONS

2.1 TRADITIONAL OPERATIONS

Nearly all the pioneers of the catering industry who started their business in a relatively small way, could be described as traditional caterers. To start a business without sponsorship, it was always necessary to raise some capital which the entrepreneurs would stand to lose if the venture was unsuccessful. It was not surprising therefore, that people followed the dominant trends of the day, which appeared successful. Catering has greatly appealed to the amateur and in the past many have failed in their attempts. Typically, the small restaurant or hotel, where the proprietor has overlooked the multitude of operating costs, have been prime targets for bankruptcy. There are now many catering business consultants – a fact which may reflect the need for small business operating advice. It is important to consider alternative ways of operating a catering enterprise and several are outlined in this chapter.

2.2 CONTRACT CATERING

Definition

Contract catering, as the name implies, is a system where a provision of catering is contracted out to an outside catering firm. For example, many firms who provide meals on their own premises for their employees arrange for catering contractors to organise and run the operation. In some cases cooked meals only are delivered and the holding and service organised by the client. In other cases the contractors may work on the client's premises full-time to run the catering as a complete operation. The key to understanding exactly what is involved in contract catering is contained in the contracts which are agreed between the catering contractor and their client. Contract catering is becoming more widespread as many organisations such as schools, meals on wheels and hospitals, are now required to put their catering out to public tender.

One important principle is *matching* the catering provision to the exact requirements of the *client*.

Where the catering is carried out using the client's premises, plant and equipment, the contractor will have been involved in the design and layout of these.

Unit

The catering operation, based on the client's premises, is known as a unit. A large catering contractor may control hundreds of such units and these will vary in size according to the needs of the client. Each unit will have its own management, which, in the case of a small unit, will be a chef/manager supported by one or two staff and in the case of a large unit, a general catering manager with responsibility for as many as 100 catering staff. Large catering contractors who operate nationwide will have a management network based on divisions and regions, all reporting to *Head Office*. Figure 2.1 illustrates the typical organisation of a firm of contract caterers.

The contract

A typical contract drawn up between a client and catering contractor will include agreements on the following points:

1. *Conditions of employment* the catering staff will usually (but not always) be employed by the catering contractor, but the rates of pay, hours and holidays will be agreed on both sides.

2. *Selling prices and portion sizes* usually, a firm's employees enjoy subsidised meals and to this end, the contract catering firm does not have a free hand in controlling portion sizes and dish prices.

3. *Style of service* this will include such aspects as the type of menus, variety of foods, healthy eating policy.

4. *Range of services* the style, number and scope of facilities to be provided such as, counter, vending operation, trolley-service, shop, directors' dining-room, etc.

5. *Fee* the fee that the contract catering firm receives from the client for providing the catering service.

6. *Surplus/deficit* the catering operation will usually (but not always) be self-financing as far as covering the costs of materials and wages. The margin of percentage loss or gain on trading will be agreed as a working figure.

Figure 2.1 *Contract catering: typical organisational chart*

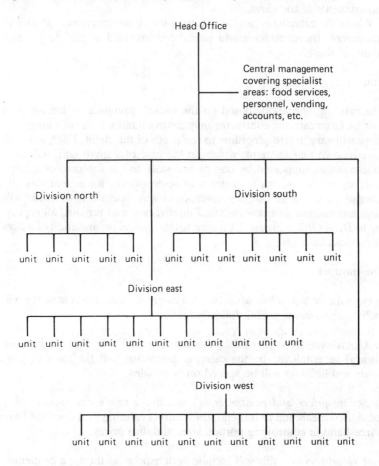

Cost allocation

Below is an example based upon a contract where the catering firm employs its own workforce and a trading break-even policy is agreed.

Contract caterer's expenses

1. Materials
2. Labour

Contract caterer's income

1. Receipts from subsidised meals
2. Other income from sales: vending, shop, etc.

3. Fixed percentage *top-up* on trading account (if required)
4. Fee for contract

Host-firm expenses

1. Premises
2. Plant and equipment
3. Depreciation
4. Deficit on caterer's income (see Contract caterer's income, item 3 above).
5. Fee for contract (see Contract caterer's income, item 4, above).

Examples of organisations

Gardner Merchant Limited   2700 units approx.
Sutcliffe Catering Group Limited   1200 units approx.
Compass   1800 units approx.

2.3   FRANCHISE CATERING

Definition

This particular catering operation is similar in principle to the breweries' tied houses which secure a sales outlet for their product. A franchise is a commercial concession by which a retailer is given the generally exclusive right to retail a company's goods or provide its services.

Organisation

The basic characteristic of a franchise is that the franchiser supplies to the franchisee various standard products, that are to be sold. It is the franchiser who controls the design and quality of the products. Most franchise firms are large companies and operate nationwide. This, together with the standardisation of the products, gives a brand name which is well known through advertising, e.g. Wimpy, Kentucky Fried Chicken, Macdonalds, etc.

This type of operation is similar, in these respects, to a system catering operation which is highly structured.

Small business investment

The financial bases of franchise units vary but often involve money being put up by both sides. The main advantage therefore, is the reduced amount of capital required in setting-up in business. There is also the reduced risk of failure because of the facilities and backing available from a larger company in such areas as marketing, advertising, business advice, tried and tested product, etc.

Control

The amount of control from the franchise company will vary in a number of respects:

1. the number and type of products;
2. the control of design and decor;
3. the money returned to the franchise company.

Examples of organisations

Wimpy Bars
Golden Egg and Spoon
Kentucky Fried Chicken
Berni Inns

2.4 POPULAR CATERING

Definition

The term 'popular catering' describes outlets that are aimed at the *mass market*.

Characteristics

The features of popular catering are:

1. menus designed to make the best use of existing facilities;
2. consistency in price, menu items, service, decor;
3. involves a systems approach (see next section);
4. usually involves fast food;
5. high technology is usually involved in the operation;
6. usually involves an emphasis on advertising and marketing.

In the large companies the advertising is nationwide. The consistency of the product quality and price is an important factor in advertising and selling.

Examples of organisation

Pizza Hut
Beefeater Steak Houses
Falstaff Grills
Happy Chef
Pastificio
Pizzaland, etc.

2.5 SYSTEMS CATERING

Definition

The term *systems catering* applies to those operations that are planned, organised and costed from start to finish and are aimed at a specific market. There is a considerable diversity of applications of systems catering, ranging from the popular to the exclusive ends of the market.

Features

1. It is aimed at satisfying particular needs.
2. Menus are restricted.
3. Dishes are completely standardised.
4. It involves the use of specialised equipment that replaces part of the traditional process of food production and service.

Examples

1. Pre-cooked meals dispensed by coin-in-the-slot from chilled compartments and regenerated in microwave ovens with tokens. This service will also include vending-machines for hot and cold beverages and all containers will be disposable.
2. A high-class restaurant serving à la carte using the 'sous vide' system of cookery. Sous-vide involves pre-portioned finished dishes, chilled in vacuum-sealed plastic pouches, which are regenerated at the time of service (see Chapter 11).

2.6 FUNCTION CATERING

Definition

Nearly all large hotels and restaurants have separate banqueting facilities to provide for special functions and these may even have their own staff and specialist management. Typical functions include: wedding receptions, cocktail parties, balls, banquets, business promotions, conferences, receptions, meetings, dress shows, special luncheons.

Function catering may also be carried out by a variety of other arrangements such as:

1. Banqueting rooms: as a specialist business, such as the Connaught Rooms in London.
2. Outside catering contractors: these may operate from food-preparation premises such as a restaurant, bakery, pub, etc. The catering is carried out in a variety of locations such as private houses, hired halls, or in a marquee.

3. Mobile kitchens: similar to outside catering but involving purpose built mobile kitchens for cooking on-site such as on film locations.

Other considerations

Function catering requires particular organisational skills, and in the case of outside caterers, plenty of improvisation ability as well. With functions there may be many points to agree with the client in addition to food and drink. These may include decor, Master of Ceremonies, a theme, and these need to be organised beforehand. One of the great attractions to outside catering as a business is the relatively low capital required to start initially in a small way.

CATERING STYLES

3.1 INTRODUCTION

French influence

As outlined in Chapter 1, the predominant style of trade cookery in this country in the late nineteenth and early twentieth centuries was French cuisine. This formed the basis of what later came to be established as the *international hotel and restaurant style* of cookery. This traditional high-class cookery is sometimes loosely referred to as haute cuisine. Whilst this style of cookery still has a strong influence today, there have been a number of additions, variations, alternatives and revolutions. These developments have been influenced, to varying degrees, by a number of factors, such as:

1. an increased demand for eating-out;
2. a wider range of customers from all social classes and nationalities;
3. commercial exploitation;
4. availability of new commodities not featured in traditional recipes;
5. differing views on healthy eating.

Scope

Along with this French influence, a considerable number of cookery styles have been evolved to meet particular markets. These fall into four broad categories:

1. Traditional French trade cookery – Escoffier tradition;
2. Bourgeoise – traditional French home cookery;
3. Nouvelle cuisine with its offshoots (see 3.4);
4. Movements – healthy eating, multi-ethnic cookery, etc.

3.2 CUISINE CLASSIQUE

Definition

This term is used to denote cookery in the style of people such as Escoffier (see 1.1). The main characteristic of this style is standardisation of such things as garnishes, dish presentation, basic preparations and cookery methods. A considerable amount of consideration and argument is directed towards the correct interpretation and perfection of classical dishes. There were several reasons why this style became so firmly established and thus influential:

1. Escoffier wrote and edited several books to make cookery *secrets* accessible. We are all familiar with the notion of the secret recipe, jealously guarded by the creator;
2. eating out was not confined to the male sex in the clubs although it was geared towards the more affluent;
3. British people were gaining employment and careers in the industry.

Language

Many of the working communications, particularly in the larger and more traditional kitchens, are in the French language. In addition to this, the names of dishes are also in French and many of these technical terms do not have equivalent English translations. For this reason, a lengthy training is involved to become competent in classical cookery, which the initiated jealously guard.

3.3 CUISINE BOURGEOISE

Definition

This term refers to traditional French home cooking which began to develop significantly in the mid-seventeenth century. As cuisine bourgeoise developed at a time of limited transportation a particular area of interest, as with cookery in other countries, is the regional variations of dishes.

A considerable number of cookery books have passed on the recipes and techniques of cuisine bourgeoise. These accounts all relate to the eating habits of the middle classes who had an interest in emulating the aristocracy. One of the best-known authorities on Victorian household management was Mrs Isabella Beeton whose books were published from 1861, and included many of the principles and practices of traditional French and English cookery.

Examples

Cuisine bourgeoise has contributed to the development of classical trade cookery, with which it has a lot in common. It signifies dishes that are not only simple and homely but also tasty and wholesome. As far as choice and use of ingredients are concerned, it differs markedly from nouvelle cuisine, which is discussed later in this chapter. Features of this style include an emphasis on pastry, confectionery and preserves.

On a menu written in French, dishes prepared in this style would be termed *à la bourgeoise*. As implied in the definition, the garnish is fairly simple and when applied to meat dishes, it consists of carrots, button onions and lardons of bacon. One of the most common versions of this style is boeuf braisé à la Bourgeoise.

3.4 NOUVELLE CUISINE

Definition

By the mid-1960s a number of restaurants chef-proprietors in France, had developed a variety of new cookery styles, which each differed in various ways from traditional cookery. These styles, although individual, shared a number of new cookery principles which established nouvelle cuisine.

This style is often described as *a picture on a plate* (see Plate 3.1) but, although a high degree of decorative work is involved, consideration needs to be given to the full range of principles.

Principles

1. Simplicity of methods and products. This includes avoiding the use of marinaded and hung meat and poultry.
2. Reduced cooking time for many commodities such as green vegetables, fish, seafood, game, pâtés and veal.
3. Fresh sound ingredients. This involves buying fresh from markets, as well as selecting pollution- and additive-free commodities.
4. Restricted menus in order to facilitate quality and value.
5. Artistic presentation – light, decorative and clean. Silver service is not used as the dishes are presented on the customer's plate.
6. Lightness avoiding the use of heavy sauces, particularly those that are flour-based. Vinegar, lemon juice and fresh herbs are used in 'finishing' dishes.
7. Simple, regional influence. Dishes are derived from simple regional dishes with no haute cuisine influence, the emphasis being on enhancing the flavours of the principal ingredients.
8. Intelligent use of new technology, e.g. microwave ovens, additive-free convenience foods, food-processors, etc.

Plate 3.1 *Nouvelle cuisine: a picture on a plate*

9. The principles of dietary balance are used with an emphasis on the popular principles of healthy eating.
10. Inventiveness – an emphasis on experimentation involving new combinations in a creative way.

Originators

There was no one person responsible for the development of nouvelle cuisine. Amongst the chefs who were involved in establishing the principles outlined were Fernand Point (founding-father), Paul Bocuse, Michel Guérard, Raymond Oliver, Jean Troisgros, Pierre Troisgros, and Roger Vergé.

Ingredients

Examples of typical ingredients used in this cuisine include freshwater fish, wild mushrooms, snails, asparagus, fresh vegetables, seafood, veal.
Examples of foods that are restricted in nouvelle cuisine include flour as used in thickening sauces with a roux, and saturated fats which are replaced with oil.

Cuisine fraîcheur

Definition

The author of this cookery style is Jean Conil, who has been responsible for several cookery books based on nouvelle cuisine. The basic idea behind this particular version is to promote healthier eating.
Consideration is given to the full range of commodities now available, which have sufficient variety to provide suitable foods from which to choose throughout the year. It is essential to feature raw as well as lightly cooked foods and sometimes these are combined in dishes.
Another important part of the rationale for this style is to encourage healthy eating by making wholesome food more attractive. This would be achieved by combining interesting and exciting commodities in dishes which are presented imaginatively.

Ingredients

Foods featured include salads, vegetables, fruits, poultry, white meats, eggs, fish, seafood, sea-plants, nuts, cheese, wild plants, yogurt, and filo pastry.
Foods not used include red meats, animal fats, refined sugar and highly processed foods.

Other considerations

Cuisine fraîcheur provides dishes suitable for both vegetarians and semi-vegetarians. In common with many of the other new styles there is an emphasis on natural flavours and experimentation.

Cuisine minceur

Philosophy

The inventor of this style was Michel Guérard, a famous French chef-patron. It is an adaptation of classical French cookery which incorporated the principles of nouvelle cuisine and places the emphasis on healthy eating by reducing the energy-value of menu items.

In cuisine minceur, foods that are regarded as harmful to health are either restricted in amount or omitted altogether and another food substituted for them, as shown by the following list of ingredients and the examples of techniques.

Ingredients

Not used: butter, flour, sugar, etc.
Restricted: fat, oil, egg yolk, etc.
Used: sugar substitute, skimmed milk powder, etc.

Examples of techniques

1. Foods are cooked without fat or oil where they have their own juices in which to cook.
2. Vegetable purée would be used as a thickening agent for sauces and stews in place of fat and flour (roux) or cream.
3. Light sabayon-based sauces are used instead of flour- and cream-thickened ones.

Cuisine gourmande

Definition

This is a development by Michel Guérard from his own cuisine minceur. While still incorporating the idea of healthy eating the dishes are more substantial.

Ingredients

Recipes do include the use of butter, eggs, cheese, pastry, alcohol, olive oil, red meat, pasta, etc., but not in excessive quantities. In most recipes, flexibility has been provided in suggestions for alternative ingredients and this is of particular help to the domestic cook.

A wider range of cooking methods can be used than in other nouvelle cuisine variations. Methods that involve the use of fat such as grilling, deep-frying, roasting and sautéing are not excluded.

Typical dishes that would feature on a menu in this style are: chilled crab consommé with chervil; hot scampi salad with mange-tout; grilled marinated blade-steak of beef; honey ice-cream.

Cuisine moderne

Philosophy

This term has been used by Anton Mosimann, formerly Chef de Cuisine of the Dorchester Hotel, in relation to nouvelle cuisine and it shares most of its principles. Particular emphasis is given to appearance which should be delicate with balanced colour, textures and light sauces. Use is made of the best fresh seasonal foods for principal ingredients and these provide the predominant natural flavour of the dishes.

Another feature of this style is small portions, with up to six courses within a typical meal.

As with other nouvelle cuisine offshoots it shares some of the principles of Chinese and Japanese cookery.

Examples

There are many examples of novel combinations creating new dishes. Three examples are: lobster salad with wild mushrooms; fillet of brill mounted on a base of pistachio mousseline on a bed of finely cut mixed vegetables; scallops with a saffron sauce and chopped tomato.

Cuisine naturelle

Definition

Another offshoot of nouvelle cuisine, cuisine naturelle is a term used by Anton Mosimann and others to indicate more *natural* cookery.

The emphasis is on simple preparations, aimed at bringing out or enhancing the natural flavour and subtleness of the ingredients. A typical example would be fresh vegetables, which in some areas of traditional cookery have not received due attention.

The particular philosophy of this style is to strike a balance between enjoying food and healthy eating.

Examples of dishes

In the preparation of dishes in this style certain ingredients such as oil, butter, cream, alcohol and salt are restricted. On the other hand, the ingredients that are particularly featured are fresh vegetables and fresh fruit. There is a strong emphasis on foods with a high fibre content.

Menu examples of some of the dishes are: marinated lemon chicken; fillet of beef with rosemary and mustard; sauté mignon of veal and fresh vegetables.

Cuisine santé

Philosophy

Cuisine santé, which was created by Christopher Buey, is aimed at the health-conscious gourmet. It attempts to overcome the criticism of those who find nouvelle cuisine and its variations too light. At the same time it departs from the classical haute cuisine by using ingredients which are much lower in energy value.

Ingredients

Fresh fruit, fresh vegetables and unrefined cereals are favoured whereas red meats, highly processed foods and fat are not. The substituting principle operates – for example, substituting yogurt for cream.

Cooking methods

The cooking methods featured are those considered to be the healthier ones such as steaming and grilling.

Cuisine du soleil

Definition

By literal translation this means 'kitchen of the sun' – a trend started by Roger Vergé. The setting for this cuisine is the Mediterranean with its natural commodities. It is an offshoot of nouvelle cuisine where the recipes are in contrast to classical ones. There should be a strong emphasis on the enjoyment of cooking through improvisation and use of imagination which extends even to basic recipes.

Ingredients

The ingredients of this trend depend upon good weather, as the name implies. The ingredients are not regarded as extraordinary bearing in mind the Mediterranean setting. The possibilities of the kitchen garden are also to be exploited to the full with this trend. Olive oil is much favoured both as a cooking medium and as an ingredient. Other common ingredients used are garlic, herbs, wine, green tomatoes, spinach, sorrel, leeks, celery, celeriac, etc.

Examples

Some examples of typical dishes include: pheasant with endive and cream; sea bream with orange and lemon stewed in olive oil; red mullet with fennel purée croûtons; rabbit in cream sauce with basil.

Cuisine spontanée

Definition

Cuisine spontanée was started by Fredy Girardet, a chef patron in Switzerland, and is an offshoot of nouvelle cuisine. Its basis is the inventiveness of the dishes which combine very contrasting textures and flavours. At the same time there is a strong emphasis on using very fresh – and if necessary, expensive – commodities and avoiding substitute ingredients in recipes.

Ingredients

Examples of some of the main commodities used in this style of cooking are: unsalted butter, fruit, cheese, good wine, frogs' legs, peanut oil, lobsters, pigeons, truffles.

Examples of dishes

Some typical examples of dishes include: asparagus with oyster sauce; foie gras with asparagus and warm vinaigrette; salad of frogs' legs and fresh broad beans; ragoût of monkfish with saffron.

3.5 OTHER MOVEMENTS AND CUISINE PRINCIPLES

There are quite a large number of different movements and traditions in cookery not covered by the previous sections. In this section, therefore, a brief account is given of some of the longer established and better known ones.

Cordon Bleu cookery

The Cordon Bleu Cookery School in this country was started in 1933 and is situated in the West End of London and at Winkfield Place, Windsor.

It provides full-time certificated courses and short courses in the field of hostess-cookery.

The full-time course content includes the study and practice of classical French, English, international and multi-ethnic cuisines. The emphasis is on small-scale high-class cookery with some continental pâtisserie later in the course. The study of wine as complementary to food is also included. Students are also brought up-to-date with the latest in domestic technology.

The course is seen as vocational in a very broad range of food-related employments.

Ethnic cookery

For centuries past people of different ethnic groups have come to settle in the United Kingdom for a variety of economic, religious, political or cultural reasons. These newcomers have included people from Asia, Middle East, West Indies, Latin America, Africa, Europe and Ireland.

Each ethnic group adds to the rich variety of cookery and provides opportunities for cross-cultural education and experimentation. The cuisines from the various ethnic groups each have their own particular characteristics which have resulted from their history, climate and available foods.

An important point to be made is that some dishes such as curry, kebabs, pizzas, hamburgers, are cross-cultural in popularity but for an authentic version of a dish, the expertise remains with the native of the country.

Some ethnic dishes are based upon certain ingredients with religious connotations, as shown in Table 3.1.

Definitions

1. The word *kosher* means *proper*, i.e. foods which are prepared and served according to Jewish dietary laws. This involves *kosher butchery* where the jugular vein of the animal is cut and the blood drained out whilst prayers are said.
2. The word *halal* means *permitted* according to the Koran. The meat is ritually slaughtered in a manner similar to kosher butchery. If halal meat is unavailable kosher meat may be used (see Chapter 12).

Vegetarian cookery

History

The vegetarian movement that started in this country in the early nineteenth century was based on two motives: first, the belief that the eating of meat aroused and stimulated animal passions and was, therefore, not conducive to mental development; secondly, as a reaction to

Table 3.1 *Religious connotations of food and drink*

Food	Buddhist	Christian	Hindu	Islamic	Jewish	Sikh
Alcohol	no	most	no	no	yes	yes
Tea, coffee	yes	yes	yes	yes	yes	no
Animal fats	no	yes	some	halal	kosher	some
Poultry	no	yes	some	halal	kosher	some
Pork	no	yes	no	no	no	no
Beef	no	yes	no	halal	kosher	no
Lamb	no	yes	some	halal	kosher	yes
Shellfish	no	yes	some	halal	no	some
Fish	some	yes	some	halal	some	some
Eggs	some	yes	some	no blood	no blood	yes
Milk/yogurt	yes	yes	no rennet	no rennet	no rennet	yes
Nuts/pulses, vegetables	yes	yes	yes	yes	yes	yes
Fruit	yes	yes	yes	yes	yes	yes

Notes:
1. Where rennet is prohibited, this is because it is extracted from the stomach of animals.
2. There are a number of Protestant Christians who are reluctant to use alcohol as a beverage.
3. Some Roman Catholics still follow ancient practice in not eating meat on Fridays although this is no longer obligatory.
4. Seventh Day Adventists do not consume pork, shellfish, animal fats, alcohol, cocoa, tea or coffee.
5. Mormons do not drink alcohol, cocoa, tea or coffee.
6. Rastafarians refuse animal products, shellfish, alcohol, salt and many processed foods.
7. Jehovah's Witnesses do not eat blood products such as black pudding. Meats are acceptable provided that the blood is drained when slaughtered.
8. All life is sacred to Hindus and many are vegetarians.

the gross over-eating and consequent unhealthiness of many of the upper classes.

Definition

Vegetarians today are defined as *people who do not eat meat, fish or poultry or any animal products, for ethical, aesthetic, religious or health reasons*. (The Vegetarian Society, 1987).

Types

There are two forms of vegetarians:

1. *Lacto-vegetarians* who eat some milk products if they have not been made by killing animals.
2. *Vegans* who avoid milk and eggs as well as meat, fish, poultry and game.

Outlets

One of the earliest *popular* vegetarian restaurants in England was Cranks, which opened in Carnaby Street, London, in 1961 and has continued to thrive.

Commodities

Animal foods are replaced in cooking by vegetarian alternatives as shown in Table 3.2.

Table 3.2 *Acceptable animal-food replacements*

Foods excluded	Acceptable replacements (for most vegetarians)
Meat, fish, poultry	nuts, beans, wholegrain cereals; seeds (sesame, sunflower, pumpkin); cheese and eggs; textured vegetable protein (TVP)
Meat or bone stock	stock made from vegetables and yeast extract
Animal fats	white vegetable fats; margarine (without whale oil)
Oils containing fish oils	100% vegetable oils
Gelatine, aspic	Agar agar, apple pectin
Animal-based flavourings for savoury dishes	vegetable yeast extracts, soy sauce; Miso, herbs and spices.

Healthy eating

During the past twenty years there has been a recognition of the part diet plays in the diseases which afflict the affluent societies of the Western world (see Table 3.3). It is important to realise, however, that there are other factors involved and a clear picture has not emerged. Despite the prophecies of doctors and dietitians, no one diet has yet been proved to be the key to a long and healthy life!

Table 3.3   *Health problems*

Health problems linked with the Western diet
obesity
heart disease
bowel diseases
tooth decay
cancer
diabetes (some types)
Other factors involved
stress
alcohol
smoking
lack of exercise
hereditary factors

In 1983 the Government intervened by issuing *Dietary Guidelines* which were to be of particular importance to caterers responsible for feeding whole sections of the community (hospital patients, school-children, prisoners). (See Table 3.4).

Table 3.4   *Dietary Guidelines (1983)*

Summary of Dietary Guidelines (1983)	
Fat	*reduce* intake, particularly saturated fat
Sugar	*reduce* intake
Salt	*reduce* intake
Fibre	*increase* intake

The concept 'healthy eating' usually refers to the application of these guidelines to catering. It is interesting to note that the term *wholefood* is often used in this context. This usually refers to the use of unprocessed food, especially whole-grain cereals and brown sugar.

'*Healthy eating campaigns*' are now commonplace in many catering outlets. The interpretations of the concept vary enormously but a recent innovation by the Health Education Authority and Institution of Environmental Health Officers (EHOs) offers an excellent way forward. The Heartbeat Award Scheme tackles the problems of *smoking, food hygiene* and *food choice*. This is a project which clearly recognises that health is not solely dependent on diet (see Figure 3.1).

Figure 3.1 *Heartbeat Award Scheme*

 ow to win the Award

Any catering establishment, public or private, restaurants, cafes, public houses, wine bars, works and office canteens, schools and hospitals, *all* can be considered for an award.

There are three simple qualifications.

1. Healthy choices, high in fibre and low in fat, must appear on the menu and be highlighted in some way. Items on a menu or menu board could be *starred* as a "healthy choice", for example. An official checklist is provided to help the caterer.

2. A minimum of one third of the seating area must be clearly reserved for NON-SMOKERS. The trend for providing non-smoking areas, especially for diners, is growing. Caterers in turn find their cleaning and repair bills are reduced when they increase their non-smoking provision. There is also the added benefit of a reduced fire risk.

3. Good standards of hygiene must be observed throughout the establishment. Food handlers must have suitable training in basic food hygiene practices.

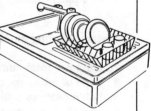

If you want to find out more about the Scheme and its benefits or make arrangements for your catering establishment to be considered for an award, contact your local Environmental Health Officer or write to:

Look After Your Heart!
Health Education Authority
Hamilton House
Mabledon Place
London WC1H 9TX

Look after your HEART!

CHAPTER 4

KITCHEN ORGANISATION

4.1 KITCHEN SIZE

The term kitchen size may refer to either the physical size or the number of staff employed.

Factors affecting physical size

1. Type of establishment.
2. Size of operation.
3. Age and design.
4. Equipment used.

Factors affecting number of staff required

1. Output – total number of meals, drinks, snacks required.
2. Type of menu required.
3. Labour-saving equipment available.
4. Use of pre-prepared foods.
5. Efficiency of work-flow, directly related to management skills.

4.2 PERSONNEL OF THE KITCHEN AND ITS ANCILLARY DEPARTMENTS

The number of staff employed in a trade kitchen can vary from one to over one hundred according to the factors outlined in the previous section. They are referred to as the *kitchen brigade*. In this section, the personnel who would be found in the large traditional kitchen will be described. Other types and sizes of kitchen are usually based on modifications of this framework.

Chef de cuisine (head chef)

Known also as executive chef, maître chef des cuisines, head chef or working head chef according to the size and style of the establishment. In large establishments the person in this position will undertake a managerial rather than a cooking role. In this managerial role the chef de cuisine will be supported by one or more sous chefs who will assist with the administration work. The chef de cuisine is responsible directly to the management for running the kitchen in accordance with the company's policy. The responsibilities will include:

1. menu planning;
2. costings;
3. control of materials: portions, wastage, security, etc.;
4. staff: rotas, engaging, induction, etc.;
5. purchasing commodities;
6. purchasing and maintenance of equipment and utensils;
7. staff welfare.

The duties will vary according to the size and character of the establishments but the main focus of a chef de cuisine's job may be summed up as that of quality controller in all aspects of the kitchen operation.

Sous chef (second chef)

This literally means *under chief* and in the case of a large kitchen this will involve responsibilities as an assistant kitchen manager. In very large kitchens there may be up to four sous chefs who would be designated as first, second, third and junior sous chef. In this case the sous chefs may be allocated particular areas of responsibility, such as staff rotas or banquets, in addition to their work of assisting with the running of the kitchen.

Chef de partie (section chef)

The next level in the kitchen-brigade hierarchy is the chef de partie. The term literally means *chief of a section*. The kitchen is divided into various sections each relating to a clearly defined set of specialist cooking tasks. Parties (sections) will be more fully discussed in section 4.4. Each different section in the kitchen has a chef in charge. The full job-title will incorporate the name of the work undertaken by the section. For example, the chef de partie in charge of the section responsible for the fish is known as the chef poissonnier. Therefore, the term chef de partie is used simply to describe a level of responsibility whilst the fuller title relates to the area of specialisation. The various chefs de partie are described below:

Chef saucier (sauce cook)

This chef de partie is responsible for the cooking of all meat, poultry, game and offal dishes including their respective garnishes and sauces, with the exception of grills and roasts which is the work of the chef rôtisseur. The saucier's responsibility will include dishes for which cooking methods such as braising, pot-roasting, (poêlé) and boiling are used. This chef is not responsible, however, for sauces such as fish and sweet which are made by the chef poissonnier and chef pâtissier respectively. The saucier's partie is the most complex as it involves the greatest variety of dishes and, hence, is usually regarded as the *star* partie and the chef saucier as a senior person in the brigade.

Chef garde manger (larder cook)

This chef de partie is responsible for the larder section of the kitchen which is usually a separate room adjoining the main kitchen. The term larder denotes a *cold* area (max 10°C) and therefore cooking does not usually take place here. The responsibilities of the chef garde manger include the storage of perishable foods, the preparation of meat and fish prior to cooking and the use of fresh and cooked items to prepare salads, sandwiches, hors-d'oeuvre and cold dishes. In large establishments the larder may contain some of the following sub-sections with a chef in charge:

1. hors-d'oeuvre (hors-d'oeuvrier);
2. butcher (boucher);
3. cold buffet (chef de froid);
4. fishmonger (poissonnier).

The larder is usually the largest section of the kitchen and because of the scope of work and range of responsibilities, the larder chef has the status of a senior chef de partie.

Chef pâtissier (pastry cook)

This chef de partie is responsible for the preparation of all hot and cold sweets including cakes, pastries and all iced confectionery. Very occasionally in large establishments a bakery is attached under the responsibility of a baker (boulanger) and this has the added advantage of producing a variety of bakery products which might not otherwise be easily obtainable. In some pastry sections a range of other specialist work may be carried out such as pulled sugar, pastillage, ice-carving and cake decoration. In large establishments this section will also include a specialist in ice-cream- and water-ice-making. There is considerable scope for very high levels of craft skill to be employed in reproducing some of the difficult classics as well as creating new dishes.

Chef poissonnier (fish cook)

This chef de partie is responsible for the cooking of all fish dishes except for plain grilled and deep-fried dishes which are done by the chef rôtisseur. The scope of work is complex, with a range of garnishes for fish dishes whether poached, shallow-fried, braised, boiled, etc. This section also prepares the butter sauces such as hollandaise.

Chef rôtisseur (roast cook)

This chef de partie is responsible for roasting, grilling and deep-frying. This in fact gives rise to a range of dishes including some that would not be obvious. The roast section is responsible for roasting meat, poultry and game with the appropriate garnishes and gravies. Deep-frying includes french-friend potatoes as well as fish. Grilling includes plain grilled fish as well as meat, offal and even lobster. In addition, this section is responsible for savouries and hot sandwiches. There is some-times a subsection for grilling under the chef grillardin (grill chef) and this is apart from any grill room that might be based in the establishment.

Chef potager (soup cook)

This chef de partie is responsible for all soups, egg and farinaceous dishes.

Chef entremettier (vegetable cook)

This chef de partie is responsible for the cooking of all vegetables including potatoes, with the exception of deep-fried items although, for some of these, the basic preparation is done by this section. This partie also supplies other parties with vegetable garnishes. In some establish-ments it is this section instead of the chef potager that makes the egg and farinaceous dishes.

Chef tournant (relief chef)

This is someone normally of chef de partie status who takes over from the others on their days off.

In addition, some staff are sometimes employed as specialists. Some are listed below.

Chef de nuit (night chef)

This chef has chef de partie status and is responsible for the whole kitchen throughout the night, to deal with any orders that might reach the kitchen via *room service*.

Chef communard (staff cook)

This cook is responsible for the preparation of staff meals, with the exception of management and certain other senior staff. The special responsibilities of this section with its regular clientele, is to pay due regard to palatability, nutritional balance and, most important of all, variety.

Breakfast chef

This chef is not in charge of a partie but is responsible solely for the cooking of breakfasts. The range of dishes cooked for breakfast is quite varied, but not as varied as for lunches and dinners. This job is usually regarded as a stepping-stone to taking responsibility as, like the chef de nuit, this chef will be in sole charge of the kitchen for a proportion of time.

Commis chef (assistant chef)

Each chef de partie will have a number of staff to assist according to the work-load of the section. These assistant cooks are known as commis and the most senior one on any partie will be referred to as first commis, the next, second commis, etc. It follows, therefore, that the next person in seniority to the chef saucier is the first commis saucier, on the vegetable section, the first commis entremettier, etc.

In theory, anybody referred to as a *commis* should be already trained. However, the term is often used indiscriminately to denote anybody who is not a chef but who does the cooking.

Aboyeur (kitchen announcer)

The main function of the aboyeur is to call out the food orders when they arrive at the hot plate and, at other times assist the chef de cuisine and sous chefs, with some aspect of the administration. The employment of an aboyeur is not as common now as years ago and the function of calling orders is usually undertaken exclusively by the sous chefs. Where aboyeurs do exist the role is normally given to a retired chef, whose knowledge of food and kitchen procedures combine with the need for a lighter task than cooking.

Ancillary staff

In addition to the staff outlined above there are many other functions apart from direct cookery which are performed by specialists often described as ancillary staff

Kitchen porters (KPs)

A number of kitchen porters are employed, usually under a head kitchen porter, who is responsible to the chef de cuisine. KPs (as they are known in kitchen jargon) are responsible for the general cleaning of the kitchen and, as the name suggests, for carrying things. It is noted that chefs are craftspeople and always clear down their own work benches and stove tops. Good and reliable kitchen porters are difficult to find and they therefore tend to enjoy a certain prestige, particularly with the chef de cuisine.

Plongeur (pot-washer)

In large establishments the washing-up of kitchen pots and other metal equipment is kept separate from the washing-up of plates, crockery, glass and silver service, which is the responsibility of the dining-room. In the French kitchen the pot-wash area is known as the plonge and the pot-washers as plongeurs.

General assistants or kitchen hands

In large establishments extra helpers are employed, unskilled or semi-skilled, as a back-up for food preparation. The tasks performed by such assistants vary. They may include vegetable preparation and locker-room supervision.

Still-room supervisor

The still-room is where hot drinks, toast and butter portions are prepared and served. Sometimes the glassware may be washed in the still-room but this depends upon the organisation of the particular establishment.

Storekeeper

The storekeeper is responsible for the storeroom and in large establishments will be assisted by one or two staff. It is usual for perishable items to be kept near the larder with the storekeeper responsible for the *dry* stores. This separation of stores control is necessary because the perishable commodities need the supervision of a skilled chef. The main duties of the stores are receiving, issuing and recording goods (see 5.1, 5.2 and 5.3).

4.3 FUNCTION

Operation 1: manual

A typical food order

Below is a typical food order for two guests from an à la carte menu (Figure 4.1). The person taking the order would of course write it by hand. Also, abbreviations would be used for many of the dishes, but not so far as to cause confusion for the chefs or the control office (see the section 'Operation 2' for computerised-system operation). The order is taken to the kitchen and given to the chef at the hot plate, or to the aboyeur, who will *call to order*. In a large kitchen this will be by a public address system to combat the background noise.

Figure 4.1 *Food order check*

```
Table 6        2 covers
                              reference:
       1 Minestrone _____ 1.
       1 Melon frappé _____ 2.
       1 Filet grillé _____ 3.
              rare
       1 Sole meunière _____ 4.
       1 Pommes frites _____ 5.
       1 Pommes vapeur _____ 6.
       2 Ratatouille _____ 7.
       1 Salade panachée _____ 8.


   date           signed
```

From the example of the *one* food order given the following points should be noted (Figure 4.2):

1. the sweet order is usually taken *after* customers have eaten their main course;
2. the sauce section and cold buffet were not involved in this order;
3. the two items in the first courses are served direct. Soup from the potager in the kitchen and melon from the hors-d'oeuvrier in the larder;
4. the roast partie does only the pommes frites on this particular order. In some establishments the grill section may do the deep-fried items, or alternatively, the sections are combined;

Figure 4.2 *Kitchen service operation*

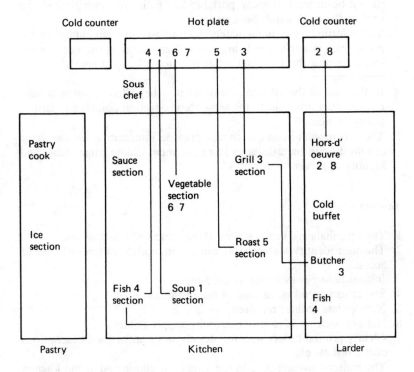

5. the raw materials of fish and meat are passed from the larder to the kitchen, ready to cook;
6. all food passes either the hot plate or, for cold items, the cold counter, and is *managed* for quality control, time and despatch by the chef at the hot plate (cold counter).

Operation 2: computer systems

Introduction

There are many different computer systems on the market for kitchen/ restaurant control. This text will consider the *restaurant key pad* system, which will have some or all of the features of operation described below.

Operation

1. The server takes the order from the customers, using a check pad.
2. The server then keys into a terminal with personal identity number and places the order. This is done by pressing keys, first establishing

the table number, date, covers and then the appropriate dishes. It should be noted that small portable key pads are available and can replace the traditional check pad.

3. The information is immediately relayed to the preparation/service points such as kitchen and bar. This will appear as a print-out in these locations and the customer's bill is automatically prepared, at the same time.

4. In the case of the kitchen, the order may be called or automatically relayed by a print-out to the separate production points, e.g. larder, pastry section.

5. These computer-print-out checks provide information on the items required (with modifications from the menu), date, time, table and identity of server.

Advantages

1. The terminals are heat-, static-, shock- and spillage-resistant.
2. The user-identity system (ID) can accommodate different levels of access.
3. Instant billing is available at any time.
4. Server can spend more time in the restaurant.
5. No separate cashier required.
6. Battery back-up in case of electricity-supply failure.
7. Clearly printed orders with full details and standardised descriptions of the dishes, etc.
8. The waiters' waiting-time in the kitchen is eliminated as the kitchen signals the availability of orders to the restaurant via a numbers board.
9. Records of all transactions are conveniently stored on hard disk.

4.4 PARTIE SYSTEM AND ADAPTATIONS

Possible arrangement of a large kitchen brigade with estimated numbers

The organisation of a kitchen by the arrangement known as the *partie system* is attributed to Auguste Escoffier (1846–1935). Escoffier came to this country in 1889 to work initially at the Savoy Hotel. The basis of his kitchen organisation combines a number of principles of which speciali-sation and even distribution of work-load are the most important.

The food and hot beverages production operation is divided into eight broad areas. A hypothetical organisation of 100 staff is shown in Table 4.1 and Figures 4.3 and 4.4.

49

Figure 4.3 *Partie system – large brigade*

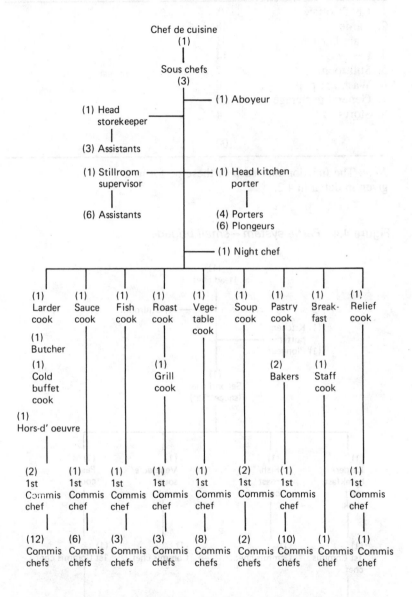

Note: This would be one possible allocation of 100 staff deployed in the traditional partie system. It must be stressed however that variations would occur from one large hotel to another even where the same number of staff were involved.

50

Table 4.1 *Kitchen staff analysis*

1. Chef's office	5
2. Larder	18
3. Main kitchen	41
4. Pastry	14
5. Still room	7
6. Wash-up: pots	6
7. General porterage	5
8. Stores	4
	100

Note: The function that each of these performs is given in detail in 4.2.

Figure 4.4 *Partie system – small brigade*

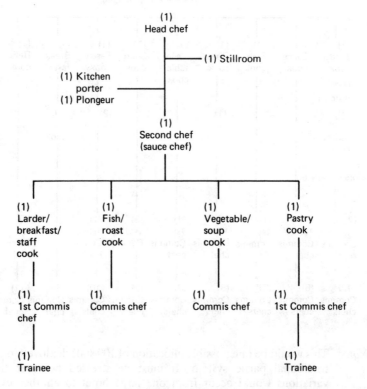

Note: In this hypothetical example of the deployment of fifteen staff there is still a hierarchy, specialisation and flexibility. These are important features to recognise, in understanding the operation of the partie system. Nearly all chefs will have a basic training in every aspect of food preparation and therefore be able to apply basic principles to new tasks where necessary.

4.5 OTHER TYPES OF KITCHEN OPERATION

In this section we will consider how kitchens in others types of catering operation deploy their staff. Table 4.2 illustrates functions and responsibilities of catering staff in hospitals and airlines (in-flight staff).

There are many other types of catering operation staffed with various combinations of skilled, semi-skilled and operative personnel. The staffing structures in each of the kitchens will vary according to the size and nature of the operation. It is also true to say that the various

Table 4.2   *Hospital and in-flight staff*

Staff hierarchy	Function and responsibilities
Hospital:	
Production catering manager	Supervision of one or more kitchens
Head cook	This could be an alternative job-title to the above.
Assistant head cook	Working cook supervising the preparation cooking and service
Cook	Production work at qualified cook level
Assistant cook	General duties such as service, vending machine update, etc.
Kitchen porter	Operation of washup machines, cleaning, etc.
In-flight:	
Head chef	In charge of a site such as Hong Kong, Gatwick
Sous chef	In charge of a shift of eight hours. (3 sous-chefs cover 24 hours, 3 × 8 hrs)
Chef, grade I	Chef de partie
Chef, grade II	Assistant to chef de partie
Chef, grade III	} Commis chef – no
Chef, grade IV	} specific duties
Production assistant	Operation of wash-up

job-titles in some operations may be used fairly loosely, particularly where job-titles do not relate to a clear national salary structure. An illustration of this would be the Armed Forces, where there is a clear salary and job-title structure, in contrast to, say, a medium-sized hotel or restaurant where there is more flexibility.

Each of the following catering operations will have a food-and-beverage-preparation staff and will use various job-titles similar to those in the French kitchen in many cases.

Sector:

educational institution catering; holiday camps; industrial canteens; leisure centre catering; motorway catering; mobile contract catering; schools meals service.

4.6 DAILY ROUTINE

By definition the word routine means:

1. *a regular course of action*
2. *performed by rule.*

Much of the work done in a kitchen is built upon routine and this assists the maintenance of standards. Examples are given below:

Specialisation The specialisation of the partie system and the job-definitions that this entails minimise arguments about who should carry out the various tasks involved.

Cleaning Routine is an important part of cleaning, particularly in conforming to the standards required by the Food Hygiene Regulations.

Mise en Place This is the preparation of food prior to service. Examples are basic sauce, tomato concassé, hard-boiled eggs, filleted fish, etc.

Pace There will be obvious differences here between a kitchen run along traditional lines and one using a cook–chill or freeze system.

Safety As food preparation involves a range of equipment including machines, there will be routine inspections to ensure that everything is in sound working order. Inspections will also be carried out to ensure that all parts of the premises are in good repair so as to prevent potential accidents.

Hygiene Many firms attempt to minimise the risk of food-poisoning with routine hygiene checks as part of a quality-assurance assessment.

4.7 PRODUCTION SCHEDULES

The menu will provide the blueprint for production and this will vary from establishment to establishment (see Chapter 7). In some cases there may be one set menu remaining unchanged for months, whilst in other establishments there may be a number of menus operating on any one day.

Production schedules

1. *A limited set menu remaining unchanged for a period of time* e.g. fast-food operation such as Macdonalds, Happy Eater, where most foods are delivered from a central source ready prepared and portioned. Business forecasting is not too crucial as most food items can be held in a preserved state.
2. *Table d'hôte as the only menu operating* e.g. a small restaurant where forecasting determines daily purchases of fresh commodities, and a range of preserved foods is stored for use if there is an unexpected increase in trade.
3. *A fairly extensive classical à la carte menu* This type of schedule requires having a wide range of foods available. A small establishment would use more convenience commodities as there would be fewer specialist staff to prepare dishes. Large establishments may change their à la carte menus daily and this gives more flexibility with ordering. In some cases large and smaller establishments may offer customers both à la carte and table d' hôte menus. In this case the two different types of menu may still share common dishes and preparation. For example, if fresh kidneys are held for grilled kidneys on the à la carte menu, they could be diverted to steak and kidney pie on the table d' hôte menu. This sort of juggling requires a firm knowledge of dishes, hygiene, costings, customer-forecasting and is the sort of thing most cooks do every day. A good *mise en place* (see 8.2) will be of particular value in these situations.
4. *Banqueting menu* In the case of banquets the numbers are usually provided at the time of ordering. With large functions in particular there will be some agreed margin to allow for last-minute fluctuations in numbers. As numbers of diners, dishes required, time of eating, and style of service are known in advance all preparations can be made before the guests arrive. In large establishments there is usually a senior chef with responsibility for functions. As large numbers have to be served at the same time the particular responsibilities of this chef are to ensure speedy and easy service, with food at the correct temperature, properly cooked and in portions of the right size.

4.8 OTHER SUPPORT STAFF

Introduction

In addition to the cooking and ancillary staff mentioned in previous sections in this chapter, there are a number of other support staff who may have some dealings with the kitchen. The ones outlined below would more likely be full-time employees in larger establishments. It is interesting to note that skilled craftspeople work in catering without catering training.

Linen keeper is responsible for all the linen and other cloths. The relationship to the kitchen will be the issue of clean uniforms and tea towels (rubbers). The linen-keeper's function also includes marking and sending to the laundry all soiled items, and organising repairs.

Carpenter deals with repairs and general maintenance in both the public areas and the work areas. This may include repairing furniture, wooden equipment, etc.

Electrician deals with all electrical repairs both 'front of house' and behind the scenes.

Plumber does all plumbing work. The potential damage to an establishment from burst pipes underlines the value of this function.

Printer Some establishments may have their own printer on the premises to print daily menus and other items.

Gardener Many hotels, particularly in the provinces, employ one or more gardeners to maintain the grounds. This includes maintaining lawns, growing herbs, fruit trees, flowers and vegetables.

Handyman literally the *Jack of all trades* who will be called to the kitchen from time to time as required.

Summary

All catering establishments need the facility of instant repairs to ensure the smooth running of the business. If a bedroom, for example, is out of action revenue is lost on a daily basis. The number and kind of other support staff employed by an establishment will vary according to circumstances of which the principal one is size.

PURCHASING, STORING
AND ISSUING GOODS

5.1 BUYING

Introduction

We are all familiar with the performance of the typical market sales-person with their easy-going, amusing, persuasive chat, and we recognise the skills involved. The fact that the customer (the buyer) also requires skills to purchase does not always seem as obvious. Unlike casual purchasing, a more formal approach is necessary in business in order to survive and therefore a knowledge of records and control procedures is essential.

In catering, the nature and size of the operation will determine who is to be responsible for buying. In general, the responsibility for buying will rest on one or more of the following: manager, chef, storeman, or buying department.

Principles of buying

Whoever has this responsibility in a catering operation will need to apply a set of well-established rules to the task:

1. a decision is made as to the *type* of foodstuff and *quality* required;
2. *quantity required*, in relation to storage and delivery dates, is assessed;
3. *method of purchasing* is determined – cash or account, market or local supplier;
4. *finance available*, within limits, is decided.

Taking all these factors into consideration the items are purchased.

5.2 STORING

Introduction

Food is *received*, *checked* and then *stored*. The proper storage of food is essential so that pilferage, deterioration and infestation can be controlled. All these factors will contribute to profit-levels and storekeeping is therefore an important and responsible job.

Principles of good storage

The storage area

There can be no standard formula for the design of storage areas because of the diverse nature of catering outlets. In all situations, however, there is a need for *dry* and *cold* stores (see Figure 5.1).

The general principles for storage in both areas are shown in Table 5.1.

Dry stores

The special requirements of dry stores (i.e. for the storage of tinned, packaged and non-perishable foods) are shown in Table 5.2.

Cold storage area

The keeping quality of perishable foods is extended if the temperature of the food is 10°C or below. Not only is this critical to stop the growth of food-poisoning bacteria but it also slows down the rate of spoilage caused by other micro-organisms and enzyme reactions.

Many establishments use the refrigerator at approximately 4°C for all perishables, making use of the fact that different areas of the refrigerator produce variations in temperature. For example, meat loses its bright red colour if not kept at chilling temperatures (0–3°C). If a chiller is not available, meat is stored in the colder areas of the refrigerator, see Figure 5.2.

If space and equipment are available, a combination of cold-storage facilities, as outlined in Figure 5.1 is preferred. The special requirements of storage areas at reduced temperatures are outlined in Table 5.3.

5.3 STOREROOM ORGANISATION

Commodities must be arranged in the stores systematically. Most systems incorporate the following principles:

1. each item must have a definite place where it can be stored;

Figure 5.1   *The ideal storage requirements of commodities*

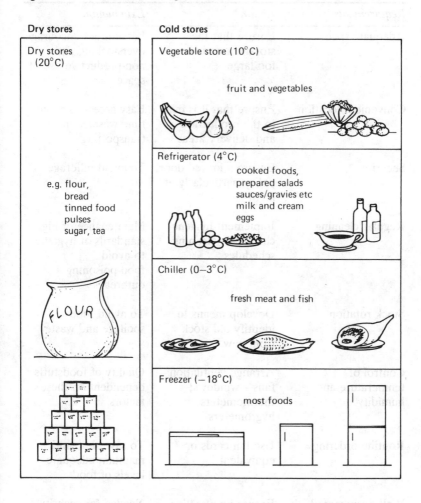

2. items used most frequently should be near the entrance;
3. food items are placed in categories to simplify storage.

The categorisation of each commodity is often difficult, for example: Do hens' eggs and caviar go together, or caviar and kippers? Does tinned turtle soup go with tinned meat extract?

Some storerooms arrange foods in alphabetical order to avoid this problem whereas others group commodities together. A typical example of the latter is given in Table 5.4. Commodities within each category would be stored alphabetically.

Table 5.1 *Storage: general points*

Requirements	Action	Explanation
Adequate space	Ensure that the storage area is not too large	Large areas encourage overstocking and non-productive use of space
Convenient location	Ensure that it is near to the production and delivery areas	Easy access to avoid time wastage in transporting
Security	Ensure a locked door policy particularly at night	To avoid pilferage
Regular cleaning	Implement hygiene checklists; cleaning schedules	Maintenance of high standards of hygiene to avoid food-poisoning outbreaks
Stock rotation	Develop means to identify old stock from new	To avoid food spoilage and waste
Control of temperature and humidity	Arrange ventilation – fans – windows; thermometers hygrometers	Quality of foodstuffs dependent on these factors
Routine ordering	Use bin cards or equivalent	To save time and maintain adequate levels of food
Well-documented system of control	Ensure an effective and efficient computerised system or paper records; no goods to be issued without a signed requisition	Needed for security, accountability and profit calculation
Prevention of cross-contamination	Provide separate areas for storage and adequate packaging	Strong-smelling foods taint others; bacteria can be transferred from raw to cooked foods.

Table 5.2 *Additional points: dry stores*

Requirements	Action	Explanation
Temperature below 20°C	Locate on north-facing wall to avoid direct sunlight	Dry goods do have an optimal shelf-life which is at its maximum in the cold.
Humidity control	Make sure there is good ventilation with door-and wall-vents and fans; foods should not be packed closely together	Damp encourages mould-growth, which in turn causes rotting and odours
Dark	Paint any windows opaque; locate away from direct sunlight if possible	Light speeds up many deteriorative changes particularly fats/oils and fruit/vegetables
Free from infestation	Tightly seal packaging; use chemicals where necessary; remove all scraps of food	Pests cause wastage and contamination; excrement is a source of Salmonella bacteria
Cleanliness	Fit with easy-to-clean (non-absorbent) shelves, such as stainless steel, plastic; keep food off floor; clean regularly	To avoid food contamination/wastage and infestation

5.4 STORAGE RECORDS

The complete stock cycle in a catering operation can be broken down into a set of logical steps. Although these may vary from establishment to establishment, Figure 5.3 is a typical illustration.

Documentation

In small establishments, stores supervision is often done by the proprietor on a day to day basis and only very simple records are kept. In large establishments more detailed records, for efficient control and use

Figure 5.2 *Temperature differences in small refrigerators*

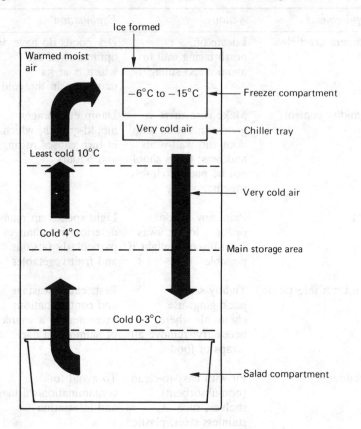

Table 5.3 *Additional points: cold storage*

Requirements	Action	Explanation
Temperature maintenance: Refrigerator 4°C Chiller 0°C–3°C Freezer − 18°C	Check and record twice daily; cool food thoroughly before storing; open doors only when necessary	Foods stored at low temperature deteriorate less rapidly
Cleanliness	Clean weekly; wipe up spillages immediately; defrost regularly	Many spoilage organisms grow at low temperatures; cross-contamination possible

Table 5.3 *cont.*

Packaging	Use suitable close filling; often airtight packaging required	Foods will dehydrate (in freezer this causes freezer burn); excess moisture forms ice and this overloads the motor. Cross-contamination prevented

Table 5.4 *Commodity classification*

1. Beverages, milk products
2. Cakes, biscuits and crackers
3. Cereals (breakfast)
4. Cereals and flour
5. Chocolate and cocoa
6. Colourings
7. Condiments and spices
8. Extracts
9. Fats and oils
10. Fish, shellfish and sea foods
11. Fruits, canned
12. Fruits, dried and glacé
13. Fruit juices
14. Fruit preserves and jellies
15. Fruits: spiced and pickled
16. Gelatine and gelatine deserts
17. Ice cream and ice-cream supplies
18. Leavening agents (e.g. fresh yeast)
19. Nut meats and nut products (for vegetarian restaurants)
20. Pickles and olives
21. Sauces and relishes
22. Sugar and related substances
23. Vegetables, canned
24. Vegetables, dried
25. Specialities (e.g. foie gras, truffles, snails)

of stock, are essential. Some of the more commonly used documents are described and illustrated below. It is important to understand that control systems differ in various respects according to the unique characteristics of the operation.

62

Figure 5.3 *Flow-chart for requisition, purchases and invoices*

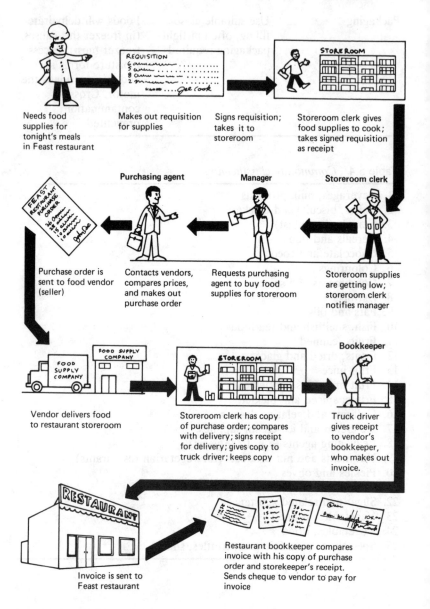

Needs food supplies for tonight's meals in Feast restaurant

Makes out requisition for supplies

Signs requisition; takes it to storeroom

Storeroom clerk gives food supplies to cook; takes signed requisition as receipt

Purchasing agent   **Manager**   **Storeroom clerk**

Purchase order is sent to food vendor (seller)

Contacts vendors, compares prices, and makes out purchase order

Requests purchasing agent to buy food supplies for storeroom

Storeroom supplies are getting low; storeroom clerk notifies manager

Bookkeeper

Vendor delivers food to restaurant storeroom

Storeroom clerk has copy of purchase order; compares with delivery; signs receipt for delivery; gives copy to truck driver; keeps copy

Truck driver gives receipt to vendor's bookkeeper, who makes out invoice.

Invoice is sent to Feast restaurant

Restaurant bookkeeper compares invoice with his copy of purchase order and storekeeper's receipt. Sends cheque to vendor to pay for invoice

Ordering/purchasing

Purchasing order book   When goods are ordered from a supplier the details of the items and quantity required are entered in this document in duplicate. Other details on the page are name and address of supplier, reference number, date, signature and date of delivery (see Figure 5.4).

Figure 5.4 *Sample purchase order as sent to a supplier*

Purchase order

No. 9905
Please quote the above number in all communications.

To: J Smith & Sons
Butcher
High Street

Delivery date: 15 : 1 : 90

Delivery instructions
deliver fresh Mon, Wed,
no later 6 pm.

Terms ACCOUNT

15% DISCOUNT

(Authorised signature)

Commodity Number	Description of items	Quantity ordered	Quantity received	Unit price	Extension
0083	LAMB B/END	4			
0077	L/LIVER	8 kg			
0079	F/ OXTONGUE	1			
0091	B/TOPSIDE	4 kg			

Sub total:

Less discount:

Total:

Delivery
Received ....
Date ....

64

Delivery

When goods arrive they must *immediately* be checked for quantity and quality against the document which arrives with them. This usually takes the form of a *delivery note* (see Figure 5.5). For example, if frozen legs of lamb are delivered they must be checked to make sure:

1. that they have not started to defrost;
2. that the wrapping is not broken;
3. that the weight corresponds to that on the delivery note.

Figure 5.5 *Sample delivery note*

Delivery note		No: 1320
From: D Sole & Sons Butcher Hastings Sussex DP3 9YT Telephone: 43567 Telex: 0889-2433	Date: 10 January 90 Your order number: 078	
To: Beauport Park Hotel Hastings Sussex		
12 x 1kg	ducks	1 box
3kg	fillet of beef	fresh
4kg	pork chops	fresh
4kg	NZ legs of lamb (PL grade)	frozen

Received by: P. Graves   Date 10/1/90

Storage

Food is taken from the delivery point without delay to be placed in the dry or cold stores. Records are kept to ensure that the required amount is stored at all times. If the records are kept with the individual commodity they are referred to as *bin cards*. If these records are kept in a central office they are referred to as *stock cards*.

Bin card   These are individual cards for each commodity, usually fixed to a shelf, bin or rack for each item. They show the quantities received from supplies, quantities issued, and stock in hand. Another key feature of this record is that it has a figure for maximum and minimum stock levels (see Figure 5.6). Therefore the storekeeper knows when and how much to order.

Figure 5.6   *Bin card*

Commodity PEARS A 2½ No 70			
Maximum stock 60		Minimum stock 8	
Date	Received	Issued	Balance
6 · 1 · 90			10
8 · 1 · 90	48		58
8 · 1 · 90		4	54
12 · 1 · 90		6	48
17 · 1 · 90		10	38

Issues

Goods should be issued from the storeroom to authorised personnel only. A simple internal requisition system is usually used. Senior members of staff write out their requirements on documents called *requisitions* which must be countersigned by the head chef. Goods are released by the storekeeper on receipt of these requisitions.

Requisition book/sheets These books/sheets are used by each department that draws stores. To make control easier there may be different colours for different departments in the organisation. An example of a requisition sheet is given in Figure 5.7.

Figure 5.7 *Requisition book/sheets*

Requisition Kitchen to Stores		Date 6·1·90	0941
Qty	Unit	Item	Number
4	kg	Patna	DG010
6	½ LBS	Butter	DA 006
2	LTR	Frying oil	DG021
4	LB	Streaky Bacon	FM014
1	TIN	Tom Purée	DG041
2	TIN	Asparagus T.	CV019
Authorised by: **JAE** Received by:			

Stocktaking

Stocktaking is a periodic check to establish the value of all goods in hand. This is usually carried out at the end of a trading-period using documents called *stock sheets*. Because of the financial implications, stocktaking is often carried out by an independent person from the accounts department or from an outside firm of accountants. The manager can therefore also establish that the storekeepers are working honestly and effectively.

Stock sheets Stock sheets list consumable items, in alphabetical order, with extra space to add additional items where applicable (see Figure 5.8).

Figure 5.8 *Stock sheet*

	page 2
Beauport Park Hotel	Date _____
Location: Dry Stores	

Stock item	Unit	Number	Unit value	Value
cont				
Tea: bags	100s			
Tea: Indian	1 kg			
Tea: China	¼lbs			
Coffee: Inst	1 kg			
Coffee: Hag	¼lbs			
Coffee: Vac	50 box			
TINNED VEG:				
Asparagus	24 box			
Beans: baked	24 box			
Beans: broad	A10			
Carrots: whole	A10			
Mixed veg	A10			
Mushrooms	Box 12			
New Potatoes	A10			
Spinach: leaf	25 box			
Sweetcorn	25 box			
Salsify	12 box			
Tomato: peeled	A10			
Tomato: whole	A10			
Tomato: purée	1 kg			

5.5 QUANTITY REQUIREMENTS

There are many factors that determine the quantity of commodities ordered direct from suppliers or requisitioned from the stores:

1. The type of menu(s) operating (table d'hôte, à la carte, function).
2. Customer number forecasts (residents, chance trade).
3. Kind of cuisine operating (traditional, popular, cook–chill, etc.).
4. Kinds of foods used, whether fresh or convenience (convenience foods would have less trimming loss and it would therefore be easier to forecast the number of portions).
5. Skills of the cooking staff with reference to cooking and trimming losses.
6. The establishment portion-size policy.

The establishment portion policy will be determined according to the kind of catering operation. For example, with a large chain such as Macdonalds, the portion-control policy is centrally directed as is the choice of equipment used for cooking and serving. At the other extreme a small hotel's portion-control policy will be much less formally determined. It is important to realise, however, that even a relatively small operation will have a large turnover as well as a narrow profit-margin so a firm and consistent portion-size and costing-policy is essential to stay in business. Differences in portion sizes, however, may operate in the same establishment between table d'hôte and à la carte menus.

To assist in estimating quantity requirements Table 5.5 gives average portion sizes for a table d'hôte or similar menu.

Table 5.5 *Average portion sizes*

Hors-d'oeuvre	Size	Fish	
smoked salmon	50 g	(off the bone):	
fruit cocktail	100 g	herring, trout,	
fruit juices	100 g	whiting, etc	
caviar	25 g	whole:	180 g
foie gras	25 g		
salami	100 g	turbot, halibut, etc.	
		cut into tronçon:	180 g
		salmon cut into darne:	180 g

Egg *	Main course	(off the bone):	
omelette	3	sole, plaice, etc,	
scrambled	3	fillets or cut as	
boiled	2	goujon, etc	120 g
poached	2		

* Size 4

Vegetables	10 portions
potatoes (old)	1.50 kg
potatoes (new)	1.25 kg
frozen vegetables	600 g (approx)
untrimmed vegetables:	
runner beans	1.5 kg
peas	3.0 kg
Mange-tout	1.25 kg
Jerusalem artichokes	1.50 kg

Soup	Size
consommé	250 cm^3
broth	200 cm^3
thick	200 cm^3

Farinaceous foods	Main course (raw weight)	Garnish
spaghetti	60 g	30 g
ravioli	120 g	60 g
rice	60 g	30 g

Meat (per portion)	Weight per portion
baked pies	180 g
chops	180 g
cutlets	2 × 90 g
escalope	120 g
hamburger	150 g
liver and bacon	180 g (incl bacon)
roasts	180 g (raw weight on the bone)
stew	120 g (off the bone)
stew	200 g (on the bone)
steamed puddings	180 g
steaks	180 g–240 g (off the bone)
tournedos	150 g (trimmed)

Poultry and game	Portions
chicken at 1.5 kg	4 portions
poussin at 400 g	1 per portion
capon at 3–4 kg	8–10 portions
duck at 2.5 kg	4 portions
grouse, partridge at 400 g	2 portions
pheasant, wild duck at 1 kg	2 portions

Cold meats (per portion)	
baked pies: Gala, game, etc	180 g (cooked)
ham, tongue	120 g (cooked)
turkey	120 g (cooked)

Trimming loss of fresh vegetables

With untrimmed vegetables the actual trimming loss will vary according to the type and condition of the items and the skill of the vegetable cook, for example, fresh mange-tout require very little trimming but in a similar state of freshness, peas require to be shelled; young broad beans require less trimming than older ones.

5.6 WEIGHTS, MEASURES AND UNITS

Despite the fact that decimalisation was introduced into this country in 1970, many foods are still available in both metric and the old imperial measures. Many chefs still work with imperial weights, recipes are still produced in both weights and even up-to-date equipment manuals often quote dimensions in imperial units. On the other hand, many young people have no idea of the length of a *yard* or the weight of a *stone*. This can cause a variety of difficulties in the work-place and it is important for all concerned to realise that while two systems exist, clarification is needed and access to ready-reckoners and conversion charts crucial.

This text can tackle this subject only briefly and Tables 5.6 to 5.10 list

Table 5.6 *Weight*

Imperial units

16 oz (ounces)	= 1 lb (pound)
14 lb	= 1 stone
8 stones	= 1 cwt (hundredweight)
20 cwt	= 1 ton

Metric units

1000 g (grammes)	= 1 kg (kilogramme)
1000 kg	= 1 tonne (metric ton)

Comparison of units

28.4 g $\approx$ 1 oz (25 or 30 g usually used in recipe conversions)
1 kg $\approx$ 2.2 lb
1 tonne $\approx$ 2205 lb

Table 5.7 *Length*

Imperial units

12" (inches)	= 1 ft (foot)
3 ft	= 1 yd (yard)
36"	= 1 yd
1760 yds	= 1 mile

Metric units

10 mm (millimetre)	= 1 cm (centimetre)
100 cm	= 1 m (metre)
1000 m	= 1 km (kilometre)

Comparison of units

2.54 cm	= 1" (inch)
39"	= 1 m
1 mile	= 1.6 km

Table 5.8 *Area*

Imperial units

9 ft^2 (square feet)	= 1 yd^2 (square yard)
4840 yd^2	= 1 acre

Metric units

1000 cm^2 (square centimetre) = 1 m^2 (square metre)

Comparison of units

1 yd^2 ≈ 0.8 m^2

Table 5.9 *Volume*

Imperial units

20 fl oz (fluid ounces)	= 1 pt (pint)
4 gills	= 1 pt
8 pts	= 1 gal (gallon)
4 qt (quarts)	= 1 gal

Metric units

1000 cm^3 (centimetre cubed)* = 1 litre

* The old metric terms millilitres (ml) and cubic centilitre (cc) commonly used to represent this unit.

72

Comparison of units

4.5 litres ≈ 1 gal
1 pt   ≈ 568 cm³
1 litre ≈ 1.75 pts

Table 5.10   *Temperature*

Fahrenheit Scale

Freezing-point of water = − 32°F
Boiling-point of water = 212°F

Centigrade Scale

Freezing-point of water =   0°C
Boiling-point of water = 100°C

Conversion of Units

Fahrenheit to centigrade ≈ minus 32; then multiply by 0.56
Centigrade to fahrenheit ≈ multiply by 1.8; then add 32

the units used in the buying and storing of food, with useful conversions between the two systems. Approximate conversion factors are used and the mathematical symbol for approximation, ≈, is used where necessary.

Figure 5.9 illustrates the difference between a pint and a litre.

Figure 5.9   *Comparison between pint and litre*

1 pint   1 litre

* milk bottle
** wine bottle

Conversions

To change from units in one system to another, multiplication by a given number is usually all that is required. These *conversion numbers* (*factors*) need not be memorised as they are readily available in textbooks, diaries, etc. It is, however, very important that you learn how to use them. Conversion factors in common usage are given in Table 5.11.

Table 5.11   *Conversion chart*

Conversion	Multiply by
acres to square metres	4050.0
centimetres to inches	0.4
cubic inches to cubic centimetres	16.4
cubic feet to cubic metres	0.03
cubic yards to cubic metres	0.8
cubic metres to cubic yards	1.3
cubic metres to gallons	220.0
feet to metres	0.3
gallons to litres	4.6
grammes to ounces	0.04
inches to centimetres	2.54
kilometres to miles	0.6
kilogrammes to ounces	35.0
kilogrammes to pounds	2.2
litres to fluid ounces	35.0
litres to pints	1.76
litres to gallons	0.22
metres to inches	39.0
metres to feet	3.3
metres to yards	1.1
miles to kilometres	1.6
ounces to grammes	28.4[*]
pints to centimetres cubed (cm^3/ml)	568.0
pints to litres	0.6
pounds to kilogrammes	0.45
pounds to grams	454.0
squre inches to square centimetres	6.5
square feet to square metres	0.09
square yards to square metres	0.8
square miles to square kilometres	2.6
square metres to square yards	1.2
square kilometres to square miles	0.4
tons to metric tonnes	1.02
tonnes to pounds	2205.0
yards to metres	0.9

[*] 25 is a figure often used in recipe conversions

Example 1
A recipes states 3 kg of flour.
You have only imperial weights in the kitchen!
Reference to Table 5.11 provides you with the information you need.

$1 \text{ kg} \approx 2.2 \text{ lbs}$

$5 \text{ (kg)} = 2.2 \times 5 \text{ (lbs)}$
$\quad\quad\quad = 11 \text{ (lbs of flour)}$

Example 2
A deep fat fryer holds 25 pints of oil. How much oil would you need to purchase to use it?
Oil is sold in litres!
Reference to Table 5.11 provides you with the information you need.

$1 \text{ pint} \approx 0.6 \text{ litres}$

$25 \text{ (pints)} = 0.6 \times 25 \text{ (litres)}$
$\quad\quad\quad\quad\quad = 13.5 \text{ (litres of oil)}$

FOOD COSTING

6.1 ELEMENTS OF COSTS

Turnover

Catering operators calculate the *total amount of takings* achieved at regular periods to check on business efficiency. These takings are referred to as *turnover* and it is important to realise that higher takings do *not* always result in higher profits.

Profit

In running any commercial catering operation a number of costs will be incurred and these have to be deducted from takings to find out how much profit has been made. In catering operations profit is described as either *net* or *gross*. In many situations gross profit is used as a basis for calculating menu prices.

Net profit

Takings − Total costs = Net profit

Gross profit (trading profit or kitchen percentage)

Takings − Food costs = Gross profit

Elements of total costs

The total costs are usually divided, for purposes of analysis, into three broad areas as shown in Table 6.1.

Table 6.1 *Elements of costs*

Area	Examples of costs
Food	commodities
Labour	wages, national insurance
Overhead	rates or poll tax, insurance, depreciation, fuel

Determining food costs

Food costs are calculated by adding (i) the value of goods used from stock, and (ii) purchases made during the month. The value of goods from stock can be worked out from monthly stocktakings which were described in Chapter 5, section 5.4.

6.2 DETERMINING THE BREAK-EVEN POINT

A break-even point is achieved when total cost equals total takings and therefore neither profit nor loss is made. To be able to determine this point, at which you begin to make a profit, a fuller understanding of total costs is necessary.

Fixed and variable costs

In all business situations some costs have to be met in full, regardless of the volume of business, whereas others will vary depending on trade. The terms *fixed* and *variable* costs are given to these situations.

Fixed

These are costs that accrue with the passage of time and are not dependent on business activity. Examples of fixed costs are rent, rates, insurance, depreciation of premises, depreciation of certain equipment, management salaries.

Variable costs

These are costs such as alcohol, food, and tobacco, which vary proportionately with the volume of business. In the case of food the materials used would be reduced in proportion to the volume of business except for a slight increase in losses of some perishables held for service and not shifted.

Semi-fixed costs

These are costs that vary with the volume of business, but not proportionately. Examples of semi-fixed costs are: gas, electricity, laundry, replacements, certain cleaning operations and the hiring of casual staff.

Examples of cost breakdown

To illustrate the analysis of turnover and the determination of profit or loss a typical example is analysed in Tables 6.2 and 6.3.

Table 6.3 is calculated from the data in Table 6.2.

Table 6.2   *Example of cost breakdown*

Category	Amount (£)	Cost classification
Sales for the month of January	40 000	Turnover
Food costs	14 200	Food cost
Salaries and wages	10 500	Labour
Employers' tax, national insurance	500	Labour
Depreciation of equipment	1 000	Overhead
Building insurance	400	Overhead
Rent	1 500	Overhead
Rates	500	Overhead
Repairs	600	Overhead
Communications (postage, telephone)	700	Overhead
Printing	300	Overhead

Table 6.3   *Percentages of cost breakdown*

Category	Cash (£)	Percentage
Materials	14 200	36
Labour	11 000	28
Overheads	5 000	13
Net profit	9 800	23
Sales	40 000	100

Example

On the basis of £20 000 sales for the same period the set of figures shown in Table 6.4 would be probable:

Table 6.4   *Percentages of cost with lower sales*

Category	Cash (£)	Percentage
Materials	7 000	35
Labour	9 000	45
Overheads	4 000	20
Net profit	0	0
Sales	20 000	100

Break-even point

The important point to bear in mind is that there will be a certain volume of turnover where fixed and semi-fixed costs are covered and this is known as the *break-even* point.

6.3   ESTABLISHING PROFIT MARGINS

In the case of foods there are various approaches to establishing profit mark-up on dishes to be sold:

1. A fixed percentage usually rounded up, e.g. cost price 27p at 60 per cent gross profit the exact selling price would be $67\frac{1}{2}$p so mark at 70p.
2. A fixed percentage but taking account of the amount of preparation rounded up or down. Some caterers charge less profit on items that require less preparation such as frozen peas and more on items such as fresh peas. It is not possible to specify a standard percentage of profit mark-up required as each establishment will have different demands, volume of business, styles of service and overheads.

In the example given in the previous section the percentage material costs for the *whole* operation worked out to be 35 per cent at the end of the month. To price an *individual* dish to make this return this would mean that we were expecting the dish to cost 35 per cent of the selling price. If the selling price happened to be £1 then the cost price would be 35p. In practice we need a formula for doing the calculation to cope with many uneven prices and different percentage margins that may be required. A calculator may be useful but you will need to know the formula to input.

Summary

Before Individual lines are marked up by a desired percentage of gross profit and this gives the selling price (see Table 6.5).
After At the end of the trading period the percentage *gross trading* profit is calculated for all sales as a collective figure and this is also referred to as the *kitchen percentage*.

Table 6.5 *Selling price—calculation chart*

Gross profit (%)	Food cost (%)	Multiply by:	Selling price (full formula based on e.g. £10 food cost)
80	20	5.0	£10 × 100 ÷ 20 = £50
75	25	4.0	£10 × 100 ÷ 25 = £40
70	30	3.3	£10 × 100 ÷ 30 = £33
65	35	2.9	£10 × 100 ÷ 35 = £29
60	40	2.5	£10 × 100 ÷ 40 = £25
55	45	2.2	£10 × 100 ÷ 45 = £22
50	50	2.0	£10 × 100 ÷ 50 = £20
45	55	1.8	£10 × 100 ÷ 55 = £18
40	60	1.7	£10 × 100 ÷ 60 = £17

Adjustments

If the kitchen percentage falls too low there may be a number of reasons for this, such as: too-low selling-prices; pilfering; careless purchasing; too-heavy trimming-losses in food preparation; too-costly staff meals; preparing too much food; poor storage, etc. When attempting to adjust the kitchen percentage, either up or down, all these factors will need to be considered.

6.4 RECIPE-COSTING

The cost price of any individual dish may be established by adding together the cost of all the ingredients and dividing by the number of portions (see Table 6.6). Obviously the more complex the recipe the more complicated the calculation, but the basic approach is very straightforward. Difficulties do arise, however, with certain ingredients such as:

(i) seasonings, spices and herbs (for items such as salt, pepper, dried herbs and spices, a small standard sum may be added);

(ii) paper items (in the case of cutlet frills and pie frills these can be treated in the same way as ingredients). On the other hand with greaseproof paper, aluminium foil, much depends upon the quantity used.

Table 6.6 *Recipe-costing example*

Dish: *Steak and Kidney Pudding*		Portions: *10*		Recipe: *683*	
Commodity	*Quantity*	*Unit cost*		*Recipe cost*	
			£	p	
Topside of beef	800 g	kg: £5	4	00	
Ox kidney	400 g	kg: £2.50	1	00	
Onion	200 g	kg: 40p		8	
Parsley	1tsp	Bunch: 80p		20	
Worcestershire Sce.	7 ml	142 ml/Bt: 40p		2	
Demi-glace	1 litre	1 litre: £1	1	00	
Suet paste (R:87)	750 g	kg: £1.20		90	
			7	24	

Price per portion = £7.24 ÷ 10 = 72.4p

6.5 STANDARD RECIPES

Standard recipes, as the name implies, set out the detail of a standard approach to the cooking and serving of a dish. The details on a standard recipe will include a step-by-step description of the preparation of the dish giving quantities, methods, equipment and serving dishes (see Table 6.7). Standard recipes will often be illustrated and include a photograph of the finished dish ready for service. In some cases nutritional data may be included as well as alternative commodities for different seasons of the year.

The advantages of standard recipes may be set out as follows:

1. portion yields are predetermined and therefore there is more efficient cost-control;
2. standards are more consistent with better quality control;
3. purchase specifications can be standardised;
4. menu-planning is assisted particularly where nutritional data is included;
5. they help to simplify staff induction/training.

Table 6.7 *Standard recipe*

RECIPE: Hamburg Steak		Yield: 10 × 100 g	Recipe: 669
ingredients	*weight*	*method*	
butter onion, finely chopped	60 g 100 g	Melt butter in a sauteuse, add onions and cook without colour.	
topside of beef (finely minced) eggs	1.5 kg 2	Place the meat in a basin, add onion, eggs, salt, pepper, pinch of grated nutmeg and mix well. Divide into 10 even pieces and shape with palate knife as fish cakes 9 cm.	
butter	150 g	Heat in a sauté pan till clarified then add steaks. Fry gently on both sides for approx. 10–12 mins.	
French fried onions (1007)	250 g	Place hamburgers in an earthenware dish and garnish with French fried onions.	
Sauce Piquante (114)	3.0 cm³	Serve sauce Piquante apart.	

Preparation time: 1 hour/Cooking time: 35 mins/Calories per portion 740

Computerised systems

Computerised food and beverage operations systems include the use of standard recipe ingredients which link to ordering. All systems include an update price facility which gives an accurate current recipe-cost.

6.6 PORTION CONTROL

To achieve portion control, service staff must be fully trained. This training should include instruction on the use of various items of equipment that aid portion control, as listed below.

1. *Machinery* Meat slicers, butter pat machines, tea measuring machines, scales.

2. *Equipment* Tartlet moulds, flan rings, pudding roll tins, dariole moulds.
3. *Utensils* Ladles, icecream scoops, measuring jugs, Parisienne cutters.
4. *Serving dishes* Soup-plates, tea and coffee cups, individual pie dishes, ramekins, sundae glasses.
5. *Preportioned commodities* Tea bags, sugar sachets, individual jars of jam, tinned pâté, individual milk and cream tubs, stock cubes, butter pats.
6. *Purchase specifications* Egg-sizes, potato-sizes and grades, size of fish, weights of chicken.

THE MENU

7.1 DEFINITION OF MENU

Catering establishments which serve food will usually produce a menu. A menu tells the customer what dishes are available at a particular meal. A menu is also a planned production schedule for the kitchen staff.

Usually menus are printed on card but they may also be in other forms such as handwritten or plastic lettering. Caterers sometimes use various gimmicks or novelty in presenting their menus as one way to attract the customer's attention.

Menu preparation should conform to a set of rules and principles and these are discussed later in this chapter.

7.2 TYPES OF MENU

Menus appear in all shapes and sizes and are as varied as the different types of catering establishments that produce them. There are, however, three categories of menus in use:

1. special function;
2. table d'hôte;
3. à la carte.

Table 7.1 summarises these three categories.

Special function menus

These are menus that are produced for a special occasion such as a banquet or party. These menus are fixed or set in content and price and these are agreed between the caterer and customer before the function.

When the function is to be in the form of a sit-down meal there will be little or no choice of dishes. When the function is to take the form of a buffet, the dishes will be from a set range, although the customers will be able to choose freely what they wish to eat. Very often in the case of a

Table 7.1 *Summary comparison of menus*

	Special function	*Table d'hôte*	*à la carte*
Price	set and does not appear on the menu	set and appears on the menu	individual and appears on the menu
Choice	none or limited	limited	wide
Cooked	beforehand	most items cooked beforehand	to order
Courses	3–6	2–4	3–13

buffet a menu will not be displayed as all the dishes are visible to the customer.

Table d'hôte menus

This type of menu provides a limited choice of dishes at a set price. All or most of the dishes on this type of menu will have been prepared by the start of the meal, e.g. soup of the day, stews, roast joints.

Á la carte menus

These menus provide the fullest choice of dishes. The four key features of this type of menu are:

1. a large selection of courses;
2. a large selection of dishes in each course;
3. items individually priced;
4. most items cooked to order.

In many cases this type of menu is compiled and used unchanged (except for price) for a number of years. It is in these cases, in particular, that the menus may be produced in very elaborate form.

It is also the case that large companies produce an à la carte menu every day for both lunch and dinner. In these cases the menus are printed by their own printers.

Some important features of the three types of menu

1. The 'special function' and 'table d'hôte' menus may include some items that require a lengthy cooking time, e.g. large joints of meat, stews, etc. but the à la carte will normally only include items that can be cooked to order.

2. Where large numbers are involved in a special function certain items that would cause service difficulties would be avoided, e.g. mixed grill, omelette, spaghetti, etc.
3. Although by definition a table d'hôte menu has a set price, occasionally certain items can be featured as extra to the fixed price.
4. The number of courses offered in all types of menu will vary according to the different establishments.
5. The three types of menu can be used for either breakfast or lunch or dinner.

7.3   EXAMPLES OF MENUS

Samples of function, à la carte, table d'hôte and vegetarian menus are shown in Plates 7.1, 7.2 and 7.3.

Plate 7.1   *Function menu*

Menu

•

Les Huitres Native
ou
Le Saumon d'Ecosse Fumé
Chablis Premier Crû 1966

Le Contrefilet Rôti à la Broche
Les Haricots Verts Fines Fleurs
Les Pommes Croquettes
Pommard 1964

La Poire Belle Hélène

Le Canapé Diane

Le Café
Liqueurs

Plate 7.2 *Table d'hôte and à la carte menus*

Starters

ICED MELON WITH CHAMPAGNE SORBET

PÂTÉ MAISON EN TERRINE

AVOCADO WITH PRAWNS

AVOCADO VINAIGRETTE

PRAWN COCKTAIL

LOCALLY SMOKED SCOTCH SALMON

VOL AU VENT aux FRUITS DE MER

FRENCH ONION SOUP WITH PARMESAN CROUTON

LOBSTER BISQUE WITH CREAM AND BRANDY

Fish Dishes

BAKED TROUT EN PAPILLOTE

DEEP SEA SHARK PROVENCALE

PAUPIETTES OF SOLE MIRABELLE

WHOLE DOVER SOLE GRILLED OR MEUNIÈRE

FRESHWATER PIKE JANNEAU

SCAMPIS BONNE FEMME

SCAMPIS DEEP FRIED

COQUILLES ST. JACQUES NANTUA

POACHED SALMON STEAK WITH HOLLANDAISE SAUCE

Specialities of the House

MEDALLIONS OF VENISON GENERAL MURRAY

SALMON EN CROUTE

DOVER SOLE BEAUFORT PARK

FILLET OF VEAL LORD BRASSEY

A CHOICE FROM THE DESSERT OR CHEESE TROLLEYS

Dishes Flambé or prepared at the table

STEAK DIANE

ESCALOPE OF VEAL MARSALA

STEAK TARTARE

MONKFISH NEWBURG

CREPE SUZETTES

CHATEAUBRIAND BEARNAISE

ROAST RACK OF LAMB

SUPREME OF CHICKEN SANDEMAN

CREPE MONTGOMERIE

Entrées and Grills

ENTRECOTE MAITRE D'HOTEL

ENTRECOTE AUX POIVRE VERT

FILLET STEAK GARNI

TOURNEDOS MARSEILLAISE

LAMB CUTLETS RAVENNA

Daily Table d'Hote

DINNER £ 12.50

HEMSTEAD PILGRIMS
(Tomato and Vegetable Soup)

TERRINE DE SAUMON FUME ST HUBERT
(Grilled and Smoked Salmon Terrine)

SAUTE DE LOTTE ARLES
(Pan Fried Monkfish in Cream and Pernod Sauce)

COQ AU VIN
(Chicken Cooked in Red Wine with Onions, Mushrooms and Herbs)

PIECE DE VEAU LIONNAISE
(Pan Fried Calves Liver in Onion Sauce)

ALL MAIN COURSES ARE SERVED WITH A SELECTION OF SEASONAL VEGETABLES

A CHOICE FROM THE DESSERT OR CHEESE TROLLEYS

TUESDAY 23rd May 1989

Desserts

SWEETS FROM THE TROLLEY

ZABAGLIONE

ICE CREAMS AND SORBETS

SELECTION FROM THE CHEESE TROLLEY

Specialities of the Season

VEAL CORDON BLEU

SAUTE OF PIGEON FORESTIERE

SUPREME OF CHICKEN ANASTASIA

DUCKLING MONTE CARLO

CREPES JARDINIERE

LASAGNE VERDI

WELSH RAREBIT

ANGELS ON HORSEBACK

COFFEES
Coffee with Cream
Decaffeinated Coffee
Gaelic and other liqueur Coffees

Plate 7.3 *A vegetarian menu*

TO BEGIN

SOUP OF THE DAY £1.75
Made with fresh vegetables and served
with our own wholewheat roll

NUT & WINE PÂTÉ £2.25
A delicious blend of nuts and red wine
served with wholewheat toast

FRESH FRUIT COCKTAIL £1.95
A light and refreshing start to a good meal

CHEESY GARLIC MUSHROOMS £2.25
A bowl of garlic mushrooms topped
with melted Cheddar cheese

GREEK SALAD £1.85
Sliced tomatoes with goat's cheese and
black olives in a light vinaigrette dressing

CRUDITÉS £1.95
A medley of raw fresh vegetables for dipping
into chilli bean dip, hummus and garlic mayonnaise

Since the early sixties Cranks has pioneered the boom in wholefood,
vegetarian cooking and continues to use only the best in wholefood
ingredients.

The wholemeal flour from which the breads, pastries, cakes and
biscuits are freshly baked each day, is stone ground and organically
grown; as are many of the grains, seeds and pulses.

Honey, molasses and raw sugars are used for sweeteners and all
our eggs are free range. All fresh fruit and vegetables are carefully
selected and wherever possible these are organically grown.

We are committed to using these ingredients with integrity, to
produce high quality, wholefood that is both natural and delicious.

MAIN COURSES

MUSHROOM STROGANOFF £4.95
Organic mushrooms in a red wine and
sour cream sauce, served with brown rice and
a mixed salad or vegetables of the day

CHEESY LASAGNE £4.50
Layers of wholewheat pasta with courgettes and
mushrooms in a delicious tomato sauce,
topped with cheese, served with a mixed salad
or vegetables of the day

SPICY LENTIL & SPINACH QUICHE £4.35
Spiced lentils and fresh spinach topped with tofu,
served with a mixed salad or vegetables of the day

CRANKS NUT ROAST £4.95
A roast of nuts and fresh vegetables with a
ribbon of chestnut stuffing, served with a red wine
sauce and a mixed salad or vegetables of the day

BROCCOLI AND CAULIFLOWER CHEESE £4.50
A mixture of broccoli and cauliflower
florets in a cheesy sauce, served with
a mixed salad or vegetables of the day

CRANKS SALAD PLATTER £4.25
A platter of today's salads served with a baked jacket
potato with your choice of topping

DISH OF THE DAY
Our staff will tell you about today's dish

SIDE ORDERS
Green Salad £1.65
Mixed Salad £1.95
Vegetables of the Day £1.95

Baked Jacket Potato:
with Butter or Margarine £1.15
Sour Cream £1.45
Cheese, Cottage Cheese or Hummus £1.80
Cranks Garlic Bread 95p
with melted cheese £1.10

DESSERTS
*All served with fresh Jersey cream,
vanilla ice cream or plain yoghurt*

CRANKS FLOURLESS CARROT CAKE £1.90
Light and moist served with cinnamon cream

CAROB AND PRUNE GATEAU £1.90
Dark, rich and delicious

SHARP TOFU CAKE £1.90
Like a cheesecake but made with tofu and
topped with blackcurrants

WHOLEWHEAT PANCAKE £1.90
Our staff will tell you today's choice

FRESH FRUIT SALAD £2.25
Seven different fruits in pure apple juice

LEMON CHEESECAKE £1.95
Deliciously creamy with the tang of fresh lemon

FRESH FRUIT TRIFLE £2.25
With Cranks cake, fresh fruit, yoghurt and
double Jersey cream

CINNAMON FRUIT £2.25
Mixed fruit flavoured with lemon and cinnamon,
folded with strained yoghourt and whipped cream

ICE CREAM & SORBETS From 90p
We have a selection of Loseley ices.

BEVERAGES
Ground Coffee, per cup 65p
Dandelion Coffee
or Decaffeinated Coffee, per cup 60p

A selection of teas is available
per pot per person 85p

All prices include VAT.
Gratuities are at your discretion

7.4 MENU COMPILATION

It is not always easy for the lay person to differentiate between well-written and badly written menus. However, the soundness of the menu contributes greatly to the meal experience because the menu is the kitchen blueprint. The principles used in menu compilation include: sound costing policy, the provision of a variety of foods demanding skills that suit the capabilities of the staff, nutritional balance, catering to include minority groups. In the following sections the full range, listed immediately below, will be examined.

1. Pricing policy based on costs.
2. Clientele.
3. Staff capability.
4. Facilities for cooking and service.
5. Balance.
6. Business promotion and marketing.
7. Availability and season of supplies.

7.5 PRICING POLICY BASED ON COSTS

Clearly this is a prime factor in any business operation. However, when considering food and drink the operation is not straightforward. Some items may require little or no preparation before being sold whilst others will require lengthy and complex preparation and cooking. Most customers will be familiar with the price of commodities that are readily available in the shops and will recognise profits on certain dishes. Further to this, price fluctuations occur in the cost of basic commodities. Despite all these points, a price has to be fixed *in advance* (see Chapter 6 for the formula and examples).

7.6 CLIENTELE

It has been said that there is little profit in trying to educate customers so it is better to give them what they want. In some catering outlets a large selection of dishes on the menu will be necessary to suit a variety of tastes. The caterer should take account of the following factors that will influence a customer's expectations:

1. the 'healthy eating' revolution;
2. minority groups – vegetarians, religious sects, etc.;
3. local tastes and produce;
4. type of occasion – celebration, business meal;
5. customers' personal resources.

7.7 STAFF CAPABILITY

The menu should match the capabilities of the cooking and service staff. Whilst this appears to be an obvious point there are many occasions when meals do not live up to a customer's expectations, because of a mismatch of skill and output. In small establishments, where fewer staff are involved in production, the standard of food may be less consistent than in larger outlets. In some cases, with a limited range of experience, the staff may not have a full understanding of the universally acceptable standards that prevail in the industry. In these cases some chefs will not have a clear idea of recipe interpretation or a model on which to evaluate their own version of a dish. Variations of classical dishes are now fairly common and some chefs have become resourceful in combining and adapting convenience foods with fresh produce. It must be stressed that there are limits to which improvisation is acceptable and that an improvised dish may even be more costly than the authentic version.

7.8 FACILITIES FOR COOKING AND SERVICE

Equipment must be adequate, particularly as improvisation often leads to poor safety and hygiene practice. It is also the case that staff are not always familiar with the full range of functions that equipment may perform, e.g. a Bratt pan for shallow frying, a stock-pot tap to withdraw clear soup from under the fat.

It is essential, for the cost-efficient use of resources, to ensure that all staff and equipment are equally involved in production. It is important to realise, as well, that any unfair overloading of work in one production or service area may lead to bad feelings and a lowering of staff morale.

7.9 BALANCE

The term 'balance' in this context means harmony of design and proportion. There are a number of aspects of a meal that need to be balanced:

(a) colour of foods;
(b) cooking processes;
(c) texture;
(d) taste;
(e) sequence;
(f) nutritive value;
(g) ingredients;
(h) words.

(a) With the set menus in particular there needs to be a variety of colour otherwise a meal will appear dull and unappetising. There are exceptions to this as in the case of *menu tone* where, for example, a chef may design a menu with all items green for St Patrick's night.

(b) Cooking processes must be varied to ensure there are not too many fried and roasted, or boiled and stewed dishes featured on the same menu.

(c) Texture, as with cooking processes, needs to be varied as too many dishes of similar texture are unappetising.

(d) Taste needs to be varied and care should be taken to ensure that there is no one flavour that predominates at the expense of others. For example: curried eggs as a first course will mask the flavour of successive dishes.

(e) There are two points to consider here:

    (i) The courses on a menu, however many, should follow the sequence of light, heavy, light. The first course should encourage the appetite, the middle courses are the largest and the final courses should be light enough to be enjoyed with the least appetite left.

    (ii) A menu will follow a traditional sequence of courses selected from the following in the order as set out below:

    1 Hors-d'oeuvre
    2 Soup
    3 Fish
    4 Entrée
    5 Relevé (served with vegetables and potatoes)
    6 Sorbet
    7 Roast
    8 Sweet
    9 Savoury
    10 Dessert

(f) An adequate diet must contain sufficient amounts of the essential ingredients for health, which are termed *nutrients*. The concept of a balanced diet has been the central theme of nutrition education, world-wide, for many years. If a diet contains a mixture of foods, one commodity rich in a particular nutrient will *balance* the lack of this in another, so that by planning menus with a good mix of ingredients nutritional balance can be achieved. Traditional examples of nutritional balance in familiar meals will already be known, e.g. fried white fish and chips – fish is deficient in energy which is compensated for by frying in oil. Potatoes add bulk to the meal, making it more digestible, and together with lemon add the otherwise missing nutrient – Vitamin C.

This concept provides sufficient practical guidelines for the hospitality industry. It is in no way adequate, however, for the growing sectors of the industry which take responsibility for the long-term nutritional health of groups of the population with widely differing needs. It is for this reason that students of catering now need more than an elementary knowledge of the nutrients to face this challenge successfully.

(g) Repetition of principal ingredients must be avoided on set menus. A cauliflower soup and cauliflower as a vegetable is one illustration of many examples of this mistake.

(h) If the same names are repeated on a set menu it may not read well, except perhaps in the case of a novelty menu. You will find many examples of similar dish names which have different ingredients in the garnish and/or sauce, e.g. Bonne Femme when applied to fish, potatoes, soup, omelette, fruits, etc.

Table 7.2 shows examples of menu balance.

Table 7.2 *Examples of menu balance*

Menu	Colour	Principal ingredients	Cooking method	Texture	Taste
Potage Solferino	red and white	tomato potato	boiling	creamy	light creamy
Filets de Sole Bercy	brown	sole cream	poaching	tender rich	medium savoury
Escalope de Veau Princesse	brown green	veal asparagus	shallow frying	crisp nutty	stronger savoury
Carottes Vichy	red	carrots	boiling	delicate	mild
Pommes au Four	light brown	potato	baking	dry	light savoury
Bavarois à l'Orange	orange white	cream orange	cold preparation	soft creamy	sweet light
Café	brown	coffee	boiled	moist	medium

7.10 BUSINESS PROMOTION AND MARKETING

The physical appearance of the menu is a factor in raising customer expectations and attracting them to eat in the establishment. In the case of special function menus a souvenir value will be a possible additional attraction. The cost of any special printing requirements and other presentation can be chosen by the customer and included in the function price.

It is a difficult management decision to weigh up additional printing costs (particularly of an à la carte menu) against possible market benefits.

In 'popular catering' (sometimes known as 'systematic catering') menus will be designed to promote a company image and consistency of products which are strong selling-points. Very often, information about available facilities such as children's parties, special function rates, will be given on the menu.

7.11 AVAILABILITY AND SEASON OF SUPPLIES

Fluctuations in the quality and price of fresh foods are directly related to the place where it is produced, the year's weather conditions, the time it comes into edible condition, and transport costs. For example, tomatoes are available all year round but vary considerably in cost.

Foods are available in a number of different states other than fresh as Table 7.3 demonstrates.

Table 7.3 *Different states in which food is available*

May be obtained:	Meat	Fish	Fruit	Vegetables
Vacuum-packed	bacon	smoked salmon	sliced apple	peeled potato
Frozen	leg of lamb	plaice fillets	strawberries	peas
Tinned	tongue	salmon	peaches	carrots
Dried	cooked minced meat	cod	apricots	peas
Smoked/salted	brisket	trout	——	——
In sugar	——	——	preserves	
In acids	——	rollmops	——	red cabbage

The change in the organoleptic quality (e.g. flavour, texture) of these foods and their relative cost will determine their use on the menu.

7.12 THE BLUEPRINT FOR OPERATIONS

As well as telling the customer what dishes are available at a particular meal the menu is the primary document informing the cooking and waiting staff what work that has to be carried out. To be able to understand a menu in this way a member of staff must be fully trained. For example, a fully trained chef would be able to identify, from the items on the menu, what personal responsibility to assume for the preparing, cooking and service. The menu also bears a direct relationship to ordering and buying. In large establishments this function is carried out by specialist staff and a constant liaison between the chef and buyer is essential to ensure the availability of items to be featured on menus, as well as price.

7.13 CLASSICAL TERMINOLOGY

In most hotels and restaurants the composition of dishes featured on the menu is denoted in the French language which also includes technical terminology. Whilst some parts of menus could easily be translated into English by reference to an ordinary French/English dictionary, the technical terminology requires a specialist reference book (e.g. Saulnier, L., *Le Répertoire de la Cuisine*).

There is a considerable amount of menu terminology most of which was created by the practice within the French kitchen of naming dishes after people and events. Table 7.4 shows some examples of these.

Some of the classical garnish names (see Table 7.5) that have constantly appeared on menus over the years, have now become firmly established and are remembered by most chefs without reference. There are, as well, many other dishes which may be drawn from classical cookery references and this provides considerable scope for menu creation.

7.14 CONSUMER PREFERENCES

Standards

There is often much confusion about standards as everyone who has discussed eating-out experiences will recall. Since the turn of the century, eating out has become the norm of a wider range of socio-economic classes. The full range of styles and standards is extremely diverse but all operations have been influenced by the traditional cuisine. This has been seen in the case of some small hotels or restaurants producing extensive à la carte menus beyond the facilities and capabilities of the staff, and may lead to the misuse of convenience foods. One establishment featuring pâté en croûte on a special function menu actually served gala pie!

The main considerations when developing standards are the first principles of marketing which are:

- identifying the type and requirements of the customer;
- identifying the product/service you are selling.

Table 7.4 *Examples of origins of names of dishes*

Actors/actresses	*Military persons*
Noisette d'Agneau Judic	Noisette d'Agneau Lucullus
Consommé Réjane	Tournedos de Boeuf Masséna
Fraise Sarah Bernhardt	Filet de Boeuf Wellington

Authors/authoresses
Oeuf Poché Maupassant
Tournedos de Boeuf Rachel
Côtelettes d'Agneau Sévigné

Mistresses
Suprême de Volaille Agnès Sorel
Crème Dubarry
Filet de Sole Montespan

Chefs
Perdreaux pôelé Carême
Filet de Sole Dugléré
Paupiettes de Sole Escoffier

Naval persons
Côtelettes d'Agneau Nelson

Composers
Oeufs sur le plat Meyerbeer
Côtes de Veau Mozart
Tournedos Rossini

Operas
Turbot Aîda
Paupiettes de Sole Manon
Bombe Tosca

Painters
Consommé Rubens

Establishments
Omelette Maxim
Côtelettes d'Agneau Réforme
Salade Waldorf

Religious connotations
Gâteau St Honoré
Cailles en cocotte St Hubert
Consommé Xavier

Events
Crème Crécy
Noisette d'Agneau Helder
Sauté de Veau à la Marengo

Royalty
Poire Condé
Ris de Veau braisé Montpensier
Fraises Romanoff

Gastronomes
Filet de Sole Baron Brisse
Consommé Berchoux
Darne de Saumon Brillat-Savarin

Singers
Filet de Truite Caruso
Pêche Melba
Omelette Patti

Geographical locations
Potage Argenteuil
Poulet sauté Piémontaise
Sauté de Veau Provençale

Statesmen
Sole Richelieu
Salade Roosevelt
Filet de Sole Talleyrand

Table 7.5 *Garnish names*

Term	Denotes (principal/ingredients)
Africaine	egg-plant, tomatoes, mushrooms, château potatoes
Ancienne	onions, mushrooms
Argenteuil	asparagus
Bohémienne	rice, tomatoes, onions
Bouquetière	artichoke bottoms, carrots, turnips, French beans, peas, cauliflower
Bourgeoise	carrots, button onions, lardons
Bourguignonne	button onions, mushrooms, lardons
Castillane	croquette potatoes, fried onions, tomatoes
Clamart	green peas
Conti	lentils
Doria	cucumber
Dieppoise	shrimps, mussels, mushrooms
Dubarry	cauliflower
Fermière	carrots, turnips, onions, celery
Fleuriste	tomato, carrots, turnips, peas, beans, château potatoes
Florentine	spinach
Hongroise	paprika
Indienne	curry sauce, rice
Jardinière	carrots, turnips, peas, beans, cauliflower
Judic	stuffed tomatoes, braised lettuce, château potatoes
Maréchale	asparagus, noisette potatoes, truffles
Maryland	sweetcorn, banana, bacon
Milanaise	spaghetti, ham, tongue, truffle
Mirabeau	anchovy, olives
Montmorency	cherries
Nivernaise	carrots, button onions, turnips, peas
Parmentier	potatoes
Périgueux	foie gras, truffles
Portugaise	stuffed tomatoes, château potatoes
Princesse	artichoke bottoms, asparagus, noisette potatoes
Provençale	small tomatoes, stuffed mushrooms, duxelles
Réforme	ham, tongue, gherkin, mushroom, beetroot, white of egg
Richelieu	stuffed tomatoes, mushrooms, braised lettuce, château potatoes
Rossini	foie gras, truffle
Soubise	onions
St Germain	green peas
Tyrolienne	fried onions, tomatoes
Vichy	carrots
Viennoise	olive, anchovy, lemon, hard-boiled egg, parsley
Washington	sweetcorn
Zingara	ham, tongue, mushrooms, truffle

Applying this to eating-out, the factors which should influence standards set are:

1. time – there will be differences here for example between a lunch when the customer will be returning to work, and a celebration dinner;
2. money – the provision will be related to what the typical customer is prepared to spend on the meal;
3. habit – the provision will be influenced by the type of food the customer enjoys most, and will also take account of ethnic, healthy eating and dietary preferences;
4. total experience – consideration here will be given to all other aspects which contribute to the atmosphere such as style of service, restaurant décor, lighting, etc.
5. legal – catering as with other businesses operates within the confines of the law. Safety, hygiene and trades descriptions laws enforce relevant standards.

7.15 NATIONAL EATING HABITS

For many years the majority of the people of Britain have had a traditional norm of three meals a day. These have included a range of traditional dishes: eggs and bacon, tripe and onions, roast beef and Yorkshire pudding, steak and kidney pudding, etc.

These eating habits are still fairly typical of some socio-economic classes in certain parts of the country. The majority of people however will experience many different types of food in different types of establishment and this development has occurred for a number of reasons:

1. For a number of years we have had catering outlets specialising in the foods of different nations – e.g. Chinese, Indian, Italian, German and Greek foods. With the influence also of the mass media and increased travel and tourism, many people will have had experience of eating such foods. This has widened people's knowledge and appreciation of foods and substantially contributed to changes in national eating habits. Examples of typical dishes that would appear on these menus are listed at the end of this chapter.
2. 'Fast food' has increased in popularity and occupies a large share of the market. The menus are restricted but make the best use of a limited range of commodities. Standardisation of product and menu are very important characteristics of this style of catering.
3. Vegetarian food has always been available either *on* or *off* the menu. More recently specialist restaurants, e.g. Cranks, have emerged to cater for vegetarians. Vegetarian diets are of varying degrees of strictness related in many cases to religious belief.

4. Health foods and whole foods have become increasingly popular. The main emphasis is on the use of organically grown, unprocessed and untreated foods. Items on such menus might feature: wholemeal pastry; brown rice; organically grown cabbage; meat from the 'Real Meat Company' which specialises in the humane rearing of animals; Carob (chocolate substitute); fresh fruit juice, decaffeinated coffee.

7.16 THE INFLUENCE OF RACE AND RELIGION

There are considerable variations between the various socio-economic and ethnic groups in food consumption. It is also a fact that many people have taken an interest in the foods of other cultures, creating a demand for eating-out as well as experimentation at home, as can be seen by:

1. the continued growing diversity of catering outlets from multi-ethnic groups, e.g. Chinese takeaways, doner/kebab, Indian restaurants, etc.;
2. the availability of different lines of commodities, cooking, serving and eating equipment and utensils in shops and markets, e.g. woks, paw paws, yams.

A large number of dishes from cuisines other than the traditional French and English are featured on menus. Table 7.6 lists a few examples both long-standing and more recent.

Racial and religious customs

It is important for the caterer to be aware of the various food customs of different races and religions as outlined in section 3.5. The following are some additional examples:

Ethiopian   100 fast days a year.
Muslims   Fasting during Ramadan involves not eating or drink-
                ing between sunrise and sunset
Western   Some Christians do not eat meat on Fridays.

7.17 GASTRONOMIC CONSIDERATIONS

Gastronomy is the art of good living through being able to appreciate food and wine.
A *connoisseur* is a critical judge.
A *gourmet* is a connoisseur of food and wine.

A caterer must have a sound knowledge and experience of food and wine. This is particularly important in the traditional commercial sector

Table 7.6 *Examples of dishes worldwide*

Bortsch	Russia
Carpet-bag Steak	Australia
Chicken Creole	Caribbean
Chilli con Carne	South America
Chop Suey	China
Clam Chowder	USA
Club Sandwich	USA
Coleslaw	USA
Cock-a-Leekie	UK
Curry	India
Fondue	Switzerland
Frankfurters with Sauerkraut	Germany
Fried Whitebait	UK
Gazpacho	Spain
Goulash	Hungary
Chicken Gumbo Creole	USA
Guava Pie	Jamaica
Hamburg Steak	Germany
Hamburger	USA
Kedgeree	India
Lord Woolton pie	UK
Minestrone	Italy
Monkey Gland Steak	South Africa
Moussaka	Greece
Mulligatawny	India
Paella	Spain
Pavlova	Australia
Pea Soup	UK
Pizza	Italy
Potted Shrimps	UK
Risotto	Italy
Sacher Torte	Austria
Scotch Broth	UK
Smoked Salmon	UK
Smorgasbord	Scandinavia
Southern Fried Chicken	USA
Spaghetti Bolognaise	Italy
Strudel	Austria
Sweet and Sour	China
Taramosalata	Greece
Treacle Tart	UK
Tripe and Onions	UK

where an establishment's reputation is directly related to the customers' perception of the standard cuisine.

Gourmet evenings may be required as special functions and such occasions may provide potential for business promotion and prestige. All the skills of menu composition including the selection of wines on the menu will be fully employed.

It must be stressed that gastronomy is about *good* food, cooking, wine and service and does not always involve very expensive commodities.

COOKERY METHODS

8.1 INTRODUCTION

This chapter is concerned with looking at various *basic cookery preparations* with the aid of the two principal classifications used in professional cookery:

1. Classification by *courses*, and this is the way that recipe books are organised in chapters or sections such as hors-d'oeuvre, soups, fish, entrées, etc.
2. Classification by preparations such as stocks, sauces, pastries, etc., as used in *mise en place*.

8.2 MISE EN PLACE

Skill

An important part of *skill* in cookery is the ability to organise in a *methodical way* and this is referred to as *working method*. This fact is not always appreciated at first, as most people new to practical cookery assume that high levels of artistic flair and creativity ensure success. Whilst this imbalanced view has been revived to some extent, with current interest in nouvelle-cuisine with its emphasis on decoration, an organised and hygienic working approach is nevertheless still essential.

Principle

The basic principle for cooking organisation and working method is *mise en place* and it is essential to understand this as it applies at all levels of working methods. The term means '*everything in place*' before an operation.

Table 8.1 *Examples of mise en place*

Basic preparation	Dish examples
1. White stock	Minestrone, tomato sauce, goulash, etc.
2. Mayonnaise	Egg mayonnaise, coleslaw, cold fish dishes
3. Duxelle	Stuffed tomato, oeufs chimay, paupiettes

Examples

Let us look at a number of different instances where *mise en place* can be illustrated.

1. *When preparing a dish completely from start to finish with no parts previously prepared*
   If a Genoese sponge is being made, all the items needed should be to hand for a smooth operation in the minimum time, but it would be disastrous if the mixture was ready and the oven had not been switched on as the mixture would collapse before it could be cooked. Therefore before starting the operation, correct working method would entail getting *everything en place*.
2. *When preparing a dish where parts of the preparation are done beforehand*
   If a Tomato Omelette is to be prepared the operation cannot begin until all necessary items are ready and to hand. It is obvious that one would not start to peel the tomatoes after the omelette is cooked so the tomato concassé would need to be *en place* as with *everything* else required.
3. *When preparing for food service time*
   Whilst *mise en place* is involved in individual operations it is also the nature of all kitchen work, particularly before service. Levels of *mise en place* will be decided with reference to many factors such as different menus and estimates of the number of customers.

Working method

Adopting a methodical approach is obviously appropriate for all skilled tasks in every kind of work. Similar examples of working method could be drawn for such areas as bricklaying, where the bricks would need to be to hand when the cement was ready. Although the bricklayer does not refer to this in kitchen terminology as *mise en place*, it is the same principle because everything has to be in place before the operation starts.

8.3 FONDS DE CUISINE

Introduction

A skilled and experienced chef will know only too well the relevance and value of 'fonds de cuisine'. The literal translation would be *foundations of the kitchen* or *foundations of cookery*.

Preparations

These foundations refer to basic stocks, basic sauces, pastries and other basic mixtures. These basic preparations and many more examples are used in the finishing-off and cooking of dishes. In this way, the flavour of dishes is greatly improved by the use of more natural commodities. Also, the reduced last-minute work-pressure allows more time to present dishes hygienically and neatly (See Table 8.1).

8.4 STOCKS

Auguste Escoffier emphasised the place of stocks in *Le Guide Culinaire* first published in 1903:
Stock is everything in cooking, at least in French cooking. Without it nothing can be done.

Figure 8.1 *Basic stocks*

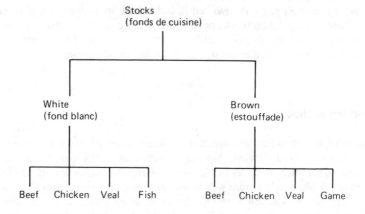

Framework

There are many different types and flavours of stock with further preparations that are developed from them. Figures 8.1, 8.2, 8.3 and 8.4 are intended to show the relationships between stock and stock-related preparations.

Figure 8.2   *Fish stock and its basic derivations*

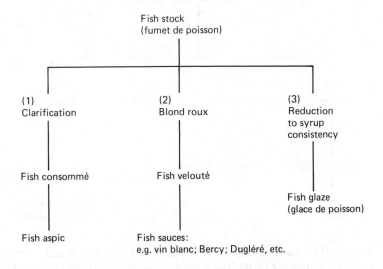

Notes: (1) Fish consommé is not a common soup. It is made from the fish stock with the addition of minced raw fish for flavour and egg-white for clarification. Fish aspic is made by adding gelatine.

  (2) Fish velouté is enriched in preparation by cooking with mushroom trimmings, freshly ground pepper and finished with a little fish glaze. Many fish velouté sauces contain dry white wine.

  (3) Fish glaze is made from fish stock reduced until it is of syrup consistency. During this process it is strained periodically through a fine chinois (see Glossary of Terms) and changed to a clean saucepan to prevent burning.

104

Figure 8.3 *White meat stock and its basic derivations*

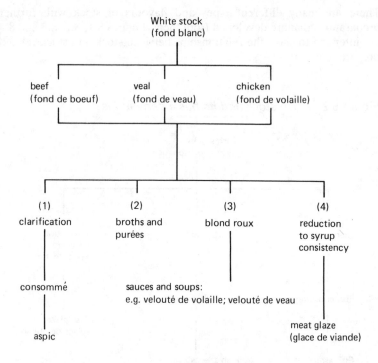

Notes: (1) Consommé is made with minced beef which increases the flavour of the stock, and egg-white to clarify. The cooking process involves long and very slow simmering where the clarification must be maintained. It is best cooked in a large stock-pot with a drain-off tap so that the clarification crust and fat at the top of the soup are not broken during straining. This gives a much better chance of preserving the clarity of the soup which is the principal presentation characteristic, particularly so that the garnish may be enhanced. If any garnishes may cause the soup to go cloudy, these are served separately.

(2) Broths are made from a good stock with finely diced meat and vegetables. All broths have some form of cereal such as barley, rice and an infusion of mild herbs.

(3) With a blond roux this stock is the basis of either a velouté soup or a velouté sauce. These are finished with a mixture (liaison) of egg-yolk and cream.

(4) The preparation of meat glaze is similar to fish glaze.

Figure 8.4 *Brown meat stock and its basic derivations*

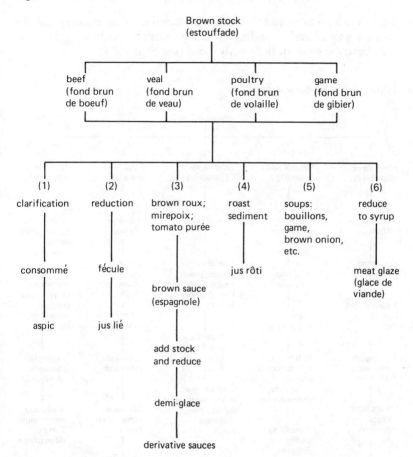

Notes: (1) A darker consommé or aspic than that made from fond blanc will result from this stock. The colour will usually resemble darkish clear amber.

(2) Jus lié is made from brown stock, bones, vegetables and other trimmings such as mushrooms. This has a long and gentle cooking before being strained and thickened.

(3) Demi-glace is refined basic brown sauce. It is made by reducing brown sauce with brown stock and skimming off the impurities that rise to the surface before straining through a fine strainer.

(4) Jus rôti is prepared by deglazing the sediment left in the bottom of roasting trays with brown stock.

(5) This stock may be used for a variety of soups both thin and thickened.

(6) Meat glaze is prepared in a similar manner to fish glaze.

106

8.5 SAUCES

There are a large number of sauces prepared in trade cookery and the clearest way of understanding these is to identify the basic sauces and then describe some of their derivations (see Figure 8.5).

Figure 8.5 *Basic sauces*

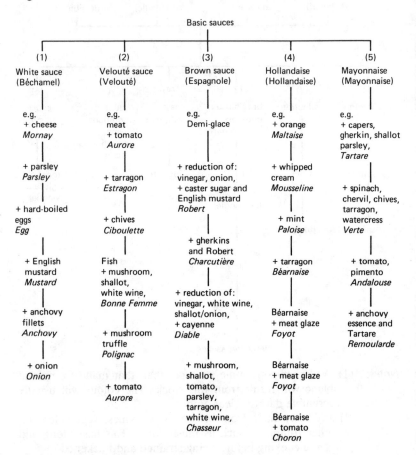

Notes:　(1)　White sauce is prepared from a white (first-stage) roux with milk and clove-studded onion. It has a number of derivative sauces, is used as a part of some cream soups, and as a binding agent.

(2)　A velouté (velvet) sauce is made from a blond (second-stage) roux. Only white stocks are used and each flavoured sauce or soup has derivations.

(3) Brown sauce is based on a brown (third-stage) roux. Where it is prepared in the traditional manner it is usually kept simmering for one or two days before being strained. It may then be stored or refined as demi-glace.

(4) Hollandaise is made by reducing vinegar with herbs and adding egg yolks with a little water, cooking gently over heat while being aerated with a whisk and slowly incorporating melted butter. It is often described as a *warm sauce* because too high a temperature would split the ingredients, breaking down the consistency. It has a variety of uses e.g. with poached fish or certain vegetables, and can be used to enrich other sauces. A principal derivation is tarragon-flavoured Béarnaise which may be served with grilled fillet steak. Béarnaise, however, is best made as a separate sauce as it should be of a thicker consistency than Hollandaise.

(5) Mayonnaise is an emulsification of egg-yolk and oil with salt, pepper, English mustard and vinegar. It has many derivatives, some of which are served with both hot and cold dishes. As a basic sauce it is usually made to a thick consistency for storage and adjusted according to use.

8.6   BASIC MIXTURES

A variety of mixtures may be used as a basis for one or more dishes. The reason behind the necessity for keeping these basic mixtures *en place* is that it would otherwise take too long to prepare certain dishes, particularly at service time.

Duxelles

Finely chopped or minced mushrooms cooked in butter with chopped shallot or onion. Used as a basis for stuffed tomatoes, stuffed aubergine, eggs Chimay, etc.

Panadas

Used in recipes for binding and extending; there are several types.

1. *Frangipane Panada*   made from flour, milk, butter, egg yolks.
2. *Potato Panada*   made from cooked sieved potatoes, milk, butter, nutmeg
3. *Bread Panada*   made from white breadcrumbs, milk, butter, nutmeg.
4. *Rice Panada*   made from rice cooked in stock, butter, nutmeg.

Stuffings

These are referred to as *farce* in the French kitchen and sometimes as *seasonings*; they are for stuffing certain joints of meat or serving as an accompaniment to roasts. Examples are chestnut, suet and mushroom stuffings.

Forcemeats

These are finely minced white-meat- or fish-based preparations used for making quenelles, soufflés and mousses. These dishes may include a panada in the preparation for extending and additional binding. Examples of forcemeat-based dishes are: *Bitok*, *Pojarskis*, *Keftédés*, *Cromeskis*, *Croquettes*, *Fricadelles*, *Fish Cakes*.

Marinades

Marinades are used for soaking various foods such as meat. The main purpose is to enhance flavour although tenderising occurs because of the acid ingredients (wine or vinegar) used. Usually the marinading liquor is used in the cooking process and is the basis of the sauce. Fish and vegetables are marinaded for certain dishes.

8.7 SOUPS

Soups that are used for first courses must be light and delicate as a means of stimulating appetite. There are other occasions where soups are served, such as after a late banquet, and lightness does not apply in the same way. Figure 8.6 describes the various types of basic soups.

Figure 8.6 *Basic soups and their derivations*

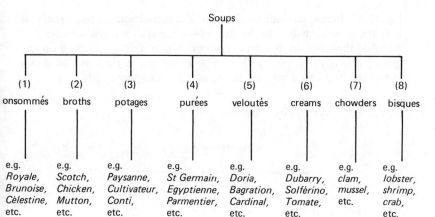

(1)	(2)	(3)	(4)	(5)	(6)	(7)	(8)
consommés	broths	potages	purées	veloutés	creams	chowders	bisques
e.g.	e.g.	e.g.	e.g.	e.g.	e.g.	e.g.	e.g.
Royale,	Scotch,	Paysanne,	St Germain,	Doria,	Dubarry,	clam,	lobster,
Brunoise,	Chicken,	Cultivateur,	Egyptienne,	Bagration,	Solférino,	mussel,	shrimp,
Célestine,	Mutton,	Conti,	Parmentier,	Cardinal,	Tomate,	etc.	crab,
etc.	etc.	etc.	etc.	etc.	etc.		etc.

Notes: (1) Consommés are clear soups prepared from a base of beef, chicken, game or fish stock. There are a considerable number of garnishes that may be added. Where consommés are served cold they will have a jelly-like consistency.

(2) Broths are one of the oldest forms of soup. They consist of good stock, vegetables, meat and mild herbs as indicated under fond blanc.

(3) Potage is a more general term for soups not included in other categories. The specialist in a large kitchen who prepares the soups is known as the potager or chef potager.

(4) Purées are passed and/or liquidised soups where the principal ingredient forms the thickening.

(5) Veloutés are from a strong-flavoured stock base made with a blond roux. They have a velvet consistency which is the origin of the name velouté. These soups are finished with a liaison of egg yolks and cream.

(6) Creams are soups that are thickened with either béchamel or velouté and finished with cream.

(7) Chowders are thick soups or stew type of seafood, vegetables, with milk or cream.

(7) Bisques are cream soups from a seafood base.

8.8 HORS-D'OEUVRE, SALADS, SAVOURIES

Figure 8.7 below sets out to illustrate a classification for the variety of *hors-d'oeuvre* available. In the case of hot items, it is often the case that many of these are in fact served warm. Where this is indicated on the menu, the term 'tiède' is used. For example, in the case of warm asparagus, this could appear on the menu as, Asperge tiède.

Figure 8.7 *Basic hors-d'oeuvre*

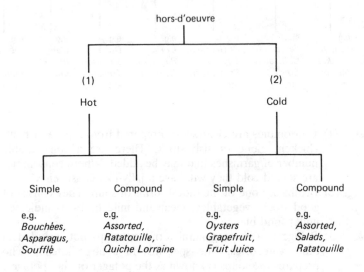

Notes: (1) Hot hors-d'oeuvre are prepared by various sections in the traditional kitchen, according to the type of cooking and commodities involved. Both hot and cold hors d'oeuvre may be featured as part of a buffet fork-luncheon as well as within a menu where they would follow the soup.

(2) There are a considerable variety of hors-d'oeuvre which include single items from caviar to grapefruit, and combinations that may be presented on a plate or from a trolley. A principal aim of an hors-d'oeuvre is to stimulate the appetite so, to this end, they must be small, neatly presented and blend in with the rest of the meal (see Chapter 7).

The general classification for *salads* is 'simple' and 'compound' (sometimes referred to as a 'combined') (See Figure 8.8). There are a few salad dishes that are served warm, e.g. Salade Tiède Nouvelle, which is cooked for two minutes. Salads are often dressed and there is a considerable number of salad dressings, such as French dressing, vinaigrette, Roquefort dressing, mayonnaise, Thousand Islands dressing.

Figure 8.8 *Basic salads and their derivations*

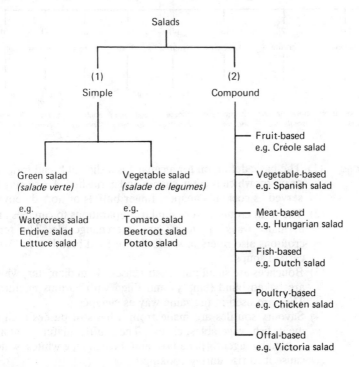

Notes: (1) *Simple salads* These salads consist of one principal item which may be fruit, vegetable or green-leaf-based. Because of their simplicity, the quality and presentation of the ingredients is of particular importance.

(2) *Compound salads* These salads are made from combinations of ingredients, often cut fairly small, sometimes marinaded and mixed with a dressing such as vinaigrette, mayonnaise, acidulated cream or other variations.

112

Savouries are classified according to their method of preparation, as in Figure 8.9 below. They are always small and delicate and may be served in a variety of situations, e.g. finger buffets, savoury course at a dinner, garnish, high tea.

Figure 8.9 *Basic savouries and their derivations*

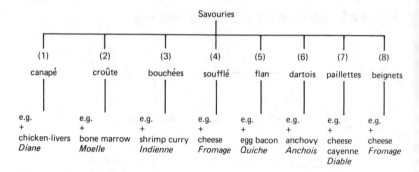

Notes: (1) The basic definition for a canapé is a slice of bread, brioche or pastry which is cut in shapes and garnished. These may be served as cocktail canapés, finger buffets or hors d'oeuvre.
(2) The term croute covers similar preparations to canapés and in many ways the terms are interchangeable. The term ·croûtons also refers to small dice of fried bread served with certain soups.
(3) Bouchées are small puff-pastry cases (4 cm diameter) which are baked blind (empty) and filled with various mixtures. They are used in the same way as canapés.
(4) Savoury soufflés are made from a basis of purées such as meat, fish, vegetables, cheese. The soufflé mixture contains a binding agent (panada), and beaten egg-whites which cause it to rise during cooking.
(5) A flan is an open tart filled with such preparations as fruit, cheese, egg, cream, stuffing. Savoury flans are used for hors d'oeuvre, as well as for light meals.
(6) Dartois consists of an oblong puff-pastry base topped with a savoury filling, then covered with another layer of pastry and baked. For service, it is cut into small pieces and used for finger buffets, etc.
(7) Paillettes are made by incorporating cheese into puff pastry by rolling it in. The paste is then cut into stick shapes and baked. These are also known as *Paillettes dorées*.
(8) Beignets are fritters which are always made small for savoury dishes. Grated parmesan, being dry and strong in flavour, is used in the beignet mixture.

8.9 EGGS, PASTA, GNOCCHI AND RICE

Eggs

There are a considerable number of ways of cooking and serving eggs. Figure 8.10 gives the classification by cooking methods. Usually eggs are cooked lightly, but care must be taken to ensure that cooking temperatures will kill harmful bacteria.

Figure 8.10 *Basic egg-dishes and their derivations*

Eggs (oeufs)	Hot	Cold
(1) scrambled (brouillés)	e.g. + tomato *Portugaise*	
(2) in cocotte (en cocotte)	e.g. + chicken and cream *Reine*	
(3) hard-boiled (durs)	e.g. + cream and onions *à la tripe*	e.g. + mayonnaise *Mayonnaise*
(4) fried (frits)	e.g. + bacon *au lard*	
(5) poached (pochés)	e.g. + cheese sauce *Mornay*	e.g. + aspic *en gelée*
(6) on the dish (sur le plat)	e.g. + onion *Lyonnaise*	
(7) omlette folded (omelette)	e.g. + onion, parsley *Maria*	e.g. + prawns *froid aux crevettes*
(8) omlette (flat) (omelette)	e.g. + tomato, capsicum, onion. *Espagnole*	e.g. + onion, potato *Paysanne froid*

Notes: (1) Beaten eggs cooked slowly in a shallow saucepan with salt and pepper and when lightly cooked finished with a little cream. The consistency of scrambled eggs should be moist and not dry.

(2) The eggs are broken into a buttered cocotte which is cooked gently in a covered bain-marie (see Glossary of Terms in Appendix). Various garnishes are added during or after cooking as the various recipes require.

(3) The eggs are placed into boiling water and cooked for 10 minutes. They are then cooled under running cold water.

(4) Eggs are best fried in an omelette pan in butter which should clarify before the egg is added. If the egg does stick on the bottom it should be moved from underneath with a blunt implement (e.g. a tablespoon handle).

(5) Eggs are poached in lightly moving water with vinegar added and no salt. Fresh eggs are essential for a good shape as well as the action of the water which should be just under boiling-point. The eggs will not stick together. When cooked, the eggs are removed to a basin of cold water and reheated in boiling salt water when required.

(6) Eggs sur le plat are broken into a buttered egg-dish which is seasoned on the bottom. They are cooked on top of the stove, finished in the oven and garnish added for service.

(7 and 8) Omelettes are made from beaten seasoned eggs. They are made in an omelette pan with butter which should clarify before the eggs are added. The process is a speedy one and omelettes are more often cooked moist and juicy, (*baveuse*). Omelettes may be presented folded or flat, with their garnishes.

Pasta

There are a considerable number and variety of pasta. There is no entirely satisfactory way of classifying them other than by size, machine- or hand-made, and by cooking method. Pastas that are boiled are usually slightly undercooked (known as *al dente*) which ensures that they are of a slightly chewy texture and this applies particularly to spaghetti.

Pasta has a tradition of variety. Figure 8.11 below gives a simple classification based on size and cooking method.

Figure 8.11 *Basic pasta dishes and their derivations*

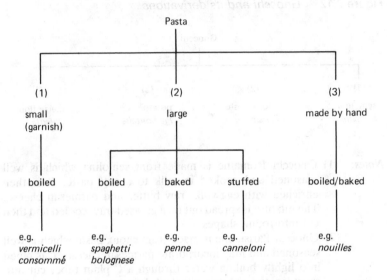

Notes (1) There is a vast range of small pasta used for garnishing such items as soups, both thick and clear. Pasta is always purchased in a dry state.

(2) The large pasta is used for main meals as well as small amounts for garnishes. One of the best-known main courses is Spaghetti Bolognaise and the best-known garnish is Lamb Cutlets Milanaise.

(3) Some pastas are made fresh as in the traditional way with no machinery involved other than a knife/pasta wheel.

116

Gnocchi

Gnocchi are a type of *dumpling* used as the basis for savouries and certain garnishes. There are four main varieties as shown in Figure 8.12.

Figure 8.12   *Gnocchi and its derivations*

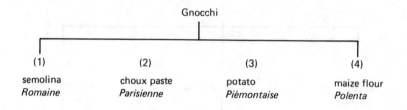

Notes: (1) Gnocchi Romaine is made from semolina which is well seasoned and cooked in milk to a stiff paste. It is then enriched with egg-yolk, raw butter and parmesan cheese. The mixture is spread out on a greased tray, cooled and then cut into round shapes.

      (2) Gnocchi Parisienne is made from choux paste which is well seasoned and may incorporate parmesan cheese. It is piped into lightly boiling water through a $\frac{1}{2}''$ plain tube, cut into short lengths and then poached. It is drained and served in a number of ways of which a light Mornay Sauce is fairly common. This gnocchi is also served as a garnish as in *Goulash Hongroise*.

      (3) Gnocchi Piémontaise is made from a mixture of baked potato pulp, flour, egg and seasoning. It is shaped into small balls and poached; drained when cooked and finished with an appropriate sauce.

      (4) Polenta is made from maize flour which is boiled with water for 25 minutes and stirred occasionally. Butter and grated parmesan cheese are added; it is then cooled and may be finished as for Gnocchi Romaine.

Rice

The simple classification in Figure 8.13 below is based upon cooking methods. There are also a number of hot and cold sweet dishes made with a rice base.

Figure 8.13   *Basic rice dishes and their derivations*

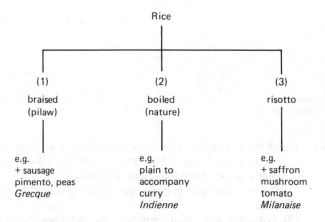

Notes: (1) The procedure for making this dish successfully can be standardised as follows: (1) The proportions of ingredients is 1 rice : 2 stock; (2) the cooking time is 20 minutes; (3) the stock must be at boiling point at all times during cooking; (4) when cooked the rice must be allowed to start to cool immediately; (5) the rice must not be stirred immediately after cooking, but left to cool for a short while first.
(2) Plenty of salted boiling water is needed for boiled rice and should be kept boiling throughout the 17 minutes cooking time for ordinary Patna rice.
(3) This is a traditional Italian dish which is cooked slowly on the top of the stove adding the stock a little at a time. Large-grain Italian rice is used for the best results.

8.10   FISH AND SHELLFISH

Fish

Fish is prepared in a number of ways for cooking and the cuts described in Figures 8.14 and 8.15 are categorised by type and size of fish.

Figure 8.14 *Round-fish classification*

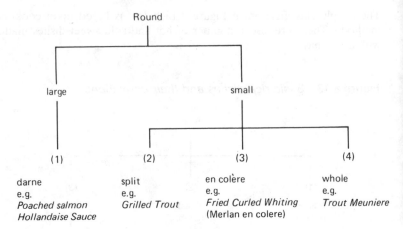

Notes: (1) A darne is a slice of a large round fish, such as salmon, cut through the bone. This term is sometimes included in the menu name, *Darne de Saumon Grillé*.
(2) Small round fish may be split open to resemble small flat fish.
(3) For en colère, skin, remove fins and eyes, push the tail through the eyes, pané (see Appendix).
(4) Small round fish may be left whole and cooked in a number of ways.

Figure 8.15 *Flat-fish classification*

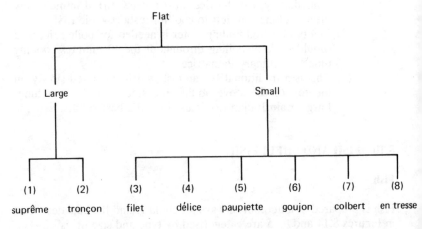

Notes: (1) These are pieces cut on a slant from fillets of large fish. A menu example would be, *Suprême de Turbot*.

(2) A tronçon is cut from a large flat fish on the bone. A menu example would be *Tronçon de Turbot*.

(3) There are four separate fillets on a small flat fish. They should be free from bones and usually skinned. An example would be *Filet de Sole Bonne Femme*.

(4) This is a fillet of fish folded. A menu example is *Délice de Sole Bonne Femme*.

(5) A paupiette is a fillet of fish, usually spread with fish forcemeat and rolled. A menu example would be *Paupiette de Merlan au Gratin*.

(6) Goujons are strips of fish cut from the fillet. They are usually breadcrumbed and deep-fried.

(7) Colbert is the name applied to Dover sole when it is semi-filleted, pané and deep-fried. Before being served the bone is removed.

(8) En tresse means fillets cut in strips, left joined at the top of the fillet, plaited (or interwoven) and breadcrumbed.

Shellfish

All shellfish may be cooked and served hot or cold. Some examples from the range of cooking methods are given in Figure 8.16.

Figure 8.16   *Shellfish classification*

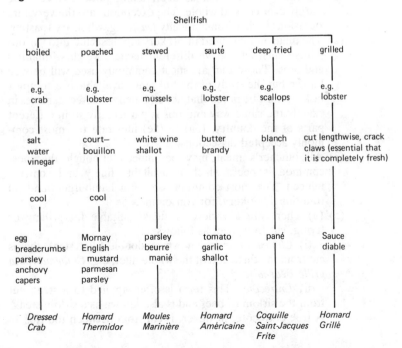

8.11   MEAT, POULTRY AND GAME

Figure 8.17 gives a classification of meat based upon the different cuts.

Figure 8.17   *Meat classification*

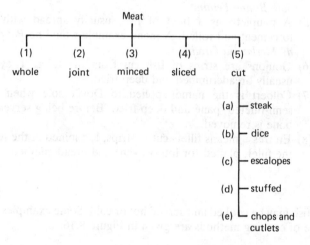

Notes: (1) Butcher's meats such as beef, lamb, pork and veal are hardly ever cooked whole. The exceptions are the very rare occasions such as some novelty *feasts* e.g. whole ox-roasting.

(2) The main animals used in cookery are dissected into various joints which each have different names, weights, qualities and uses. Those that are most commonly used will be well known but the study of the full range available is a complex task. It must be noted that not all butchers dissect carcases in exactly the same way and this is particularly so in different parts of the country. (5a) to (5e) illustrate the most commonly accepted dissections.

(3) All butcher's meat may be minced although the most common is beef, which is available finely and coarsely minced. The most common use is for hamburgers and, in traditional cookery, for consommé.

(5) (a) There are a variety of steaks suitable for grilling or frying, cut from beef as follows:

(i) *Chateaubriand*   Known as double fillet steak this is cut from the thick end of the whole fillet, e.g. *Chateaubriand grillé Béarnaise*.

(ii) *Entrecôte*   This term is often applied to a steak cut from the sirloin of beef and is also known as a sirloin steak. A true entrecôte, however, is cut from between the ribs.

    (iii) *Filet Mignon*   A small or thin fillet steak.

    (iv) *Fillet Steak*   A steak cut from the fillet of beef.

    (v) *Minute steak*   A steak usually cut from the sirloin of beef and battened out.

    (vi) *Point steak*   A steak cut from the point end of a rump of beef.

    (vii) *Porterhouse Steak*   A double thickness T-bone steak.

    (viii) *Rump Steak*   A steak cut from the rump of beef.

    (ix) *T-bone Steak*   A steak cut through the loin of beef including the fillet and bone which gives the characteristic T-shape.

    (x) *Tournedos*   A steak cut from the thinner part of the fillet of beef and usually used in garnished sauté dishes, e.g. *Tournedos Rossini*.

(5) (b) Certain dishes require diced meat and this will usually involve the coarser cuts. In the preparation excess fat and gristle may be trimmed off.

(5) (c) The most common meat to be prepared as escalopes is veal and it is battened out with a cutlet bat. A preferred practice is to envelope the escalope in cellophane to avoid it breaking up during preparation.

(5) (d) The most common example of meat prepared with stuffing is *Beef Olives*.

(5) (e) There are a variety of chops, cutlets and other cuts from lamb, veal and pork.

    (i) *Chop*   This is a cut from the loin of pork or lamb, e.g. *Côte de Porc grillé*.

    (ii) *Cutlet*   This is cut from the best end of lamb or veal, e.g. *Côtelette d'Agneau*.

    (iii) *Côtelette Double*   This is a cutlet of double thickness with two bones.

    (iv) *Chump chop*   This is cut from the chump end of the loin of lamb and is usually grilled or braised.

    (v) *Crown chop*   A chop cut through a saddle of lamb (the two loins not separated).

    (vi) *Noisette*   This is a heart-shaped piece cut from the loin of lamb and boneless. It is used mostly for garnished sauté dishes.

122

Poultry

The term applies to all domestic fowl kept for breeding (see Figure 8.18).

Figure 8.18 *Poultry classification*

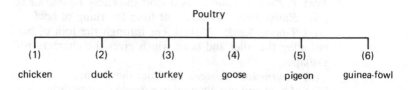

Notes: (1) A variety of sizes are used, as follows:

(a) *Poussin*   A baby chicken which is used for a variety of dishes including grills and pôelé. The weight range is 300–500 g.

(b) *Grain*   A prime chicken in the weight range of 750 g–1 kg, used for a variety of cooking methods such as roast, grill, sauté, baked (pies), sûpremes.

(c) *Reine*   A prime chicken in the weight range of 1–2 kg, used for roasting, boiling, sauté, etc.

(d) *Poularde*   A large fully-grown bird in the weight range, of 2–3 kg, used for boiling, casserole, galantines, etc.

(e) *Poule*   The largest chicken in use in cookery, approximately $3\frac{1}{2}$ kg, used for soups, salads, vol-au-vents, etc.

(2) Ducks may be roast or braised, the most common example being, *Canard à l'Orange*. The weight range for ducks is 2–3 kg, and for duckling, $1\frac{1}{2}$–2 kg.

(3) Turkey have a considerable weight range from approximately 3–22 kg. There are a variety of suitable cooking methods such as roast, pôelé, etc.

(4) More common in France, the goose weighs between 3–5 kg and may be cooked as for other poultry such as turkey. It is most commonly roast and has darkish meat.

(5) Pigeons are prepared in similar ways to other poultry. There is a variety of species but they are not a common feature on many menus in this country.

(6) Guinea-fowl are cooked in similar ways to chicken. They are more often used for special banquets.

Game

The word *game* applies to all wild animals and birds traditionally hunted and used in cookery. The main ones are shown in Figure 8.19. Other

Figure 8.19 *Game classification*

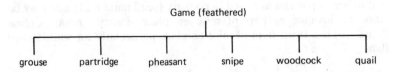

game used (furred) are venison, rabbit and hare. All game tends to be both tough and dry. It is therefore hung before cooking and in some cases marinaded as well. A well-known example of this is Jugged Hare (*Civet de Lièvre*). See Table 12.9, p. 281

8.12 VEGETABLES

The subject of vegetables is a considerable one but Figure 8.20 below gives a fairly simple cooks' classification. Classification is of course not always easy, as for example when attempting to decide whether the tomato is a fruit, vegetable or salad.

It is important to remember, however, that these classifications are given as a means of trying to make the study manageable, by considering groups with common characteristics rather than individual items.

There is a wide range of types of vegetables (see Figure 8.20) and these have a variety of uses as: a vegetable; a garnish; an ingredient in a dish. In principle, vegetables should be cooked fresh and as far as possible this usually happens. However, some are precooked for à la carte service, as well as table d'hôte, e.g. tomato concassé, spinach, ratatouille, duchesse potato mixture, etc.

Figure 8.20 *Vegetable classification*

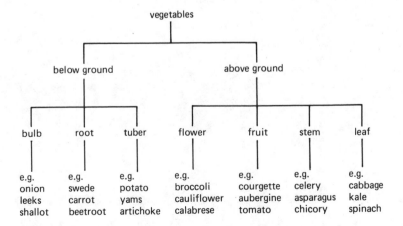

8.13 PASTRIES, SWEETS AND DESSERTS

A number of pastries are used in cookery (see Figure 8.21) and may be made in advance as part of mise en place. Pastry Cream (Crême Pâtissière) is a usual item of mise en place particularly for soufflés and flans.

Figure 8.21 *Types of pastry*

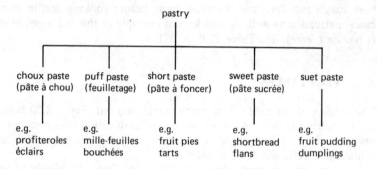

COOKING PROCESSES

9.1 THE COOKING PROCESS

Commodities are brought to the kitchen to be prepared for eating. *Food preparation* is a broad term to describe the many operations the chef may apply to food for this purpose. Many such operations do not involve heat – for example, marinading to improve taste and texture; garnishes to improve appearance; mincing to improve texture; seasoning to improve flavour. If heat is applied at any stage of preparation the food is said to undergo cooking.

Why food is cooked

Heat has been used in the preparation of food for millions of years (see section 1.6). The advantage to early man must have been primarily the increased *palatability* of cooked food. As cooking processes developed, meals changed from a collection of a few raw foodstuffs to the rich *variety* of cooked dishes which are enjoyed today. These flavour, colour and texture changes still remain the most important reasons for cooking food. Food which has been heat-treated may also *last longer, be safer to eat* and *easier to digest*.

Fresh foods are perishable and their shelf-life is short. Many bacteria and enzymes which cause food to deteriorate, however, are destroyed by heat and keeping-quality is therefore improved. Other techniques of food preparation such as salting, smoking and the use of vinegar also extend the life of foods.

Many pathogens and toxic substances associated with food are destroyed at cooking temperatures. It is crucial, however, for food handlers to realise that cooking will not always make food safe to eat (see Chapter 14).

During cooking the chemical structure of food is altered. In some cases this begins the digestion of some nutrients – for example, proteins. In other cases it can change the food so that the nutrients are more available for the process of digestion. An example of this is cooking vegetables, so that cell walls are softened to release valuable nutrients, which might otherwise pass through the body undigested.

How food is cooked

The process of cooking requires the *transfer of heat energy throughout the food* by a combination of *conduction, convection* and *radiation*. A brief summary of these methods of transferring heat is given below. Further details can be found under the individual process sections.

Conduction

Heat is transferred throughout solids by conduction. This takes place in the heating of (i) solid food and (ii) cooking equipment. Solid materials such as metals, which allow heat energy to spread easily through them are termed *good conductors*. They are needed for hot plates, pans, oven shelves and any other equipment which is directly involved in transferring heat to food. Solid materials which prevent heat passing through them easily are termed *insulators* – examples are wooden spoons and the insulating material, such as polystyrene or fibre wadding, in the walls of ovens and refrigerators.

Convection

Heat is transferred through liquids and air by convection. This takes place in the heating of (i) the cooking medium (ii) the air inside ovens. Convection currents can be seen in the movement of peas in a pan of boiling water. The water in contact with the surface of the pan will be heated by conduction. It will expand as it gets hotter, become less dense, and rise as does a hot-air balloon. As it rises, the space it leaves will be filled with cold water from around it, and this in turn will be heated and will rise. The resulting circular motion is known as a *convection current*. In the case of an oven, small gas flames can heat the air in the entire oven space in a few minutes by convection currents.

Radiation

Heat can be transferred by radiation. Heat from the sun, for example, reaches us after radiating through miles of the vacuum which we call outer space! When these so-called *waves* reach our body they transfer their heat energy to us and we feel warm. Food can also be heated by the direct heat of the sun or in a similar manner by a grill or toaster. In these cases the heat waves involved are called *infra-red waves* which represent one type of radiation. In a gas oven about 23 per cent of the heat produced is due to radiated infra-red waves, compared with about 42 per cent in an electric oven. Figure 9.1 shows other types of radiation which are involved in transferring other types of energy.

Infra-red and microwaves have application in cooking food, and gamma rays are being used in some countries, although not yet in the UK, as a method of preservation. This latter process of *irradiation* is extremely effective but also controversial on health grounds. It is gamma rays which are used in nuclear power stations and tragedies such as Chernobyl (1986) are slow to fade from memory.

Figure 9.1 *Types of radiation*

light   ultra-violet

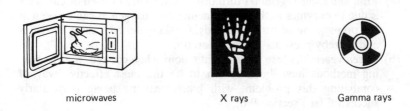

microwaves   X rays   Gamma rays

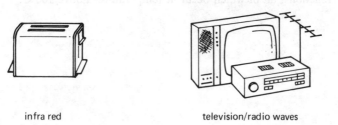

infra red   television/radio waves

Changes which take place during cooking

Heating food brings about permanent changes in *texture*, *colour* and *flavour*. This section summarises the main changes which take place during cooking.

Texture changes

(a) *Proteins* are complex molecules which slowly unfold on heating. This change in their nature (*denaturation*) causes foods to become firmer and *set* as, for example, with eggs. The effects of denaturation on meat proteins is more complicated. Some of the protein (meat fibre) sets whilst other protein leaks out with tissue fluids to form the meat juices. Collagen, a connective tissue protein, dissolves out of the meat with slow, moist cooking, producing tender dishes from poor quality cuts (see Chapter 12).
(b) *Starches* absorb water when heated to thicken and form a gel. Most baked goods owe their texture to the water-trapping properties of flour/water mixtures.
(c) *Cellulose*, the basis of fibre in plants, softens if heat is applied. This process is speeded up if water is used as a cooking liquor.
(d) *Fats* melt and soften foods during cooking. They can also hold air (e.g. in creamed cake mixtures) to produce lightness and volume.

Colour change

(a) *Fruit and some vegetables* turn brown if they are bruised or cut. This is due to enzymes in the food reacting with oxygen as can be seen in the preparation of fruit for salads. Cooking destroys these enzymes and thereby prevents this discoloration.
(b) *Green vegetables* lose their bright colour when cooked. Short cooking methods have been shown to be the most effective way of combating this problem, with batch-steaming being particularly successful (see section 9.6).
(c) *Meat pigments* change from red to brown at temperatures of above 65°C.
(d) *Browning reactions* with heat are typically seen in baked and confectionery goods. They are usually a combination of the following reactions, all of which occur at temperatures above 100°C.

	Explanation	*Example*
Dextrinisation	breaking down starch molecules into smaller molecules, termed *dextrins*	toasted bread
Caramelisation	reactions between sugar molecules	toffee
Maillard browning	reactions between sugar and protein molecules	surface of cakes

Flavour changes

The heat of cooking causes chemical changes in the food, producing a range of new flavours. Many of these are volatile and create character-istic cooking odours which help to stimulate the appetite. It is important to realise that this is a good reason both for cooking food and for consuming hot food. It is a critical factor in feeding the young, for example, who need to eat large quantities of food in relation to their body size.

Nutritional value

The effects of cooking on the nutritional value of food are varied and will be discussed in relation to individual techniques/foods later in the chapter. Whilst nutritional value is certainly often reduced by cooking this does not normally motivate the caterer to change or adapt cooking procedures. Within catering operations the *saleable value*, rather than the *nutritional value*, has been the prime consideration in both the purchase and processing of food. In recent years, however, nutrition has become much more important in:

1. Institutional catering, e.g. hospitals, school meals, meals-on-wheels.
2. Health cuisine restaurants, e.g. vegetarian, wholefood.

These issues will be discussed in more detail in Chapter 13.

The process approach

Cooking has classically been divided into *moist techniques* which involve water as a cooking medium, and *dry techniques* which do not involve water as a cooking medium (see Figure 9.2). This classification is subdivided to include the commonly used cooking processes which form the basis of this chapter. Microwaves can be used to cook food and microwave cookery is therefore included in this chapter.

130

Figure 9.2 *Dry and moist cooking processes*

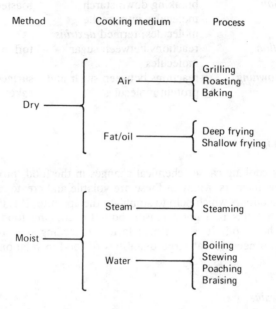

9.2 BOILING

Description of the process

This is a *moist* method of cooking in which *foods are immersed in liquid which is either at, or brought to, boiling-point.* This liquid may be water, stock, milk or court bouillon.

Heat transfer

Heat is *conducted* through the equipment surfaces to the liquid in contact with them. The liquid transfers this heat to the food by *convection* currents. Heat is absorbed by the surface of the food and passes through it by *conduction* and the food cooks. Figure 9.3 illustrates this.

Equipment

Boiling can be carried out in *small equipment*, such as saucepans, on the stove top, which may be solid, open or of the induction type. Specialist large equipment is also available, for instance, boiling pans, stockpot stands, stockpots, tilting kettles, and bratt pans. For details of any of this equipment see Chapter 10.

Figure 9.3 *The boiling process*

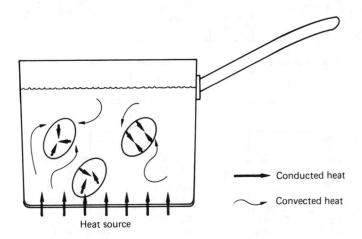

Conducted heat

Convected heat

Heat source

Routine care of equipment

(a) Equipment should be cleaned after use. The use of hot water and detergent is usually adequate. Burning can occur if the liquid level is allowed to reduce too much and soaking and abrasives may then be required.
(b) Equipment should be maintained and serviced according to manufacturers' instructions.

Suitable foods and cooking procedure

Boiling liquid may be used in the preparation of food in two ways:

1. the *complete cooking* of food;
2. the preparation or partial cooking of food items, termed *blanching*.

This section deals primarily with the cooking of food by the boiling process which is outlined in Figure 9.4. Techniques of blanching and examples can be found in Figure 9.5.

Rapid boiling

When liquids boil they rapidly produce large bubbles which burst explosively at the surface. There is rapid evaporation of water as steam, and the food may dry out and burn if the level of water is not constantly monitored. Very few foods can be cooked by prolonged boiling as they would shrivel, toughen or fall to pieces. In this respect the term 'boiling'

Figure 9.4 *Boiling techniques*

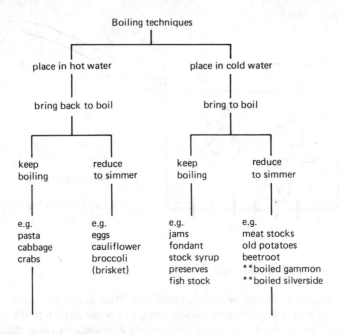

**On the menu these are referred to as 'boiled' whilst in the kitchen they
are actually simmered.

is misleading. *In practice most foods are either placed in boiling water, or
brought to the boil, and then cooked by simmering at lower temperatures.*
Well-known exceptions are starchy foods such as pasta, which are
prevented from sticking by constant boiling.

Simmering

This is a gentle heat treatment which causes small bubbles to rise slowly
from the liquid. The food remains whole, with a better texture and more
flavour. The water does not evaporate so quickly and less vigilance is
required to maintain the correct level of liquid.

Cooking from hot or cold liquid?

There is much debate as to the necessity for the traditional practice of
placing some foods into hot water and some into cold, prior to boiling/

Figure 9.5 *Blanching techniques*

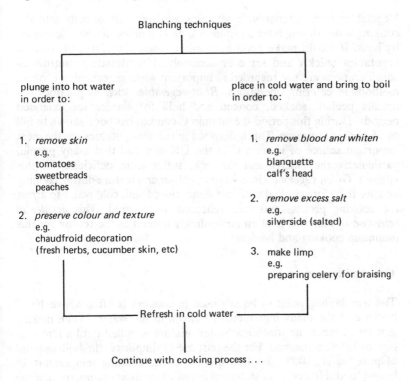

simmering. *Many foods could be placed into either with little difference to the palatability of the cooked product.* It is, however, easier and safer to use cold water in the large-scale preparation of food. This also deters the impatient chef from using water from the hot-water system if adequate supplies of boiled water are not available – only water from the cold tap is safe for cooking! Some foods – e.g. fish – break up if placed directly into hot liquid, whilst it is easier to produce clear stock if the ingredients are gently brought to boiling-point from cold.

Cooking with/without a lid

Most foods are boiled with a lid to speed up the process. Exceptions are leafy vegetables which produce an undesirable flavour if volatile acids are not allowed to escape, and stocks/jams where a function of the cooking is to evaporate water and *reduce* the water content.

The cooking of vegetables

Vegetables lose water-soluble vitamins and minerals directly into the cooking water during boiling, vitamin C and thiamine are also destroyed by heat. It would make good nutritional sense, therefore, to cook *all* vegetables quickly and serve immediately. Unfortunately, nutritional considerations are not regarded as important when determining cooking methods in catering operations. *Root vegetables* such as potatoes are usually peeled, soaked, cooked and held for service for extended periods. During this period the vitamin C content has been shown to fall by 75 per cent or more! This is despite the fact that potatoes are the most important source of vitamin C in the UK diet and that many people, particularly the elderly and the sick, suffer from deficiency of this vitamin. *Green vegetables* lose flavour, colour and texture during cooking and are therefore cooked until just done, rinsed with cold water to arrest the cooking process and then reheated as required. This *accidental retention of nutrients* is often misleadingly quoted as the reason for this minimum cooking and holding!

Time and temperature

The true boiling-point of liquids used in cookery is often above 100°C because of the many ingredients dissolved in the water. When making jam for instance the fruit/sugar/water mixture is boiled until a temperature of 105°C is reached. For the purpose of simplicity, the boiling-point of pure water, 100°C, is often quoted as the cooking temperature of boiled food. However, as stated earlier *most foods are simmered and not boiled*. The temperature of simmering is even more difficult to establish and can range from 65°C–90°C. Because cooking temperatures are variable it is therefore impossible to give accurate cooking times, unless equipment is thermostatically controlled, and skill is therefore needed to assess when foods are ready. Approximate cooking times can be useful until experience is gained.

Approximate cooking times
25 minutes per 500 g   meat
30 minutes per 500 g   poultry
20 minutes per 500 g   vegetables

The boiling process in catering operations

This is the most commonly used cooking technique, involving a wide range of foodstuffs. No special equipment is needed and any type of fuel can be utilised. The use of water as a cooking medium makes boiling an economical way of cooking foods although soluble nutrients are leached into the cooking liquor. Some of these can be recovered, however, if the liquor is used in the preparation of stocks and sauces.

Safety rules

Boiling liquids can be the cause of serious burns

1. The boiling utensil should be matched with the quantity of food to be cooked. If not enough space is available water will spill as it boils.
2. The food handler should take care when placing foods into, or removing items from, boiling liquids.
3. When reducing liquids, adequate ventilation should be available to remove steam from the atmosphere. Condensation can cause slippery floors and dampness on electrical appliances.
4. Safe practices should be observed in operational procedure, clothing and footwear (see Chapter 15).

9.3   POACHING

Description of the process

This is a *moist* method of cooking in which *food is placed in liquid which is brought to, and maintained at, a temperature just under boiling-point.* The cooking liquid may be water, milk, stock, wine, stock syrup or court bouillon.

Heat transfer

Heat is *conducted* through the cooking utensil to surfaces of the food in contact with it. It is carried to all areas of the cooking liquid by *convection* currents. Heat reaching the surface of the food is transferred through the food by *conduction*. Figure 9.6 illustrates conduction and

Figure 9.6   *The poaching process*

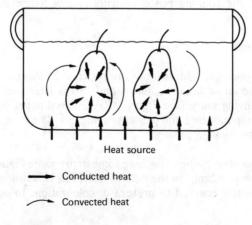

Heat source

⟶ Conducted heat

⟋ Convected heat

convection in poaching. If steam is trapped by a lid or greased paper it will increase the speed of cooking (see Steaming, section 9.6).

Equipment

Poaching does not require special equipment. Deep-poaching is often carried out in saucepans and shallow-poaching in trays, saucepans or ovenproof dishes of suitable dimensions. Fish can be poached in purpose-made *fish-kettles* which may also be used for service.

Care of equipment

(a) Equipment should be cleaned after use. Hot water and detergent are usually adequate.
(b) Care should be taken when using tin-lined copper fish-kettles or pans. The lining of tin must be intact to protect the customer from copper poisoning. Abrasive cleaning chemicals and materials should be avoided.
(c) Fish-kettles of aluminium or copper will need to be cleaned carefully to keep the attractive appearance of these expensive utensils. This is particularly important if they are used for service (see Chapter 10).

Suitable foods and cooking procedure

Foods requiring gentle handling and low-temperature cooking are often poached. It is an ideal method for eggs, fish and fruit required whole. Despite the fact that it is a moist method it is not suitable for butcher's meat because of the minimum temperatures employed. Poultry, however, can be poached satisfactorily, increasing flavour, moistness and tenderness. When the cooking liquor is used in the final dish the nutritional value is also increased. Most foods are placed into cold water although eggs are a common exception. These are placed in hot liquid to set (*denature*) the egg-proteins (in the egg-white) so as to retain its shape. The rest of the cooking process occurs at low temperature to avoid toughness.

Depth of liquid

1. *Shallow-poaching* Most foods are poached by this method. A minimum amount of liquid is added and this is later used to make an accompanying sauce (see Figure 9.7). Greased paper or a lid can be used to trap moisture and prevent drying out. The item can be basted during the cooking process.

2. *Deep-poaching* When poaching some items, more liquid is used than in shallow-poaching. In the case of fruits this is because they have to be completely covered to prevent discolouration. In other cases, as

Figure 9.7 *Shallow poaching*

with eggs, a depth of water is needed to prevent food sticking to the cooking dish, or other pieces of food, during cooking (see Figure 9.8).

Details of poaching procedures and foods used can be seen in Table 9.1 and Figure 9.9. Most types of poaching can take place in the oven or on the stove top.

Figure 9.8 *Deep poaching*

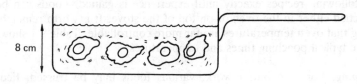

8 cm

Figure 9.9 *Poaching procedures*

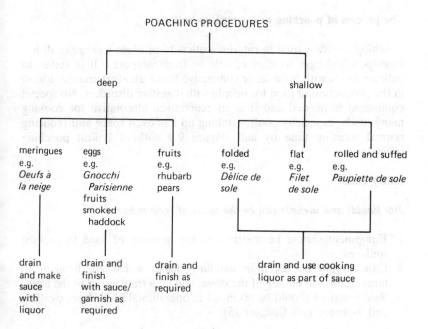

POACHING PROCEDURES

deep   shallow

meringues	eggs	fruits	folded	flat	rolled and suffed
e.g.	e.g.	e.g.	e.g.	e.g.	e.g.
Oeufs à la neige	*Gnocchi Parisienne* fruits smoked haddock	rhubarb pears	*Délice de sole*	*Filet de sole*	*Paupiette de sole*

drain and make sauce with liquor	drain and finish with sauce/ garnish as required	drain and finish as required	drain and use cooking liquor as part of sauce

Table 9.1 *Approximate poaching times/temperatures*

	cooking time		cooking temperature
Fillet of plaice	5–10 min	}	
Whole small trout	20 min	}	just below boiling-point
Eggs	3 min	}	no movement of water
Whole pears	25 min	}	

Time and temperature

Because of the delicate nature of poached food it is important to gauge correctly the time and temperature for cooking. A few minutes over might cause fish to fall to pieces or fruit to disintegrate completely. Skill in the techniques of poaching, as in most methods of cooking, depends on following recipes exactly until experience is gained. Foods can be poached either in the oven or on top of the stove. It is worth remembering that oven temperatures are far more controllable. Table 9.1 shows some typical poaching times and temperatures.

Shaping: For cold buffet work, various foods may be trussed, tied, wedged, etc., prior to poaching to give the desired shape when cooked. Large fish will normally be poached in a fish-kettle which has a drainer so that it can be lifted without breaking.

The process of poaching in catering operations

Poaching is widely used in catering outlets to produce a range of dishes from poached eggs to fillet of sole to fruit compotes. It is suited to delicate foods with little fat or connective tissue and is therefore, useful in the production of food for people with digestive disorders. No special equipment is needed and it is an economical alternative for cooking many foods, especially poultry, taking up less oven space and reducing normal roasting time by half. Figure 9.9 outlines typical poaching procedures.

Safety rules

Hot liquids and utensils can be the cause of serious burns.

1. Equipment should be matched to the quantity of food to prevent spillages.
2. Care should be taken in handling dishes which are brought to temperature on the top of the stove, and then transferred to the oven.
3. Safe practices should be observed in operational procedure, clothing and footwear (see Chapter 15).

9.4   STEWING

Description of the process

This is a *long, slow, moist* method of cooking in which *small pieces of food are simmered in a minimum amount of liquid. The liquid, which may be water, stock or prepared sauce, is always served with the food.* The stew is cooked in a dish with a tightly fitted lid, either on top of the stove or inside the oven. Figure 9.10 illustrates the process in the oven.

Figure 9.10   *The stewing process – in the oven*

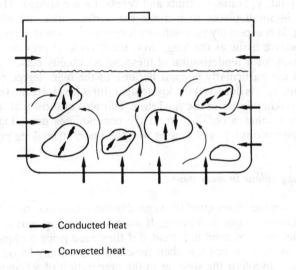

➤ Conducted heat

➤ Convected heat

Heat transfer

Heat is *conducted* through the cooking utensil and to the surfaces of the food in contact with it. It is carried to all areas of the cooking liquid by *convection* currents. Heat reaching the surface of the food then passes through it by *conduction*, the food then cooks.

Equipment

Stewing can be carried out in a variety of *small-scale kitchen equipment*. Saucepans or oven-proof dishes can be used providing they have tight-fitting lids. Specialist *large equipment* is also available, e.g. *bratt pans*, and *boiling pans*. For details of this equipment see Chapter 10.

Care of equipment

(a) Equipment should be cleaned directly after use. Hot water and detergent are usually adequate but, if sticking or burning occurs, soaking and abrasive cleaning materials may be necessary.
(b) Care should be taken to prevent damage to lids which need to be close-fitting to stop moisture from escaping.
(c) Equipment should be maintained and serviced according to manufacturers' instructions.

Suitable foods and cooking procedure

Meats, poultry, seafoods, fruits and vegetables are stewed. The food is cooked in small pieces to increase the surface area and allow even cooking. It is especially successful with coarse meats with large amounts of connective tissue as the long, slow, moist cooking provides the ideal requirements for tenderisation of these poorer quality cuts.

Stews are particularly popular because of the high degree of flavour retention. This is due to (i) the low temperatures involved and (ii) the use of the cooking liquor in the final dish. This also ensures that maximum nutritional value is obtained from the commodities used. Figure 9.11 shows the various types of stewing with their normal cooking procedure.

Developing colour in meat stews

If a brown colour is required the vegetables and meat may be browned in hot fat (*seared*) prior to stewing. If no colour development is required vegetables must be carefully sweated if they need prior cooking. White meats may be blanched and then rinsed to remove any blood or scum which may discolour the stew, as in the preparation of a blanquette.

Consistency

The cooking liquor thickens and changes colour during cooking as soluble components of the food pass into the water. These soluble components may be fat, soluble proteins, starches, sugars, vitamins, minerals or flavourings. They are often called *extractives* and they are further concentrated as water is lost as steam. In some instances these extractives will thicken the stew without the addition of thickening agents, as is the case with Irish stew. In others the consistency will need to be adjusted, by the use of suitable thickening agents, and then carefully monitored during cooking, to gain the correct degree of thickness.

Figure 9.11 *Stewing techniques*

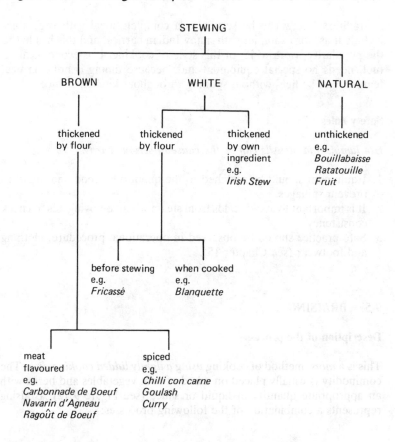

Thickening agents

Stews are usually thickened with flour during cooking but may be thickened after cooking is complete, with egg and cream *liaison*. In certain other kinds of stews the flour is *singed*, in the oven, with the main ingredients, before the liquid is added.

Time and temperature

Stewing involves cooking temperatures of approximately 80°C. This equates to an oven temperature of between 150°C and 180°C. It is important not to overcook as this causes drying-out of liquid, discoloration and breaking-up of food, and flavour-deterioration. Cooking times vary depending on the type of food, quantity, quality and temperature. It is normal for stewing to be a long process of often two or more hours.

The process of stewing in catering operations

A traditional stew can be served as a complete meal with vegetables included, as, for example, with many Indian curries, and this has led to the popularity, worldwide, of this style of cooking. It is economical on fuel, needs no special equipment and, because timing is not a critical feature, can be held without spoiling throughout kitchen service.

Safety rules

Hot liquids and utensils can be the cause of serious burns.

1. Equipment should be matched to the quantity of food and liquid to prevent spillages.
2. It is important to avoid scalds from steam when removing lids to check consistency.
3. Safe practice should be observed in operational procedure, clothing and footwear (see Chapter 15).

9.5 BRAISING

Description of the process

This is a *moist* method of cooking *using a tightly lidded cooking dish*. The commodity is usually placed on a bed of root vegetables and herbs with an appropriate quantity of liquid or sauce (see Figure 9.12). Braising represents a combination of the following processes:

Figure 9.12 *The braising process*

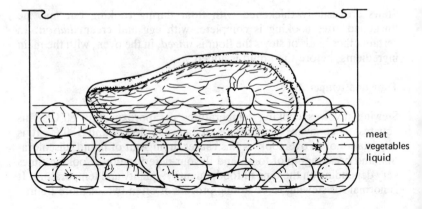

meat
vegetables
liquid

1. *stewing*   less liquid involved
2. *pot-roasting* water, not fat, main ingredient in cooking liquor.
3. *steaming*   water vapour trapped under lid

Heat transfer

The food cooks by a combination of (i) heat produced from the steam, and (ii) heat conducted and convected through the container and the liquid in which the item is cooked.

Equipment

Braising can take place in a specially designed pan, called a *braisière*, or in a tight-lidded earthenware dish. If large quantities are required then *bratt pans* may be used, although these are not suitable for braised dishes which require glazing.

Care of equipment

(a) Equipment should be cleaned directly after use. Hot water and detergent are usually adequate but soaking and abrasive cleaning agents may be necessary.
(b) Care should be taken to avoid damage to lids which need to be tightly fitting in order for foods to braise effectively.
(c) Equipment should be maintained and serviced according to manufacturers' instructions.

Suitable foods and cooking procedures

Poultry, meat and vegetables can all be braised. It is a particularly suitable method for tough, fibrous vegetables which require a lot of softening and also for the coarser, cheaper cuts of meat (see Figure 9.13). The normal braising technique is outlined in Figure 9.14. The bed of root vegetables used are generally overcooked and discoloured after braising and are strained off and used in the preparation of sauces.

Thickening

The liquid in which the food is cooked is usually served with the braised items as a sauce. It is thickened by one of the following methods.

(a) The items to be braised are *dredged in flour* before cooking so that the liquor thickens during cooking, e.g. braised steaks.

Figure 9.13 *Braising types*

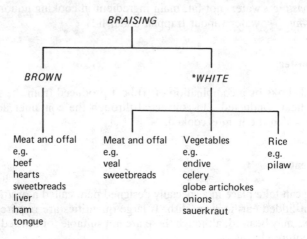

*White braising involves white stock and natural ingredients, ie. not browned

(b) *Espagnole* is diluted with an equal quantity of stock and used as the cooking liquor, e.g. braised beef.
(c) The liquor remains *unthickened during cooking*. It is made into a sauce when cooking is completed. This can be by the addition of butter or a ready-made base such as a velouté, e.g. braised sweetbreads.

Braising meat and offal

Browning Braised dishes are classed as either *white* or *brown*. Brown braising involves the colouring of meat in hot fat (*searing*) before cooking. Large joints need to be flash-roasted to obtain the same effect.

Glazing Some meat dishes are *glazed* towards the end of the cooking period. The lid is taken off the braising pot and the cooking liquor is spooned over the commodity at regular intervals. This procedure, called *masking*, is the equivalent to basting except that the liquid is not fat. The water present in the liquid evaporates from the surface of the food leaving behind a gelatinous, shiny glaze, e.g. *Ris de veau Financière*.

Marinating Some meats are soaked in flavoured alcohol or acid, to tenderise and improve flavour and colour, prior to cooking, e.g. *Civet de Lièvre*.

Figure 9.14 *The braising procedure*

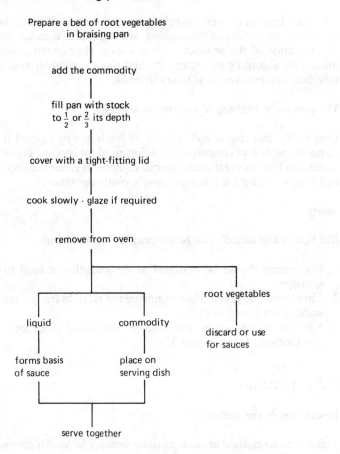

```
Prepare a bed of root vegetables
       in braising pan
              |
       add the commodity
              |
       fill pan with stock
       to ½ or ⅔ its depth
              |
     cover with a tight-fitting lid
              |
     cook slowly - glaze if required
              |
        remove from oven
```

Larding If very lean meats are required braised, they need to have fat added to them to prevent excessive shrinkage and drying out, e.g. *Boeuf braisé à la mode.*

Braising vegetables

Fibrous vegetables, such as celery, are washed and then placed into boiling water for 10 minutes and then rewashed in cold water. Without this initial *blanching* celery hearts could not be cleaned effectively. After blanching they are also limp enough to be shaped and tied to produce traditional braised dishes.

Time and temperature

Foods are braised at oven temperatures of around 150°C until the food is well-done or tender. Overcooking will produce discolouration and disintegration of the product. This is a long, slow cooking method but times vary according to commodity and size. Vegetables and meat can take between one and four hours to braise.

The process of braising in catering operations

Despite the fact that a wide variety of foods can be braised it is not a common method of cookery. It is mainly used for cooking poorer quality meats and fibrous vegetables. Special equipment is not required but skill and time is, making it a comparatively costly operation.

Safety

Hot liquids and utensils can be the cause of serious burns.

1. Equipment should be matched to the quantity of food to prevent spillages.
2. Care should be taken when removing the lid of braising pans to avoid scalds from escaping steam.
3. Safe practice should be observed in operational procedure, clothing and footwear (see Chapter 15).

9.6   STEAMING

Description of the method

This is a *moist* method of cooking *using steam. The food is surrounded by steam under varying degrees of pressure.*

Heat transfer

Steam is produced when water is heated. The water molecules absorb the heat and turn into a gas. If this gas (steam) then meets a cool surface it will condense back into water and give off the heat it absorbed initially. This is why steam burns so painfully when it condenses on the skin!

How steam cooks food

If food is placed in a cabinet of steam some of the steam will condense back into water as it touches the cooler food. The food absorbs the heat and this heat is conducted through the food causing it to cook. Figure 9.15 illustrates this.

Figure 9.15 *Steaming without pressure*

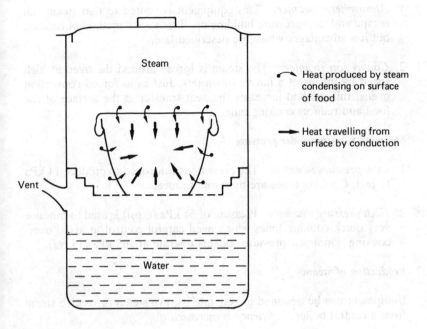

Pressure steaming

If the steam is not allowed to escape into the atmosphere, pressure will build up. This increase in pressure causes water to boil at temperatures of above 100°C. The *greater the pressure*, the *higher the temperature*, the *faster the cooking*. For example, at 34 kPa (5 psi) pressure water boils at 109°C and contains six times more heat than water at 100°C.

Units in which steam is measured

Steam is measured in units called *Kilopascals (kPa)*. This replaces the old units *pounds per square inch (psi)* and *kilonewtons per metre squared (kn/m^2)*.

Conversion: 1 kPa = 1 kn/m^2
7 kPa ≈ 1 psi

Equipment

The technical details of the variety of steamers available to the trade can be found in Chapter 10.

Steamers working without pressure

1. *Atmospheric steamers* This equipment is vented so that steam can escape and stop pressure building up. This a slow method of cooking but has advantages which are described later.

2. *Convection steamers* The steam is forced around the oven at high speed by means of a fan or steam jets. Just as in forced convection ovens, this method increases the heat transfer at the surface of the food and reduces cooking time.

Steamers working under pressure

1. *Low-pressure steamers* The pressure is controlled to produce 14 kPa (2 psi). Cooking times are therefore reduced.

2. *High pressure steamers* Pressure of 54 kPa (8 psi) is used to produce very quick cooking times which need careful control to avoid overcooking. Domestic pressure cookers operate at 105 kPa (15 psi).

Production of steam

Equipment can be designed to generate its own steam or receive steam from a central boiler. *Efficiency is increased if*:

(a) *air* is excluded from the equipment before steam is introduced and cooking commences;
(b) *moisture in the steam* is removed to produce what is termed *dry* steam (a feature of expensive new equipment).

Routine care of equipment

(a) Equipment should be cleaned regularly, with non-caustic detergent and warm water. The doors should be left slightly ajar after cleaning to allow for air circulation.
(b) Equipment should be maintained and serviced according to manufacturers' instructions.
(c) Equipment that generates its own steam will need to have the 'boiler' drained, cleaned and refilled at least once a week.

Suitable foods and cooking procedures

Steaming is a method of cooking which *does not develop colour*. Even though food can overcook, it will not burn or dry out, because of its constant contact with moisture at its surface. This moisture presents a problem for dry foods as they can easily become *soggy* if not covered carefully. Most other foods are cooked in perforated containers so that excess moisture can drain away. It is an unsuitable method for items which require a crisp, brown surface, such as short-crust pastry or cakes. Despite these drawbacks many foods including vegetables, fish and puddings, are successfully cooked with steam. In industrial catering, 'boiling' chickens and bacon joints are also often cooked by steaming. Poor-quality cuts of meat can be effectively tenderised and are often used to make savoury steamed dishes. Figure 9.16 gives examples of commonly steamed dishes with an indication of general cooking procedure.

Food at all stages of preparation, ranging from fresh to pre-cooked and frozen items, can be steamed successfully. The *retention of shape, texture, flavour and nutrients is high* making this an extremely successful cooking operation. Vegetable steam cooking saves considerable time, fuel and nutrients because the traditional blanching, refreshing and reheating is avoided. Small batches can be cooked on demand, in minutes, and then taken directly from the steamer to the customer.

Figure 9.16 *Steaming procedures*

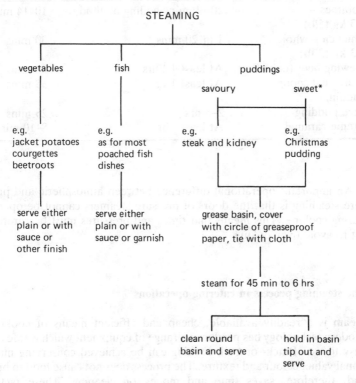

* Some suet-based items are immersed in boiling water, cooked by a process of rapid boiling, in which escaping steam is trapped by a lid. The items are therefore cooked under pressure and this may be classified as steaming, e.g. Jam Roly-poly.

Time and temperature

Steaming without pressure is a slow operation but if forced convection is introduced faster cooking times are achieved. Steaming under pressure reduces cooking times dramatically, as temperatures relate directly to pressure and range from 100°C to 122°C. Large and dense items cook more slowly but if using high pressure these differences are of only marginal importance, e.g. 1 minute or 8 minutes (See table 9.2).

Table 9.2   *A comparison of traditional/high-pressure cooking times*

Food	Time to cook by conventional method	Cooking times at 8 psi/ 54 kPa
Potatoes – 2.3 kg (5lb)	20–40 mins boiling method;	10–14 mins
Chicken – whole 1.3 kg (3 lb)	1 hr 20 mins	30 mins
Stewing beef (cubed)	At least $1\frac{1}{2}$ hrs	30 mins
Individual sponge puddings	At least 1 hr	35 mins
Rice pudding	2–3 hrs	25 mins
Creme caramel	At least $\frac{1}{2}$ hr	8–10 mins

An important operational difference between atmospheric and pressure steaming is that the doors of pressure steamers cannot be opened during cooking. This means that times and pressures must be carefully set to avoid overcooking.

The steaming process in catering operations

Steam is a readily available, cheap and efficient means of cooking. Modern technology has produced a range of equipment which is safe and easy to use. Batch- or bulk-cooking can be achieved conserving nutritional value, colour and texture. The process does not cause food to burn and, therefore, saves time and money on cleaning. These factors combine to give a cooking process which is both low on labour and high on productivity thereby ensuring it a place in all modern catering operations.

Safety rules

Steam can be the cause of serious scalds.

1. Before use, check that the water level is correct for self-generating equipment.
2. Switch off all steam controls and reduce pressure before opening.
3. Stand behind the door as it opens, to shield the body from steam.
4. Follow manufacturers' instructions.
5. Safe practice should be observed in operational procedure, clothing and footwear (see Chapter 15).

9.7   BAKING

Description of method

This is a *dry* method of *cooking in an oven*. The texture, surface and volume of baked goods are modified by steam. This is produced by the food as it cooks (secondary steam), or can be injected into the oven (primary steam) if required.

Heat transfer

The heat source in the oven *radiates infra-red heat energy* (see section 9.1) and also heats the air in the oven cavity directly by producing *convection currents*. The surfaces of the food will absorb heat from both sources and also from the hot trays and racks by *conduction*. The food will be cooked through by the *conduction* of this surface heat. Figure 9.17 illustrates this.

Equipment

The process of baking can be carried out either in a *batch* or in a *continuous* operation. The latter process involves a conveyor-belt system where raw food enters one end of a *tunnel oven* and cooked food is removed from the other end. This is the method by which bread is manufactured in factories.

In a batch operation any style of oven can be used. In catering operations these usually fall into the following categories:

1. traditional *general purpose* oven;
2. forced-air-*convection* ovens;
3. *combination* ovens (a) microwave/convection (b) convection/steam;
4. specialist *pastry* ovens;
5. specialist *pizza* ovens.

These ovens are described in detail in Chapter 10.

Figure 9.17 *Baking process*

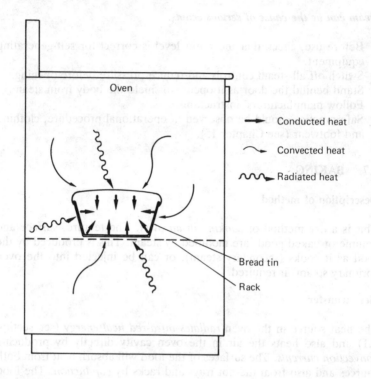

Routine care of equipment

(a) Ovens should be regularly cleaned. Hot water and detergent are usually adequate. Deep cleaning at 3-monthly intervals is recommended.
(b) Baking trays and moulds should be kept lightly oiled. To prevent sticking it is common practice to scrape and wipe clean after use, washing with hot water and detergent only when absolutely necessary.
(c) Equipment should be maintained and serviced according to manufacturers' instructions.

Suitable foods and cooking procedures

The process of baking is usually associated with flour products; egg and milk dishes; fruit; vegetables, and fish. The baking of meat usually involves fat and is therefore classified as roasting. Figure 9.18 illustrates the application of the three methods to different foods and Figure 9.19 shows the cooking procedures for the main groups of baked foods.

Figure 9.18 *Baking methods*

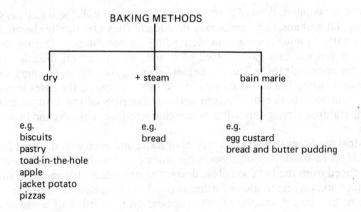

Figure 9.19 *Baking procedures*

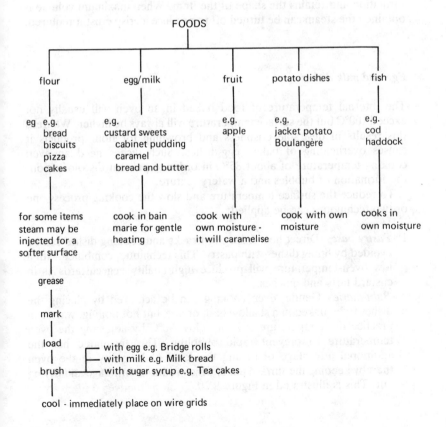

Flour products

These are combinations of flour and liquid (water or milk) to which eggs, sugar, fat and aerating agents may be added. They are usually classified into batters, doughs or pastes depending on consistency. During the baking process tiny gas bubbles of steam, air or carbon dioxide are produced causing the mixture to expand. During cooking and cooling the gelatinised starches and denatured proteins set, trapping the gases inside the item to produce the desired texture. Because of the high surface temperatures, drying-out will produce characteristic crispness and brown colour.

Most foods contain large quantities of water and even with dry heat the atmosphere inside the oven soon becomes damp with *secondary steam* produced from the hot food. This delays the premature drying-out of the surface and therefore allows further expansion of aerated goods. Despite this natural steam, cracks will often appear on the surface of bread and cakes as gases break the hardened surface to escape. Bakery ovens which inject *primary steam* into the oven cavity are therefore often used for the production of bread. The constant moisture on the surface prevents crust formation and retains the shape of the item. When maximum volume is obtained the steam can be turned off to produce a crisp crust if required.

Egg and milk dishes

The internal temperature of food baked in an oven will usually not exceed 100°C but the surface temperature will always be higher. Whereas this results in desirable crispness and browning for flour products it causes overheating of baked egg-dishes. Such dishes need an even cooking temperature of about 85°C in order to prevent discolouration, the formation of bubbles and a watery texture.

To reduce the surface temperature and slow the cooking process one of two techniques can be applied:

1. *Pastry base* Direct heat from oven racks and cooking dishes can be avoided by lining dishes with pastry. This technique, combined with a low oven-temperature will produce high-quality egg custards as in custard tarts and quiches.
2. *Bain-marie* Gentle, even cooking can be achieved by placing the dishes to be baked in a shallow bath of hot, but not boiling, water. In practice the temperature is kept below 90°C by adjusting the oven temperature to prevent rapid bubbling. This technique has the additional advantage of raising the level of humidity in the oven thereby keeping the surface moist which reduces shrinkage and drying out. This is illustrated in Figure 9.20.

Figure 9.20 *Individual egg custards in a bain-marie*

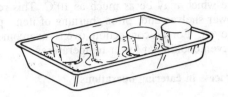

Fruit and vegetables

Baking fruit and vegetables is a relatively simple operation where whole or stuffed items are cooked, with relatively little preparation, in the oven. The major change taking place is the softening of cellulose with some drying-out of the surface. Fruits such as apple are sprinkled with sugar to encourage surface browning by caramelisation.

Fish

Many of the baked fish may be stuffed with any one of a variety of preparations, including veal forcemeat, duxelle, and fish forcemeat.

If a large fish is used and it is to be presented whole, as for a buffet, it may be shaped (trussed in a letter S) before cooking. The fish is cooked in the oven with butter and oil and constantly basted to enhance colour and moistness. Any sauce or glaze will be made with the cooking liquor as the base.

Time and temperature

Oven temperatures range from 120°C to 270°C with times varying according to item, size and degree of cooking required (see Table 9.3). Internal temperatures do not rise above 100°C but surface temperatures can be above 130°C. The browning reactions, which this high surface-temperature produces, are outlined in section 9.1.

Table 9.3 *Examples of cooking times and temperatures of baked foods*

Oven	Temperature	Time
Pizza	270°C	10 minutes
Jacket potatoes	230°C	60 minutes
Victoria sandwich	205°C	15 minutes
Baked egg custard	170°C	60 minutes

Cooking temperatures also vary according to oven type (see Chapter 10). General-purpose ovens have stagnant heat areas creating variations in temperature which may be as much as 10°C. This results in slower cooking on lower shelves and, often, burning of items placed near the sides of the oven. Forced-convection ovens overcome this problem creating fast, even cooking at lower temperatures.

The baking process in catering operations

Baked goods, particularly flour-based items, are extensively produced in catering operations and in food-processing factories. Bread is one of the UK's staple foods and bakery technology is highly developed to cope with the quantity required by the customer.

Safety rules

High oven temperatures with steam can be the cause of burns and scalds.

1. Care is needed in moving heavily loaded trays, into and out of ovens, to prevent burns and scalds from the hot and steamy oven atmosphere.
2. The food-handler should take care when removing baked items from trays/tins/moulds.
3. Safe practice should be observed in operational procedure, clothing and footwear. (see Chapter 15).

9.8 ROASTING

The term roasting is given to three different techniques of cooking. In all cases the term refers to a *dry* method of cooking *involving either the addition of fat/oil, or the use of foods with a high fat content*. The three techniques are:

1. spit-roasting;
2. pot-roasting;
3. oven roasting.

The three methods will be discussed briefly below. A full account of oven roasting will then be outlined as this is the most popular method of roasting in use today.

Spit-roasting

This is the traditional use of the term roasting and is only applicable to the cooking of meats. It could be more accurately described as slow *grilling* as it involves cooking by radiated heat, on a spit, over a very

Plate 9.1 *Traditional spit-roasting*

fierce, glowing fire (see Plate 9.1). The spitted roast cooks in the open air retaining the full flavour of the food and also that imparted by the fuel used, for example, wood. The meat is prevented from drying-out by the constant rotation of the spit which allows the meat to baste itself with the hot fat which oozes from the surface. Some caterers specialise in providing this outdoor service for special functions and they enjoy the opportunity to display their skill and talent. A modern equivalent is the electrically heated rotisserie or revolving spit fitted to some grills and ovens.

Pot roasting (poêlé)

A traditional technique of 'old cookery' involves *roasting meat* on a bed of *root vegetables* using *butter* in an *enclosed* container (Figure 9.21). The meat cooks in a steamy atmosphere, produced as water seeps out of the vegetables, speeding up the cooking time. After cooking the lid is removed to allow browning and the juices left are used as a base for a sauce. The enclosed steam makes this a moist method of cooking and therefore not a true roasting.

Figure 9.21   *Traditional pot-roasting*

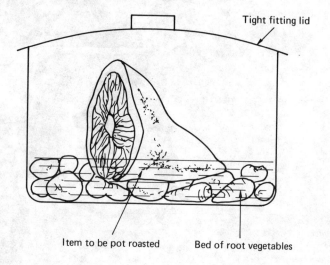

Tight fitting lid

Item to be pot roasted   Bed of root vegetables

Oven-roasting

Method

'Oven-roasting' refers to cooking foods in an *uncovered dish, in the oven, without any water*. Fat is either produced during the cooking process (for example, meats) or added (for example, vegetables) to the food. For this reason it is often described as *baking food in a quantity of fat.*

Heat transfer

The heat source in the oven *radiates infra-red heat energy* and also heats the oven cavity directly by producing *convection currents*. The surface of the food will absorb heat from both sources and also from the hot trays and racks by *conduction*. The food will be cooked through by the *conduction* of this surface heat (see Figure 9.22). It is usual for the surface of the food to lose water into the atmosphere and become crisp.

Figure 9.22 *The process of roasting*

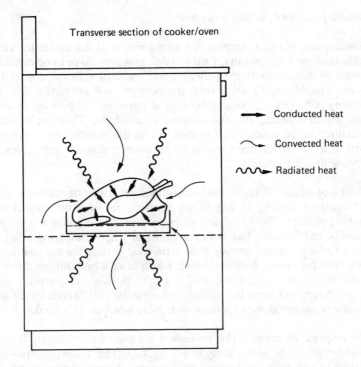

Transverse section of cooker/oven

→ Conducted heat

∿ Convected heat

∿∿ Radiated heat

Equipment

Oven-roasting can take place in any oven producing dry heat. Ovens can be classified into the following categories:

1. traditional *general purpose* oven;
2. forced-air-*convection* ovens;

3. combination *microwave-convection* oven;
4. combination *steam-convection* oven.

These ovens are all described in more detail in Chapter 10.

Routine care of equipment

(a) Equipment should be cleaned after use. Ovens may need regular deep cleaning using caustic degreasants if in heavy use. This is particularly important if used extensively for roasting as grease deposits are spilt and spattered throughout the oven cavity.
(b) Equipment should be maintained and serviced according to manufacturers' instructions.

Suitable foods and cooking procedure

Roasting is a popular method of cooking *meats*. It is suitable for veal, pork, lamb and also poultry. Cuts of beef, however, have to be carefully chosen as this dry method of cooking will not soften fibrous connective tissue. Tougher cuts such as shin, for example, will never tenderise by roasting (Chapter 12). *Vegetables* such as potatoes and parsnips, with a high starch-content, are also roasted successfully. They retain their structure, soften inside and become crisp on the outside. With constant basting from hot fat they brown to produce traditional vegetables to serve with roast joints.

The use of oil/fat Roasted food has a moist yet crisp exterior because of the constant coating of hot fat/oil which it receives throughout the cooking process. The fat/oil also seeps inside the food giving it a unique richness and flavour. The difference is clear when comparing a baked and a roasted potato. *Basting* is the term used to describe the coating of food with fat during roasting. Foods which have a high fat content will baste themselves as did the wild animals spit-roasted centuries ago, whilst others will need the addition of some type of fat/oil, which will usually be spooned over the item at regular intervals as it cooks.

The roasting of meats The procedure adopted for all meats is very similar and can be seen clearly in Figure 9.23. The following terms are outlined to identify the reasons for following these techniques and the adaptations required for vegetables.

(a) *Trivet* The roasting tray will quickly reach a much higher temperature that that in the oven cavity as heat is conducted along the metal shelves and throughout the dish. If the meat were to be placed directly onto the tray this would cause initial *scorching* and eventual *frying* of the meat in the hot oil collected in the bottom of the tray. The resultant inedible, burnt crust would then have to be discarded.

Figure 9.23 *Roasting meat*

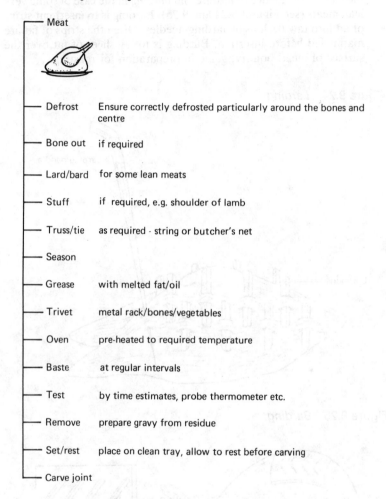

Roasting meat (stages)

- Meat
- Defrost   Ensure correctly defrosted particularly around the bones and centre
- Bone out   if required
- Lard/bard   for some lean meats
- Stuff   if required, e.g. shoulder of lamb
- Truss/tie   as required - string or butcher's net
- Season
- Grease   with melted fat/oil
- Trivet   metal rack/bones/vegetables
- Oven   pre-heated to required temperature
- Baste   at regular intervals
- Test   by time estimates, probe thermometer etc.
- Remove   prepare gravy from residue
- Set/rest   place on clean tray, allow to rest before carving
- Carve joint

The meat is therefore raised off the floor of the dish with either a metal rack (*trivet*), bones or in some cases vegetables. All three of these items are often loosely described as trivets but the literal translation refers only to the first one.

In contrast, the roasting of vegetables requires no trivet. Potatoes and parsnips prepared for roasting have a much larger surface area than the typical roast joint prepared for the same number of covers. It is therefore important that every source of heat is utilised to give a crisp, brown surface in the relatively short cooking-time.

(b) *Larding and barding* Techniques for incorporating fat/oil into roasted foods can vary from simply adding it to the roasting pan to the elaborate practice of *larding* and *barding* in the case of some very lean meats (see Figures 9.24 and 9.25). Larding is to insert cut strips of fat into raw flesh using larding needles. Often the strips of fat are marinaded before insertion. Barding is to lay slices of fat over the surface of meat, poultry, game in preparation for roasting.

Figure 9.24 *Larding*

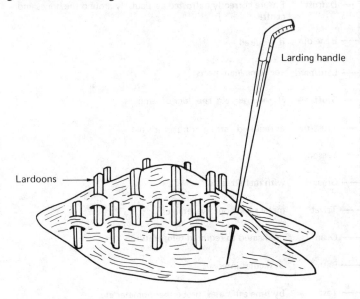

Larding handle

Lardoons

Figure 9.25 *Barding*

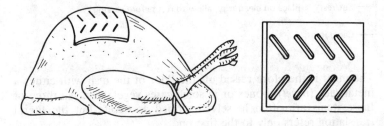

(c) *Setting* of the roasted joint refers to the practice of leaving the item at room temperature for up to 30 minutes after it has been removed from the oven. The main advantage of this procedure is to allow easier carving and thereby better portion-control.

(d) *Speed of cooking* is dependent on oven temperature unless micro-waves are involved. There is much debate and research as to the best technique for reducing shrinkage and moisture-loss during roasting. In many cooking processes a *searing action* (high temperature for a short time) is used to add to the *colour* of the end-product, but it has been shown repeatedly that it does not *seal pores* nor *seal in juices*! In the case of roasted items, in almost all circumstances, there is sufficient browning in the cooking process even at low temperatures, to make the practice of searing unnecessary. However, it is still common practice to put roasts into hot ovens and then to reduce to lower temperatures to complete cooking. This is despite evidence which shows that *cooking losses are reduced* and *flavour conserved* with *slower, longer* cooking at constant temperature. It must be pointed out however that many chefs still believe that the practice of *searing* roast joints in the cooking process is the only way of obtaining the true roast flavour.

Time and temperature

Large joints of meat are generally roasted *fairly slowly* in ovens at temperatures of around 175°C. Vegetables can be roasted more quickly at higher temperatures.

Cooking times and temperatures vary considerably, however, depending on many factors, including:

(a) type of oven, e.g. forced-convection ovens cook more quickly than traditional ovens;
(b) position in oven, e.g. in traditional ovens the top is always hotter than the bottom and cooking times will vary;
(c) quantity of food, e.g. one portion of roast potatoes will cook more quickly than twenty portions. This is because the large quantity of cold food will reduce the initial oven temperature;
(d) weight and shape of food, e.g. a rolled and stuffed joint will take longer to cook than one of a similar size on the bone;
(e) degree of cooking required, e.g. pork should always be cooked at a higher temperature than lamb (the general rule is that red meats are underdone and white meats are cooked through, paying particular attention to any internal bones).

Roasting meats to perfection There is considerable skill involved in roasting red meat, poultry and game. Initially a decision is made as to the temperature of cooking. It is important to realise that to enable large joints to cook throughout, without overcooking on the outside, it is necessary to lower the temperature and extend the cooking time (see Tables 9.4 and 9.5).

Table 9.4 *Cooking times for roast poultry*

	Weight	Temperature	Time
Spring chicken	$\frac{1}{2}$ kg	220°C	30 mins
Large chicken	$2\frac{1}{2}$–5 kg	175°C	2–4 hours
Turkey	10 kg	125°C	6 hours

Table 9.5 *Degrees of cooking for meat*

Degree of cooking		Internal temperature	Appearance
Blue	au bleu	≈ 60°C	Flesh blueish red/blood
Rare	saignant	≈ 65°C	Pink flesh, blood
Medium	à point	≈ 70°C	Pink centre
Well done	bien cuit	≈ 80°C +	Firm, no blood

The time of cooking is roughly gauged by reference to tables or simply by experience (most tables indicate between 15 and 25 minutes per $\frac{1}{2}$ kg if meat is placed into a pre-heated oven). The cooking is then carried out and checked towards the end for 'doneness'. This is best carried out with a thermometer designed for the purpose – a meat probe. This should pierce the largest muscle away from fat or bone. Most meats are considered just cooked when they reach an internal temperature of 70°C, but pork and chicken should always be cooked to temperatures of over 85°C to ensure the meat is free from parasitic worms and pathogenic bacteria such as Salmonella.

The process of roasting in catering operations

Oven-roasting is a traditional method of cooking and very popular in the UK especially on Sundays! It is a relatively simple operation, oven temperatures being easy to control with any type of fuel/oven producing good results.

Excess fat is rendered from meats during the cooking process and can be skimmed off and discarded. This suits the tastes of many customers who are interested in low-fat diets. The natural juices, however, are used to enhance flavour and nutrients are thereby conserved.

Safety rules

1. The correct degree of cooking of meats must be accurately measured to protect the consumer from parasitic worms and pathogenic bacteria.
2. Care should be taken when handling oven trays to prevent spillages of hot fat.

3. Safe practices should be observed in operational procedure, clothing and footwear (see Chapter 15).

9.9 GRILLING

Method

Grilling is a method of cooking using *dry, radiant heat of high intensity* (see Figure 9.26). The term *broiling* is used in the USA to describe a similar process, particularly in relation to chickens (broilers).

Figure 9.26 *The process of grilling*

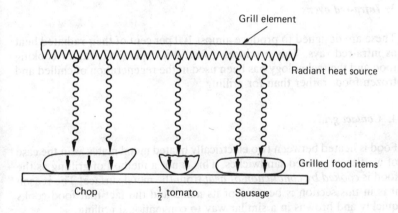

Heat transfer

Radiated heat travels from the heat source to the food surface. Its heat energy is absorbed by the surface of the food and is then conducted throughout the food.

Equipment

A variety of equipment can be used to grill food. The technical data is given in Chapter 10.

1. *Over-heat grills*

The food is placed on grids (called *grill bars*) over a heat source which may be charcoal, wood, gas or electric. Traditionally this type of grilling occurred out in the open in the form of a barbecue. An indoor equivalent uses volcanic rock which is heated by gas or electricity until it glows red, thereby simulating glowing coals without the smoke!

2. *Under-fired grills*

The food is cooked on greased grids, bars or trays under a heat source which is usually gas or electric. The trade term for this piece of equipment is a *salamander* and it can also be used for toasting, glazing and gratinating.

3. *Infra-red ovens*

These are designed to produce almost 100 per cent of their radiated heat as infra-red rays. This produces a fast, but expensive, way of cooking food and the technology has been used in the regeneration of chilled and frozen food, rather than for grilling.

4. *Contact grills*

Food is heated between two electrically heated metal plates as in the case of waffles or toasted sandwiches. This is not a method of grilling as the food is *cooked by conduction of heat* from the metal surface! The reason it is in this section is because of its name and the fact that food cooks quickly and browns in a similar way to conventional grilling.

Routine care of equipment

(a) Food adhering to the grill bars should be scraped off when cooking is completed.
(b) Equipment should be *cleaned* on a daily basis or more often if used frequently. Grease tends to spray over the entire surface of the equipment and surrounding floor area. Detergents and hot water should be used to remove all traces of grease to prevent a build-up which would then be difficult to remove. Deep-cleaning on a regular basis might involve the use of degreasants or steam. Care must be taken to remove any food adhering to grill bars as this will burn on if heated continuously.
(c) Equipment should be maintained and serviced according to manufacturers' instructions.

Suitable foods and cooking procedures

The method of grilling is suitable for prime cuts of meat and poultry as long as they are evenly and thinly cut. It is not suitable for cuts which contain a high proportion of connective tissue as no water is used in this method, and cooking times are too fast. Fruits and vegetables are mostly unsuitable as they shrivel up with intense dry heat although exceptions are well-greased mushrooms and tomatoes. Figure 9.27 summarises the various procedures termed grilling and gives examples of suitable food for use with this process.

Figure 9.27 *Grilling procedures*

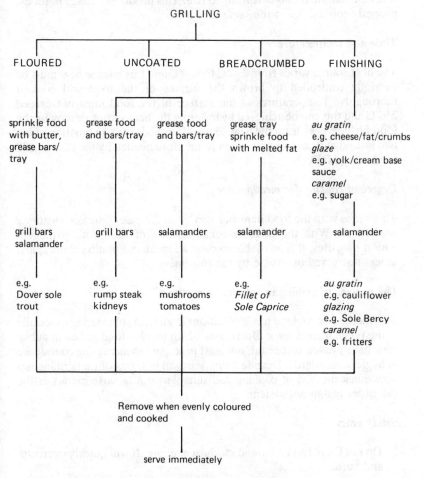

NB: Items may need basting during grilling to prevent dryness.

Size

Foods to be cooked by grilling must not be thicker than about 3 cm in order to brown, cook thoroughly and not burn or dry up. Certain types of meat can be batted out to reduce the thickness, as in the case of steaks or cutlets. Meat can also be skewered, as with kebabs, to allow quicker penetration of the surface heat.

Uniformity

Preparing all the items to be cooked to a uniform size avoids the problem of overcooking some items whilst others are undercooked. When cooking dishes such as mixed grill, it is useful to begin cooking the larger items first and add the others according to size. This produces a range of foods, properly cooked, all at the same time.

Time and temperature

The heat source varies from 230°C to 980°C and this intense heat must be carefully controlled to brown the surface of the food and cook it thoroughly. Temperatures at the surface of the food must not exceed 250°C and this can be achieved by lowering the heat setting or moving the food further away from the heat source. In practice, a combination of the two is used and constant attention is therefore needed by the chef to grill food successfully.

Degree of cooking for meat/poultry

This varies with the food item and also, as in the case of steaks, customer preference. With the possible contamination of flesh with pathogens and/or parasites, it is advisable to cook all meat and poultry thoroughly, unless instructed otherwise by the customer.

The process of grilling in catering operations

This method of cooking has applications in all fields of catering especially in the popular *steak bars*. Operations which involve food grilled in public view have proved successful, not least in respect to increasing confidence in hygiene standards. Despite being wasteful in terms of fuel grilling is a very quick method of cooking and suitable for à la carte menus or the call-order restaurant system.

Safety rules

1. Do not leave food unattended whilst cooking. It will quickly overcook and burn.

2. Keep floor areas free from spilt grease as this can lead to slippery and dangerous floors.
3. Exercise great care when adjusting grill bars or salamander racks. They are heavy and contain hot food and oil.
4. Safe practice should be observed in operational procedures, clothing and footwear (see Chapter 15).

9.10 DEEP-FRYING

Description of the process

Food is immersed entirely in hot fat/oil. It is not in contact with any surface of the frying vessel.

Heat transfer

Convection currents in the pre-heated medium carry heat to the surface of the food. The interior is heated by *conduction* of the heat from the surface (see Figure 9.28).

Figure 9.28 *Heat transfer during deep-frying*

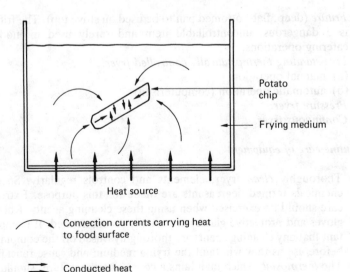

Potato chip

Frying medium

Heat source

Convection currents carrying heat to food surface

Conducted heat

Equipment

Deep frying can be carried out in any of the pieces of equipment listed below. Details can be found in Chapter 10. The main components are shown in Figure 9.29.

Figure 9.29 *The main components of modern fryers*

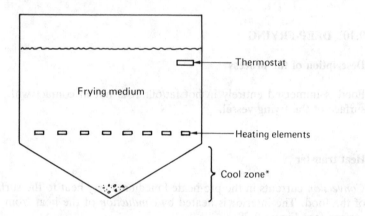

* This area remains at lower temperatures because it is under the heating elements. Food particles accumulate here thus prolonging the life of the oil and preventing burnt spots appearing on the food.

1. *Friture* (deep, flat-bottomed pan to be used on stove top). The friture is a dangerous, uncontrollable item and rarely used in modern catering operations.
2. *Free-standing thermostatically controlled fryer:*
   (a) manual operation
   (b) automatic operation (computerised)
3. *Pressure fryer.*
4. *Continuous fryer.*

Routine care of equipment

(a) Thoroughly *clean* fryer, elements and controls regularly. Special chemicals termed degreasants are made for this purpose. Extreme care should be exercised when using these cleaning agents. Rubber gloves and protective glasses are usually recommended. It is important that any cleaning agents are thoroughly rinsed off the equipment before use as they will taint the frying medium and cause rancidity.
(b) The *thermostat*, which maintains a constant temperature, should be checked for accuracy at least twice a year.

The frying medium

The frying medium can be fat (solid at room temperature) or oil (liquid at room temperature). These are chemically similar substances only differing in the type of triglycerides present (see p. 314). Such substances possess properties which make them an ideal medium for transferring heat and cooking food:

1. they heat up very quickly and operate at very high temperatures, therefore working quickly and efficiently;
2. foods absorb between 8 and 50 per cent of the frying medium as they are cooked and this alters their taste, texture and nutritional value. For this reason bland foods low in energy are often cooked in this manner.

Choice of the frying medium

There are a number of factors to be taken into consideration when choosing a frying medium.

Heat stability

As the temperature is raised all fats or oils begin to decompose. The temperature at which this occurs is called the *smoke point* when the triglycerides break down to produce a blue haze of 'acrolein'. The frying medium will foam, darken and taint the food. The longer it is used the lower the temperature at which smoke is produced and this may eventually lead to frying at low temperatures to avoid a smoke-filled atmosphere. It is therefore important to choose fats/oils with high smoke points (see Table 9.6).

Table 9.6 *A comparison of frying media*

Lipid	Smoke point	Recommended frying temperature
Butter	140°C	unsuitable for deep frying
Lard	168°C	≈ 150°C
Corn oil	221°C	≈ 183°C
Formulated vegetable fat	224°C	≈ 185°C

The constant heating and cooling of the frying medium and the use of water-based foods also affects the triglycerides. They may break up and produce off-flavours (rancidity) or combine to form sticky substances (polymers) on the sides of the fryer. In both cases the addition of anti-oxidants and stabilisers helps to reduce these problems.

Taste

It is important to choose a frying medium which complements the foods cooked. For example, lard and dripping are used successfully for fish and chips but their animal flavour is not appreciated in all foods. Indeed the emphasis has been on the use of completely tasteless, odourless products derived from plant sources such as processed cotton-seed oil.

In summary, if it is to be used routinely the frying medium should be a *specially formulated product with a high smoke point and added stabilisers and anti-oxidants*.

Care of the frying medium

Having chosen a suitable oil or fat great care must be taken in its use. Incorrect handling of the frying medium will mean increased costs and poor-quality products. The following points should be observed in all situations.

1. *Use at the correct temperature* Food should be fried below the smoke point (a thermostat is essential) at the recommended temperature. Any frying medium that is smoking below cooking temperature should be discarded. It is important to heat up the oil/fat slowly to avoid scorching and set to a *standby* temperature (120°C) when not in use for short periods.
2. *Skim and filter regularly* The frying medium should be skimmed after each use. It should be filtered daily for a friture, but less often for cool-zone fryers where manufacturers' instructions should be followed. Many models have self-filtering devices built into them.
3. *Avoid contact with air/moisture/metals* These substances speed rancidity and, therefore, the fryer should be kept sealed when not in use; food should be dried off as much as possible before frying, and copper utensils in particular should not be used.
4. *Maintain the correct 'turnover'* A fryer in constant use will lose up to 20 per cent of frying medium each day, most of this being absorbed by the food. New fat/oil can be added on a daily basis and under ideal conditions the fat/oil in the fryer will never have to be discarded. This daily addition of fat/oil without discarding the old is called *turnover*. Obtaining the right turnover along with proper frying methods will produce good fried products and save money.
5. *Do not mix with other fats* Animal and fish fats are usually unsuitable for deep frying because of their relatively low smoke point. For this reason items such as uncoated oily fish, bacon and beefburgers should not be cooked by this method. Contamination with such fats will cause excessive discolouration, smoking and rancidity.
6. *Do not salt foods over the fryer* Salt, either table salt or that in cured products such as bacon, speeds up deterioration.

7. *Do not overload* A common operating fault, particularly during hectic service periods, is to overload the fryer in the belief that it speeds up production. In fact in doing so the temperature drops so low that longer frying times are necessary and a greasy end-product is produced.

8. *Use food at room temperature if possible* The colder the food the longer the cooking-time and the greater the absorption of fat. It is therefore not desirable to use foods straight from the freezer unless they are specifically formulated for this purpose. This is the case for some pre-cooked foods which only require heating through and browning. Many raw frozen foods, however, will tend to brown on the outside and remain uncooked inside if cooked from frozen.

9. *Discard thick, rancid, dark, foaming, smoking fat/oil.*

Suitable foods and cooking procedures

Deep-frying is a fast, dry process unsuitable for large items of food or cuts of meat containing a lot of connective tissue. Using a variety of coatings many menu items can be cooked in this way. Figure 9.30 illustrates some of the foods commonly deep-fried, and the relevant cooking procedures.

Protective coatings

The sudden contact of the food with temperatures of above 150°C may lead to burning or overcooking of its surface. It is for this reason that protective surface coatings, such as batter, are commonly used. This coating also, as it hardens, reduces moisture-loss from the foods and oil/fat absorption from the medium. For delicate foods this coating may also function to keep the food from breaking-up. Firm foods with a high water content such as raw potato produce a constant layer of steam between the potato and the oil/fat which is as protective as the batters mentioned above. It is important to realise that in all cases the outer surface browns and hardens (producing crispness) to give a variety of appetising colour, flavour and texture characteristics to the product.

Time and temperature

The *time* needed to process food items will be determined by a range of factors, apart from temperature which is considered later.

1. *The function of deep-frying*

(a) reheating pre-cooked food   e.g. croquette potatoes
(b) partially cooking raw foods   e.g. blanching chipped potatoes
(c) completely cooking items   e.g. fried fish
     from raw

Figure 9.30 *Deep-frying*

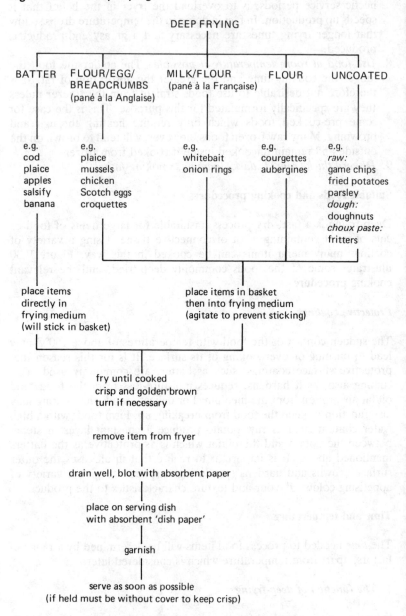

2. *The volume of food to be processed*

The greater the volume of food the longer the cooking-time.

3. *The recovery time of fryer*

This is the time taken for the fat/oil to return to the desired temperature after the cold food is added and is directly related to the efficiency of the fryer. Frozen food often adds an extra 25 per cent on to the cooking time.

4. *The ratio of food : fat/oil*

A minimum ratio of 1 : 6 and maximum 1 : 10 should be followed for efficiency. Always follow manufacturers' instructions.

5. *Size, shape and uniformity of food*

Large pieces of food require longer cooking. If all pieces of food in the fryer are roughly the same dimensions they will require the same cooking time.

6. *The pressure at which food is fried*

Fryers have been developed which stop the steam – produced during normal frying – from escaping. As with the traditional high pressure steamer (pressure cooker) this results in shorter cooking times. Foods also retain more moisture making them more tender and preventing drying-out. Recent studies suggest 75 per cent moisture-retention compared to 50 per cent in normal frying. However, crispness can be lost in this process and it is not suitable for items such as chipped potatoes.

The *temperature* at which fried food is cooked is critical to the acceptability of the product. Food fried at the right temperature is golden brown (except for blanched items), crisp on the outside and with a minimum of absorbed fat. Foods fried at too high a temperature develop a dark brown, hard crust often with an uncooked centre. Foods fried at too low a temperature soak up fat, become soggy, lack colour and are unpalatable.

Most oils/fats designed for deep-frying have a specific temperature range of between 165°C and 195°C (see Chapter 12). Within this range 180°C is the best temperature to use and most fryers will be set at this temperature for most foods. At this temperature minimum cooking times and absorption of fat/oil are achieved.

Lower temperature/longer times are required for some foods

In some cases the advantages of using the frying medium at lower temperatures outweigh the problems of grease absorption and longer cooking times.

Examples

1. *Blanching*   Chipped potatoes can be cooked without colour so that at a later stage in production they can be reheated and browned at a higher temperature.

2. *Cooking white meat*   To ensure thorough cooking, particularly of pieces on the bone.

3. *Dense food items*   Items such as Scotch eggs require a longer period in the fryer to ensure thorough cooking.

4. *Aerated goods*   For items such as choux paste which need to aerate, time must be allowed for chemical and physical raising to take place.

The deep-fat fryer in catering operations

Deep-fat fryers are used extensively in all types of catering outlets. Outlined below are some of the many advantages the process has to offer if used with due care and attention to the many points outlined in this section.

1. *Ease of service pressure*   Foods can be partially cooked prior to service and then finished off on demand, e.g. chipped potatoes, whitebait.

2. *Cooking times*   Cooking times are invariably fast which is another reason why fried foods are the mainstay of fast-food menus.

3. *Quality assurance*   Because of the short cooking times involved food can be cooked immediately prior to service, producing a fresher product of uniform size and easy to handle for service.

4. *Level of skill*   The process has been easily automated to produce computerised fryers which need little skill to operate. Maximum use has been made of this feature in fast-food operations.

Safety rules

The hazard of hot oil/fat to premises (in the form of fire) and to the food handler (in the form of burns) cannot be overemphasised

1. All operators must be trained not only to use the equipment, but also in fire drill procedure.
2. The correct level of frying medium should be used. This will be marked on most fryers. The use of open-top fritures should be avoided but if used they should be only *one-third* full.

3. The fryer must not be overloaded as this may cause hot oil/fat to overflow.
4. Drain wet foods and then dry with absorbent paper. This prevents splatters of hot fat reaching the skin of the food-handler.
5. Use the basket to drop foods into fryer if possible. For other foods carefully place foods into the fryer *away from* the food-handler.
6. Do not leave fryers unattended unless they are fully automatic.
7. Reduce the temperature of the oil/fat when not in use for short periods. The ideal standby temperature is 120°C.
8. Do not operate above the correct temperature. The oil/fat may reach its *flash-point* at which temperature it ignites spontaneously.

9.11 SHALLOW-FRYING

Method

This is a *dry* method of cooking. *Food is cooked in a small quantity of fat/oil in a pre-heated shallow pan or on a greased metal surface* (see Figure 9.31). *Dry-frying* is a term which has recently been used to describe shallow-frying without oil/fat. Foods with a high fat content can be placed on preheated surfaces and can then cook in their own juices.

Figure 9.31 *Shallow-frying techniques*

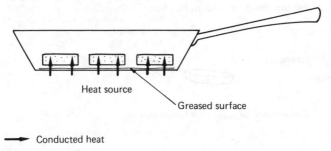

Heat source

Greased surface

→ Conducted heat

Heat transfer

The food cooks by direct heat conduction from the metal surface. The frying medium may aid the process if a sufficient depth is used or may merely serve as a thin lubricating layer to stop sticking and burning (see deep-frying).

Equipment

Shallow-frying is a widely used cooking process and can be applied to many different situations. The equipment used varies according to

Figure 9.32 *Equipment for shallow-frying*

1. *Plat sauté pan*

This may be used with or without a lid.

2. *Sauteuse*

Deeper, but sloping sides for ease of palette knife manipulation.

3. *Frying pan*

Sloping sides as the sauteuse. Sometimes flat handle pans are used for fish and round handle pans for meat.

4. *Omelet pan*

Curved sides for rolling the folded omelet.

5. *Wok*

Steep sides and bowl shape for stir frying.

6. *Bratt pan* – see Chapter 10.

various factors such as, availability and the preference of the chef (see Figure 9.32).

The frying medium

Because of the severe heat of the metal cooking surface the frying medium forms a lubricating, protective layer between food and utensil. Because of the greasy nature of fats/oils they are ideal lubricants and can also operate at the high temperatures reached on the hot metal surface. The fat/oil is used only once in most shallow-frying operations, either being incorporated into the dish or discarded after use.

Choice of frying medium

Consideration must be given here to the menu item to be shallow-fried. If there is a long *cooking-time* involved a robust, high smoke point fat/oil should be used. If the frying medium is to be used in the final dish, *flavour* must be considered. In all cases the ability to *prevent sticking* will be of prime importance especially when the item is to be shaped or tossed.

Butter

Butter has remarkable anti-sticking properties if used correctly. It should be added to the pre-heated pan and heated until bubbles subside and it just begins to brown. At this point the butter is said to have clarified. Foods added once the butter has clarified will not stick. They will also develop good colour and have a delicious flavour. Butter does have a low smoke point and will burn easily so skill is needed in this operation. It is also an expensive commodity and, although the basis of traditional French cuisine, has been replaced by vegetable oils in many situations. It is worth noting that some oils, such as olive oil, are as expensive as butter.

Lard and dripping

These are both stable at shallow-frying temperatures/times but do taint the products with an animal flavour. They were used extensively until the market was flooded with refined vegetable oils/fats during the latter part of this century.

Vegetable oils and fats

Many of these are specially designed for high-temperature frying and are useful if long cooking-times are involved. Poor-quality oils often give an undesirable after-taste to fried items (often described as sweetness) and it is therefore essential to use a well-defined product.

Figure 9.33 *Shallow-frying*

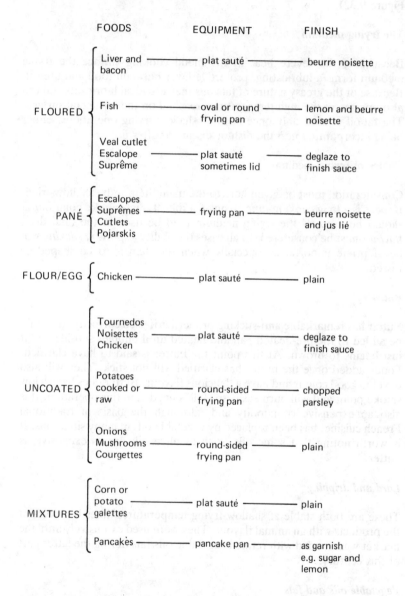

FOODS	EQUIPMENT	FINISH
FLOURED		
Liver and bacon	plat sauté	beurre noisette
Fish	oval or round frying pan	lemon and beurre noisette
Veal cutlet Escalope Suprême	plat sauté sometimes lid	deglaze to finish sauce
PANÉ		
Escalopes Suprêmes Cutlets Pojarskis	frying pan	beurre noisette and jus lié
FLOUR/EGG		
Chicken	plat sauté	plain
UNCOATED		
Tournedos Noisettes Chicken	plat sauté	deglaze to finish sauce
Potatoes cooked or raw	round-sided frying pan	chopped parsley
Onions Mushrooms Courgettes	round-sided frying pan	plain
MIXTURES		
Corn or potato galettes	plat sauté	plain
Pancakes	pancake pan	as garnish e.g. sugar and lemon

Butter and oil mixture

To obtain a good flavour at a reasonable price, this mixture is often used. It operates well at most temperatures and the skill needed to use butter, without burning, is not as important

Suitable foods and cooking procedure

Many types of food can be shallow-fried as can be seen in Figure 9.33. Large items must be cut into thin pieces to ensure thorough cooking. The absence of water in this cooking process makes it unsuitable, however, for poor-quality meats with large amounts of connective tissue (see Chapter 12). A certain amount of fat is absorbed by the food and, therefore, the energy value of food items will be increased by this method of cooking. Figure 9.34 details the procedures for shallow-frying. Most procedures for shallow-frying, although the same in principle, fall into the categories: meunière, sauté, griddle and stir-fry.

Meunière

Literally this term means 'in the style of a miller's wife'. It describes a method of cooking which applies mainly to fish. Fish cooked in this way is seasoned, lightly floured (presumably the connection with the miller) and shallow-fried in butter or oil. The fish is sprinkled with lemon juice, garnished with a slice of lemon and finished with beurre noisette and chopped parsley. Vegetables – for example, chicory – can also be prepared in this way.

Figure 9.34 *The general procedure for shallow-frying*

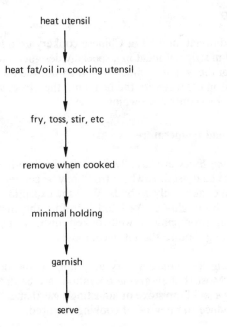

heat utensil

↓

heat fat/oil in cooking utensil

↓

fry, toss, stir, etc

↓

remove when cooked

↓

minimal holding

↓

garnish

↓

serve

Sauté

This word has two commonly used interpretations:

(a) *to sauté* means to cook in hot fat over strong heat in a sauté pan. The pan is shaken during cooking, tossing the food, to ensure even cooking without burning. Examples are sauté onions, potatoes and kidneys.

(b) *a sauté* is a dish produced by shallow frying tender meats or poultry. The items are first cooked in a sauté pan, removed and kept warm. The sauce is made by first draining off the fat from the sauté pan, deglazing with wine or stock and finishing according to the recipe. The meat and sauce should be combined immediately prior to service.

Sauté dishes are either white or brown. For brown sauté the items are coloured in the cooking process – for example, Poulet sauté. For white sauté they should be started in a cold pan to produce an uncoloured (white) finish as with *Suprême de Volaille à la Crème*.

Griddle

A deep metal plate with or without ridges which can be used to shallow-fry if greased with a little fat/oil. Sausages and hamburgers are suitable for this method.

Stir-fry

A traditional method of Chinese cookery used for fast frying vegetables and thin strips of meat in a specially designed utensil termed a *wok*. The base of the wok is rounded with high sides so that only a small amount of food is in contact with the heat and, therefore, stirring is the only action needed to control browning.

Time and temperature

Cooking times are usually short for shallow-fried items because of the intense heat used. A whole trout may be cooked in 20 minutes whereas a pancake takes only seconds. With the exception of steaks all foods need to be thoroughly cooked and therefore the chef must use considerable skill in producing a well-cooked dish, with the correct degree of browning, before the fat decomposes!

Cooking temperatures vary according to the depth and texture of the food. Most shallow frying operations are controlled by moving the pan across a solid top stove or adjusting a gas flame. This requires experience to produce the degree of cooking required.

Appropriate times and temperatures for some shallow fried items are given in Table 9.7 as an indication of the cooking method. In practice there are many other variables to consider such as quality, size of equipment, etc.

Table 9.7   *Time and temperatures for shallow-frying*

	Time	*Temperature*
Fried eggs	$\approx$ 2 min	$\approx$ 95°C
Steak (well-done)	$\approx$ 20 min	$\approx$ 130°
Fillet of fish	$\approx$ 15 min	$\approx$ 150°C
Sauté potatoes	$\approx$ 10 min	$\approx$ 180°C
Crêpes	$\approx$ 30 sec	$\approx$ 190°C

The use of shallow-frying in catering operations

This is a fast method of cooking prime-quality foods. It can produce a range of textures and colours providing a variety of items and courses such as banana flambé, eggs and croûtons. It is limited however, unless thermostatically controlled equipment is available, as it is labour-intensive and that labour has to be skilled.

Safety rules

The hazard of hot oil/fat to the premises (in the form of fire) and the food handler (in the form of burns) cannot be overemphasised.

1. The cooking equipment should be of the correct size to prevent spillages.
2. Pans must be moved carefully on the stove top to prevent splattering and burns.
3. Safe practice should be observed in operational procedure, clothing and footwear (see Chapter 15).

9.12 MICROWAVE COOKERY

Description of the process

This is a *dry* method of cooking which involves *radiated microwave energy* which is used to *create heat* in food.

Heat transfer

The radiated energy, in the form of microwaves, affects only some of the molecules in the food. These are the electrically charged molecules, of which the most important in food is water. For simplicity, this text will refer to microwaves affecting *only* water molecules.

1. Microwaves penetrate the food to a depth of between 2–5 cm.

Figure 9.35 *Microwave cookery*

1.

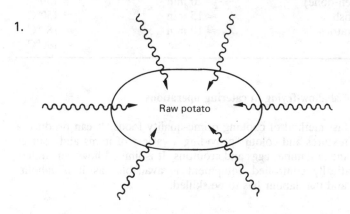

ᔥᔥᔥᔥᔥ► Microwaves

2. Microwaves pass on their energy to water molecules. The water molecules then VIBRATE (move) 2000 million times per second! This movement produces a band of HEAT inside the food.

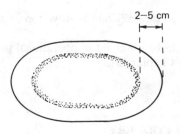

2–5 cm

▨▨ Water molecules
moving causing
heat

3. The heat produced in this area is CONDUCTED (solids) or CON-VECTED (liquids) throughout the food.

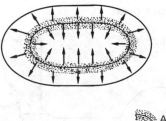

Area of heat within food

4. Food is heated from all directions producing very fast cooking times.

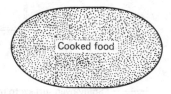
Cooked food

Traditional cooking involves loss of heat to the oven, to the equipment and to the kitchen itself. Microwave cookery, in comparison, offers a quick and efficient method of cooking. The reasons for this can be summarised:

(a) cooking begins immediately the power is switched on;
(b) cooking begins within the food and heat travels in all directions speeding up the process;
(c) heat energy is not absorbed by the oven walls nor by the air inside the oven;
(d) heat energy is not absorbed by the cooking dishes;
(e) microwave ovens need only 13 amp electrical supply (low power rating).

Equipment

The microwave oven

Microwaves are produced from electricity by a *magnetron*. They are then directed into an oven and distributed evenly by a *fan*. A shiny oven surface allows the waves to be reflected in all directions to promote fast, even cooking (see Figure 9.36).

Figure 9.36 *A microwave oven*

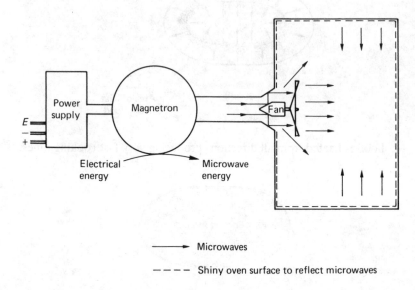

———→ Microwaves

– – – – Shiny oven surface to reflect microwaves

Adaptations of basic equipment

Turntable Convection currents are slow to develop and, therefore, many microwaves are fitted with a turntable to simulate 'stirring'.

Browning attachments Microwave cooking produces no browning of the surface as temperatures inside the oven are not high enough to produce the surface changes referred to in section 9.1. Modern developments to increase surface browning include:

(a) *browning dishes* These are ceramic dishes coated with a layer of material which absorbs microwaves and gets hot. Food placed on the hot surface will sear as if in a hot frying pan.
(b) *infra-red heaters* These are positioned in the oven so that at the end of cooking browning can be achieved quickly.
(c) *micro-aire cookers* These are conventional ovens with the facility to produce microwaves. They combine both systems to produce a high level of versatility, speed and cost-effectiveness.

Temperature probes Because the food may be cooked inside whilst the surface remains cool, traditional *eye judgement* to determine if food is cooked is impossible. Thermometers which will pierce the surface of the food and measure internal temperatures are, therefore, useful. These are called *temperature probes* and are available ready-installed in some ovens, usually referred to as *computerised* microwave ovens. They are especially useful in cooking meat and poultry to avoid undercooking and dangers of food poisoning (see Figure 9.37).

Figure 9.37 *Microwave temperature probe*

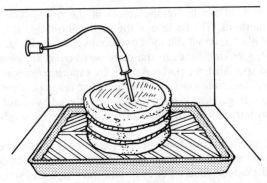

A temperature probe inserted into a joint of meat means that you can judge the cooking by its temperature.

Cooking dishes Cooking dishes, of such materials as glass, china and plastic, contain very little water and microwaves will pass through them. They do not, therefore, get hot except by normal conduction from the food as it cooks. It is a common and unfortunate mistake to assume that dishes from the microwave will be cold when removed! This method of heating food is ideally suited to regeneration of chilled foods using disposable decorative cardboard/plastic containers. Problems occur, however, with the use of metallic dishes/foils as the microwaves are reflected. This not only lengthens cooking time but damages the magnetron. Manufacturers have flooded the market in recent years with *microware*. This is specially formulated, lightweight, plastic equipment produced solely for this method of cooking.

Care of equipment

1. The oven should be cleaned after use with warm, soapy water.
2. The oven should be serviced and maintained according to manufacturers' instructions.

Suitable foods

Prime cooking Most foods contain a large proportion of water and can, therefore, be cooked, from raw, in a microwave oven. Although most suited to dishes which do not need to develop colour, a variety of techniques can be applied if this is required. Baked flour products are not particularly successful as *crispness, colour* and *aeration* are difficult to achieve. Cheaper cuts of meat do not have the time to dissolve out the collagen and tend to remain *chewy*.

Reheating/defrosting Microwave cookery is ideally suited to reheating cooked food and defrosting frozen food.

Time and temperature

Food will cook at similar temperatures in the microwave oven as in traditional methods. The surface of the food will not be the hottest part, as described above, and if the food overcooks it will be *inside* that begins to char first. Cooking times in the microwave oven are determined by reference to specialist recipe books and by experimentation. The latter may be costly and time-consuming initially but reaps positive benefits in the long term. In general, cooking times are reduced by about 75 per cent compared with traditional processes. Cooking-time will be influenced by:

(a) *type of food* Porous foods, like minced beef or mashed potatoes, microwave faster than dense ones like steak or whole potatoes.
(b) *size and shape of food* Foods of uniform shape and size cook more consistently as in traditional cooking. Because of the unusual method of heat transfer small, spherical shapes are ideal. Round shapes cook more evenly than squares or rectangles, which absorb more energy at the corners. Food in a shallow dish will cook faster than the same quantity in a deeper dish. Ring shapes are ideal for microwaving as energy penetrates the food from top, bottom, sides and centre, producing minimum cooking times.
(c) *amount of food* Cooking time is directly related to food quantity. This is because the microwave energy remains constant, but has to be shared among an increased volume of food, therefore requiring a longer period to cook the food.
(d) *power rating* The *power output* of microwave ovens varies from between 500 and 700 watts. The lower the output the longer the cooking time.
    Variation in power output for an individual oven is also possible. The amount of microwave energy released into the oven over a time period is controlled by the *variable cooking control setting* (see Table 9.8). The energy is periodically turned *off* and *on* to produce slower cooking, heating and defrosting. Table 9.9 gives some examples of approximate cooking times.

Table 9.8   *Typical microwave power controls*

Variable control setting	Approximate percentage of microwave power
Full power	100
Roast	70
Simmer	50
Defrost	30
Warm	10

Table 9.9   *Examples of approximate cooking times (maximum power)*

Cod fillets 450 g	4 min
Gammon joint 450 g	7 min
Jacket potatoes (2)	9 min
Cabbage 450 g	7 min
Scrambled eggs (2)	2 min

Microwave cooking techniques

Covering foods

Lids or clingfilm (specially formulated) are used to trap steam and moisture to tenderise and speed cooking. To hold in heat and prevent spatters without steaming, paper towels can be used. Paper can also be used under breads, baked potatoes, etc., to absorb moisture and keep the surfaces crisp and dry.

Releasing pressure from foods

Foods with a tight-fitting skin must be pricked prior to cooking to stop them bursting because of rapid build-up of steam. This applies to foods such as baked potatoes, sausages, egg-yolks and also to clingfilms used to cover food.

Arranging foods

Individual items such as fairy cakes or potatoes should be placed in a ring around the outside of the turntable. Spaces should be left between the foods so that energy can penetrate from all sides. The centre of the oven receives least energy and is therefore left empty.

Foods with thin or delicate ends, like drumsticks or asparagus spears, are placed with the thick or tougher portions to the outside of the dish.

The parts which need more cooking will receive more energy, so the food will cook evenly, see Figure 9.38.

Figure 9.38 *Microwave cooking techniques*

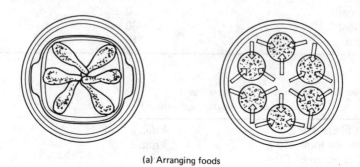

(a) Arranging foods

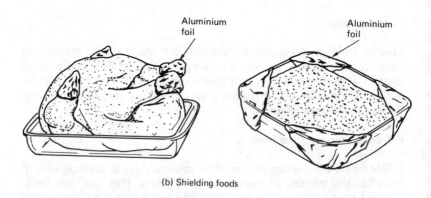

(b) Shielding foods

Shielding food

Areas which attract the most energy, like the wing tips and breast bone of a turkey, or the square corners of a cake, need protecting to prevent overcooking. Small pieces of foil can be used for this purpose as they deflect the microwaves away from these areas. Covering meats with a sauce also shields the meat and prevents drying out, see Figure 9.38.

Stirring foods

This technique is used in all forms of cookery to distribute heat evenly. Foods should be stirred from the outside to the centre once or twice during cooking and before service. Foods will not scorch or stick, so there is no need to stir constantly as with conventional processes.

Rearranging foods

Closely packed solid food may need repositioning, during the cooking cycle, to achieve the same effect as stirring in a liquid-based food.

Turning foods

Large items such as turkeys and roasts need to be turned over as microwave ovens usually receive most energy at the top. Smaller items may be turned once during cooking but for ovens with a turntable this is not always necessary.

Colouring foods

Colour can be developed using one of the modifications of microwave equipment as outlined above. Foods can also be finished off under a grill or use can be made of the many *browning powders* on the market. Experimentation with normal kitchen ingredients provides numerous ways of achieving surface colour:

- butter and paprika brushed over the surface of poultry
- soy sauce, tomato sauce and Worcestershire sauce brushed onto meat joints
- grated cheese and breadcrumbs on chicken pieces
- frostings and toppings as decorative finishes for cakes after cooking
- the use of highly coloured ingredients such as brown sugar
- bread can be brushed with diluted meat extract and sprinkled with poppy seeds, nuts etc.

Standing time

This is one of the most important microwaving techniques. Heat is in the food, not the oven, and many foods build up enough internal heat to continue to cook by themselves after they are removed from the oven. Letting roasts, large whole vegetables and cakes stand to finish cooking allows the centres to cook completely without overcooking.

The microwave in catering operations

Despite the many advantages over conventional cooking the microwave has been slow to 'take off' in the trade. Its use in defrosting and reheating on a small scale has been unparalleled but development into *volume* processing has been slow. However, it has flexibility. When properly integrated into the food production and food service system it can do much to reduce costs and serve foods of high quality.

A summary of the main advantages and disadvantages of the use of the microwave are shown in Table 9.10. It must be stressed that, as with all technology, aspects may soon be dated.

Table 9.10 *Advantages and disadvantages of microwave cookery*

Advantages	Disadvantages
Faster than conventional	Browning of surfaces requires extra attention
Cheaper than conventional	Not suited to all foods
Rapid and safe defrosting	Cooking times difficult to establish
Reheating without overcooking	Limited capacity oven
Variety of cooking and/or service dishes	Metallic or metallic trimmed equipment cannot be used
Less washing-up	

Safety

1. Microwave ovens should be kept properly maintained according to manufacturers' instructions.
2. The door rim and seal must be kept free of grease to avoid leakage of radiation.
3. The oven must not be operated when empty as this leads to damage of the magnetron.
4. Foods and covers that are likely to burst must be pierced or vented to avoid burns to the food-handler.
5. Safe practice should be observed in operational procedure, clothing and footwear (see Chapter 15).

KITCHEN EQUIPMENT

10.1 KITCHEN EQUIPMENT AND MACHINERY

There is an extensive range of kitchen equipment and machinery and various ways of classifying it. The particular classification adopted in this book attempts to deal with equipment under the following functions: cooking equipment (subdivided into the different processes used in cooking); holding equipment; food preparation; beverages production and serving equipment; washing-up equipment, and waste-disposal equipment.

A Cooking equipment

Baking, roasting, braising

General-purpose oven As the name suggests, these ovens are used for a variety of cookery activities. They may be fuelled either by gas or electricity. Less common types are oil or solid fuel. Sizes vary according to use and often – in the form of the familiar 'stove' – they are combined with a top for boiling. A number of stoves together may form the familiar 'range', known alternatively as an 'island' or 'suite'. Ovens may be (i) a part of other combinations including counter-top or open kitchen service; or (ii) a part of a modular arrangement, combining with other modular equipment such as bain-marie, deep-fryers, etc. Both gas and electric ovens have thermostatic controls but unlike the forced-air convection ovens the inside temperature is uneven, generally being hotter in the top part.

Convection oven As the principle of heating in an ordinary oven is convection, these ovens may more accurately be described as *forced-air convection ovens*. Fuelled by either gas or electricity these ovens have a fan to force the circulation of the hot air inside. Advantages include:

(i) more rapid cooking saving up to 25 per cent time;
(ii) less energy is needed – up to 10°C lower temperature setting;
(iii) uniform cooking
(iv) more effective use of oven space.

Other features may include:

1. various numbers of shelves from six to eleven;
2. roll-in rack system with size suitable for gastronorm containers;
3. interior light;
4. viewing door;
5. timer;
6. a 'snorkle' attachment to recycle exhausted hot air giving approximately 20 per cent energy-saving;
7. self-draining floor;
8. automatic door-switch;
9. cook-and-hold option.

Bakers/pastry oven These ovens are purpose-built with the oven compartments in the form of large single decks. They are heated from top and bottom for the even cooking of bread and pastry items. Because of their flat shape they are stacked two or more deep, either as single-deck separate units joined together or multi-deck manufactured models. Some ovens may include the following features:

1. independent control for each deck;
2. steaming system – to produce primary steam if required;
3. variable top and bottom heat;
4. built-in canopy.

Pizza oven Heated by either gas or electricity, the main feature of these ovens is high and rapid temperature recovery. Both floor and counter models are available and they may be decked or single and usually include a timer for cooking.

Microwave ovens These ovens use microwave energy which penetrates the foods and cooks by frictional heat (see 9.12). It is important to note that these ovens cook by time and not temperature and also have controls for adjusting the amount of microwave energy released into the compartment for cooking, reheating and defrosting.

A fan to circulate the microwaves is included with all models and this is to reduce hot and cold spots. There are a considerable number of facilities that may be included with various models of microwave ovens such as:

1. see-through window in door;
2. oven light;

3. signal bell;
4. automatic defrost device;
5. pre-set push-button programmes.

Combination microwave and convection oven   This type of oven has a single compartment which can be used as microwave, or convection, or a combination of both methods simultaneously. Where microwave and convection are used at the same time this optimises the advantages of both methods.

Roast-and-hold oven   These ovens are designed for the low-temperature roasting of meat. They have a probe which measures the internal meat temperature when cooking and when this reaches a selected temperature the oven reduces heat automatically. A saving of up to 25 per cent meat shrinkage is claimed for this type of oven over the general-purpose oven.

Regeneration oven   Regeneration can be achieved in a variety of ovens such as: infra-red, microwave, forced convection, high pressure wet/dry steam and various combinations.

Steam convection oven   The size of these ovens varies from 6 to 40 grids. They operate on the principle of two independent heating units for cooking by convection and steaming and the transfer from one mode to another is automatic. The particular advantage of this type of oven is the quality of the finished product in terms of nutrition and texture.

Plate 10.1 illustrates the various types of ovens.

Boiling

Boiling pan   (See Plate 10.2, p. 199) Pans for boiling are available either as (i) round casting, or (ii) squared casting to fit in with modular arrangements of other equipment. Both gas and electric direct heating are available as well as steam jacket operated by either main steam supply or single built-in steam-generator. Sizes vary from 45 to 180 litres. Some features that may be included are:

1. lift-out inner pan (not steam jacket type);
2. table models;
3. cold-water input swivel arm;
4. comprehensive safety controls;
5. counterbalanced hinged lids;
6. lift-off lids.

Boiling table – induction   A solid top which turns itself on and off automatically when pans are placed on top. This only works however with cast iron and steel (but not stainless steel) pans as the current flows

Plate 10.1 *Ovens*

in response to these metals only. Pans of other metals may be used if they have a ferro-magnetic metal bottom.

Boiling table – oven top For heating pans by electric rings or gas burners. The number of rings/burners vary from two to ten. Boiling tables may be free-standing on floor or counter-top or more commonly as part of a stove range.

Boiling table – solid top This provides cooking functions similar to those of the open-top boiling table. They have a solid cast-iron cooking area usually incorporated as part of a stove range. Free-standing counter-top models are also quite common. Solid tops may be fuelled by gas or electricity. The gas type are lit from the top, under a centre ring which becomes the hottest part of the stove when fully heated. The top of the electric type consists of a number of solid plates which can be heated separately and can combine plates of differing sizes, the larger ones usually at the back. After they are turned off, solid tops should be cleaned with emery paper and then wiped with a greased rag.

Stockpot stands These are low boiling tables specially designed to allow safe and easy movement of heavy stockpots on and off the stove top. They are heated by gas or electricity, and are open or solid-top standing usually 40–60 cm from the ground. They may be finished in enamel or stainless steel. Some models have adjustable feet.

Tilting kettle These are for bulk boiling or stewing. They are heated either directly by gas or electricity or by a steam jacket fed by a central system or built-in steam-generator. Usually made from stainless steel, they have variable controls for rapid boiling or simmering and a tilting device to make it easy to remove finished products. The capacity of the tilting kettle varies from 15 to 100 litres. The table-top models will usually be in a smaller size than the floor models. Other features may include:

1. in-built drip gutters on table models;
2. self-locking tilt mechanism;
3. automatic return to vertical.

Plate 10.2 illustrates a commonly used boiling pan.

Plate 10.2 *Boiling equipment*

Deep-frying

Thermostatically controlled deep-fryer   The temperature of the frying medium is automatically maintained at an appropriate level to minimise fire risks, and avoid greasy or overcooked food. Electric and gas models are available, the latter providing the best temperature control and reducing the fire-risk to a minimum. Most models incorporate a *cool zone* (see Chapter 9).

Fryers designed for the catering trade are either manual or automatic. Fully automatic (computerised) models are pre-set so that at the end of the cooking period (time/temperature pre-selected for individual foods) the basket lifts out of the frying medium and drains. Both floor-standing and counter-top models are available and may be in single or multiple units. Other features may include:

1. timer switch;
2. computerised controls for automatic time and temperature;
3. overriding safety thermostat;
4. filter-drain system;
5. oval or rectangle pans and baskets;
6. swing-up heating elements to facilitate cleaning, with automatic cut-off of power;
7. coupling to fire-fighting system;
8. basket lifts;
9. basket-support rail;
10. overflow drain;
11. double-coil element for fast reheating;
12. batter plate for free-frying.

Pressure deep-fryer   A tight-fitting lid traps moisture as it is driven off the food as steam and the build-up of pressure reduces cooking-time. This type of fryer retains more moisture in the food than the conventional fryer but food required crisp is not successfully cooked using this equipment (see Chapter 9).

Continuous fryers   In the large-scale production of food, batch-frying can be replaced with a continuous operation. Food is fed onto one end of a conveyor-belt system and fried food collected at the other end.

Oil filters   This is an external facility for cleaning oil in deep-fryers. The oil is pumped out through reusable filters and recycled. There are several different makes on the market and manufacturers make various claims for extended oil life, cost recovery and speed.

   Plate 10.3 illustrates deep frying equipment.

Plate 10.3 *Deep-frying equipment*

Grilling

Over-heat/salamander grill Food is cooked on grids, bars or trays under a heat source which is gas or electric. Some of the early gas models incorporated an electric fan for instant heat for glazing. Salamander grills may be free-standing, wall-mounted or built-in to part of a range. Whilst some models are multi-purpose others are built to operate for a limited range of items, as are the meat grills found in steak houses. Other features may include:

1. drip tray;
2. insulated handles;
3. two separate brander shelves;
4. brander-shelf mounted on rollers;
5. stainless steel or vitreous enamel finish.

Under-fired grill Most commonly fuelled by gas which heats a bed of fire bricks. Food is cooked on grill bars which slant above the fire bricks. This gives the grilled items a distinctive pattern of dark criss-cross lines when the food is turned over and round on each side whilst grilling. The large stainless-steel versions which incorporate an air-vent are known as the 'silver grill' and this piece of equipment would be a feature in a Grill Room.

Contact grill It is important to realise that despite the name, the cooking method achieved by this equipment is not grilling (see Chapter 9). These 'grills' are heated by electricity and have a top and bottom cast-iron surface. Food is sandwiched between these surfaces so that both sides of the food are cooked simultaneously by conduction. The surfaces usually have a ribbed design so that a conventional grill pattern will be branded onto items. There are versions of the contact grill with different-shaped cooking plates for different operations such as grilling meats, toasted sandwiches or waffles.

Plate 10.4 shows some types of grills.

Steaming

Steaming equipment is made from aluminium or stainless steel, to prevent rusting, and designed to operate at atmospheric, low or high pressure. All the equipment described below is manufactured to modular and gastronorm specifications.

Atmospheric-pressure steamer Steam is produced either internally, from a cistern of water, or externally from a steam generator. The water is heated – by either gas or electricity – to generate steam and food cooks in the steamy atmosphere produced. There is a vent situated at the

203

Plate 10.4 *Grills*

204

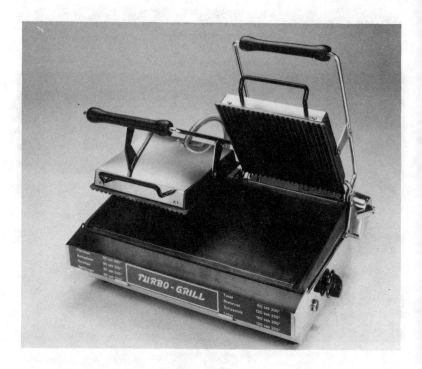

top of the cooking compartment for excess steam to escape and ensure that atmospheric pressure is not exceeded. These steamers are usually fitted with a double door-latch to allow safer access during cooking.

Convection steamer   Convection steamers cook at atmospheric pressure but differ from atmospheric pressure steamers because the air/steam is forced to circulate by means of a fan or high-velocity jets of steam. Food cooks quicker than in traditional atmospheric steaming but slower than in high-pressure equipment. Models are available as single, double or triple compartments.

Low-pressure steamer   This is similar in size and operation to the atmospheric steamer but has a steam-pressure valve for adjusting the steam pressure. The food will be cooked quicker than in an atmospheric steamer and the usual cooking pressure is 14 kPa (2 psi). There are usually safety door-latches to prevent opening under pressure.

High-pressure steamer   This may operate with either an internal or external steam supply. The main advantage with an external steam supply is the extra convection produced by the steam jets which reduces cooking time. A valve controls the pressure at approximately 54 kPa (8 psi) whilst cooking. A safety device is often fitted to the doors so that the steam pressure is reduced before the doors can be opened. Single-, double- or triple-door models are available all with automatic timing and cut-off devices.

Plate 10.5 illustrates a low pressure steam oven.

Plate 10.5 *Low pressure steam ovens*

206

Multi-purpose

Bratt pan   These are relatively new pieces of equipment suitable for large catering operations. They are shallow, square vessels which are used for a variety of cooking operations such as boiling, braising, poaching, shallow-frying and stewing. Particular features are the large surface area and tilting facility. They are heated by either gas or electricity and are usually floor-standing. Other features may include:

1. modular shape;
2. balanced tilting action;
3. counterbalanced lid;
4. hand-wheel tilting mechanism.

Plate 10.6 illustrates the Bratt pan.

Plate 10.6   *Bratt pan*

B Holding equipment

Hot food

Bain-marie This is basically a well containing hot water into which pots are placed to keep their contents hot for service. Bains-marie may be free-standing or incorporated into a cooking range. They may also be a part of a service-counter arrangement, being open as previously described, or enclosed with fitted containers and lids. They may be heated by gas, electricity – or sometimes in the case of the enclosed type – by direct steam. After use they are cleaned by draining off the water through the run-off, refilling with detergent water, rinsing and refilling.

Hot cupboard (hotplate) Hot cupboards are containers used to keep cooked foods hot for service, they may also be used for heating service dishes and plates. Hot cupboards may be heated by gas, electricity or steam. The top of the hotplate may be used as a hot-service counter and may be kept at a higher temperature than the interior. The waiter-waitress service models will have doors on both sides. They are usually made of stainless steel and adapted into all kinds and combinations of gastronorm service units. Many hot cupboards will incorporate a bain-marie which will usually be of the fitted type, giving a neat and hygienic appearance.

Temperature control is extremely important as palatability is severely affected by reduced temperatures or the dried appearance of overheated food. Legislation, to protect the customer from food-poisoning, requires food to be kept above 63°C and hotplates are usually maintained at this temperature. Higher temperatures will be used if doors are on both sides. Some other features include:

1. adjustable shelves;
2. recessed controls.

Small portable models are obtainable and have locking wheels.

Plate warmers/dispensers These are units for heating and storing plates for service. The plates are stacked onto a round plate-size sprung platform which raises the pile as plates are removed (self-levelling). These may stand alone, be mobile, or be part of a service arrangement. They may be single, double or quadruple stack models and take up to eighty plates each per stack.

Plate 10.7 shows a bain-marie.

Plate 10.7 *Bain-marie*

Cold food

Cold rooms   Maintained at a temperature of 10°C, these walk-in rooms are designed for the storage of perishable foods which do not require temperatures as low as a refrigerator. They may incorporate a walk-in freezing compartment and are designed in a variety of sizes usually tailored to suit an individual kitchen size. Other features may include:

1. open or sliding doors;
2. inside-door release;
3. internal light;
4. modular shelving;
5. hanging rails.

Refrigerator   This is a container for the cold storage of perishable food. The temperature will vary according to the intended use:

General purpose	4°C
Fresh meat	0°C–2°C
Fresh fish	0°C–2°C
Salad	6°C

In large establishments it is more usual to have separate refrigerators for different commodities, e.g. wet fish would be stored in a wet-fish cabinet; dairy and grocery products, fresh meat, etc. (see Chapter 5) in their respective cabinets.

Blast chillers These are large units which are designed to cool hot food to chilling temperatures in a minimum amount of time. Once the food is brought to the required temperature it is removed to chilled storage units. Blast chillers are usually used as part of a cook–chill system and details can be found in Chapter 11. The chiller operates with fans to assist the rapid and uniform cooling of the food by currents of cold air cooled by liquid nitrogen or similar refrigerant. Blast chillers are available for coping with loads of between 20 kg and 60 kg. The larger loads are accommodated by trolley loading.

Blast freezers These are part of the technology essential for the rapid freezing of raw or cooked food. They are used in catering as part of cook–freeze operations. Small or large models are available for dealing with loads in the range of 11kg to 400 kg. As with blast chilling the larger loads are trolley loaded and once temperatures below − 18°C are reached the foods are wheeled into freezer storage units.

Frozen food storage cabinet A container for the storage of frozen foods at a temperature of below − 18°C. Sizes vary from small, single-door cupboards to walk-in freezer rooms.

Holding equipment for cold food is shown in Plate 10.8.

C Food preparation equipment

Bowl choppers (cutters)

These are usually table-top models and are used for cutting raw meat, fish, pâtés, coleslaw, breadcrumbs, etc. The blade action also includes a mixing function as well. The texture of the chopped product will be finer the longer the chopping operation. There is a built-in safety device so that the blades will not rotate if the cover is removed.

Food mixers

These may be bench-top or floor-standing. Apart from whisking, mixing and kneading, machines also have attachments for adding a mincer,

210

Plate 10.8 *Holding equipment for cold food*

(b) refrigerator *(c) blast chiller*

vegetable slicer, cheese-grater and in some cases a liquidiser. Bowl sizes vary as follows: bench models: 4–20 litres; floor models: 20–100 litres.

Food-mixers used in the bakery and confectionery industries will usually be larger and may have different mixing actions. Other features may include:

1. collar or extension rim;
2. between three and ten speed controls;
3. automatic timing switch;
4. bowl lift;
5. up to 6 hp motor on larger models.

Food processors

These vary from small domestic 2–4 litre size to 30–45 litre floor-standing cutters/mixers. All types have a see-through cover and safety switch-off when the cover is removed. These machines are used for cutting, kneading, slicing, blending and liquidising. Other features may include:

1. varied speeds;
2. various attachments for different operations.

Ice-cream-making machines

There is a variety of machines available from the bucket 6 qt capacity (manual or electric motor) to 100 litre per hour stainless steel electric. Some machines may combine the production of several products such as soft ice-cream, milk shakes.

Ice-making machines

There is a variety of machines giving different outputs. Apart from the machine size, room and water input temperature effect output as well. Outputs usually range from 500 to 10 000 cubes per hour. Storage capacity of machines varies from 11kg to 160 kg. Machines will usually have facilities for changing the size and shape of the ice-cubes.

Meat-slicing machines

Slicing machines may be either hand-operated or electrically-powered. They may be gravity-fed which means that the feeder-shelf to the blade slants so that the item is moved onto the blade by its weight. Alternatively, the feed may be automatic which means that it is held horizontally and moved along automatically as the machine handle rotates. The electric machines are either belt- or gear-box-driven and will have a blade within the size range 8″–14″. Health and safety factors are of the utmost importance in the design, operation and cleaning of these machines. All machines have a blade-guard which incorporates a safety micro-switch. A no-volt release switch and a mushroom panic button are also included for safety. All parts are detachable to facilitate cleaning. The controls are always obvious and easily accessible. The thickness gauge will operate from 0 to 16 mm. Other features may include:

1. blade removal tool;
2. sharpening device;
3. detachable last-slice device.

Potato peeler

These are electrically powered to stir the potatoes against the abrasive drum interior with a water input for continual washing. They operate with a carborundum peeler plate which may be fine- or coarse-grained in combination with abrasive drum sides. Pedestal, mounted or bench models are available and sizes vary from 3.5 kg capacity producing 100 kg per hour, to 25 kg capacity producing 600 kg per hour. Sealed plugs and switches are used for safety because of the damp operation conditions. Other features may include:

1. timer for controlled peeling;

2. waste ejector;
3. chute guard;
4. changeable peeler plates;
5. adjustable positions for waste and water outlets;
6. permanent diamond serrations in peeler chamber.

Vegetable preparation machine

There are a variety of types ranging from attachments to food-mixers to dedicated stand-alone models. All machines perform a variety of operations such as grating, slicing, shredding, dicing and chipping, with the use of interchangeable cutting blades. According to machine size, the prepared food output varies from between 26–2 600 kg per hour. The operations and types of food vary from vegetable julienne or sliced tomatoes to grated cheese or nuts. The largest types which are capable of 6 000 lb output per hour have a continuous-feed-hopper.

Types of food preparation equipment are shown in Plate 10.9.

Plate 10.9 *Food preparation equipment*

(a) potato peeler   *(b) mixing machine*

214

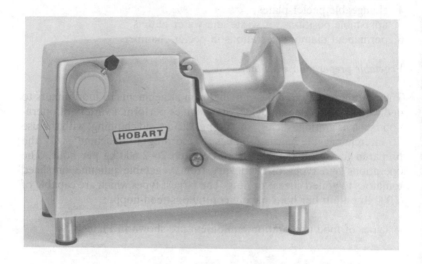

(c) bowl chopper

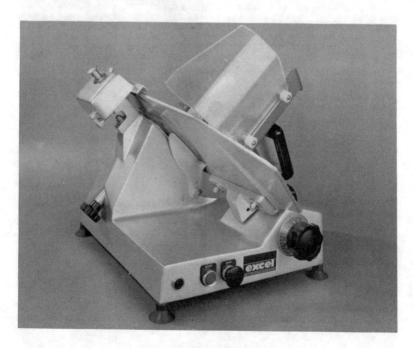

(d) slicing machine

(e) food processor

(f) vegetable preparation machine

D Beverage production and serving equipment

Beverages vending machines

These provide a range of hot beverages, usually from powdered ingredients. Some machines include cold drinks as well. Self-service machines may be either coin- or credit-card operated.

Café sets

Used with undercounter pressure boilers for making and storing black coffee at the rate of between 20 and 200 litres per hour, these also have a container for heating and storing milk at serving temperature. Other features may include:

1. level gauges for the storage containers;
2. incorporated 'café filtre';
3. twin urns;
4. push-button controls;
5. steam-injection system.

Carbonated drinks dispenser

These machines are capable of producing up to 150 litres per hour of carbonated cold drinks. They operate in conjunction with different flavoured syrups. They may be counter-top or free-standing models and single- or double-console. There may also be a thickness control for the drinks mix.

Espresso coffee machine

The traditional hot-beverage machine for the production of espresso or cappuccino coffee. These machines may have between one and four fusion units and the function of these is to produce the individual cups of coffee with pressured steam at the rate of 5 seconds per cup. In addition there will be a number of steam jets for heating milk for making cappuccino.

Filter coffee machines

Electrically operated, there is a considerable range of models and makes available, some of which are capable of producing up to 150 cups of fresh coffee per hour. The water is either poured in manually, or plumbed in. The boiling water passes through freshly ground coffee in a filter which then passes into a serving jug below. Serving jugs when full of coffee are kept hot on small round hotplates. Multiple units are available.

Hot-water boiler/dispenser

These may be heated by either gas or electricity and may be fitted or free standing. There is a wide range of capacities up to 54 litres. The fitted type may be operated by expansion or alternatively by pressure with a gauge and valve for steam. The output of continuous boiling water for beverages ranges from 100 to 250 litres per hour.

Milk-shake machines

These may be counter- or console-models with single- or four-flavours available. They may also be push-button with built-in syrup containers and pump-operated. The usual output is eight shakes per minute with a storage capacity of up to 60 litres.

E Washing-up equipment

Conveyor dish-washers

These operate on the conveyor-belt principle as the name implies. The soiled items are loaded at one end and pass through the pre-wash, wash, rinse and, if included, drying tunnels, emerging at the other end ready for use. Outputs vary up to as much as 9 000 plates per hour. They are usually stainless steel, heated by electricity or steam and have variable belt-speed controls.

Front-loading batch dish-washers

The usual design is a single compartment with one or two sliding trays onto which soiled items are placed. All models have a selection of automatic programmes for lightly- to heavily-soiled items. Some models will have trays to specialise in particular items such as plates only, glasses only, etc. Programmes vary from 1 to 10 minutes and outputs may be as much as 1000 items per hour. Most commercial machines are made from stainless steel. Other features may include:

1. override programme facility for heavily soiled items;
2. internal automatic detergent dispenser;
3. pull-down or rounded-slide-door types available;
4. some models have a round rotating-tray operation.

Glass-washing machine

Similar in operation to the front-loading batch-washers although counter models are available as well which may fit under a bar counter. Some machines are incorporated in units with counter, sink and storage racks. Some models will have a variable timer for different glasses.

Pass-through batch dish-washers

These operate with push-in trays at one side and pull-out at the other. The push-in and pull-out operation can be at an angle for corner models. Outputs may be up to 1100 plates per hour. Other features may include:

1. pre-wash sink;
2. overhead manual spray.

Pan and utensil washer

Similar to the front loading batch dishwasher, usually floor standing. They take heavily soiled items and have a timer included. They are powered by a motor unit and have a hydraulically driven shaft (thus making it electrically safe) and an assortment of interchangeable brush heads. They are usually situated over a pot wash sink but may be detachable for use in other areas of the establishment.

Plate 10.10 illustrates washing-up equipment.

F Waste-disposal units

All types of food production generates waste which must be removed as soon as possible. Waste-disposal units (see Plate 10.11) reduce the volume of waste by (i) producing a slurry of soft food-waste and disposing of it down the drain or producing a semi-dry pulp; (ii) crushing both hard and soft waste and compacting it into a dense, solid material to be disposed of in the normal way. There are bench, trough or free-standing stainless-steel models available.

10.2 SMALL KITCHEN UTENSILS AND THEIR USES

The smaller items of equipment and utensils used in cookery are classified in this section by the materials from which they are made. In the cases where items are made from more than one material the most obvious feature decides the classification. In this type of classification some items – e.g. rolling pins which are made of either wood or stainless steel; mixing bowls which may be made of a number of materials – may appear more than once.

A Cast aluminium

Examples of cast-aluminium equipment and utensils

Saucepans, stockpots, mixing bowls, measures, colanders, fish kettles, sauteuses, frying pans, dariole moulds, pie dishes, ham press, roasting pans, bain-marie pots, etc. (see Plate 10.12).

Plate 10.10   *Washing-up equipment*

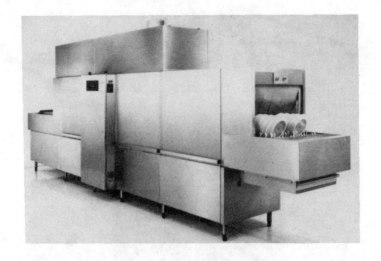

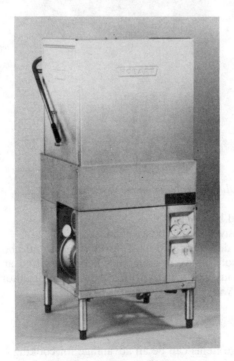

(b) batch dishwasher

Plate 10.11   *Waste-disposal unit*

Cleaning cast-aluminium equipment

1. Soda should be avoided.
2. Harsh abrasives should be avoided.
3. Hot water, detergent and hard-bristle brush should be used.
4. As it is a soft metal, it sometimes becomes pitted and tends to be slightly porous, particularly with grease, therefore thorough cleaning in very hot water with detergent is essential.

Considerations

1. Heavy gauge items can be an advantage for cooking.
2. Thin gauge items may easily become dented.

Plate 10.12   *Examples of aluminium items*

1 Saucepan   2 Turbot kettle   3 Stew pan   4 Bain-marie pot   5 Oblong pie dish   6 Pudding sleeve   7 Jelly mould

3. Aluminium is a soft metal therefore any stirring should be done with a wooden implement, not metal.
4. Certain foods such as red cabbage and artichoke bottoms become discoloured if cooked in aluminium.
5. Some items may combine with black cast-iron handles.

B   Cloth

Examples of cloth items

1. Piping bags – made from waterproof nylon, strong cotton, canvas (used with a variety of tube shapes and sizes for such things as duchesse potatoes, meringue, etc.)
2. Muslin cloth – made from cotton (used for straining certain soups and sauces).
3. Tammy cloth – made from unbleached calico (used for straining certain soups and sauces, although now rarely seen in use).
4. Jelly bags – made from flannel (used for straining sweet and savoury jellies).
5. Oven pockets – made from hessian, sometimes separate or linked.

Cleaning cloth items

1. As soon as possible after use all materials should be cleaned by washing in hot detergent water, rinsed and dried.
2. Heavier and more porous materials should be periodically boiled.

222

Consideration

1. Muslin and particularly Tammy cloths are not so much in common use these days as they were a few years ago in the French kitchen. It is however possible that they could reappear more for nouvelle cuisine dishes which tend to feature very finely strained sauces.
2. Piping bags tend to split with rough usage and hard laundering. When purchasing therefore, some estimate of the expected use needs to be established.

C Copper

Examples of copper items

Saucepans, stockpots, Pommes Anna moulds, dariole moulds, braising pans, bains-marie, salmon kettles, casseroles, roasting trays, sauteuses, sugar boilers, egg-white bowls, etc. (see Plates 10.13 and 10.14).

1 Whisking bowl   2 Flat saute pan (plat a' sauteuse)   3 Bain-marie pot
4 Bavarois mould   5 Charlotte mould   6 Bombe mould   7 Bain marie
sauce pot   8 Sugar boiler   9 Russe   10 Sauteuse   11 Pommes Anna
mould   12 Savarin mould   13 Petite savarin mould   14 Plat
a'sauteuse   15 Dariole mould

Cleaning copper equipment

1. As nearly all copper utensils are tin-lined, care should be taken not to use heavy abrasives for cleaning.
2. Very hot water with detergent and a firm-bristle brush should be used.
3. To clean copper surfaces which tend to tarnish easily a DIY preparation made from $\frac{1}{3}$ salt, $\frac{1}{3}$ flour, $\frac{1}{3}$ silver sand mixed to a smooth paste with vinegar, is used.

1 Stockpot (marmite) 2 Stew pan 3 Salmon kettle (rondin) 4 Braising pan (braisiére) 5 Oval cocotte 6 Trout kettle

Considerations

1. Next to silver, copper is the best conductor of heat.
2. It has a prestigious aspect when used in cookery and is favoured particularly by traditionalists.
3. Copper resists corrosion, is tough (large items do not need to be thick gauge) and wears well.
4. Copper is very expensive compared with some alternatives.
5. Utensils used in cookery are tin-lined to protect the food from the 'green rust' which forms on the surface of copper.
6. As the tin lining eventually wears with use it needs retinning which is expensive.
7. Exceptions to the tin-lined rule are: (i) sugar boilers – because of the higher temperatures involved; (ii) egg-whites whisking-bowl because of the whisk scraping.

8. Care is needed to ensure that tin-lined items do not burn dry as tin melts at 231°C compared with copper at 1083°C.

D Earthenware and china items

Examples of earthenware and china items

Solid dishes, pie dishes, casseroles, soufflé dishes, egg dishes, raviers, pudding basins, crescent salad plate, ramequin, marmites, oyster plates, shells, game-pie dish, etc. (see Plate 10.15).

1 Round shallow casserole 2 Petite marmite 3 Marmite (pot au feu) 4 Oval casserole 5 Soufflé dish 6 Oval sole dish 7 Oval eared dish 8 Crescent shaped salad dish 9 Small round casserole 10 Oblong hors d'oeuvre (ravier) 11 Eared cocotte (eggs en cocotte) 12 Round eared dish (oeuf sur le plat) 13 Scallop shell 14 Small eared individual pot (pot au chocolate) 15 Ramekin

Cleaning earthenware and china

1. Avoid extreme changes of temperature if plunging into hot water for cleaning.
2. Hot water with detergent and brush or scouring pad are used when not using a dish-washer.

Considerations

1. Very expensive and breakable.
2. Avoid stacking unevenly or too high.
3. Definitions:
   earthenware – vessels made from baked clay.

porcelain – fine kind of glazed earthenware.

china – general term for fine porcelain and fine glazed earthenware.

E Glass

Certain items of glass equipment and utensils such as measuring jugs, bowls, etc., are available. Many kitchens, bakeries, cake factories, etc., have a policy of *'no glass'* where food is prepared. Glass items such as sundae dishes, coupes, salad bowls, etc. may be used in food *service*.

F Iron: cast and wrought

Examples of iron items

Frying pans, omelette pans, fritures, oval fish-meunière pans, woks, pancake pans, baking sheets, cake tins, spatulas, paella pans, Swiss roll tins, etc. (see Plate 10.16).

1 Flat handled fry pan   2 Round handled fry pan   3 Omelette pan   4 Baking tray   5 Pancake pan (deep)   6 Meuniere pan   7 Deep roasting pan

226

Cleaning iron items

There are three approaches to cleaning according to the state of the equipment:

1. Wipe with a clean lightly greased cloth or kitchen paper.
2. Use salt as an abrasive with kitchen paper or rag to clean and then lightly grease.
3. Wash in hot water with detergent, use abrasive as necessary, rinse, dry and lightly grease as above.

Considerations

1. Most iron items of equipment are used for frying or baking and the less contact they have with water in cleaning the less likelihood of food sticking.
2. Iron is liable to rust so all equipment must be dry and lightly greased.

G Non-stick metal

Examples of non-stick metal items

Saucepans, frying pans, roasting trays, Yorkshire-pudding moulds, cake tins, savarin moulds, flan tins, etc.

Cleaning non-stick metal items

1. Avoid abrasives that may damage the surface (should not be necessary if non-stick!)
2. Hot water, detergent and brush should be used.

Considerations

1. To preserve the non-stick surface avoid high temperatures or burning dry.
2. Try to avoid the use of metal stirring implements.

H Paper

Examples of paper items

1. Greaseproof paper – available in various thicknesses and used for small piping bags (e.g. for royal icing), lining cake tins, protective cover for food (cartouche), etc.
2. Hand towels – small double-folded, thick, coloured, absorbent paper. Used for drying hands once.

3. Kitchen paper – usually off-white thick absorbent paper, used for draining deep-fried foods, etc.
4. Silver foil – has a variety of uses from protecting foods to stiffening table-napkin buffalo horns.
5. Cutlet frills, pie collars, buffet skewers – all decorative and quite expensive. Hand-made from clean white firm paper.
6. Doyleys – many different sizes and either round or more usually oval. Made from good-quality firm white paper. Used by placing on food service dishes and arranging food on top such as, sandwiches, pie dishes, etc.

I Plastic

Examples of plastic items

Bowls, measuring jugs, gastronorm containers, hors d'oeuvre dishes, scrapers, coded cutting boards (polythene), etc.

Cleaning plastic items

1. Hot water with detergent, use brush, rinse dry.

Considerations

1. Avoid putting hot food into plastic as it may taint the food.
2. Plastic is easily disfigured or burnt if left near heat.
3. Relatively cheap.
4. Non-breakable.

J Stainless steel

Examples of stainless steel items

Bowls, measuring jugs, colanders, conical strainers, buckets, egg-rings, butchers' tray, funnels, ladles, tongs, fish slices, rolling pins, spoons, gastronorm trays, etc. (see Figure 10.5).

Cleaning stainless steel items

1. Hot water, with detergent.
2. Scouring pad or brush may be used if necessary.
3. Rinse dry.

Considerations

1. Stainless steel is a comparatively poor conductor of heat.
2. Good-quality stainless steel is expensive.

228

3. It does not rust or tarnish or discolour food in any way.
4. When used for saucepans it is combined with another metal for the base such as aluminium, copper, etc.
5. Used fairly extensively for small utensils.

Plate 10.17 *Examples of stainless steel items*

1 Ladle, medium 2 Serving spoon, plain 3 Serving spoon, perforated
4 Ladle, small 5 Ladle measure 6 Slice 7 Bucket 8 Jug measure
9 Flour sieve 10 Basin 11 Grater 12 Mixing bowl 13 French slicer
(mandolin) 14 Flour scoop 15 Pie dish 16 Butcher's tray 17 Balloon
whisk 18 Whip whisk

K Tinned steel

Examples of tinned steel items

Potato-ricer, baking tins, piping tubes, pastry cutters, conical strainers, bowl strainers, spiders, metal sieves, whisks, cake wires, balers, passoirs, mouli strainers, soup-passing machines, nest frying-baskets, watercress baskets, etc. (see Figure 10.6).

Plate 10.18 *Examples of other metal items*

1 Strainer (Passoir) 2 Vegetable ladle 3 Skimmer 4 Slice 5 Fine conical strainer 6 Potato snower 7 Frying basket 8 Conical strainer (chinois) 9 Flan ring 10 Custard cup 11 Boat shaped mould (barquette) 12 Shallow patty tin 13 Oval fancy 14 Petite savarin 15 Brioche 16 Genoise tin 17 Balloon whisks)

Cleaning tinned steel items

1. Depends upon the item being cleaned; many involve mesh.
2. Mesh items should be placed in water immediately after use to avoid drying and sticking.
3. All tinned steel items are washed in hot water with detergent, rinsed and dried.

Considerations

1. When using sieves and fine strainers avoid banging to force mixture through.

L Wood

Examples of wood items

Chopping boards (although these are being replaced with plastic), rolling pins, spatulas, mixing spoons, sieves, salt boxes, triangles, mushrooms, etc.

Cleaning wood items

1. Be sure to watch for cracks and crevices.
2. Avoid scraping items as this may splinter the wood.
3. Wash in very hot water with detergent; use a scrubbing brush but do not soak items.
4. Dry immediately and place somewhere to dry further.
5. Certain items, such as triangles, will not need washing, whilst others will need to be washed very often, e.g. chopping boards.

Considerations

Wood is porous and retains bacteria, grease, dirt and flavours, and for reasons of hygiene, therefore, it is being replaced by other materials for direct food preparation. Wooden chopping boards should not be used. Stainless steel tables are replacing wooden tables.

M Wrought steel

Examples of wrought-steel items

Frying pans, fritures, baking trays, roasting trays, nelson trays.

Cleaning wrought-steel items

As with both wrought- and cast-iron this metal is liable to rust so the same rules apply.

Considerations

The same factors apply to wrought- steel as to cast- and wrought-iron.

10.3 PERSONAL EQUIPMENT AND UTENSILS

Cooks have traditionally owned their own knives and other small tools. Most catering students are expected to purchase a basic set of tools, mostly consisting of knives, before they start their college course. This system does of course help to perpetuate the tradition of ownership of craft tools! This section will consider the important points related to all knives and hand tools used in food preparation, although not all will be the personal property of a typical cook.

Knives

Figure 10.1 shows some examples.

Figure 10.1 *Kitchen knives*

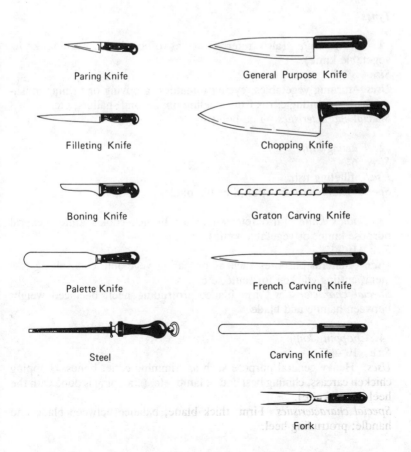

Paring Knife

General Purpose Knife

Filleting Knife

Chopping Knife

Boning Knife

Graton Carving Knife

Palette Knife

French Carving Knife

Steel

Carving Knife

Fork

Materials

Blades steel – liable to rust, stain, metal scarring and pitting, if not maintained constantly; stainless steel – rust and stain resistant.

Handles wood – porous, liable to work loose and crack; hardwood – liable to work loose and crack; moulded plastic – firm, non-slip surface and shape, hygienic.

Handles may be colour-coded, e.g. for cooked or raw preparations, for fish etc. They may be riveted to blade to add strength, though this is not necessary with moulded plastic.

Storage wallet – thick canvas with sized slots to accommodate tools; box – either wood or metal, usually home-made or adapted from another use; attaché case – purpose built, moulded interior, and expensive.

Types

1. *Paring knife* (also referred to as office knife, turning knife, vegetable knife).
Size 3″–4″
Uses – turning vegetables, eyeing tomatoes, grooving or turning mushrooms, segmenting citrus fruit, peeling onions and shallots, etc.
Special characteristics – fine point.

2. *Filleting knife*
Size 6″
Uses filleting fish.
Special characteristics thin, flexible blade.

3. *Cook's knife* (also referred to as: French cook's knife, general purpose knife, or vegetable knife).
Size 10″–12″
Uses General purposes such as preparing vegetable cuts, dicing raw meat, cutting chicken for sauté, etc.
Special characteristics firm blade, protruding heel, balanced weight between handle and blade.

4. *Chopping knife*
Size 10″–14″
Uses Heavy general purpose such as trimming cutlet bones, chopping chicken carcass, chining best end of lamb, etc. (chopping is done with the heel of the knife).
Special characteristics Firm, thick blade; balance between blade and handle; protruding heel.

5. *Palette knife*
Sizes 6"–12"
Uses A large number of varied uses such as: turning shallow-fried items
e.g. fillet of sole meunière; spreading soft mixtures e.g. whipped cream;
shaping preparations e.g. pommes Byron; mixing, e.g. butter for spreading, etc.
Special characteristics according to use the blade may be flexible or
fairly stiff. There is an alternative handle known as a 'cranked handle'
and this is used more in confectionery work.

6. *Boning knife*
Size 6"–7"
Uses boning butcher's meat as well as skinning and removing gristle.
Special characteristics the blade is fairly narrow and tapers to a point.
The handle should be of moulded plastic shaped to accommodate the
boning 'fist' hold.

7. *Carving knife* (also known as ham knife)
Size 8"–14"
Uses carving mostly large pieces of cooked meat:

(a) hot and cold, on the bone;
(b) 'off' the bone if mechanical slicer not used;
(c) the carving knife is often used by chefs or waiters in the dining-room,
    to carve in front of the customers;
(d) other items will be carved such as smoked salmon, smoked ham, etc.
    and a separate knife may be used for these.
(e) if a carving knife is used for bread then the serrated or scalloped type
    ('Gratton edge') is preferable.

Special characteristics the blade is usually thin.

8. *Butcher's steel*
Size 10"–14"
Uses for keeping a sharp edge on all knives used for cutting. A lot of
skill is required to use a steel successfully and instruction is essential.
There are also a number of safety hazards when using a steel such as
holding the point of knife too near chin; not having all the hand
protected by the guard if the thumb is not in the right position; and
distractions.
Special characteristics there are various grades from coarse to fine. The
steel is magnetic and fine metal shavings stick to the steel.

9. *Carborundum stone*
Size 10"–12"
Uses gaining a quick and very sharp knife edge.
Special characteristics easily broken, normally used by skilled cooks.

10. *Cooks' fork*   (also known as a roasting fork or meat fork)
Sizes   5″–10″
Uses   holding meats firm when carving, lifting cooked meat slices, turning roasting meats and birds, etc.
Special characteristics   there are two shapes: (i) curved which may have a guard; (ii) straight without guard (long-pronged).

Figure 10.2   *Small tools*

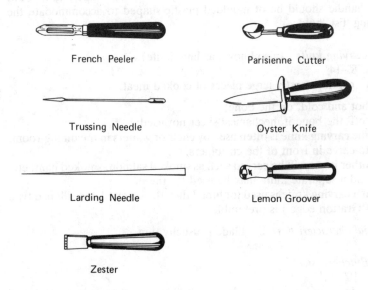

French Peeler

Parisienne Cutter

Trussing Needle

Oyster Knife

Larding Needle

Lemon Groover

Zester

Small tools

Figure 10.9 shows examples of these.

1. *French peeler* (also known as: potato peeler)

Uses   for peeling fruit, potatoes (if not by machine), eyeing potatoes, etc.
Special characteristics   Double-bladed for use with either hand. Often in water so a wooden handle will soon become loose.

2. *Lemon decorator* (also known as a groover).

Uses for grooving lemon, cucumbers, carrots, and other fruit and vegetables to give a cartwheel effect to slices, also used for other decorations.
Special characteristics there are two types of lemon decorator, one vertical, the other horizontal giving a choice of manipulations.

3. *Lemon zester* (known also as a zester)

Uses to remove the zest from citrus fruits for sauces, sweets, etc.
Special characteristics none.

4. *Vegetable scoops* (also known as parisienne cutter, parisienne scoop)

Size 12 mm–28 mm
Uses there are a variety of shapes and sizes for different purposes:

(a) small, round, for garnishes such as those for soups;
(b) medium, round, for parisienne potatoes, melon balls, scooping the inside out of tomatoes, etc.;
(c) oval, medium, for garnishes, melon balls, etc.;
(d) oval, medium, serrated, for decorative work on buffets, etc.

Special characteristics there is a fairly extensive range but the most popular is the medium plain round used for parisienne potatoes and melon balls.

5. *Trussing needle*

Sizes 8″–12″
Uses for trussing all poultry and game, also other items needing trussing.

6. *Larding needle*

Size 8″–12″
Uses for passing fat through lean meats.
Special characteristics there are two types (i) end jaws for clasping the strip of lard; and (ii) open end.
There is also a larding pin which is an implement with a handle, used to pierce meat whilst containing the strips of lard.

7. *Oyster knife*

Size 3″–4″
Uses for opening oysters which is done immediately before service.
Special characteristics there are two types in use (i) with a safety guard,

and (ii) plain. The end is sharpest and care needs to be taken that the point of the knife does not slip upwards against the hand or arm. Instruction is essential before attempting to open oysters.

8. *Garnishing knife*

Size 4"
Uses for decorative cuts with its serrated edge. Items will vary such as citrus fruit, slices of pâté, etc.
Special characteristics usually only made from stainless steel as if tarnished the edge would be difficult to clean.

9. *Apple corer*

Size 25 mm round hole
Uses removing the core from apples when they need to be cooked whole e.g. baked apple; removing the centre from apple slices, e.g. fritters, etc.
Special characteristics these sometimes combine with a single-bladed potato-peeler.

10.4 KITCHEN PLANNING – SPACE

Introduction

Kitchen planning is a highly specialised task and usually calls upon the advice and work of a number of experts. Large catering operations will have their own architects who will work with management and other specialists to draw up plans. In the next two sections the subject will be introduced. The demands upon a kitchen will vary considerably with the type, size, organisation and industrial sector. Trade kitchens vary enormously, as will be appreciated when we consider the difference between say, a small contract catering unit and a large luxury hotel. Despite the differences all kitchens will function better if they have been scientifically planned. This section will be concerned with those factors that determine the size of a kitchen. The next section will consider some of the principles of lay-out.

Estimating kitchen space

It does not follow that the larger an establishment the larger the kitchen. Space is costly and this may be reduced if some food items such as, pastries, bread, sous vide (see 11.3), are bought in ready prepared. Modern equipment and system may also increase production output in more limited space such as, cook–chill (see 11.2), cook/freeze (see 11.4).

The list of considerations is given below, although it must be remembered that all are interrelated.

1. Nature of the operation – whether residential or non-residential; geographical position for supplies.
2. Scope of the operation – whether serving a single outlet or multiple, such as banquets, outside functions.
3. Numbers of meals – whether this is always known in advance or is estimated.
4. The length of meal times – the number of sittings.
5. The type of food service – whether dealing in set meals or providing a choice such as table d'hôte and à la carte. In the case of choice, obviously, more food is required to be prepared and/or held.
6. The system operating – if purpose-built equipment is used, as mentioned above; cook–chill or cook–freeze. In these cases the kitchen area needed would be greatly reduced, particularly if only functions were catered for.
7. The use made of modular equipment – modular equipment is built to standard sizes so that it fits together.
8. Arrangement of ancillary functions – whether functions such as dishwash, plate-wash, vegetable preparation, are in the kitchen area.
9. Age of the building – some older establishments may have fairly large kitchens which were built before space planning was a prime consideration.

10.5 KITCHEN PLANNING – LAYOUT

We now look at the arrangement of the sections and equipment in the kitchen. The design of a kitchen will need to take account of the following points.

1. Flow of work

Kitchens are production units concerned with the following sequence of operations:

(a) incoming supplies of raw and prepared materials;
(b) storage of materials;
(c) preparation of materials;
(d) cooking and assembly of materials;
(e) service as arranged;
(f) cleaning function – related to production: workshop, equipment and utensils;
(g) cleaning function – related to services: crockery and cutlery.

2. Internal travel

The arrangement of the kitchen with all ancillary functions, contained in the sequence outlined above, will need to minimise the distance staff have to travel to carry out their duties. Any professional caterer knows only too well the value of time, as in any business the cost of labour is extremely expensive.

3. Comfort of working conditions

The siting of all equipment that produces hot air and steam will need access to ventilation. More flexibility is possible if a ceiling-duct ventilation system is installed, as this draws off the hot atmosphere evenly throughout the kitchen. Adequate working space is essential to avoid any feelings of restriction. Adequate staff-changing facilities are also an important point to be included in the considerations for kitchen planning.

4. Compliance with legislation

Both the Health and Safety at Work Act and the Food Hygiene Regulations put the onus on employers to ensure that premises are adequate.

5. Vision

With planning in both restricted and unrestricted space, the necessity of being able to see all the activities in a kitchen from one place may be overlooked. This is important for supervision and not only affects the size and siting of equipment but extends as well to the use of thick glass partitions to ancillary areas such as the wash-up and larder.

6. Services

The siting of electricity, gas, water, and drainage are early planning points. If equipment is to be mobile, then obviously more connections would be required, and specially-designed heavy-duty connections for all services should be available.

7. Standard equipment

The use of standard-size equipment (see Kitchen equipment terminology – next section) will normally decrease the amount of space required. As functions are streamlined with standard-sized containers and equipment it is easier to estimate space requirements accurately.

10.6 KITCHEN EQUIPMENT TERMINOLOGY

Adaptable

This term refers to kitchens which are designed to allow large-scale equipment to be reorganised for different arrangements of food production and service. This requires services such as gas and electricity to have multi-points. These kitchens are used in some colleges for teaching.

Gastronorm

This is an international modular system which refers to standard sizes of all containers and appliances (e.g. ovens, hotplates, etc.) within a trade kitchen. The advantage of this system is that the same container can be used to prepare, freeze, store, cook and serve any foods. The containers are not all the same size but they relate to one another so multiples of various sizes can be put together. A fractional reference relates to the area size. (This is based on 1/1 as standard size) see Table 10.1 and Figure 10.3.

Table 10.1 *Gastronorm sizes*

Module Size	Exterior Measurements mm mm	Interior Measurements mm mm
2/1	650 × 530	623 × 503
1/1	530 × 325	503 × 298
2/3	352 × 325	325 × 298
1/2	325 × 265	298 × 238
1/3	325 × 176	298 × 149
1/4	265 × 162	238 × 135
1/6	176 × 162	149 × 135
1/9	176 × 108	149 × 81

Alternative depths for all sizes:
  40 mm
  65 mm
 100 mm
 150 mm

Euronorm

In principle this is a similar system to gastronorm. The two systems, however, are not interchangeable because the sizes differ.

Figure 10.3 *Gastronorm shapes*

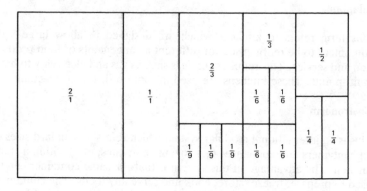

Modular

This term refers to kitchen equipment which is of standard size and can be put together in different combinations. The gastronorm system often includes modular equipment.

Regeneration

This is a term that has come into use to describe the reheating of chilled or frozen food (see cook–chill, cook–freeze and sous vide).

NEW TECHNOLOGY

11.1 INTRODUCTION

Catering for large numbers of people has always produced problems at service time. Traditional approaches have involved extended mise en place (e.g. peeling and then soaking of vegetables overnight) and various levels of pandemonium as service begins. More problems emerge in certain specialist sectors of catering where food has to be transported along hospital corridors or miles of roads to school kitchens. Container insulation, time schedules, overcooking during transport/holding and the prevention of temperatures dropping below palatable levels constitute a nightmare for supervisors. The quality and hygienic safety of such food has been constantly criticised.

Despite these problems the vast majority of catering operations have changed little in over a century, retaining much of the craft-based, labour-intensive, traditional system described in Chapter 2. This *low tech* approach has been attributed to the past availability of cheap labour that would accept long and anti-social working hours and poor working conditions. Recently, however, the industry has found uses for technology and technological systems in the form of **cook–chill, sous-vide,** and **cook–freeze.** The successful installation and operation of such systems is a complex process, fraught with problems, and this chapter is only intended as an introduction to these systems.

11.2 COOK–CHILL

Cook–Chill is a catering system based on the conventional cooking of food, followed by rapid *chilling*, storage/transport at chilling temperature (0°C–3°C) and subsequent *regeneration* (reheating) immediately prior to service.

The principles of cook–chill

The cook–chill operation differs fundamentally from traditional catering, as can be seen from Figure 11.1 and 11.2 below.

Figure 11.1 *Traditional catering*

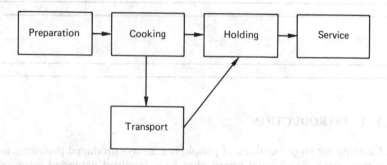

Figure 11.2 *Cook–chill system*

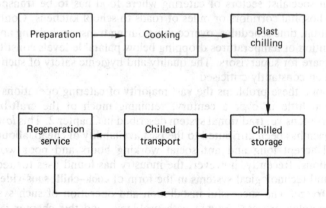

Menu items can be portioned before cooking, after cooking or after regeneration

(a) Chilling

The principle of cooling food to temperatures below that of normal refrigeration (4°C) but above the temperature that will cause ice-crystal formation (0°C) is called 'chilling'. This temperature range (0°C–3°C) extends the life of the product.

In a cook–chill system food is cooked and then rapidly cooled in a *blast chiller*. When the temperature is down to 3°C the food is transferred to a *chilled store* where it is held at 0°C–3°C. If required it can be transported in temperature-controlled vehicles to a holding unit from where the food can be regenerated and consumed.

At all stages in the system temperatures are monitored either manually with temperature probes (see Plate 11.1) or automatically by the equipment used.

Plate 11.1 *Temperature probes*

(b) Regeneration

If cold food is placed in a traditional oven for reheating it will take a considerable time to reach the required temperature throughout. Everyone is familiar with the sight of burnt surfaces, tough edges and the cold centres of traditionally reheated food! Many advances have been made in this area, so that technology now exists to *reheat without overcooking*. The technique is termed 'regeneration' and can be applied to almost all cooked foods, with excellent results. The temperature of regenerated food is critical for palatability and safety and is monitored with the use of temperature probes.

(c) The central production unit

Cook chill kitchens producing food to be regenerated at more than one other site are termed Central Production Units. Large C.P.U.'s resemble

244

a factory style operation with production line techniques and high levels of mechanisation. Fig 11.3 illustrates the relationship of the C.P.U. with the satellite kitchens /end units and Fig 11.4 the typical stages in a cook chill operation.

Figure 11.3 *A central production cook–chill system*

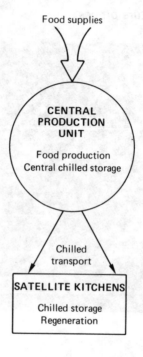

Types of equipment

The cook–chill equipment varies widely particuarly in relation to size of operation, and technological developments continue to improve ease of use and economy. The methods of regeneration and packaging show considerable diversity at the present time. Regeneration equipment can be based on microwave, infra-red, high-pressure steam or forced-convection technology (see Chapter 10). Food can pass through the cook–chill cycle in a number of packaging materials, including thermo-plastic, porcelain, china, ceramic, stainless steel, aluminium foil and disposable ovenable board. Recent developments have produced containers in which the food can be cooked, sealed, chilled, regenerated, served and then discarded. This not only speeds up the operation but the minimal handling of *open* food reduces the risk of contamination.

Figure 11.4 *Flow chart of a cook–chill production system*

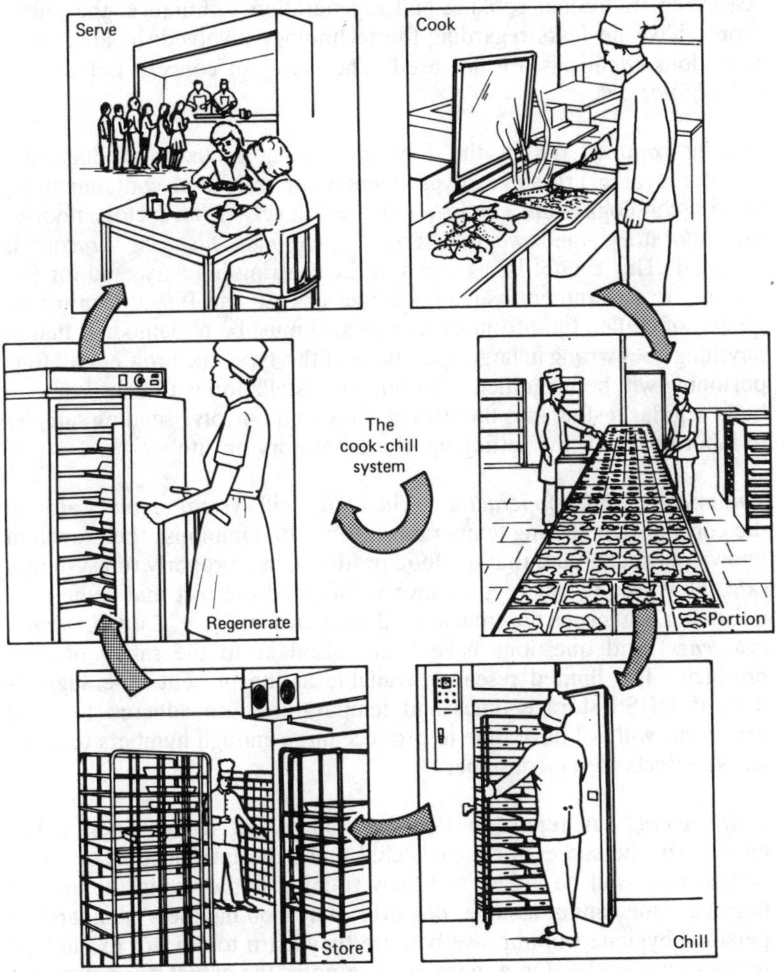

Quality systems

When attempting to analyse cook–chill systems it is useful to look at the four areas which are of main concern to both consumer and caterer:

(1) safety;
(2) acceptability;
(3) nutritional value;
(4) cost effectiveness.

(1) Safety

Assuming traditional cooking and regeneration techniques, the public should have no fears regarding the technology involved: irradiation or hazardous chemicals are not used. The factor of concern is therefore *microbiological*.

Quality control Within the food processing industry products are monitored at every stage of production for microbial contamination. Food technologists are employed at every level – from factory floor to the laboratory – and what is termed *good manufacturing practice* is assumed. This cannot be assumed in the catering industry, and for this reason the government issued guidelines in 1980 and 1989 to control the quality of chilled food from such outlets. It must be remembered that, if anything goes wrong in large operations of this type, the problems of food poisoning will be magnified. The time of installation is the ideal time to build regular testing into the system. This could involve sending samples to laboratories or the setting up of a laboratory on site.

The safety of chill temperatures The cook–chill system revolves around the concept that chilling temperatures (0°C–3°C) minimise the growth of known pathogens and that the food produced in a properly run system is safe. However recent reports have highlighted the fact that some food poisoning organisms do grow at chill temperatures (e.g. *Lysteria monocytogenes*) and questions have been raised as to the safety of such products. The limited research available at the present time suggests that, if DHSS storage times and temperatures are adhered to, such organisms will not have time to produce large enough numbers to cause any ill effects to the consumer.

Staff training A report in 1989 concluded that training was a key element in the success of a cook–chill unit. The introduction of a new system may well be linked with new training initiatives in the area of hygiene. One cannot assume, however, that food handlers' standards of personal hygiene will improve because they learn to use, for example, a temperature probe. On a more positive note, the actual work-flow in a cook–chill system may bring better standards of hygiene. For example, if chefs are not in a panic to organise 450 meals in the space of 30 minutes they may well be working in a calmer atmosphere, so that, if a tray of food is dropped, they may have time to pick it up and wash it. If pears are being placed in the bottom of a cooked flan, there will be time to select a clean cloth to dry them with rather than a dirty tea-towel.

DHSS guidelines – hygiene control throughout the system Cook–chill systems are in operation within catering in this country under the non-mandatory guidelines published in 1980 and 1989. Guidelines are essential to control large-scale production of food using techniques which were hitherto only employed in food processing factories. They outline time and temperature requirements and a variety of other aspects summarised below. Recent observations of hazardous malpractice in hygiene control have led to calls to the government to implement legislation to enforce adherence to the guidelines by all cook–chill users.

Time and temperature The strict control of time and temperature has been shown to be essential, not only in the prevention of food poisoning but to the success of the unit (Anne Walker, *Success or Failure in Cook–Chill Catering*, Bradford: Horton Publishing, 1989). The main requirements of the guidelines in respect to time and temperature are summarised in Table 11.1. Other components of the guidelines include:

- good quality of primary ingredients;
- temperature monitoring of storage areas;
- measurement of cooking temperatures for meat/poultry;
- establishment of cleaning schedules;
- prevention of cross-contamination;
- separation of high- and low-risk foods;
- monitoring of times and temperatures of operation;
- a system of stock rotation, with adequately labelled chilled products, which will prevent use of outdated stock;
- end product microbiological standards.

Table 11.1 *Government guidelines (1980)*

Guidelines	Explanation
Chilling to start within 30 minutes of the completion of cooking	} } } Fast cooling to stop pathogens } multiplying
Temperature down to 3°C within 90 minutes	} }
Storage at 0°C–3°C	Chill temperatures to slow growth of pathogens and spoilage microbes
Maximum life 5 days, including day of cooking and day of use	Precaution to minimise risk of food-poisoning
Food must be reheated to an internal temperature of 70°C	Temperature at which most pathogens are killed

(2) Acceptability

This is generally associated with appearance, taste, smell and texture of food. Recent studies have indicated that 2 days is the optimal time for preserving the major sensory qualities of cooked chilled food. (Zacharias (1960)

The Operation

The method of operation, of course, significantly affects these qualities.

(a) Fast chilling prevents overcooking and loss of flavour and moisture. Equipment must therefore be efficient and the packaging must not insulate the food from rapid chilling or reheating.
(b) Food should ideally reach the customer within five minutes of leaving the regeneration unit. This means that the food will be at an acceptable temperature.
(c) Attractive presentation can be achieved easily by the use of a wide range of containers suited to this process. Last minute 'finishing touches' can also be accomplished by staff no longer subject to the pressures of traditional service.

Menu Development

What is very apparent is that menu items going through a cook chill cycle, if the system is properly controlled, may be as *good* or as *bad* as using traditional techniques. The *quality of ingredients* and the *skill* employed to cook them is just as important in a high tech system as a low tech system! However, some items do need recipe modification and research and development is a vital part of the process of producing chilled food successfully.

(3) Nutritional value

The major losses of nutrients occur in the *cooking process* and the introduction of a chilling system will therefore make little difference to the nutritional value of most cooked foods. However, the losses of heat-sensitive vitamins will probably be improved, as the traditional holding at hot plate temperature is replaced with quick regeneration.

Care should be taken to ensure wide menu choice to avoid cumulative losses of nutrients. As with all nutritional situations, variety of cooking methods, as well as of commodities, ensure the adequacy of the diet.

The following points may offer guidance to those concerned with maintaining nutrient levels in foods:

(a) the quicker the food is chilled, the less the nutrient loss;

(b) the longer the food is chilled, the greater the nutrient loss; food consumed within 2–4 days is optimal for vitamin retention;
(c) packaging with as little air as possible retards rancidity and other spoilage.

(4) Cost effectiveness

Despite the high capital expenditure, a reduction in overall catering costs has been shown to be the prime motivation in changing to a cook–chill system (Walker, 1989). This is usually dependent on a strategy of reducing labour costs, which has led to many industrial disputes. It would seem, from observations of successful units, that loss of overtime and week-end work must be counter-balanced by an increase in basic wage rates.

Advantages of the cook–chill system

A well planned and well operated system can produce food of excellent quality at a marketable price. Despite the many obstacles that face catering managers attempting to bring forward such technological change, the positive advantages, listed below, are attainable:

1. Food is indistinguishable from freshly cooked.
2. Hot food holding and transport eliminated.
3. Little restriction on menu selection.
4. Peak production periods eliminated, therefore better management of time and skills.
5. Regular working hours can be established, reducing labour cost.
6. Government control provides basis for a more hygienic system.
7. Space requirements no greater than for traditional systems. The even spread of production allows better utilisation of space. This is based on a rapid turnover of chilled food.
8. Using the same dish for all steps from cooking through to service reduces the tasks in the kitchen and therefore saves money.
9. More consistent quality and portion control throughout all stages of production.
10. Can be used for individual or multiportion packs or for full meals or components of meals.

11.3 SOUS-VIDE

Introduction

The development of sous-vide owes its origin to experimental work concerned with reducing weight loss in the preparation of a very

250

expensive goose-liver paste (foie gras) in France. Its literal translation means 'under vacuum' and this gives a clue to the meaning of the term.

Definition

Sous-vide is a system of catering where food is vacuum packaged, either before or after cooking, and then rapidly cooled to chilling temperatures (0–3°C). It is then stored/transported at this temperature with subsequent regeneration as required. (See Figure 11.6)

Sous-vide production systems

Food is placed in vacuum packs and stored at chill temperatures of 0°C–3°C until required. This type of vacuum pack, which is to be later heated, is termed a *cook pouch*. The recommended life of cooked food chilled in a pouch is max 21 days (1989) and therefore adds a considerable extension to normal cook–chill systems. As Figure 11.6 shows the food can be cooked traditionally and then vacuum packed *or* can be placed raw in the pouches and then cooked. This latter cooking method is termed *vacuum cooking* and results in a lower weight loss and keeps the food intact during cooking. Some pouches are designed so that after filling they can be dipped in hot water for a few seconds to *heat-shrink* the loose material and folds of the package to form a 'second skin'. This is particularly useful for meat cookery.

To make sure temperatures are correct for serving and cooking, small temperature probes are used. A single probe is used to monitor the temperature of one item in a batch of similar dishes.

Foods prepared in this way are handled with the same equipment and care as for cook–chill. Government guidelines for hygiene are applicable (see p. 247). Below is therefore only an account of the packaging of the sous vide product and its uses. Plate 11.2 illustrates the sous-vide product.

The sous-vide pouch

Regeneration of the sous-vide product is usually achieved by using low pressure steam/combination ovens or by simply boiling in water.

The plastic material of the pouch is actually two films of different materials (called laminates) which together give the properties required below:

- **excludes oxygen**
  Foods spoil during storage, developing surface slime, 'off' flavours and changes in taste, colour or texture. This spoilage may be caused by microbes, oxygen or enzymes in the food, but in all cases is reduced with low temperature. Changes are further reduced by surrounding

Plate 11.2 *The sous-vide product*

the food with a material – usually polythene – which will be a barrier
to the atmosphere.
- **remains stable at cooking temperature**
  A material is required which will be stable at low temperature and also
  at cooking temperature of up to 100°C.
- **allows clear visibility of the cooked food**
- **is tough enough not to be damaged in transit or storage**
- **heat-seals easily and effectively**
- **is non-toxic**.

Uses of sous-vide

Sous-vide systems offer all the advantages of cook–chill which were
outlined in the previous section. The system is used primarily where a
3-day storage is too restrictive. Table 11.2 shows the main advantages
and disadvantages when comparing cook–chill with sous-vide.

Examples

In the case of hospitals, special diet requirements may not have been
forecast but could be more easily available with this system because of
the longer storage life of the sous-vide food. In the commercial sector, à

Table 11.2 *Advantages and disadvantages of the sous-vide system*

Advantages	Disadvantage
• Sous-vide systems offer most of the benefits of cook chill outlined in last section	More storage space required for 3-week cycle
• individual dishes reheated in 3–4 minutes	The longer the time in chiller the greater the cost
• 21-day life gives flexibility with menu choice	Vacuum-packing equipment and pouches expensive
	* Microbiological hazards if system mis-used

* The vacuum packaging excludes oxygen and spoilage is reduced. Some pathogens, however, do not need oxygen to multiply (see Chap. 14) and the product must be kept at the correct temperature for only the specified time to prevent microbiological hazards.

la carte menus with extensive choices may be more realistically supported. In all cases it must be remembered that the system may be adopted as a food-production system belonging to the business or, alternatively, the food may be bought-in.

11.4 COOK–FREEZE

Definition

Cook–freeze is a catering system based on conventional cooking followed by rapid freezing to below minus 18°C. Food is held at this temperature during storage/transport with subsequent regeneration (reheating) immediately prior to service.

The cook–freeze system

The process of cook–freeze is illustrated in cook–chill guidelines for hygiene are applicable (see p. 247).

Equipment

• a blast-freezer for rapid cooling of food;
• a freezer for storing frozen foods;
• packaging which is strong enough to avoid damage and to stop food drying out in the freezer.

Figure 11.5 *The cook–freeze system*

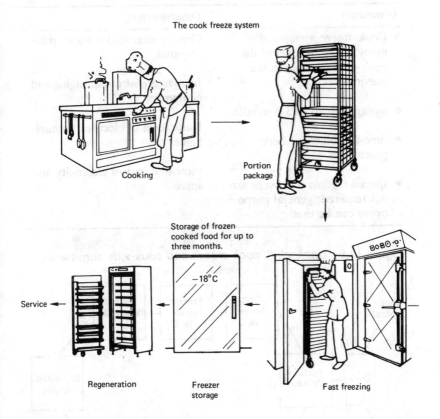

The cook freeze system

Cooking

Portion package

Storage of frozen cooked food for up to three months.

−18°C

Service

Regeneration

Freezer storage

Fast freezing

Uses of cook–freeze systems

The massive amount of storage space needed for a catering unit to freeze and keep cooked food makes this a less attractive prospect to the caterer than cook–chill and sous-vide. If frozen food is required it is more likely that caterers will negotiate specifications with food-manufacturers and buy in as required. Indeed this is what is happening in the larger hospitals and in some expanding contract-catering firms. Table 11.3 lists the advantages and disadvantages of cook–freeze systems, while Figure 11.6 summarises the three methods discussed in this section.

11.5 INFORMATION TECHNOLOGY

There are a number of special applications for computers in catering operations which may include accommodation services; room manage-

Table 11.3 *Advantages and disadvantages of cook–freeze*

Advantages	Disadvantages
• Cook–freeze systems offer many of the benefits of the cook–chill outlined in the previous section	Greatly increased storage space required
• storage for up to 3–6 months	Increased cost of packaging and equipment
• time-flexibility for better purchasing	Noise level of electrical motors higher
• special regenerator ovens are not required; general purpose ovens can be used	Increased cost of electricity and space

Figure 11.6 *Cook–chill, cook–freeze and sous-vide summarised*

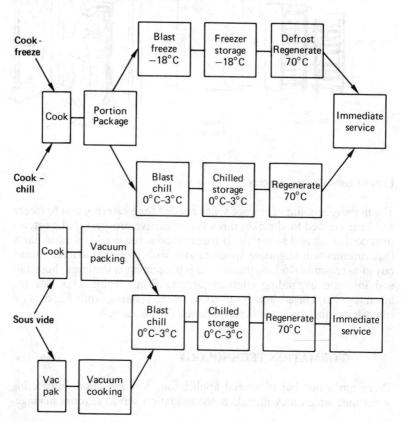

ment; accounting and control; marketing; food and beverage preparation, and service in hospitals, hotels, fast-food operations, etc.

Computers are used extensively in all areas of the industry. Some large companies will have a controlled mainframe system whilst smaller organisations may select from a variety of software packages. A great deal of software has been produced especially for the catering industry and new versions and/or updates appear regularly. Table 11.4 gives a broad overview of some of the functions assisted by computers.

Table 11.4 *Overview of some computer applications*

Function	Operation	Notes
Food stock control	Storeroom Kitchen	Accounting for stock levels, stock movement, reordering, stock-taking, gross-profit calculation
Recipe costing	Mass-produced meals	Gross-profit forecasting and control; stock analysis
Customer orders, large scale	Large scale	Mass customer meal requirements for specific meals in advance, e.g. hospitals
Restaurant key pad system	Restaurant	Guest's meal order entered on computerised terminal which notifies all relevant sections – kitchen, bar, accounts
Stocktaking	Bar cellar	Physically checking the movement of stock, gross-profit calculation and forecasting
Vending sales	Multi-locations	Analysis of sales: by machine, cost price, stock level, numbers sold, etc.
Room bookings	Reception	Taking and checking reservation for rooms and checking occupancy; customer's bill posted immediately

CHAPTER 12

COMMODITIES

12.1 COMMODITIES: THE FOODS WE EAT

Food is required to sustain life. Without it we would die. The ingredients (nutrients) needed by man to stay alive and healthy are outlined in Chapter 13. All animal and plant cells contain varying amounts of these nutrients but some also contain poisonous substances (toxins). Man throughout the world has utilised his own particular environment to find non-toxic varieties of plants and animals and to develop ways of preparing others to make them safe to eat, e.g. Aboriginal Australians eat large larva called 'Witchety Grubs'; the Chinese have fermented toxic soya beans to produce safe 'soy milk' and 'soy sauce'; the Welsh use seaweed (laver) to make a traditional bread; and cassava boiled in an open pan is the staple diet of many people in the tropics. In a *closed* pan cyanide builds up in the liquid in deadly amounts!

This chapter aims to identify the commodities seen on the UK market, their quality points and uses within the catering industry. The nutritional value of foods is indicated by charts, and further discussed in Chapter 13. The methods of preserving foods are outlined in Chapter 14 and the various preserved and processed varieties are indicated under the relevant foods. The chemical additives used in food manufacture are discussed as a part of 'Food quality' in Chapter 13 (section 13.7).

This text is by no means comprehensive and offers merely an introduction to the foods used in cookery in the 1990s. Legislation and a high level of food-processing require caterers, more than ever before, to be fully aware of the components of the meals which they cook and serve. The chapter is divided into two sections – foods from animals, and foods from plants.

12.2 FOOD FROM ANIMALS

MEAT

Meat is the body-tissue of animals, eaten as food. The term includes muscle (lean meat), connective tissue, fat, and edible internal organs (offal). Throughout the world a great variety of animals are included in the diet of man, ranging from monkeys to worms, but this text is restricted to those animals most commonly eaten in the UK and which are classed as butcher's meat, poultry and game.

The changing market

Throughout this century changes have taken place which have affected the customer's meat requirements dramatically. Factors such as family size, social customs, proportion of disposable income spent on food and the introduction of new protein foods, have all played a part in the evolution of eating habits.

The most important challenge to the meat industry at the present time is the negative image of animal fat, in a country where many adults are obese and suffering from heart disease. Customer preference, therefore, is for *less visible fat* and has led to:

(a) the breeding of animals with less fat;
(b) slaughtering at an earlier age to minimise fat deposits;
(c) the closer trimming of meat cuts;
(d) continental-style meat-cutting which involves separation and preparation of individual muscles from the carcase.

Experimentation with carcase-cutting has also served to satisfy the increased demand for quick-frying and grilling steaks. Scrag-end of lamb, for example, can be boned out to give high-quality meat for frying. Joints of beef such as thick flank, can be similarly upgraded by slicing individually prepared muscles to give good-quality steaks.

It is imperative that students entering an industry which consumes 20 per cent of the UK meat market should keep up-to-date with the highly skilled and adaptable British butchers. Caterers cannot afford to be blind to the changes within the meat industry and no useful purpose can be served by living in the past. We hope that this book will be a bridge from the old traditional teaching to the reality of the twenty-first century.

Butcher's meat

Cattle, sheep and pigs are intensively reared in large numbers for the UK market. Table 12.1 summarises the main characteristics of these animals.

Table 12.1 Characteristics of animals bred for meat

Meat	Name	Age	Quality	Outlet	Carcase weight (approx)	Hanging Period	Muscle colour	Fat
Beef	Young bull / Steer castrated male / Heifer young female	} ≈ 18 months	Good quality beef	} Wholesale/retail	200–230 kg	14 days*	Cherry red	Creamy white
	Cow beef older female	variable	Poor quality beef	} Manufacturing and catering industry	variable	14 days	Usually darker meat	May be yellow**
	Mature bull beef old male	variable	Poor quality beef					
Veal	Bobby veal	2–3 weeks	Poor quality	Wholesale/retail	18–23 kg	3–5 days	Pale pink	Little fat
	Quality veal	4–6 months	Good quality	Wholesale/retail	100 kg	3–5 days	Pale pink	Good cover white fat
Lamb	New season lamb	< 6 months	Best quality***	Wholesale/retail	15–25 kg	5–7 days	Dull red	} Firm cream white
	Old season lamb	6–12 months	Good quality	Wholesale/retail	15–25 kg	5–7 days		
Mutton	Mutton old breeding ewes	variable	Poorer quality	Manufacturing and Fast-food outlets e.g. kebab houses	variable	5–7 days	Dark red	
	old breeding rams	variable	Poorer quality					
Pork	Sucking pig	2–3 days	Best quality pork	Special functions	4.5 kg–11 kg	2 days	Very pink	White
	Porkers	16–18 weeks	Quality pork	Wholesale/retail	41 kg–50 kg		Pink	White
	Cutters	18–20 weeks	Quality pork	Wholesale/retail	50 kg–64 kg		Pink	White
	Baconers	20–22 weeks	Processed into quality bacon/ham	Wholesale/retail	68 kg–73 kg		Pink	White
	Heavy hogs	more than 26 weeks	Poorer quality pork	} Manufactured meat products	82 kg+		Pink	Large fat deposits
	Mature boar	variable	Poorer quality pork		82 kg+		Pink	} Fat cover variable
	Mature sow	variable	Poorer quality pork		82 kg+		Pink	

* some joints can be hung for up to three weeks, e.g. sirloin and fore-rib
** some breeds produce a yellow fat (Guernsey), and grass-fed cows always produce a deeper colour fat
*** all New Zealand lamb is graded according to conformation (shape) and fat cover

Slaughtering

Animals are taken to registered abattoirs where they are anaesthetised, killed and then dressed. The term 'dressing' is used to describe the process of removing both offal and non-edible parts to produce the *carcase*. Traditionally it has been accepted that the main factors which affect the final quality of meat are breed, feed, age and sex. In recent years it has become clear that what happens to animals prior to slaughter has a major effect on the quality of the carcase. Animals that are calm, well-fed and rested produce good-quality meat. Of particular importance is the glycogen level in the muscles, which is depleted if animals suffer stress immediately prior to slaughter. After death, glycogen is turned into lactic acid and the acidity increases (from pH 7 to approximately pH 5.5) producing meat with good colour, good texture and high water-holding capacity. If however there is no glycogen left in the muscle, acidity does not develop and poorer-quality dark meat is produced.

Kosher/Halal meat (for use by Orthodox Jews and by Muslims) To conform with religious tradition animals are slaughtered, often at a local abattoir, by slitting the throat so as to cause the blood to pour out.

Maturing meat The muscle fibres lose their extensibility after death to produce a stiffness described as *rigor mortis*. The actual process is not reversible but softening does occur due to proteolytic enzymes breaking up this tight structure. The time needed for rigor to pass varies with individual animals. The carcase is hung in chilling conditions for this period and therefore the process is known as *hanging*. Longer periods do not improve tenderness but have considerable advantages in terms of flavour development. It is for this reason that prime cuts of beef, for example sirloin, are often hung for extended periods (e.g. two weeks) for discerning customers.

Growth promoters

It is common practice for male animals to be castrated prior to rearing for meat. This prevents the development of male characteristics and encourages a more even hind quarter to fore quarter ratio. Animals are also more docile and easier to handle. The disadvantage of this procedure is that it slows down growth rates by approximately 10 per cent and chemicals have been used for many years to marginalise this effect. These chemicals are either (a) antibiotics which increase the size of the carcase; or (b) the very effective hormones which directly increase the size of muscles. Consumer groups have protested about the undesirable residues to be found in the carcase meat of animals treated in this way, and the recent ban on the growth-promoting hormones has led to an increased interest in rearing uncastrated male animals. This, however, does require intensive farming methods with animals being penned and reared indoors, which may prove to be equally distasteful to the British public.

Cooking meat (see Chapter 9)

Meat contains muscle fibres, fat and connective tissue which all play a part in the development of tenderness in the final dish. The parts of the body which are used most develop thicker muscle fibres, more connective tissue and generally more fat. The area across the back (e.g. loin, rump) is therefore considered to produce the best-quality meat, with fine-grained, large muscles and little fat or connective tissue. The remaining portion of the carcase produces coarse grained meat with more connective tissue and fat. By adjusting the cooking method to suit the individual cuts it is possible to tenderise all meat. The concept of tough meat is really only applicable to very old animals (of which there are few on the market) or to the cooking process. Hence the old adage 'God sent the butcher, the devil sent the cooks'. The effect of cooking can conveniently be considered under the following headings: muscle fibres, connective tissue, and fat.

Muscle fibres Protein, of which muscle fibres are composed, will denature and become firm on cooking. It will lose extractives (soluble proteins, vitamins and minerals) and shrink. A balance between increased palatability and overcooking needs careful attention. Dry cooking methods may result in tough, dry meat. Moist methods may produce significant shrinkage and weight loss.

Connective tissue This fibrous protein is found in two distinct types in the animal body:

1. *White connective tissue (collagen)* is found in sheets separating muscle bundles. The quantity varies from 3–18 per cent (compare fillet steak and shin of beef) causing toughness if not removed by cooking. Moist heat will cause it to dissolve out into the cooking liquor as gelatine. Dry heat will have no effect on collagen and this is why it is only suitable for cuts with minimal amounts of this type of connective tissue.
2. *Yellow connective tissue (elastin)* is the yellow *gristle* which is usually cut away from meat before cooking. It remains tough and unpalatable whatever method of cooking is used.

Fat Melts on cooking, playing an important part in the development of flavour, colour and tenderness. Lean meat can easily become dry and flavourless and it is for this reason that larding and barding (see p. ooo) are common techniques in the preparation of lean cuts and continental-style items.

Nutritional value

Meat offers a good profile (range) of essential amino-acids and valuable B vitamins. Fat content is variable and can range from 3 to 30 per cent. Red meat contributes significantly to the body's requirement for iron – a mineral found only in limited quantities elsewhere. Figure 12.1 shows the proportions of nutrients in stewing steak.

Figure 12.1   *Proportions of main nutrients in stewing beef*

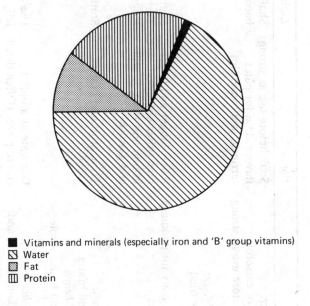

■ Vitamins and minerals (especially iron and 'B' group vitamins)
◨ Water
▨ Fat
▥ Protein

Storage

Meat should be stored at chilling temperatures to maintain colour and extend keeping quality. Under normal conditions all meat except pork can be considered to have a shelf-life of around seven days. Pork is prone to rancidity and best cooked within two to three days.

Offal

The edible parts of the animal not on the carcase are termed offal. The main offal items of pork, beef and lamb are outlined in Table 12.2. The high levels of B vitamins and iron are of particular importance in liver and kidney as they are the most commonly eaten offal in the form of pies, pâtés and grills.

Table 12.2 Offal

Common name	Beef	Pig	Lamb
Liver	*Ox liver:* Braise or casserole. Soak before use as strong flavour. *Calves' liver:* Usually fried	Soak before use as strong flavour. Use for pâtés, terrines, and casseroles	Shallow fry as in liver and bacon
Kidney	Used mostly for puddings and pies	Paler, longer and larger than other kidneys. Leave in loin and roast or grill and garnish.	Sauté as for Rognons Turbigo; grill as for Rognons grillés
Heart	*Ox hearts:* Slice and braise. *Calves' hearts:* Stuff and braise whole.	Trim, stuff and braise	Stuff, then roast or braise
Head (whole skull area)	*Calves' head:* Cook skin, cheeks, and tongue in a blanc.	Decorate as a buffet centre piece. (Often diced and used in brawn).	Use for stocks or savoury jelly

Brains	Soak to remove blood then poach in water, aromates and vinegar. Serve as part of Calves' Head. May be fried whole or chopped	Poach, fry or cook in cream
Cheek (facial muscle)	Cook with calves' head in a blanc and serve as part of the dish.	Use diced as a main ingredient in brawn. Smoked and known as *bath chaps*, boiled and served cold
Tongue	*Ox tongue:* Salt, boil, skin and press. Serve cold. May be served hot e.g. Langue de Boeuf with Sauce Madère.	Usually one per portion braised; may be pressed and served cold
Sweetbreads (thyroid gland and pancreas)	Calves' sweetbreads are prepared in a variety of ways such as: fried, steamed, stewed, braised. Washed and soaked before use.	Prepared in a variety of ways as for calves' sweetbreads.

Table 12.2 (continued)

Common name	Beef	Pig	Lamb
Tripe (stomach wall)	Three kinds of ox tripe are honeycomb, blanket or thick seamed. Usually stewed, e.g. tripe and onions		
Chitterlings (intestinal wall)		Used as case for sausages. May be grilled or fried.	
Trotters (feet)	Calves' feet are used in certain braised beef dishes. May be used for calves' foot jelly	Boiled to make savoury jelly for pies. Boiled or grilled and served with a hot sauce	
Lambs fry (testicles)			A delicacy. Most usually lightly fried
Tail	Oxtail is jointed and is a prime braising dish	Used for soups and stews.	
Lights (lung)	Not normally used as a main dish in the UK except in times of food shortage, such as the two World Wars. Sometimes used in the preparation of pâté de foie.		
Melts (spleen)	Not normally used for main dishes but may be used in other countries for sausages.		

Animal fats including lard, dripping and suet are discussed with vegetable oils later in the chapter.

Beef

The beef carcase is split along the backbone into two halves, and then each *side* is cut through between the tenth and the eleventh rib to produce the *fore quarter* and *hind quarter*.

Cutting

Traditional beef-cutting involved the preparation of primal cuts on the bone, whereas today the majority of the carcase is boned out and many of the traditional cutting lines are therefore not relevant to modern butchery. Indeed, many caterers will now buy vacuum-packed boned-out beef which bears little resemblance to cuts they may once have purchased or have tediously learned for examination purposes! The main cutting lines used are shown in Figure 12.2 for clarity but most carcases are only cut in this manner by the retail butcher. Wholesale stewing steak, braising steak and minced beef for example, are sold to the caterer ready-prepared and may be derived from more than one part of the carcase. It is most unlikely, for example, that a chef would order shin of beef for making beef consommé; he would either use meat available in the stores or would order lean minced beef.

Marbled flesh

As an animal increases in size, fat begins to be deposited inside the muscles (intramuscular fat) causing a flecked appearance known as *marbling*. For many years this has been associated with beef quality although tests by the Food Research Institute have failed to detect differences. With the present practice of breeding for less fatty carcases, and therefore less marbling, it is an unrealistic and misguided concept for quality grading.

Tenderised beef (marketed under the name 'Proten' beef)

The proteolytic enzyme papain extracted from pawpaws (a tropical fruit) can be injected into animals before slaughter. It has been shown to be harmless to the animals but has a tenderising effect on meat fibres during cooking. The international meat firm Swifts hold the patent for this method but are now selling the licence to other abattoirs. Under new legislation all meat treated in this way will have to be clearly identified.

Figure 12.2 *Primal cuts of beef*

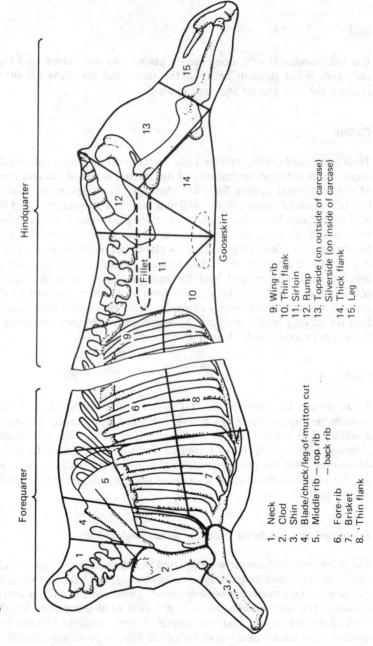

Forequarter

1. Neck
2. Clod
3. Shin
4. Blade/chuck/leg-of-mutton cut
5. Middle rib — top rib
   — back rib
6. Fore-rib
7. Brisket
8. Thin flank

Hindquarter

9. Wing rib
10. Thin flank
11. Sirloin
12. Rump
13. Topside (on outside of carcase)
    Silverside (on inside of carcase)
14. Thick flank
15. Leg

Fillet

Gooseskirt

Vacuum packaging

Most wholesale beef for the catering trade is now vacuum-packed. It is easier to handle and extends storage to between four and thirty weeks at chilling temperature. The polythene/nylon film is impervious to oxygen thereby slowing spoilage but changing the colour from cherry-red to a dark purple/red. Although this is an unattractive colour it is of no importance because as soon as the pack is opened the normal colour returns.

Table 12.3 explains preparation and cooking methods for forequarter beef, and Table 12.4 does the same for hindquarter beef, in each case with examples of typical menu items.

Veal

Veal on the UK market may be home-produced or from animals bred in Holland. Quality veal is derived from animals specially reared for this purpose and is distinct from Bobby veal derived from male calves culled from dairy herds at a few weeks old (see Table 12.5).

Cutting

Bobby veal carcases are small and are cut similarly to lambs with the same terminology used, e.g. shoulder, breast. Most of this veal is used in manufacturing.
   Quality veal carcases are larger and cut similarly to beef with the same terminology used, e.g. silverside, fore rib, brisket. Figure 12.3 shows the most-commonly-used cutting lines and terminology for this type of veal.

Flesh colour

The flesh of young animals is pale pink and this is maintained in veal production by feeding the animals on a milk (iron-free) diet coupled with restricted activity.

Lamb

The lamb carcase is traditionally left whole or split down the backbone into two sides. Much of the lamb on the British market is New Zealand in origin. It is usually transported frozen with a keeping quality of up to 6 months. There have been considerable improvements in packaging in recent years to reduce the colour changes associated with frozen meat. As with vacuum-packaging the colour returns when the package is opened but the retail customer still prefers the colour of fresh meat. The low prices and availability of New Zealand lamb, however, make this a popular choice both wholesale and retail. All New Zealand lamb is

Table 12.3 *Beef: Forequarter*

Primal cuts	Methods of preparation	Cooking methods	Menu examples
Shin	1. Boned and sliced/diced/minced	} stew	Bolognese Sauce Pies
Clod and sticking piece	1. Boned and sliced/diced/minced	}	Goulash
Brisket	1. Boned-out and rolled joint	Slow roast or pot roast Salt or pickle	Roast beef Pressed beef
Middle ribs	1. On the bone 2. Boned-out joint 3. Boned-out and sliced	Roast Roast Braise	Back rib, Top rib Roast beef Braised steak
Chuck Blade Leg-of-mutton cut (triceps muscle)	1. Boned and sliced/joint 2. Prepared and sliced 3. Prepared and sliced	Braise, roast Braise, fry Braise	Braised beef Feather steak, Blade fillet Braised steak
Fore-rib	1. On the bone 2. Boned-out and rolled joint	Roast Roast	Carvery roast beef Roast beef
Forequarter thin flank	1. Boned, defatted and minced 2. Processed into beefburgers and sausages	Sauté, boil, bake Griddle, fry	Cottage pie, Meat loaf Hamburgers, Sausages

Table 12.4 *Beef: Hindquarter*

Primal cuts	Methods of preparation	Cooking methods	Menu examples
Wing rib	1. On the bone or boned and rolled 2. Boned and cut into steaks (steaked)	Roast Grill	Roast wing rib of beef Carbonnade of beef
Sirloin	1. Bone-in/boneless joint 2. Bone-in steaks 3. Boneless steaks	Roast Grill Grill, sauté	Carvery and special functions – roast beef T-bone steak Minute steak, entrecôte bordelaise
Fillet	1. Trimmed fillet 2. Fillet steaks	Bake, roast Grill, sauté	Beef Wellington, Chateaubriand Grilled fillet steak, Tournedos Rossini
Rump	1. Boneless joint 2. Boneless steaks	Braise (not common) grill	Pièce de Boeuf à la Mode Grilled rump steak
Hindquarter thin flank	see Forequarter flank	see Forequarter flank	
Thick flank (top rump)	1. Cut into two joints 2. Prepared and cut into steaks	Roast Grill, fry	Roast or pot roast beef Steaks
Silverside	1. Cut into two joints 2. Can be cut into steaks	Roast Grill, fry	Roast silverside of beef Steaks
Topside	1. Cut into joints, e.g. corner cut 2. Prepared and cut into steaks	Roast Grill, fry	Roast topside of beef Beef olives
Leg (commonly sold as shin of beef)	1. Boned-out and dice/slice/mince 2. Boned-out and minced	Stew	Casserole of beef, cottage pie
Skirt	1. *Goose skirt* cut across grain into pieces 2. Diced or sliced	Stir fry Stew, braise	Chinese style dishes, Strogonoff Ragoût de Boeuf

Table 12.5 *Veal*

Primal cuts	Methods of preparation	Cooking methods	Menu examples
Knuckle/leg/shin	1. Cut in rounds with bone in 2. Boned and diced	Stew Stew, bake	Osso Bucco Veal pie
Topside (Cushion) Silverside	1. Boneless steak or thin slice battened-out 2. Whole boneless joint	Sauté, grill Roast, braise	Schnitzels, escalopes Noix de veau Bourgeoise
Thick flank	1. Boneless steak or thin slice battened-out 2. Whole boneless joint	Sauté, grill Roast	Schnitzels, escalopes Roast veal
Rump or fillet	1. Boneless steak or thin slice battened-out	Sauté, grill	Schnitzels, escalopes
Loin	1. Bone in joint 2. Boneless rolled joint 3. Bone in chops or cutlets 4. Boneless steak or thin slice battened-out	Roast Roast Sauté, grill Sauté, grill	Selle de veau Orloff (two loins not split) Roast veal Côte de Veau Bonne Femme Médallion de veau à la crème
Chuck Fore-rib	1. Boneless steak or thin slice battened-out 2. Boneless rolled joint	Sauté, grill, deep fry Roast	Schnitzel Roast veal
Neck and clod	1. Boned and diced	Stew	Blanquette de veau
Breast/brisket	1. Boneless joint 2. Processed into mince	Roast, braise Sauté	Roast stuffed breast of veal Pojarski, Bolognese Sauce

271

Figure 12.3 Primal cuts of veal

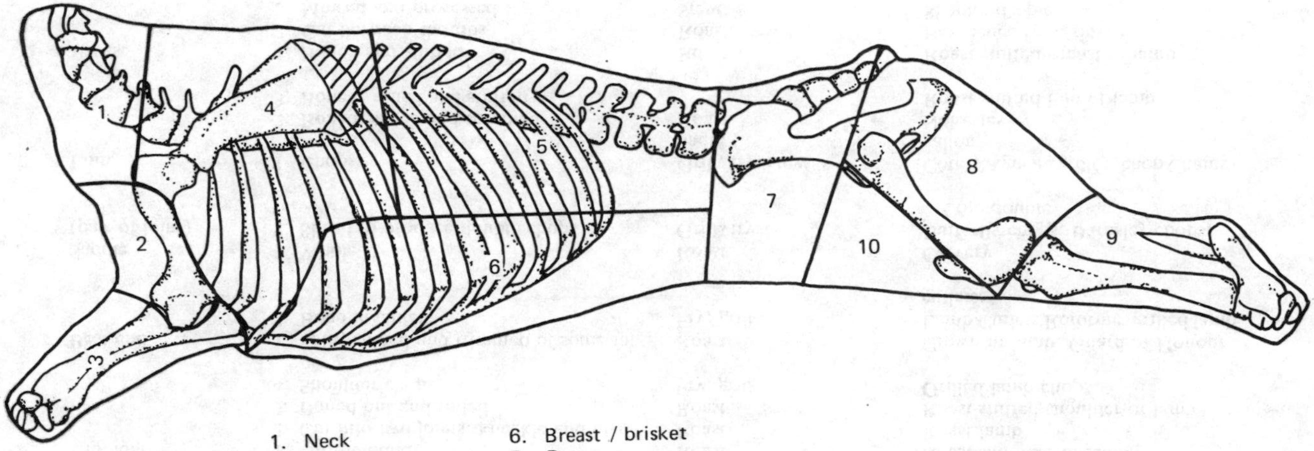

1. Neck
2. Clod
3. Knuckle/leg
4. Chuck
5. Loin
6. Breast / brisket
7. Rump
8. Silverside } also known as cushion
   Topside
9. Knuckle
10. Thick flank

Table 12.6 *Lamb*

Primal cuts	Methods of preparation	Cooking methods	Menu examples
Scrag Middle neck	1. On the bone 2. Boned-out (lamb *fillet*)	Stew Roast, grill, fry	Hot-pot, Irish stew Kebabs
Shoulder	1. On the bone 2. Cut into two joints: knuckle and blade 3. Boned-out and rolled 4. Shoulder chops	Roast Roast Roast Fry, grill	Roast shoulder of lamb Roast lamb Roast stuffed shoulder of lamb Grilled lamb chops
Best end	1. Split, chined and trimmed of some fat 2. Bone-in cutlets	Roast Fry, grill	Crown of lamb, Guard of Honour Lamb Cutlets Réforme, grilled lamb cutlets
Saddle (pair of loins)	1. Whole 2. Sliced to produce double chops	Roast Grill, fry	Carvery Butterfly chops, Barnsley chops, Côte double
Loin	1. Chops 2. Boned, sliced and trimmed 3. Boned, rolled and stuffed	Grill, fry, stew Sauté Roast	Côte d'Agneau grillée, chop Champvallon Noisettes Roast stuffed loin of lamb
Breast	1. Boned and stuffed 2. Cut between the ribs 3. Minced and processed	Roast Roast, stew Stew	Roast stuffed breast of lamb Barbecued spareribs Shepherd's pie
Leg	1. Whole 2. Split into knuckle half and fillet half 3. Fillet half sliced	Roast Roast Grill	Gigot d'Agneau Rôti Roast lamb Gigot chops
Chump	1. On-bone chump chops 2. Chump steaks	Grill Grill	Grilled chump chop Grilled chump steak

graded in relation to carcase shape (conformation) and fat cover. Relevant details are shown in Table 12.6 and the most commonly used cutting lines and terminology can be seen in Figure 12.4.

Figure 12.4 *Primal cuts of lamb*

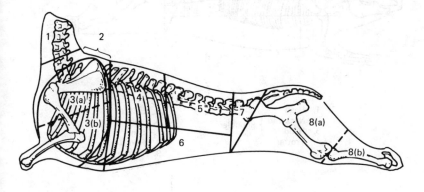

1. Scrag	5. Loin
2. Middle neck	6. Breast
3. Shoulder Blade $\frac{1}{2}$ (a)	7. Chump
Knuckle $\frac{1}{2}$ (b)	8. Leg Fillet $\frac{1}{2}$ (a)
4. Best End	Knuckle $\frac{1}{2}$ (b)

Pork

The pork carcase is traditionally left whole or split down the backbone into two sides. Methods of production usually involve intensive rearing under controlled conditions indoors. Pigs are prolific breeders and this coupled with early slaughtering produce a very economic food (see Figure 12.5).

The eating of pork meat is taboo (forbidden) in certain religions although the origins of this habit are obscure. Certainly pork is the most fatty of the butcher's meats, liable to go rancid and very indigestible for babies. It may also carry parasitic infections which can affect humans, so very thorough cooking of pork is accepted practice. Table 12.7 shows methods of preparation and cooking.

Cured meats

Thousands of years ago it was discovered that if the surface of meat was rubbed with *salt* its keeping qualities could be extended and it was cured of its tendency to spoil easily. This so-called *curing* was due primarily to the dehydrating effect of salt on micro-organisms. It was later discovered

Figure 12.5 *Primal cuts of pork*

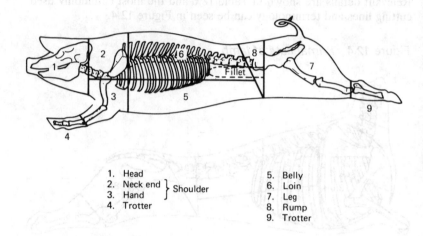

1. Head
2. Neck end ⎫ Shoulder
3. Hand ⎭
4. Trotter

5. Belly
6. Loin
7. Leg
8. Rump
9. Trotter

that small amounts of potassium or sodium nitrate were also present, as impurities, in the salt and further enhanced the preserving action. Bacteria in meat convert nitrate to *nitrite* which causes red myoglobin (the pigment in muscle) to turn a pink colour, stable even during cooking. The nitrite also has some flavour effects and has specific action against *Clostridium botulinum*, the most dangerous food poisoning organism.

Modern methods of curing involve using pure sodium chloride (common salt) with measured amounts of nitrate and nitrite. Despite the traditional use of nitrate the addition of nitrite is considered by some scientists to be dangerous. Nitrite is thought to react with other chemicals, during cooking and in the body, to produce *carcinogens,* and its use is strictly regulated by law.

Methods of applying the salt vary from rubbing it into the surface or soaking the meat in brine, to injecting brine into the main arteries and pumping it throughout the carcase. If a curing technique is based on a salt solution the term *pickled* is often used to describe the process. Cured meats may also be dried and smoked.

Bacon

The main meat cured in this country is pork. Cured pork is called bacon and various types are on the market:

green or unsmoked bacon   cured
smoked bacon   cured and then smoked
sweet cured bacon   sugar is added to the curing brine

Table 12.7 Pork

Primal cuts	Methods of preparation	Cooking methods	Menu examples
Belly	1. On the bone 2. Boned and stuffed 3. Processed into sausages	Roast, stew Roast Fry, grill, bake	Barbecue spare rib Roast stuffed belly pork Toad in the hole
Hand	1. Traditionally sold on the bone 2. Boned and rolled 3. Processed into pie-meat or sausages 4. Some muscles removed, sliced	Roast Roast Bake, fry Stew	Roast pork Roast pork Pork pie Goulash
Neck end	1. Blade-bone joint 2. Cut into riblets 3. Boneless steaks	Roast Grill, fry, roast Grill, fry	Roast pork Grilled spareribs Grilled shoulder steak
Loin	1. Separation of fillet 2. Pork chops (loin chops) 3. On bone or boned and rolled	Pot roast Grill Roast	Tenderloin Grilled pork chop Roast loin of pork
Leg	1. Whole leg or carvery cut 2. Boneless joints 3. Boneless steaks	Roast, boil Roast Grill	Roast leg of pork and apple sauce Roast pork Grilled pork steak
Chump	1. Cut into chops 2. Boned and cut into lean steaks (pork fillet)	Grill Grill, fry	Grilled chump chop Escalope of pork
Head	1. Meat removed and processed	Boil	Brawn
Feet	1. Whole	Boil, grill	Grilled pigs trotters and mustard sauce

Modern refrigeration has reduced the need for highly salted products and bacon is now treated to give mild flavours and a partial preserving effect. It is often vacuum-packed to extend its shelf life at 5°C to 7 days. Figure 12.6 shows the most common cuts of bacon.

Figure 12.6 Bacon

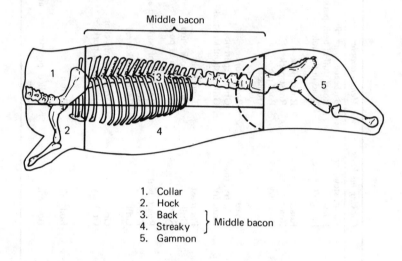

1. Collar
2. Hock
3. Back
4. Streaky } Middle bacon
5. Gammon

Ham

Prime legs of pork, with their fine-grained muscle, have traditionally been separated from the rest of the carcase and cured separately to produce specialist ham. Parma ham, for example, is produced from pigs fattened on parsnips. York ham is cured for four months and is only ready when it is covered with green mould. Bradenham ham is pickled in a mixture of molasses, brown sugar, salt and spices. Many such prized hams are eaten raw whilst others are boiled and served hot or cold.

Picnic and *shoulder hams* are made with meat from other parts of the carcase. The meat is boned and pressed into shape with only a light cure and in no way reflects the cost or quality of the traditional hams outlined above.

Other cured meats

Some cuts of beef – for example, silverside – are traditionally cured to form *salt beef*. Ox, sheep's and pig's tongues are similarly treated to produce cold pressed meats. Meat products such as sausages can be cured and smoked to produce a host of varieties as are seen in continental delicatessens.

Processed meat products

Meat from any part of the animal can be used in the manufacture of meat products, which include sausages, pâtés and such regional delicacies as faggots and brawn. The meat may be cured and smoked (e.g. salami) and is usually minced and mixed with a number of other ingredients such as cereals, herbs, cream, eggs, onion or blood. They do however have limited keeping quality and preservatives are often added.

The content and labelling of these products are controlled by detailed legislation. It is worth remembering that minimum meat content indicates both fat and lean in approximately 50 : 50 ratio. This is because the word 'meat' includes both fat and lean and is normally accepted to be in this proportion on the carcase. It may well be that the caterer seeing a label stating 65 per cent meat does not appreciate that this may be half fat! In commercial catering this may not be relevant but for the welfare sector it is such knowledge that is critical to economic nourishment.

POULTRY

This is a term used to describe birds which have been domesticated to supply man with either meat or eggs.

This section deals with the rearing of poultry for meat and details of the main birds involved can be found in Table 12.8. By far the greatest number eaten in this country are chicken and turkey and the following points relate mainly to this section of the market.

Methods of rearing chicken and turkeys for meat

1. *Broilers*

Thousands of cross-breeds, with extremely fast growth rates, are intensively reared in large, barn-style housing with constant regulation of feed, water, temperature, light and ventilation. When the birds reach the required weight they are slaughtered and prepared for sale (fresh or frozen) at automated processing factories. The giblets (neck, heart, liver, stomach) are either retained to be processed separately or sold with the bird.

2. *Roasters*

Male chickens show better growth rates and can be reared separately to produce large roasting birds.

Table 12.8 Poultry

Bird	Age	Approximate size	Yield	Quality Points	Shelf-life	Purchase state	Cooking methods	Examples of use
Baby chicken (Poussin)	4–6 weeks	350 g	1 per portion	delicate flesh high % bone	1 week at 0°C	whole bird fresh or frozen	Roast, bake, sauté, grill	Poussin en Crapaudine
Double spring chicken	6–8 weeks	450 g–680 g	½ per portion	delicate flesh	1 week at 0°C	whole bird fresh or frozen	Roast, bake, sauté, grill	Poussin Polonaise
Small roasting chicken (poulet de grain)	8–10 weeks	900 g–1.3 kg	2–4			} whole bird with or without giblets } chicken pieces	Roast, poêlé, sauté, grill, poach, braise	Poulet rôti á l'Anglaise
Medium roasting chicken (poulet reine)	10–12 weeks	1.3 kg–1.8 kg	4–6	} white flesh	1 week at 0°C	} boneless breaded nuggets	Roast, poêlé, sauté, grill poach, braise	Poulet poche aux riz, sauce suprême
Large roasting chicken (roosters) (poularde)	12–16 weeks	1.8 kg–2.3 kg	6–8			} burgers } chicken pies	Roast, poêlé	galantine de volaille

279

	Age	Weight	Flesh/fat	Storage	Form	Portions	Cooking method	Uses
Boiling fowl (old egg-laying bird) (Poule)	12–18 months	1.8 kg–3 kg	some fat which can be rendered and used for sauté	1 week at 0°C	whole bird fresh or frozen	Depends upon use but main course equivalent: 4–12	Boil	stock vol-au-vent chicken salad sandwiches etc.
Turkey	6–10 months	3 kg–14 kg	heavy breasts and small bone	1 week at 0°C	whole bird fresh or frozen	allow ½ kg undrawn weight per portion	roast, poêlé	Traditional roast turkey
Geese	over 4 months	3 kg–7 kg	dark flesh high fat	1 week at 0°C	whole birds fresh or frozen	as for turkey	Roast, braise	Roast Goose
Duck	over 4 months	1.50 kg–3 kg	dark flesh high fat	1 week at 0°C	whole birds fresh or frozen	4–6	Roast, braise	Canard à l'orange
Duckling	10–16 weeks	1 kg–1.5 kg	dark flesh high fat	1 week at 0°C	whole birds fresh or frozen	2–4	Roast	Caneton
Guinea fowl 12+ weeks	12+ weeks	1.5 kg	dark flesh tender	1 week at 0°C	"	2–3	Roast, casserole	Pintade rôti
Pigeon	8–10 weeks	0.25kg–1.5 kg	dark flesh	1 week at 0°C	"	1–2	Roast, bake	Pigeon pie

3. *Free range*

Some chickens, a few turkeys and most other poultry are allowed access to open paddocks during daylight hours. Strict EC legislation protects the 'free range' label and large supermarket chains also regularly visit supplying farms to monitor conditions.

Growth promoters

The feed of poultry, as for most farm animals, is specially formulated to produce optimal growth rates. It may also contain antibiotics to increase food utilisation but the use of hormones has now been banned because of undesirable residues in the flesh. It used to be common practice for breeders to insert hormone pellets into the neck to castrate cockerels chemically. These were then fattened to produce large roasting birds called capons. At the present time roasters are sometimes called capons or capon-style chickens.

Cooking poultry

With the exception of the water birds (ducks, geese) poultry flesh is lean with very little fat or connective tissue. Fat is therefore often added during the cooking process and roasting techniques are commonly used to enhance and develop flavour in flesh which might otherwise be bland. Poultry show a clear distinction between light and dark muscle. The active leg and wing muscles develop more juiciness and flavour on cooking for which some customers show a preference. Catering packs of frozen white/dark meat are useful if requirements are known in advance.

Nutritional value

Poultry meat offers good quality protein with little fat except for water birds. Figure 12.7 shows the proportions of nutrients in cooked chicken.

GAME

This term traditionally refers to animals which are killed in the wild. Although several types are now also being reared domestically, they are still classified as game. The numbers of both *furred* and *feathered* game animals eaten in this country are small and they are therefore processed by the retailer. Animals active in the wild develop a darker coloured and tougher textured flesh. They are usually hung, for periods of a few days to weeks, to improve flavour and tenderness. Hares are hung uncleaned, wild rabbits and deer are gutted immediately, whole game birds are drawn but unplucked. Table 12.9 lists some examples of game with the appropriate season.

Figure 12.7 *Proportions of main nutrients in cooked chicken*

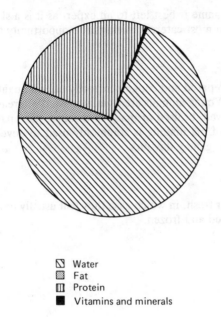

▧ Water
▩ Fat
▥ Protein
■ Vitamins and minerals

Table 12.9 *Game*

Examples	Season	Approximate hanging time	Approximate portions per animal
Feathered game			
* Grouse	12 August–15 December	3–4 days	1–2
* Partridge	1 September–1 February	7–8 days	1
* Pheasant	10 October–1 February	6–14 days	2–4
Snipe	12 August–31 January	7–10 days	$\frac{1}{2}$
Woodcock	12 August–31 January	7–10 days	1
Wild duck	12 August–1 March	8–10 days	2
Furred game			
Hare	September–March	2–3 days	6–8
* Rabbit	September–April	2–3 days	4–6
* Venison	July–March	up to 3 weeks	variable

* Animals also reared domestically

Choosing game

The grading of game is best left to an expert as it is a skill acquired by experience, with most caterers having little opportunity to learn.

Cooking game

Wild animals prepared and cooked correctly offer a quality rarely tasted in modern life. Young animals are usually roasted whereas older tougher animals are stewed, braised or made into soups, pies, pâtés or terrines. The technique of marinading is commonly used to develop tenderness and complement gamey flavours.

Availability

Purchased either fresh, in which case they will usually have feathers/fur, or ready prepared and frozen.

FISH

Fish present more variety than most other classes of food. There are more than 1500 different marketable fishes worldwide with over fifty commonly seen on the European market. The bulk of this catch consists of cod, hake, herring, mackerel, pilchard and anchovy.

Classification

This is a difficult procedure as many variations exist. Table 12.10 attempts to group the many different *animals commonly fished from seas, lakes and rivers*. Turtles and frogs are added to this list, as are various forms of shellfish.

Availability

Most sea fish are in season all the year round but there are restrictions on the fishing of shellfish. Freshwater fish are governed by the fishing season. Frozen fish are available to supplement demand throughout the year. Freshly frozen fish are often of such quality that most customers cannot distinguish them from fresh.

With the exception of trout and salmon which may be farmed most fish are acquired by pursuit rather than by domestication. Trout in a trout farm are fed on specially formulated meal which produces a distinctive coloured flesh but very poor flavour.

Table 12.10 *Animals commonly fished from seas and rivers*

Category	Types	Examples
Fish (cold blooded aquatic, scaly skin, lay eggs)	**Freshwater fish**	trout, salmon, salmon trout, eel
	Sea-water fish	
	1. *Pelagic (oily)* live at or near surface of sea	herring, mackerel, tunny
	2. *Demersal (white)* live at or near bottom of sea	*Round*: cod, haddock, whiting, coley, ling, monkfish, pollack
		Flat: plaice, skate, halibut, brill, turbot, sole, dab, Dover sole
Fish offal	**Roes** 1. *Hard* (female)	caviar, salmon roe, lumpfish roe
	2. *Soft* (male)	soft herring roe
Shellfish	1. *Crustacea* external skeleton, jointed legs	crab, lobster, shrimp, crawfish, scampi
	2. *Molluscs* soft muscular body, most have external shell	*univalves*: whelk, snail *bivalves*: mussel, oyster *others*: squid, octopus
Reptiles (cold-blooded four-legged, scaly skin, lay eggs)	**Turtle**	green turtle, terrapin
Amphibia cold-blooded, lay eggs in water, four legs	**Frogs**	green frogs

Keeping quality

Fish are caught by nets or lines and usually squirm about until they suffocate. This stressful death depletes muscle glycogen and post-mortem acidity is unable to develop, thereby causing fish to be a very perishable food. The polyunsaturated oil in the flesh begins to go rancid and proteins begin to produce ammonia within hours of death. The maximum shelf-life of top-quality fish is five days but they are often kept this long on deep sea fishing boats. The general rule is that fish should be delivered and cooked on the same day. If it is to be stored this is best at chilling temperature, preferably in a separate cabinet.

Table 12.11   *Fish: quality points*

Fresh fish	scales	glossy, bright, adhering to the skin
	flesh	firm and elastic, not separating from bone
	skin	undamaged, covered with natural glaze
	gills	pink, no slime
	eyes	bright, not sunken
	smell	pleasant, salty
Frozen fish	surface	no sign of dehydration ('freezer burn')
	fillets	clean cut, no stickiness
	packaging	no damage, clear label
Fresh shellfish	alive	heavy in relation to size
		molluscs tightly closed
		crustacea showing signs of activity

Cooking fish

Apart from a few shellfish most fish in this country is eaten cooked but the Japanese are well-known for their raw-fish dishes. Care must be taken to examine the flesh for parasites which are normally inactivated by the cooking process.

Fish muscle is white or grey/pink depending on the quantity of oil dispersed in it. The muscle fibres are shorter than those of other animals and are formed into *flakes* with connective tissue between them. This connective tissue easily gelatinises to yield a delicate structure which can quickly disintegrate in moisture or dry out in hot air. Cooking times for fish are therefore short with dry methods enhancing the taste as water evaporates from the surface, concentrating flavours. Moist methods yield a flavoursome cooking liquor which can form the basis of an accompanying sauce. The negligible energy value of white fish makes deep-frying a good choice of cooking method (see Chapter 9, section 9.10).

Fish products

The short shelf-life of fish and its abundance in certain localities and at certain times of the year have led to the development of smoked, salted and dried fish. Smoked herrings and mackerel are examples of commonly eaten products of this kind. Exotic varieties such as Bombay Duck feature on Indian menus throughout the world. Recent debate about the health hazards of smoked food have led to the alternative use of dye in many traditionally smoked fish products in Europe and America.

Canned salmon, tuna, sardines, pilchards and mackerel are popular around the world and fish is also processed into fish fingers and fish cakes. Research into other ways of marketing fish have led to experimentation with products such as fish sausages and fish crisps.

Fish offal in the form of hard and soft roes are not uncommon menu items but it is the prized caviar and its substitutes which are the best-known.

Health hazards associated with shellfish

Shellfish are filter-feeders who constantly wash through their bodies large quantities of water. Any bacteria or chemicals in the water may accumulate in the fish. Contaminated shellfish from polluted water are known to have caused outbreaks of cholera and mercury poisoning. Allergy is also commonly attributed to shellfish and caterers could bear this in mind when formulating table d'hôte menus.

Nutritional value of fish

Fish offers protein of high biological value and oily fish are a valuable source of fat-soluble vitamins. Forms of fish in which the bones are eaten provide one of the few good sources of calcium and Vitamin D in the diet apart from milk, and items such as sardines are to be recommended for growing children and the elderly. Figure 12.8 shows the proportions of the main nutrients in cod fillets.

Figure 12.8 *Proportions of main nutrients in cod fillets*

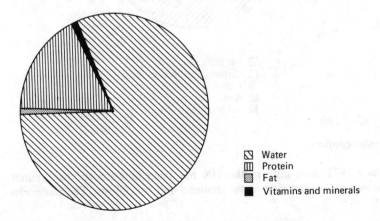

Water
Protein
Fat
Vitamins and minerals

MILK AND MILK PRODUCTS

Milk is legally defined as the secretion obtained, by normal milking methods, from the lactating mammary glands of a healthy, normally fed cow. Although other animals can produce milk for human consumption it must be labelled accordingly, e.g. goats' milk.

Nutritional value

Cows' milk contains a high-quality protein though significantly less valuable for babies than human milk. Allergic reactions to cows' milk are common in infants possibly causing colic, asthma, and eczema. It is therefore advisable for mothers to breast-feed until the age of at least six months. The whole range of vitamins and minerals is present in milk with the exception of iron. The fat content is low in liquid milk but milk does contain significant quantities of Vitamins A and D, and forms one of our major sources of calcium. Figure 12.9 shows the proportion of the main nutrients in milk.

Figure 12.9 *Proportion of main nutrients in fresh whole cows' milk*

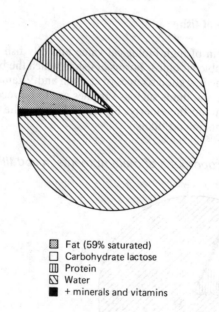

☒ Fat (59% saturated)
☐ Carbohydrate lactose
⦰ Protein
⧄ Water
■ + minerals and vitamins

Pasteurisation

Since 1922 most milk in the UK has been heat-treated to eliminate known pathogens such as tuberculosis and brucellosis. The pasteurisation process only slightly affects nutrients, taste and appearance and has been the key to effective distribution and development of milk and milk products. Unless clearly stated all milk, for sale as a liquid or to be further processed into milk products, has undergone this treatment.

Homogenisation

The fat in milk rises to the surface, on standing, to give the familiar cream line. For many types of liquid milk this is undesirable and the process of reducing the fat-globule size has been used to keep the fat permanently dispersed. The process is also used extensively in cream and yogurt production to increase viscosity. In this way products look richer and creamier than they would normally and are also more stable.

The industry

The UK milk industry is a highly organised, modernised and diverse operation as can be seen from the extensive range of products on the market. In recent years the healthy image of milk has been slightly tarnished as an animal product containing largely saturated fat. The industry's response has been to produce skimmed and semi-skimmed varieties of most products. Unfortunately it is often forgotten that milk-fat carries with it many valuable nutrients (especially Vitamins A and D) and that many community groups, especially children and old people, do not necessarily benefit, financially or nutritionally, from low-fat products.

Specialist milks

People of the Jewish faith may choose to use milk and milk products which have been prepared according to religious tradition. These *Kosher* milk products are available in most large towns.

Liquid milks and milk products are classified and briefly described in Tables 12.12 and 12.13. Further details can be obtained from the Milk Marketing Board.

Cheese

Cheese manufacture and varieties are further discussed because of their contribution to the diet of people across the world, their extensive use in food preparation and the variety with which the caterer is confronted.

Process

Milk is allowed to sour with acid, as in the natural process, or with rennet. The resulting clot is stirred, cut or strained to allow the liquid

Table 12.12 Liquid milks

Types	Varieties	Packaging 1pt bottle	Packaging Others	Keeping quality at 4°C	Minimum fat content %	Other characteristics
Untreated	Whole milk	Green top	} not available	} up to 3 days	3	Bottled under licence from herds which are TB-free and brucellosis-tested.
	Channel Island and South Devon milk	Green top gold band			4	Not allowed to be sold to catering establishments. Cream line
Pasteurised Mild heat treatment to destroy pathogens. (72°C for 15 secs)	Whole milk	Silver top		} up to 5 days	3	No cream line, distinctive flavour
	Channel Island and South Devon milk	Gold top			4	Yellow cream line
	Homogenised whole milk (H)	Red top	} Fully labelled waxed cartons		3	No cream line, distinctive flavour
	Semi-skimmed milk (H)	Silver/red striped top			1.5	
	Skimmed milk	Blue/silver check top			0.03	Blueish white
Sterilised Severe heat treatment to destroy microbes and most bacterial spores (100°C for 30 min)	Whole milk (H)	Silver cap		} 2–3 weeks unopened	3	Cooked flavour and yellowing due to caramelisation; popular in the Midlands
	Semi-skimmed (H)	Blue cap	} sky-blue-topped polyprophylene bottles		1.5	
	Skimmed	Red cap			0.03	
UHT Heat treatment to destroy microbes and most bacterial spores (132°C for 1 sec)	Whole milk (H)	} not available in bottles	} fully labelled cartons	} 4 months unopened	3	Slightly yellow change particularly noticeable in milk products
	Semi-skimmed milk (H)				1.5	
	Skimmed milk				0.03	
Fortified *added nutrients	e.g. Calcia, Vitapint	} detailed label on carton as required by legislation		} up to 5 days	Details on label as required by legislation	Added skimmed milk powder and/or vitamins A, D, calcium
Flavoured added flavour	e.g. chocolate milk drink			} up to 5 months		Expanding market; popular from vending machines

Key H = homogenised

Purchasing units: pasteurised and sterilised milk – 10cm³, 200cm³, 1 litre, 2 litre, 1 pt, 2 pt, 3 gallons, 5 gallons

Table 12.13 *Milk products*

Name	Process	Most commonly used varieties		Purchase units
Dried milks	Dried by spraying liquid milk into heated chamber or over hot rollers	Dried whole milk Dried skim milk Filled milk	baby milks most commonly used dried skim milk with vegetable fat added	} Sold in approximate reconstituted volumes } (pints and litres)
Concentrated milks	Water content reduced by 60% and canned	Evaporated milk Condensed milk	colour change, ie yellowish sugar added. Rich/creamy.	$\frac{1}{4}$, $\frac{1}{2}$, 1pt, cans/tubs $\frac{1}{4}$, $\frac{1}{2}$, 1pt, cans/tubs
Fermented milks	Bacteria added to change texture and flavour	Natural yoghurts Yoghurt dessert drinks Fruit flavoured yoghurts	} Whole milk yoghurt (whole milk) } Low fat yoghurt (skimmed milk) } Very low fat yoghurt (semi-skimmed milk)	Fresh/frozen; individual cartons or 1 gallon catering packs.
Cream	Separation of fat from milk; sold in relation to quantity of fat	Clotted cream Double cream Whipping cream Single cream Half cream Sterilised half cream Sterilised cream " Aerosol	minimum fat content 55% minimum fat content 48% minimumf fat content 35% minimum fat content 18% minimum fat content 12% minimum fat content 12% minimum fat content 23% UHT whipped cream	} Also available in cans, } plastic cartons, } (sterilised) UHT cartons } and aerosols
Butter	Churning separates out water to give solid fat	Butter – salted – unsalted Concentrated butter	minimum 82% butter fat minimum 96% butter fat	500g, 1kg packs/ individual 6g portions
Ice cream	Frozen milk-solids including milk-fat, sugar, emulsifiers, stabilisers	Dairy ice cream	Large variety of products. Label needs careful interpretation to evaluate quality and cost. Must not be allowed to melt as refreezing impossible.	} Sold by volume – } $\frac{1}{2}$, 1, 2 litres, etc
	As above but milk-fat replaced by vegetable fat	Ice cream		
Cheese	Milk clotted and separated into curds (for cheese) and whey (by-product)	Over 400 varieties (see text)	Low fat, Full fat varieties	Sold by weight

* *Whipping cream* sold to caterers may have added sugar and stabilisers
Whipped cream may have added sugar and stabilisers
** *Imitation cream/Dessert topping* cream substitutes based mainly on fats/oils; must be labelled as such on menus in catering establishments

290

Figure 12.10 *Cheese production*

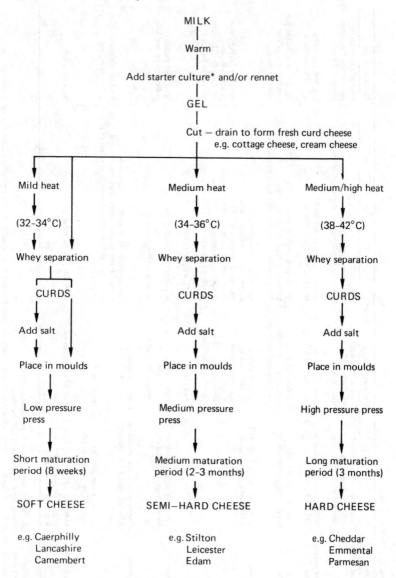

* Acid producing bacteria

whey to drain away. The curds are treated in a number of different ways which are illustrated in Figure 12.10. The combination of setting agent, time, temperature, pressing, moulding and maturing have been refined to produce at least 400 distinct varieties. The type of animal, type of grass it feeds on, and many more environmental conditions give rise to a uniqueness that science is slow to match. Parmesan cheese, for example, has been made in no place other than that of Parma in Italy. This is certainly not for want of trying.

Nutritional value

Cheese represents a concentrated source of energy and high quality protein. Figure 12.11 shows the composition of an average cheese.

Figure 12.11 *Proportions of main nutrients in cheese*

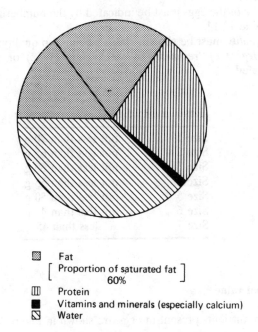

	Fat
	Proportion of saturated fat 60%
	Protein
	Vitamins and minerals (especially calcium)
	Water

EGGS

Types of eggs

Eggs from hens, turkeys, ducks, geese, quails and gulls may be used in cookery but the term refers to hens' eggs unless otherwise stated.

Methods of production

Hens have been cross-bred to produce breeds which lay up to seven eggs a week for the first 18 months of their lives. They are reared by one of the following methods:

1. free range   with access to open paddocks;
2. deep-litter   freedom to roam in large barns;
3. battery   restricted to cages with one or more birds.

EC labelling

Regulations came into force in 1973 in regard to the sale of hens' eggs:

(a) the *package* must be clearly marked to indicate the identity of the packers;
(b) the *size* of the eggs must be indicated by the numbering scale shown in Table 12.14.
(c) the *quality* must be shown, class A being top quality;
(d) the *degree of freshness*, by week code (1–52) or date, must be indicated.

Table 12.14   *Egg sizes*

Size 1	not less than 70 g
Size 2	not less than 65 g
Size 3	not less than 60 g
Size 4	not less than 55 g
Size 5	not less than 50 g
Size 6	not less than 45 g
Size 7	less than 45 g

Nutritional value

The main nutrients present in eggs are shown in Figure 12.12.

12.3 FOOD FROM PLANTS

During the history of man, trial and error has led to the use of over 3000 species of plants as food. Of these, less than 200 have been cultivated to produce the range of commodities we use today. These are summarised in Table 12.15.

Figure 12.12   *Proportions of main nutrients in raw eggs*

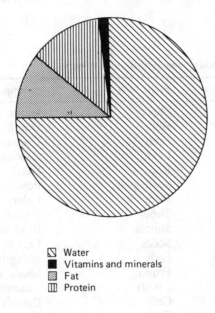

☒ Water
■ Vitamins and minerals
▨ Fat
▥ Protein

Fresh vegetables

This term is used by caterers to refer to the *soft edible plant products which are usually eaten with meat, fish or a savoury dish and are commonly salted or at least not sweet.* They are derived from many parts of different plants and have extensive uses in catering. These are summarised in Table 12.16.

Effects of cooking

Many vegetables are made more palatable by cooking. The starch they contain is gelatinised (softened) and fibres tenderised. The effect on vitamins and minerals is discussed in 13.2 and 9.1.

Nutritional value

Mainly composed of water, these plant products contain fibre and some vitamins. Avocados and olives contain high proportions of oil. Many root vegetables are important sources of starch and form the staple diet of many people. Figure 12.13 illustrates the main nutrients in fresh vegetables.

Table 12.15 *Foods from plants: a summary*

Commodity group	Plant part	Example
Fresh vegetables	Flower	Globe artichokes
	Bulb	Onion
	Fruit	Cucumber
	Leaf	Cabbage
	Root	Swede
	Seeds/pods	Peas
	Stem	Celery
	Tuber	Potato
	Shoots	Bean shoots
Pulse vegetables	Seeds	Lentils, beans, peas
	Pods	Mangetout
Fungi	Fruiting body	Mushrooms, cepes, morels
	Cells	Baker's yeast
Fruits	Fruit	Apples, cherries, kiwi, etc
	Stem	Rhubarb
Nuts	Seeds	Almonds
Cereals	Seeds	Wheat, barley, rye
Other starches	Palm pith	Sago
	Tuber	Arrowroot
Sugars	Stem	Cane
	Root	Beet
	Trunk	Maple syrup
Oils	Seeds	Soya
	Fruits	Olives
Seaweed	Algae	Laver
Beverages	Leaf	Tea
	Seeds	Cocoa, coffee
Flavours	Various parts of plants	Herbs and spices
Colours	Various parts of plants	Herbs and spices

Table 12.16 Fresh vegetable chart

Name	Category	Season	Uses	Alternative name
Artichoke (globe)	Flowers	JJAS	ABCG	
Artichoke (Jerusalem)	Tubers	JFD	AD	
Asparagus	Stems	MJJ	ABCDG	
Aubergine	Fruits	JJASO	A	Egg plant
Avocado	Fruits	JFMAMJJASOND	B	Avocado pear
Beans (broad)	Pods	JJA	A	
Beans (French)	Pods	JJASOND	ACG	Fine beans
Beans (runner)	Pods	JAS	A	
Beans (sprouts)	Shoots	JFMAMJJASOND	AC	
Beetroot	Roots	JFMAMJJASOND	AC	
Breadfruit	Fruit	JFMAMJJASOND	AC	
Broccoli	Flowers	FMAMJJAS	A	
Brussels sprouts	Leaves	SON	A	
Cabbage (green)	Leaves	JFMJJASOND	ACG	
Cabbage (spring)	Leaves	JFM	AG	
Cabbage (red)	Leaves	JFASOND	AI	
Cabbage (white)	Leaves	JFMAMJJASOND	AC	
Cabbage (Chinese)	Leaves	JFMAMJJASOND	AC	Chinese leaves
Calabrese	Flowers	JFMAMD	A	Purple broccoli
Carrot (new)	Roots	MJ	AG	
Carrot (old)	Roots	JFMAMJJASOND	ACG	
Cassava (sweet)	Tuber	JFMAMJJASOND	A	
Cauliflower	Flower	JFMMJJASOND	ADG	
Celeriac	Roots	JOND	BF	

Table 12.16 (continued)

Name	Category	Season	Uses	Alternative name
Celery	Stems	JFMAMJJASOND	ACH	
Chard	Leaves	JOND	A	Swiss chard
Chicory	Leaves	AMJJA	AC	Endive
Chillis	Pods	JFMAMJJASOND	H	Chilli peppers
Chives	Bulbs	FMAMJJAS	GH	
Corn salad	Leaves	FM	C	Lamb's lettuce
Courgette	Fruits	MJJA	AG	Zucchini
Cucumber	Fruits	JFMAMJJASOND	ACG	
Custard squash	Fruit	JFMAMJJASOND	AE	
Dudi	Fruits	JFMAMJJASOND	A	
Eddoe	Roots	JFMAMJJASOND	AC	Malanga, Dasheen
Endive (Belgian)	Leaves	JFMAMJJASOND	AC	Chicory
Fennel	Stems	JJASO	AGH	
Garlic	Bulbs	JFMAMJJASOND	H	
Ginger root	Roots	JFMAMJJASOND	H .	
Gourd	Fruit	JFMAMJJASOND	A	
Horseradish	Roots	JFMAMJJASOND	H	
Kale (curly)	Leaves	JFM	A	
Karela	Pods	JFMAMJJASOND	A	
Kohlrabi	Stems	AMJJ	A	
Leek	Bulbs	JFMAJJASOND	AD	
Lettuce (cabbage)	Leaves	AMJJAS	ACG	
Lettuce (cos)	Leaves	ON	C	Romaine

Lettuce (iceburg)	Leaves	JFMAMJJASOND	C	
Mangetout	Pods	AMJJAS	A	Sugar pea, Snow pea
Marrow	Fruit	JJAS	A	
Okra	Pods	JFMAMJJASOND	AG	Ladies' fingers, Gombo
Onion	Bulbs	JFMAMJJASOND	AGH	
Onion (button)	Bulbs	AMJJAS	AGI	
Onions (spring)	Bulbs	FMAMJJAS	C	
Padrushka	Root	JFMAMJJASOND	DH	
Parsnip	Roots	JOND	A	
Pear (vegetable)	Fruit	JFMAMJJASOND	C	Chow-chow
Peas	Pods	MJJAS	ACG	
Pimento	Fruit	ASOND	ACG	Pepper, Capsicums
Plantain	Fruit	JFMAMJJASOND	A	
Potato	Tubers	JFMAMJJASOND	ACG	
Potato (sweet)	Tubers	JFMAMJJASOND	AG	
Pumpkin	Fruit	JFMAMJJASOND	ADE	
Radicchio	Leaves	JFMAMJJASOND	C	
Radish	Roots	FMAMJJASON	BC	
Ridge cucumbers	Fruits	JFMAMJJASOND	ACDI	
Salsify	Roots	JOND	AG	Oyster plant
Samphire	Leaves	JFMAMJJASOND	AI	
Sea kale	Stems	JFMAMJD	A	
Shallot	Bulbs	JFMAMJJASOND	HI	
Sorrel	Leaves	FM	DGH	
Spinach	Leaves	ASON	A	
Sweetcorn	Fruit	JJAS	A	
Sweet potato	Tubers	JFMAMJJASOND	A	

Table 12.16 (continued)

Name	Category	Season	Uses	Alternative name
Swede	Roots	JFMAMJND	A	
Tannia	Tuber	JFMAMJJASOND	A	
Taro	Tubers	JFMAMJJASOND	D	
Tindoori	Fruits	JFMAMJJASOND	G	
Tomato (common)	Fruit	JFMAMJJASOND	ABCDFG	
Tomato (cherry)	Fruits	JFMAMJJASOND	BG	
Turnip	Roots	FMAM	ACG	
Watercress	Leaves	JFMAMJJASOND	CG	
Yam	Tubers	JFMAMJJASOND		Indian potato

Key: Uses as: A. Vegetables
B. Hors-d'oeuvre
C. Salads
D. Soups
E. Pie
F. Sauce
G. Garnish
H. Flavouring
I. Pickling

Figure 12.13 *Proportions of main nutrients in fresh cabbage*

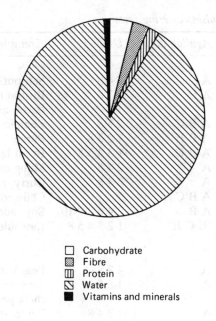

- ☐ Carbohydrate
- ▨ Fibre
- ⊞ Protein
- ▨ Water
- ■ Vitamins and minerals

Season and availability

Many fresh vegetables e.g. tomatoes are available all year round, although the price will vary considerably. Some vegetables are imported from a variety of countries to ensure a continual supply, e.g. exotic vegetables available in the large stores. The availability of other vegetables will depend upon the climate in any one year. Taking these factors into account, it follows that data on season is difficult to present in a useful way. It is however important to know when fresh items, not available all year round, are likely to be available and details are given in Table 12.16.

Pulse vegetables

These are the dry seeds of the legume plant family and include beans, peas, lentils and the familiar peanut (groundnut). Many varieties are grown worldwide and there is an increasing range available in the UK because of the influence of vegetarian and multicultural cookery trends. Table 12.17 includes both commonly used and some less-familiar types and also indicates if they are available as fresh vegetables.

300

Table 12.17 *Pulses: catering facts*

Pulses	Availability	Uses	Examples of uses
Beans			
Black-eyed	A	2 4 8	Salt pork, curry
Boston	A D	2 7 8	Boston beans with bacon and treacle
Broad	A B C	2 5 8	Zampino, curry
Butter	A B E	1 2 3 8	Purée Tourangelle, curry
Flageolet	A B C	1 3 4 5 8	Roast lamb flageolets
Mung	A	2 4 8	Mung-bean flan, curry
Pigeon Pea	A	2 4 8	Curry, side dish
Red Kidney	A B C	2	Chile con carne, curry
Soya	A B	2 4 6 8 9 10	Soy sauce, soya protein
White Haricot	B C E	1 2 3 4 5 8	Cassoulet of pork
Peas			
Blue	A	4 7 8	Peas with mint
Chick	A	1 2 8	Sausage and chick pea casserole
Green	A	1 2 4 8	Purée St Germain
Yellow	A	1 2 4 8	Pease pudding
Lentils			
Green	A	1 2 4 8	Baked ham and lentil purée
Puy	A	1 2 4 8	Lentilles au beurre
Yellow	A	1 2 4 8	Crème de Lentille, curry
Red	A	1 2 4 8	Soups

Key: *Availability*
A. Dried
B. Fresh
C. Canned (brine)
D. Canned (sauce)
E. Frozen

Uses
1. Soups
2. Stews
3. Hors d'oeuvre
4. Accompaniment
5. Salad
6. Sauce
7. Vegetable
8. Vegetarian
9. Textured protein
10. Oil

Nutritional value

Leguminous plants produce seeds rich in protein (see Figure 12.14). This is low in some essential amino-acids, however, and must be mixed with other protein foods in the diet to provide an adequate diet (see 13.3)

Figure 12.14 *Proportions of main nutrients in baked beans in tomato sauce*

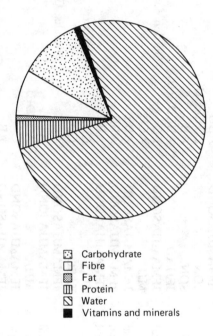

    ▦ Carbohydrate
    ☐ Fibre
    ▨ Fat
    Ⅲ Protein
    ◩ Water
    ■ Vitamins and minerals

Fungi

Moulds, e.g. mushrooms, truffles

The *fruiting bodies* of some species of mould are eaten, often as a delicacy, whilst other moulds are used to ripen cheeses and ferment foods such as soy sauce. The limited part they play in the diet makes moulds of little nutritional value.

Yeasts e.g. baker's yeast

A few types of yeast are used extensively in the manufacture of wine, beer and baked products. Yeast and yeast extracts (e.g. Marmite) contain high levels of many B vitamins, but normal *consumption is too small* to warrant their being described as good dietary sources.

Table 12.18 Fresh fruits: catering facts

Name	Category	Season	Uses	Alternative name
Apple (Bramleys)	Top	JFMOND	CDEFHIJ	
Apple (Granny Smith)	Top	JFMAMJJASOND	ABG	
Apple (Cox's Orange)	Top	JND	ABGK	
Apple (Golden Delicious)	Top	JFMAMJJASOND	ABG	
Apple (Grenadier)	Top	SON	CDEFHIJ	
Apple (Laxtons)	Top	SON	AB	
Apricot	Stone	JFJAD	ABCDEHJ	
Avocado pear	Tropical	JFMAMJJASOND	EG	Garden pear
Babaco	Misc.	MJJ	ACF	
Banana	Tropical	JFMAMJJASOND	ABE	
Banana (canary)	Tropical	JFMAMJJASOND	ABE	
Banana (red)	Tropical	JFMAMJJASOND	ABE	
Bilberry	Soft	JJAS	CDJ	Blueberry
Blackberry	Soft	JASO	CDJ	
Cape gooseberry	Soft	JFMAMJJASOND	AC	Physalis, Goldenberry
Cherimoya	Tropical	JFMAMJJASOND	A	
Cherry	Stone	MJJA	ABCDEJ	
Citron	Citrus	JFMAMJJASOND	C	
Clementine	Citrus	JFMAMJJASOND	AB	
Crab apple	Top	JJAS	CDHIJ	
Cranberry	Soft	JFMAMJJASOND	CDHJ	
Currant (black,red,white)	Soft	JAS	CDJ	
Custard apple	Tropical	JFMAMJJASOND	AB	Anona fruit
Damson	Stone	SO	CDJ	
Date	Stone	JFMAMJJASOND	ABEI	

Fruit	Category	Season	Code	Notes
Doere berry	Tropical	JMAMJJASOND	C	
Durian	Tropical	JFMAMJJASOND	A	
Feijoa	Tropical	JFMAMJJASOND	ADG	
Fig	Tropical	JFMAMJJASOND	AB	
Gooseberry	Soft	JJA	CDEHJ	
Grape	Misc.	JFMAMJJASOND	ABF	
Grapefruit	Citrus	JFMAMJJASOND	G	
Grapefruit (pink flesh)	Citrus	JFMAMJJASOND	D/H	
Greengage	Stone	ASO	CDHJ	
Guava	Tropical	JFMAMJJASOND	A	
Jack fruit	Tropical	JFMAMJJASOND	A	
Kiwi-fruit	Tropical	JFMAMJJASOND	ABG	Chinese gooseberry
Kumquat	Citrus	JFMAMJJASOND	CJ	
Lemon	Citrus	JFMAMJJASOND	CDEFGHJI	
Lime	Citrus	JFMAMJJASOND	CDEFGHJI	
Loganberry	Soft	JA	CDJ	
Loquat	Tropical	JFMAMJJASOND	ACJ	Japanese medlar
Lychee	Tropical	JFMAMJJASOND	ABCE	
Mango	Tropical	JFMAMJJASOND	AEI	
Mandarin	Citrus	ASO	B	
Medlar	Top	SO	AJ	
Melon (cantaloup)	Misc.	JJA	AG	
Melon (charentais)	Misc.	JJAS	ABG	
Melon (gallia)	Misc.	MJJA	AG	
Melon (honeydew)	Misc.	JFMJJASOND	AG	
Melon (ogen)	Misc.	JFMAMJJASOND	AG	
Melon (water)	Misc.	MJJAS	ABG	
Mangosteen	Tropical	JFMAMJJASOND	AB	

Table 12.18 Fresh fruits: catering facts

Name	Category	Season	Uses	Alternative name
Mulberry	Soft	JA	BHJ	
Nectarine	Stone	JFMAMJJA	B	
Nisperies	Tropical	JFMAMJJASOND	A	
Orange	Citrus	JFMAMJJASOND	ABCDEFGHJ	
Orange (mineola)	Citrus	JMAMJJASOND	AB	
Orange (Seville)	Citrus	JFMAMJJASOND	J	
Ortanique	Citrus	FMAM	BJ	
Passion fruit	Tropical	JFMAMJJASOND	AC	Grenadilla
Paw-paw	Tropical	JFMAMJJASOND	AE	Papaya
Peach	Stone	JFMMJJASD	ABCDEHJ	
Pear (conference)	Top	ON	AB	
Pear (William)	Top	SON	ABCD	
Pear (prickly)	Misc.	JFMAMJJASOND	AC	Cactus pear
Persimmon	Misc.	JFMND	ACGK	Kaki fruit, Sharon fruit
Pineapple	Tropical	JFMAMJJASOND	ABEG	
Plantains	Tropical	JFMAMJJASOND	C	
Plum	Stone	JFMJJASO	BCDJ	
Plum (Santa Rosa)	Stone	JFMAMJJASOND	ACD	
Plum (Kelsey)	Stone	JFMAMJJASOND	ACD	
Pomegranate	Misc.	JOND	B	
Pomelo	Misc.	JFMAMJJASON	G	
Quince	Misc.	MND	CIJ	
Rambutan	Tropical	JFMAMJJASOND	A	
Raspberry	Soft	JASO	CHJ	
Rhubarb	Misc.	JFMAMJJAND	CD	

Sapodilla	Tropical	JFMAMJJASOND	A	
Satsuma	Citrus	JFMAMJJASOND	AJ	
Soursop	Misc.	JFMAMJJASOND	C	
Star fruit	Tropical	JFMAMJJASOND	A	
Strawberry	Soft	JJA	ACJ	
Strawberry (wild)	Soft	MAMJJAS	A	
Tamarillo	Misc.	JFMAMJJASOND	AB	Java plum, jambolan
Tangerine	Citrus	JFMAMJND	AB	
Ugli fruit	Citrus	JFM	A	Tangelo

Key:

Categories
1. Top fruit
2. Soft fruit
3. Stone fruit
4. Citrus
5. Tropical/sub-tropical
6. Miscellaneous

Use
A. Uncooked sweet
B. Fruit basket
C. Cooked and served cold
D. Cooked and served hot
E. Meat dish garnish
F. Fish dish garnish
G. Hors-d'oeuvre
H. Sauce
I. Preserves – savoury
J. Preserves – sweet
K. Salad

Fruits

This term is used by caterers to refer to plant products which are *soft and edible with fragrant aromatic flavours. They are naturally sweet or are sweetened during cooking.*

The range of fruits available is extensive. Traditionally, fruit available in this country was classified into top fruit (apples and pears), soft fruit (berries), stone fruit (plums, peaches), citrus fruit (oranges and lemons), and miscellaneous items like rhubarb. With the import and development of so many other varieties, classification is difficult and not of much use in the wholesale trade. Table 12.18 attempts only a basic classification and summarises the main catering uses of both common and exotic varieties. Many fruits are available canned and frozen.

Nutritional value

Mainly composed of water, fruits contain valuable supplies of Vitamin C (see Figure 12.15). Starchy fruits such as the banana and bread-fruit are staple foods in some countries.

Figure 12.15   *Proportions of main nutrients in apple*

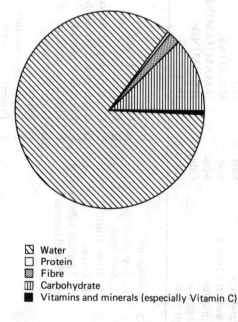

◪ Water
☐ Protein
▨ Fibre
▥ Carbohydrate
■ Vitamins and minerals (especially Vitamin C)

Season and availability

The availability of fresh fruits is similar to fresh vegetables.

Dried fruits

Many fruits were traditionally sun-dried to extend their keeping qualities. The processes are often more sophisticated now, but the method of preservation – removing water – remains the same. The sugar in the fruit is concentrated as they are dried and they are therefore much sweeter than the original fruit. Examples of fruits commonly available dry include grapes (sultanas, raisins, currants); plums (prunes); apples; apricots; figs and dates.

Nuts

The fruits of many plants produce nuts which can be eaten raw, cooked or used as a garnish. They are available in a variety of forms and these and their common uses are detailed in Table 12.19. Dessert nuts (in their shells) are available during the autumn and winter months.

Nutritional value

Nuts contain large amounts of oil which makes them valuable both as a cash crop (coconut) and in the diet as an energy source. Protein is also present in quantities far higher than in most plant products. It is low in some essential amino-acids, however, and must be mixed with other protein foods to provide an adequate diet (see 13.3). For diagram showing main nutrients, see Figure 12.16.

Cereals and other starchy foods

Cereals are cultivated grasses whose small dry fruits are known as grain. They have been used as a source of food since as early as 3000 BC and still form the basis of most people's diet. The prominence of cereals as food plants is due to their ability to grow in almost any climate or soil, the ease of cultivation and their high yield. Wheat, barley, oats and rye have been the most important cereals in the Middle East and Europe; rice in Asia; corn in the New World and sorghum (millet) in Africa. Table 12.20 shows the common products derived from cereals.

Milling and refining

Traditional preparation of cereal grain has involved removing the tough outer layers (bran) to make them more easy to cook and eat. This is often now a highly mechanised process able to remove bran and germ to leave only endosperm. Details of the typical grain and the milling process are outlined in Figure 12.17. The removal of the germ reduces the fat content and therefore extends keeping quality. It does however reduce fibre, protein and B vitamins and there is much debate as to the health implications of the latter. Indeed, outbreaks of beri-beri were almost

Table 12.19 Nuts: catering facts

Nuts	Availability	Uses	Example
Almond	A B C D E F	1 2 3 4 5 7	Shallow-fried Trout with Almonds, Indian rice pudding, sweet dishes
Brazil	A B D H	1 2 3 4 7	Lentil and brazil nut roast
Cashew	B D I	4 6	Nut cutlet, vegetable cutlets, Indian puddings, savouries
Chestnut	A B H	1 2 3 4 5 6 7	Marron glacé
Coconut	A C E F	1 2 3 4 5 7	Madeleines, vegetable curry, chutney, rice dishes
Hazel	A B D	1 2 3 4	Praline
Macadamia	A B	1 2 3 4	Macadamia nuts with avocado
Peanut	A B I	4 7	Peanut butter, savoury snacks, vegetable cutlets, Indian sweets
Pecan	A B D	1 2 3 4	Pecan pie
Pistachio	A B D	1 2 3 4 5 6 7	Galantine of chicken, rice dishes, Indian pudding (Barfi)
Walnut	A B C D F G	1 2 3 4 5 6 7	Waldorf salad

Key: Availability
A. In shell
B. Shelled whole
C. Blanched
D. Chopped
E. Flaked
F. Ground
G. Pickled
H. Preserved in syrup
I. Salted

Uses
1. Cakes
2. Pastries
3. Sweets
4. Vegetarian dishes
5. Garnish
6. Stuffings
7. Meat dishes

Figure 12.16 *Proportions of main nutrients in almonds*

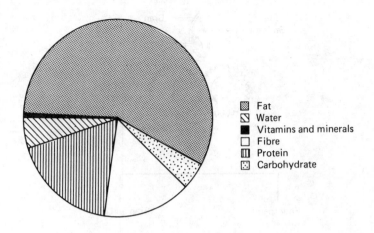

Fat
Water
Vitamins and minerals
Fibre
Protein
Carbohydrate

Table 12.20 *Cereal products*

Cereal	Main product	Catering uses
Wheat	Soft flour	Sponge cakes, short pastry
	Strong flour	Bread, puff-pastry, batters, roux
	Brown flour	Brown breads, rolls, etc.
	Semolina	Gnocchi Romaine, puddings
	Processed whole grain	Breakfast cereals
Corn	Cornflour	Thickening sauces, blancmange
	Processed grain	Breakfast cereals
Barley	Extract	Brewing
	Malt flour	Bread
Rye	Rye meal	Breakfast cereals
	Rye flour	Bread
Rice	Long grain (Patna)	Savoury rice dishes
	Short grain (Carolina)	Sweet dishes
	Wild	Savoury dishes
	Paper	Macaroons
	Processed grain	Breakfast cereals
Oats	Rolled oats	Porridge
	Oatmeal	Oatcakes, ginger cake

Figure 12.17 *Grain and the milling process*

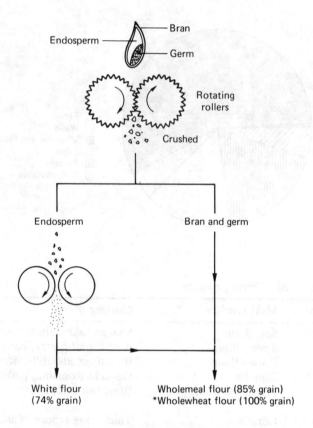

White flour (74% grain)

Wholemeal flour (85% grain)
*Wholewheat flour (100% grain)

Stoneground wholewheat flour is produced in the traditional way by grinding the grain between stone rollers

unknown until the modern rice milling – to remove the bran and germ – began in Asia. At the present time refined wheat flour, the UK's staple cereal product, is fortified with thiamine, niacin, iron and calcium.

Nutritional value

A comparison of Figures 12.18 and 12.19 reveals the main differences in the nutritional composition of white and wholemeal flour.

Wheat

Wheat is an extremely versatile raw material, when compared with other cereals, primarily because of the high quantities of protein found in the

Figure 12.18 *Proportions of the main nutrients in white flour*

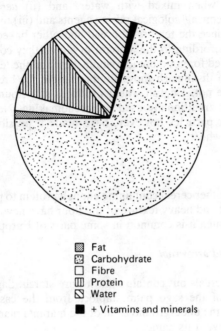

Fat
Carbohydrate
Fibre
Protein
Water
+ Vitamins and minerals

Figure 12.19 *Proportions of the main nutrients in wholemeal flour*

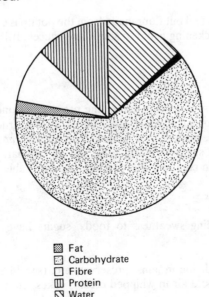

Fat
Carbohydrate
Fibre
Protein
Water
Vitamins and minerals

endosperm. This protein, known as *gluten*, is able (i) to stretch and become *elastic* when mixed with water, and (ii) *aerate* with gases produced by chemical/biological raising agents and (iii) to *heat-fix* during cooking to produce the texture of bread and other baked goods.

Flours vary according to the amount of gluten they contain. Over 10 per cent is needed for good bread manufacture and the terms *strong* and *soft* are used to distinguish those flours suitable for breadmaking and those which are not. English wheat produces soft flour and imported wheat has been traditionally used for breadmaking. New methods of separating flour particles however, have made it possible to get hard flour from soft wheat.

Rye

Rye is the only other cereal containing enough protein to produce bread. The dark colour and heavy texture of the flour have never been popular in the UK although it is common in some parts of Europe.

Sago, tapioca and arrowroot

These are not cereals but contain almost pure starch. Sago is produced from the pith of the sago palm, tapioca from the cassava root and arrowroot from the underground stem of the maranta plant whose arrow shaped leaves give it its name.

Potato

Potato is not a cereal but flour made from the potato is commonly used in catering as a thickening agent in soups and sauces. It is usually referred to as *fécule*.

Sugars

Natural sweetness in food is due to the presence of one or more of the different types of sugar molecules. These include fructose, galactose, glucose, sucrose, maltose and lactose. The term *sugar* usually refers to sucrose or table sugar with which we are all familiar. This, and other sweet products in common use, are described in Table 12.21.

Function in foods

Apart from adding sweetness to foods, sugars have other functions, including

1. preservative action in jams, preserves, etc. (see 14.8);
2. crystals can hold air in whipped cream, cakes, etc.;

Table 12.21 *Sugars*

Sweetener	Source	Process	Main ingredients	Catering uses
Table sugar	Sugar beet Sugar cane	Soaked to remove sugar and then water removed from sugar solution by evaporation. Refined to remove colour and · flavour. Can be processed further into castor/icing sugar	99% sucrose	Icing sugar, cakes, sauces
Raw brown sugar	Sugar beet Sugar cane	Partially refined	Sucrose plus some colour and flavour	Rich fruit cakes
Brown sugar	Sugar beet Sugar cane	Refined white sugar with colour added	Sucrose and colour	cakes, coffee
Molasses	Sugar beet Sugar cane	By-product of refining	Sucrose, flavours, colours, gum	Used in some breads and cakes
Honey	Bees	Bees collect nectar from flowers, this contains sucrose. They swallow it, partially digest it and regurgitate into beehive	Glucose and fructose	Honey cakes, table syrup, in drinks
Golden syrup (corn syrup)	Starch	Produced by acid breakdown of starch	Glucose and maltose	Treacle tart, gingerbread
Liquid glucose	Starch	Produced by acid breakdown of starch	Mainly glucose	Fondant
Maple syrup	Maple tree	Bark cut and syrup flows out	Mostly sucrose, flavour and colour	Sauce for waffles and pancakes

3. caramelisation to produce colour and toffees, etc.;
4. production of crystalline confectionery goods.

Nutritional value

Sugar provides energy for the body in a readily available and acceptable form. It does not however, contain any other nutrients in significant amounts (no, not even honey!) and intake must not lead to an unbalanced diet. This, and other considerations are discussed in 13.3. Figure 12.20 illustrates the nutritional value of sugars.

Oils and fats

These are *greasy* substances of animal or plant origin which produce *energy* for the body on digestion. Table 12.22 shows the sources and characteristics of commonly used oils and fats. If they are solid at room temperature in temperate climates such substances are known as *fats*,

Figure 12.20 *Nutritional value of sugar*

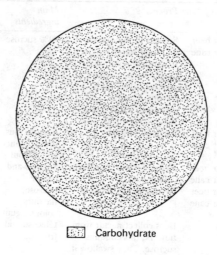

Carbohydrate

and if liquid they are known as *oils*. A useful scientific term that refers to both is *lipid*. All lipids contain 99 per cent of molecules called *triglycerides*. These molecules each contain three fatty acids which may be *saturated* with hydrogen or *unsaturated*. Some of the fatty acids are essential to the body, as vitamins are, and are termed *essential fatty acids*.

Fats contain a high proportion of saturated fatty acids and are usually of animal origin. They also contain a substance called cholesterol.

Oils contain a high proportion of unsaturated fatty accids and are usually of plant origin.

In recent years there has been a lot of discussion as to the best type of lipid to eat. This is discussed in Chapter 13.

Nutritional value

A comparison of Figures 12.21 and 12.22 shows the difference between oils/fat from respectively vegetable and animal origin.

The vegetable oil products

Vegetable oils are refined and used for:

1. *Frying* The characteristics of refined vegetable oils, especially those formulated for this purpose, make them ideal for both deep- and shallow-frying. Full detail of these properties is given in 9.10 and 9.11.

Table 12.22 *Sources and characteristics of fats and oils*

Source	Name	Characteristics and uses
Animal		
pig*	lard	A pure fat used for pastry, frying
beef*	suet	Hard fat from around the kidneys needs to be grated for use in puddings and pastry.
	butter	Used as a spread and in baked goods for flavour. Expensive.
	dripping	Fat collected when meat is cooked or rendered.
Marine		
whale	whale oil	Used extensively for margarine until world control of whale killing.
fish*	herring anchovy pilchard	Unsaturated oils which tend to go rancid quickly. Used extensively for animal feed.
Tree and-Bush		
red palm	red palm oil	Tropical tree fruit used, in countries of origin, for cooking. Used commercially to produce margarine and other fats.
coconut	coconut oil	Extracted from white flesh of coconut. Used to produce margarine and other fats.
olive	olive oil	Grown in Mediterranean countries, the small, green fruit of the olive tree. Extracted simply by squeezing the fruit to produce an expensive table oil.
cocoa bush	cocoa butter	Extracted from the seeds. Used in manufacture of cocoa products and in pharmaceutical industry. The most expensive fat available.
Oilseeds		
maize groundnut (peanut) soya bean rapeseed* sunflower safflower sesame cottonseed	vegetable oils	Oil extracted using heat and solvents and then refined by removing acid, colour and odours. Used extensively for frying as oils or in manufacture of margarine and other fats.

* Produced in UK

Figure 12.21 *Main components of oil from vegetable source*

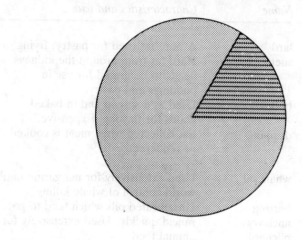

Saturated portion

Figure 12.22 *Main components of fat from animal source*

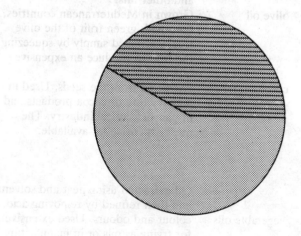

Saturated portion

2. *Margarine production* Since the process of hydrogenation was developed, which allowed liquid lipids to be changed to solid lipids, the glut of vegetable oil on the market has been used extensively to manufacture margarine. Hydrogenated fat, water, flavour, colour, emulsifiers and stabilisers are mixed together and then *plasticised* – a process which is a combination of cooling and kneading and which enables a suitable texture to be formed.

3. *Bakery fats* The technology of hydrogenation and the development of plasticity has led to the development of a whole range of products designed for the specific requirements of different bakery goods. Many of these are white as colour can be introduced into recipes from egg or other ingredients. A good example is the fat which is produced for puff-pastry. It is so *plastic* that it can be rolled out like plasticine and literally placed between layers of paste!

Beverages

1. *Cocoa and chocolate*

Derived from the seeds of the tree *Theobroma cacao* originally from South America. The Aztec emperors were known to drink golden cups of 'foaming chocolate' – a mixture of cocoa bean, water, spices and pepper. The cocoa drink was prized for its energy value, stimulating power (caffeine) and aphrodisiac properties. Christopher Columbus brought cocoa beans to Europe in 1502 and the drink reached England in 1657 with sugar and milk replacing the pepper and water. Not until the mid-1900s was chocolate sold for eating. It is a concentrated form of energy widely used as an emergency ration by land, air and sea forces.

Nutritional value The nutritional value of chocolate is illustrated by Figure 12.23 below.

Figure 12.23 *Proportions of main nutrients in chocolate*

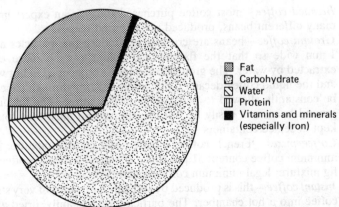

- Fat
- Carbohydrate
- Water
- Protein
- Vitamins and minerals (especially Iron)

Cocoa products Details of processing and the variety of products obtained from the cocoa bean are detailed in Figure 12.24, 12.25 and 12.26.

The use of couverture This is what the pastry chef will use to decorate gâteaux, etc. The high triglyceride content of cocoa butter makes this an easy product to melt and spread but when it sets it has usually lost its sheen and texture. The long factory process, perfected over the last two decades is still a skilled job in the kitchen. It is known as *tempering*. Techniques vary, but all include temperature control, in an effort to obtain the correct size and distribution of triglyceride crystals. See Figure 12.25

2. Coffee

Produced from two main species of the tropical tree, *Coffea arabica* (*arabica* beans) and *Coffea canephora* (*robusta* beans) the former being the better quality. The tree produces red berries on its stem (like holly) each of which contains two 'coffee' seeds. The seeds at this stage are green and when roasted become brown. The longer the roasting the stronger the flavour. The roasted beans are ground so that when hot water is applied their flavour can be extracted easily.

Coffee took Europe by storm in the 1630s when seeds from Ethiopia were used to produce coffee for the new fashionable coffee houses of London and cafés of Paris. Despite condemnation by various religious sects (which still practise abstinence today) because of its caffeine content, its popularity has grown. Today Europe consumes 55 per cent of world supplies of which three-quarters is produced in Latin America.

Nutritional value the nutritional value of coffee, without milk or sugar, is negligible. It does however have strong stimulant action.

Coffee types

(a) *Blended coffee* – most coffee purchased today is an expert mix of many different beans, produced under brand names.
(b) *Ground coffee* – beans are crushed to produce fine particles about 1 mm wide so that the flavour and colour can be more easily extracted by water. The ground coffee must be steeped in hot water and the liquid coffee decanted off, filtered slowly through paper, or be constantly allowed to percolate over the coffee. The flavour of ground beans will easily be lost on storage and must therefore be kept in sealed containers.
(c) *Coffee mixes* 'French coffee' – coffee and chicory mixture: legal minimum coffee content 51 per cent; 'Viennese coffee' – coffee and fig mixture: legal minimum coffee content 85 per cent.
(d) *Instant coffee* – this is produced by spraying a fine mist of very strong coffee into a hot chamber. The particles are 'instantly' dried and a

Figure 12.24 *The production of cocoa*

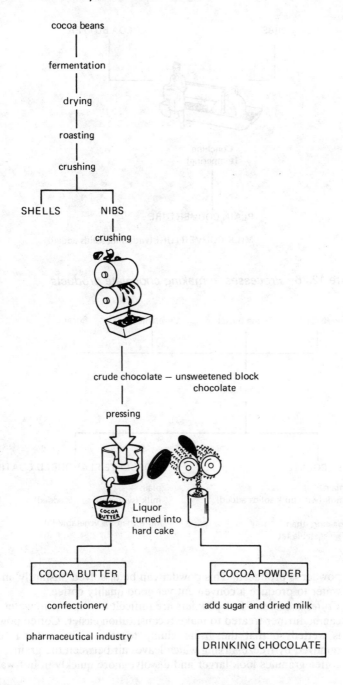

cocoa beans

|

fermentation

|

drying

roasting

crushing

SHELLS   NIBS

crushing

crude chocolate — unsweetened block
chocolate

|

pressing

Liquor
turned into
hard cake

| COCOA BUTTER | | COCOA POWDER |

confectionery   add sugar and dried milk

pharmaceutical industry

| DRINKING CHOCOLATE |

320

Figure 12.25 *The production of chocolate couverture*

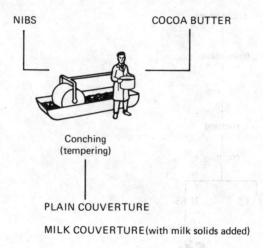

NIBS

COCOA BUTTER

Conching
(tempering)

PLAIN COUVERTURE

MILK COUVERTURE(with milk solids added)

Figure 12.26 *Processes in making chocolate products*

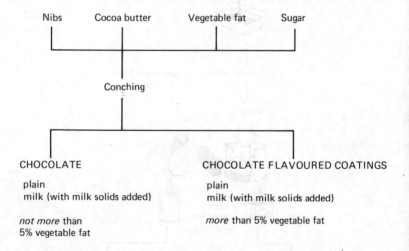

Nibs   Cocoa butter   Vegetable fat   Sugar

Conching

CHOCOLATE

plain
milk (with milk solids added)

not more than
5% vegetable fat

CHOCOLATE FLAVOURED COATINGS

plain
milk (with milk solids added)

more than 5% vegetable fat

powder is produced. This powder can be dissolved 'instantly' in hot water to produce a convenient yet good quality coffee.
(e) *Coffee granules* – fine powders are difficult to disperse in water and can be further treated to make reconstitution easier. Coffee powder is wetted so that the grains clump together. The water is then removed by freeze–drying which leaves air between the grains. The coffee granules look larger and dissolve more quickly in hot water.

(f) *Decaffeinated coffee* – green coffee beans can be treated before roasting to remove the stimulant caffeine.
(g) *Espresso* – made by forcing steam and water through ground coffee to produce a very fast cup of coffee. The speed at which coffee could be served led to the popularisation of this Italian technique. Since the introduction of instant coffee it has declined in popularity.
(h) *Coffee essence* – concentrated coffee used for flavouring.

3. Tea

Tea is obtained from the leaves of the evergreen bush *Camellia sinensis* which grows in tropical and sub-tropical areas of the world. The Chinese were the first people to discover that a drink could be made from the dried leaves of the tea plant; they called it *cha*. It was brought to England in the seventeenth century and became popular. Over a hundred years ago tea plants were cultivated in the mountains of India and Sri Lanka (Ceylon) with great success and now most of the tea we drink comes from areas, such as Darjeeling and Assam, in these countries.

Types and grades of tea   The three types of tea are black, green and oolong. The differences between them relates only to the method of processing. Leaves from a single plant may yield any of these types. In the production of black tea the leaves are rolled to release the juices which are oxidised by the air (as a cut apple browns) to a coppery red colour. This process is called fermentation and is followed by drying which produces a very dark coloured leaf. Green tea is unfermented and dried while green, preserving its colour. Oolong is semi-fermented so it has some of the characteristics of both black and green tea. Black tea represents 98 per cent of the world market.

The grades of tea are determined by the size of the leaves and their position on the stem of the plant. Table 12.23 outlines the main categories of tea. After drying all tea is sieved in four sizes, the largest being the whole leaf and the smallest – termed dust – is often used in tea bags.

Tea is shipped to its destination in airtight boxes and then blended by experts to give the properties required by the retail market.

Purchasing tea   Tea may be sold under brand names, country of origin, (e.g. Ceylon, China); area of origin (e.g. Darjeeling); leaf quality (e.g. Pekoe); or size (dust, whole, leaf). Overall quality may well be difficult to predict and trial and error are usually employed to find suitable teas for specific catering needs.

Nutritional value   The nutritional value of tea, without milk and sugar, is negligible. It does, however, have stimulant properties.

Table 12.23 *Types of tea*

Type	Process	Grading	Names
Black*	fermentation drying	Young, orange tinted leaves from tip of stem	Orange pekoe
		Leaves from middle of stem	Pekoe
		Larger leaves from base of stem	Souchong
Oolong	semi-fermented drying	any leaf	Oolong
Green	drying only	smallest leaves rolled into balls	Gunpowder
		medium-sized leaves rolled lengthwise	Young hyson
		large leaves rolled into balls	Imperial

* Black teas are sometimes scented by the addition of dried blossoms such as Jasmine. Earl Grey is an example of a scented tea.

Flavours

The flavour of food can be described as a mixture of smell and taste and has a great influence on the acceptability of foods. Flavourings used in foods can be classed as one of the following:

1. natural flavourings;
2. synthetic flavourings;
3. flavour enhancers.

1. *Natural flavourings* Many plants have parts which are strong-smelling and can be described as *aromatic*. Over the centuries cooks have found that the use of some of these have enhanced the flavour/colour of certain foods. Those plants grown in *tropical climates* are generally referred to as producing *spices* and those grown in *temperate climates* are termed *herbs*. Some plants produce a very concentrated oil which can be extracted to produce odorous liquids. They are termed *essential oils* and some have been used to flavour foods whilst others are used in the perfume industry.

(a) *Herbs* are usually the leaves or stems of temperate plants and are therefore often green in colour. Many herbs have a medicinal role but this section will deal only with those which have a well-established use in cookery (see Table 12.24).

(b) *Spices* can be derived from many parts of tropical plants and are usually available in powder form. Some – such as cayenne – are very strong whilst others have only a mild flavour. Many spices (e.g.

Table 12.24 *Herb chart: A caterer's guide*

Name	(1)	(2)	Examples of uses
Angelica	C	3	confectionery decoration, sweets
Balm	B	1	beverages
Basil	B	125	pasta, salads
Bay	B	26	bouquet garni, syrups
Bergamot	B	12	salads, beverages
Borage	AB	1	Pimm's cup, salads
Bouquet garni	CB	12	(parsley stalk, bay and thyme branch)
Burnet	B	1	salads, beverages, sauces
Camomile	A	2	tea
Celery	BC	16	Irish stew, soups, celery salt
Chervil	B	12	decoration, salads
Chives	C	12	salads, omelettes, hors-d'oeuvre
Comfrey	AB	1	beverages
Costmary	B	2	soups, game and veal dishes
Curry leaf	B	1	curry
Fennel	CD	12	fish, salads, stuffings, curry
Fenugreek	BD	1	salads, curry
Hop	A	1	salads, tea
Lemon balm	B	12	salads, beverages
Lovage	CDE	13	confectionery
Marigold	A	1	rice, soups, salads
Marjoram	B	12	omelettes, soups, stews
Mint	B	12	sauce, salads, curry, chutneys
Oregano	AB	12	pizza
Parsley	BC	126	bouquet garni, garnishing
Rosemary	B	2	veal and lamb dishes
Sage	B	2	pork and duck stuffings
Sorrel	B	1	soup
Tarragon	BC	124	Béarnaise sauce, fish dishes
Thyme	B	12	soups, stews

Key:(1) *Parts used*:   (2) *State*:
    A. Flower   1. Fresh
    B. Leaves   2. Dried
    C. Stem   3. Candied
    D. Seeds   4. Pickled
    E. Roots   5. In oil
                6. Powdered

paprika and turmeric) are used for colour as well as flavour (see Table 12.25).

(c) *Essential oils* are available in liquid form usually in small bottles. Examples include oil of peppermint, vanilla, orange and lemon.

Table 12.25 *Spice chart*

Name	(1)	(2)	Examples of use
All spice	C	12	pickling, confectionery, savoury dishes
Aniseed	AB	12	confectionery
Caraway	C	1	confectionery, savoury dishes, cheese, curry
Cardamom	CD	1	rice dishes, curry
Cassia	E	1	confectionery
Cayenne	C	2	stews, oysters, whitebait, curry, cheese, shrimps
Chilli	G	2	stews, curry, meat dishes
Cinnamon	E	12	curry, syrups, confectionery, rice dishes
Cloves	D	12	confectionery, pickling, beverages, curry, rice dishes
Coriander	D	12	curry, pickles, à la grecque, lamb and pork stews
Cumin	D	12	curry, pickles, rice dishes
Dill	D	1	fish, egg dishes, sauces
Fenugreek	D	12	curry, (this can be classified as herb or spice)
Ginger	F	123	confectionery, melon, beverages, all meat curries
Horseradish	F	13	sauce
Juniper	D	1	sauerkraut, game and pork dishes
Mace	E	12	savoury pies
Methi	D	1	curry, rice dishes
Mixed Spice		2	caraway/cloves/nutmeg/mace/cinnamon/coriander/ginger
Mustard	D	1	mayonnaise, meat dishes
Nutmeg	D	12	sweets, mashed potato
Paprika	G	2	goulash, cheese dishes, chicken dishes, soups, curry
Pepper	G	12	savoury dishes
Poppy	D	1	bread, confectionery, beverages
Saffron	B	12	rice, paella, bouillabaisse, cakes, soups
Spearmint	A	1	peas
Tamarind	C	1	some vegetable curries
Turmeric	F	12	curry, pickles
Vanilla	C	1	sweets, ices

Key: (1) *Parts used*   *State*
     A. Leaves   1. Whole
     B. Flowers   2. Powdered
     C. Pod   3. Pickled
     D. Seeds
     E. Bark
     F. Roots
     G. Fruit

Synthetic forms of some of these oils are available. The term essence or flavouring is used for natural and synthetic flavours and the caterer would need to ask the supplier for details. There are currently hundreds of flavours on the market with no details as to their origin and the government will eventually introduce labelling legislation for consumer information and safety.

(d) *Alcoholic beverages* usually have a flavour suitable for cooking. Some examples are given in Table 12.26.

Table 12.26 *Alcoholic beverages*

Name	Flavour and/or base	Example of use
Bénédictine	various herbs	soufflés
Beer	hops	Carbonnade de Boeuf
Brandy	wine	Pêche flambé
Champagne	Champagne grapes	Saumon au champagne
Chartreuse	various herbs	ice sweets
Crème de Menthe	mint	soufflés
Curaçao	orange	Crêpes Suzette
Grand Marnier	orange	Soufflé Grand Marnier
Kirsch	cherry	melon, pineapple
Madeira	Madeira grapes	Madeira sauce
Maraschino	cherry	Grapefruit Maraschino
Rum	molasses	Babas au rhum
Sherry	grapes	Sherry trifle
Whisky	barley	Chicken à la King

2. *Synthetic flavourings* Natural flavours are complex mixtures of a number of chemicals, often occurring in very small quantities. They are therefore very difficult to reproduce synthetically. Synthetic flavourings are substances that can be prepared in laboratories and used to flavour food. They are either:

(a) *synthetically prepared nature-identical compounds* which are exact copies of one or more of the components found in any natural flavour e.g. *citric acid* – one of the major components in citrus fruits; *vanillin* – the main component of oil of vanilla. They are often cheaper to produce but inferior to natural flavours.
(b) *artificial food flavours not found in nature* are substitute chemicals which are totally different chemicals which happen to have a flavour resembling a natural product, e.g. saccharin – 300 times as sweet as the sugar sucrose; ethyl vanillin – an ester with a flavour similar to vanillin.

3. *Flavour enhancers* Some substances have the ability to increase or enhance the natural flavour of food without contributing to the flavour itself, e.g. *salt* – substance used since antiquity, around the world, to increase the palatability of both savoury and sweet foods; *Monosodium glutamate* (MSG). This substance has been used in the Far East (in the form of seaweed) for centuries. The refined chemical is used extensively in processed food to enhance the meaty flavour of savoury items. In this form it has been associated with allergic responses in some people.

Colours

Colours can be added to food to enhance colour, produce new colours, or to maintain uniformity of colour. This latter aspect has become of considerable importance as the processing of food has expanded this century. Within catering the use of colours is not widespread, except for decorative purposes, and this could well be a point which could be marketed more effectively. The commonly used colouring agents can be grouped into two categories (i) synthetic compounds; and (ii) natural colours from animal/vegetable origin.

1. *Synthetic compounds*   Over a hundred years ago coal-tar dyes were developed for the textile industry and their advantages soon became apparent to the food industry. Many are now thought to be toxic with long-term health hazards such as cancer a possibility. The EC is gradually reducing the number in use and it seems likely that the use of all coal-tar dyes – e.g. tartrazine, sunset yellow, Red G – in food will eventually be prohibited.

2. *Natural compounds*   There has been renewed interest and research in the use of natural colours because of consumer anxiety about coal-tar dyes. They are however more prone to colour breakdown, being adversely affected by air, light and heat which explains why the few synthetic colours still allowed are used predominantly. Examples of natural food colours are: annatto (derived from a type of palm); caramel blackjack (from sugar); cochineal (from an insect); saffron (from a species of crocus), and chlorophyll (from green leaves).

The pressure from consumer groups has recently mobilised a lot of companies to remove synthetic colours from food which is specifically intended for children. There are fish fingers on the market, for example, which are coloured with turmeric/annatto and sausages coloured with cochineal. The black tasteless product derived traditionally from burning sugar, legally termed caramel, is an inexpensive way of colouring most meat products *naturally*.

NUTRITION AT WORK

13.1 INTRODUCTION

Nutrition is the study of food in relation to health. The main body of nutritional knowledge is barely a century old and is still far from understood. It is for this reason that there is such debate and controversy over food-related issues. Harold McGee, a well-known American author, aptly describes the development of the nutritional fads, which do little to promote the basic guidelines of good nutrition education:

> The pattern is predictable: scientists open up a new area of knowledge, and before it has been entirely explored and understood, the popular theorists exploit it as the long awaited Answer. When proteins, carbohydrates and fats were the only known nutrients, fads centered on each of them. Vitamins are discovered, and out come the Vitamin Bibles. Along comes fibre, and along comes the life-saving high fibre diet. (*The Cooking and Love of Food*, London: George Allen & Unwin, 1984)

The message is clear, a little patience and moderation are called for!

13.2 THE NUTRIENTS AND A HEALTHY DIET

Food must supply the body with ingredients, needed for everyday function, which it cannot manufacture itself. These essential ingredients are termed *nutrients*. Some are required in small amounts, others in larger quantities, but without any one of them the body cannot function. The main nutrients are outlined in Tables 13.1 and 13.2. The detail is not exhaustive and some of it may be controversial, but it serves merely to guide the caterer into an appreciation of the primary role of the food which he prepares.

Table 13.1 Sugars, starches, fats, proteins: a catering guide

	Sugars	Starches	Protein		Fibre	Fats	
			Animal	Vegetable		Saturated	Unsaturated
Source	Sugary foods; cakes, drinks Sugar, jams, sweets, honey	Cereals: bread, flour, and other products. Sago, tapioca, cassava, potato, etc.	Meat, eggs, cheese, milk, fish, poultry, etc.	Bread and other cereals, nuts, pulses, etc.	(1) Fruit and vegetables (2) Unrefined cereals	Butter, eggs, milk, cheese, meat	Vegetable oils, soft margarine, nuts, fish, poultry
Function	A source of *energy*, readily available to the body. Some involved in structure of cells; others have physiological function e.g. hormone production	Source of *energy*. Forms the staple diet of most of the world's population	(1) Essential for growth and repair (2) Forms major part of: enzymes, hormones and antibodies (3) Produces energy for the body. (cf. 13.6) Excess protein in the diet is converted to sugar by the body. This is an expensive way of obtaining energy.		Aids the passage of food through the intestines. Small proportion of fibre digested by the action of bacteria in the intestine. This is important physiologically but has little effect on the total energy value of the diet.	Concentrated energy store for the body. Especially useful for growing children or very active adults. Also contains: (1) Essential fatty acids – important for brain development. (2) Vitamins A, D, E, K (3) Cholesterol (found in animal fats)	
Health issues	(1) Dental caries are probably increased as a result of eating sticky sweet foods.	Implicated in obesity, but this is unlikely to be the main cause because of bulky natures of starchy food.	Overdose effects from taking excessive intakes of protein are unknown.		*Shortage* of fibre, (particularly from cereals) has been implicated in diabetes, heart disease,	(1) Obesity – excessive energy intake can lead to obesity (2) Heart disease – fats have been strongly implicated in	

	Sugar	Starch	Protein	Fibre	Fat
Effects	(2) Heart disease: sugar has been implicated. (3) Appetite depressants: small quantities of sugar can reduce consumption of other valuable nutrients. (4) Junk food – sugar is a major component of *unbalanced foods* containing many calories but few other nutrients. (5) Excessive intake can lead to obesity.			cancer of colon, bowel disorders, etc.	the debate concerning heart disease. Saturated (animal) fats have been associated with a high level of blood cholesterol – an indicator of heart disease. Relevance now questioned as blood cholesterol levels appear to fluctuate independently of dietary intake. The debate continues. (3) Cancer – polysaturated recently implicated in cancer; monosaturates, such as olive oil, now recommended by some nutritionalists
Government recommendations	Average sugar intake should be reduced	No specific recommendations, but if sugar and fat are cut, more energy foods in form of starchy food will have to be included in the diet.	Intake not altered but a greater percentage from vegetable sources has been recommended.	Recommendations suggest fibre should be increased from 20g to 30g per day	Total fat intake reduced to provide 30 per cent of energy requirement. Saturated fats to account for only 10 per cent of energy intake. No recommendations for lowering cholesterol.
Implications for caterers	Diabetic diets Low calorie sweeteners, desserts, drinks	More starchy foods in diet Fewer processed foods	Vegetarian diets More use of nuts, pulses and other vegetable proteins	High-fibre diets Wholemeal bread, pastry, pasta, cereals, etc.	Low-fat diets Low-cholesterol diets Less saturated fat. (i.e. less from animal sources).

Table 13.2 *Vitamins and Minerals: a catering guide*

Nutrients	Common sources	Function	Deficiency	Excess	Incidence	Implications for caterers
Vitamin C *Ascorbic acid*	*Plant* Fresh fruit Fresh vegetables (potatoes a regular source) *Animal* Very small quantities in liver/fish roe	Essential for the *cementing* substance in bones, teeth, connective tissue and blood vessels. Needed for absorption of iron. (Used extensively in food manufacture as an antioxidant and as a bread improver) *No proof* that Vitamin C cures colds	*Mild* Tendency to bruise easily; slow healing of wounds; lowered resistance to infection; tooth decay *Severe* Scurvy: internal bleeding, weakened muscles, soft spongy gums, pain in joints, tooth loss, death	Excess forms oxalic acid stones in the kidneys	*Deficiency not uncommon:* (a) elderly who do not eat enough fruit and vegetables. (b) long-term hospitalisation can produce symptoms. (c) disease and related drug therapy can produce symptoms	(1) No store in body: fruit and vegetables must be consumed daily. (2) Easily destroyed by: storage – loss by oxidation chopping – loss by oxidation soaking – loss in water cooking – loss by action of heat Holding – loss by action of heat (cf Chapter 9)
The B Vitamins *Thiamine B1*	*Plant* Unrefined cereals Fortified cereal products Pulses *Animal* Lean meat Offal	Works with enzymes to release energy from foods	*Mild* Weight loss, fatigue, emotional disturbance *Severe* Beri beri: muscular degeneration, heart irregularities, emaciation or oedema	High doses may cause deficiency in other B vitamins.	Deficiency became common in nineteenth century Asia as a result of milling the cereals which formed the staple diet, ie. polished rice. Common in alcoholics whose diet contains insufficient thiamine to metabolise the energy content of alcoholic drinks. Linked with antisocial/aggressive behaviour of US adolescents who have lived on highly refined (junk) food.	(1) No store in body – must be consumed every day (2) Easily destroyed by heat and lost in cooking liquids (water soluble)

	Sources	Function / Metabolism	Deficiency	Overdose	Notes	Storage
Niacin B2	*Plant* Unrefined cereals Fortified cereal products Pulses *Animal* Meat Offal	Amount required relates directly with consumption of energy foods.	*Mild–severe* Pellagra: diarrhoea; depression; dermatitis	*Overdose* risks include duodenal ulcer, abnormal liver function and high blood sugar	Deficiency associated with the spread of maize, as a staple diet, across America and Third World *without* the traditional cooking procedures which allowed niacin to be utilised. Decline now due to introduction of mixed diets.	(1) No store in body – must be consumed every day (2) Stable to heat of cooking but lost in cooking liquids (water soluble)
Riboflavin	*Plant* Green vegetables Marmite Fortified cereal products *Animal* Liver Eggs Meat extract Fresh milk	If sufficient quantities are not eaten, toxic substances build up in the muscle as energy foods cannot be metabolised.	*Mild* Growth slow; lesions on lips and eyes, scaly skin	High doses may cause deficiency in other B vitamins	Deficiency prevalent in the very poor across the world, and alcoholics (see above)	(1) No store in body – must be consumed every day. (2) Stable to heat but lost in cooking liquids (water soluble) (3) Destroyed by ultra-violet light

Table 13.2 *Vitamins and Minerals: a catering guide*

Nutrients	Common sources	Function	Deficiency	Excess	Incidence	Implications for caterers
Pyridoxine B6	Widespread in meat, vegetables and cereals	Needed for protein metabolism Formation of anti-bodies and haemoglobin	Tiredness/ depression Anaemia Tooth decay	Large doses may bring de- pendency leading to deficiency when one returns to normal amounts.	Requirements increase enormously whilst taking oral contraceptives or during pregnancy. Deficiency symptoms often develop during pregnancy, especially dental caries (free dental care for pregnant women in UK).	(1) No store in body – must be consumed daily (2) Increase foods rich in B6 if feeding pregnant/lactating women. (3) Lost in cooking liquid.
Folic Acid	*Plant* Dark green leaves of vegetables *Animal* Liver White fish	Needed for protein metabolism and formation of haemoglobin	Anaemia	No risk identified.	Deficiency often develops during pregnancy due to increased requirements. In UK folic acid/ iron supplements are advised during this time. Mild deficiency may be widespread. Absorption affected by some drugs.	(1) Heat-sensitive and water-soluble – 90 per cent usually lost by cooking (2) No store in body (3) Rich food sources to feature on daily menus (4) Minimum cooking and holding

Vitamin	Sources	Function	Deficiency	Excess	Notes	Conservation
Cyanocobalamine B12	*Animal* Meat Dairy produce (animal foods only)	Needed for the development of the nervous system	Damage to digestive system and spinal cord. The disease *pernicious anaemia* can be cured by Vitamin B12. Lack of B12 is not the cause of pernicious anaemia, the symptoms of which develop spontaneously and are unrelated to dietary habits.	Large doses may bring dependency leading to deficiency when one returns to normal amounts	Vegan vegetarians at risk from deficiency. Lacto- vegetarians drinking milk and eating milk products are not affected.	(1) Minimum cooking and holding times (2) Incorporate milk/milk products in meals for vegetarians
Vitamin A *Retinol*	*Animal* Dairy foods Fortified margarine Liver *Plant* Beta-carotene, found in green and orange plants, converted to retinol in the body. *Supplement* Fish liver oils	Essential for: (1) health of tissue lining the throat, eyes, lungs, etc (2) production of retinol pigment	*Mild* Dryness of skin, poor teeth formation, *lowered resistance to infections* Night blindness *Severe* Xerophthalmia (scaling of eyes) Blindness Sterility	Excess is toxic causing headache; dizziness; hair loss; loss of appetite; yellowing of skin Can be fatal *Overdoses* caused by over-use of supplements particularly common in children and health faddists	Mild *deficiency* possible in winter months. Also caused by disorders of the digestive tract.	(1) Store maintained in body. (2) Not lost from foods during cooking (3) Diet in winter may be inadequate. Maintain supply of fresh vegetables.

Table 13.2 *Vitamins and Minerals: a catering guide*

Nutrients	Common sources	Function	Deficiency	Excess	Incidence	Implications for caterers
Vitamin D *Calciferol*	*Diet* Limited supply from margarine, oily fish, eggs, butter *Sunlight* Human body adapted to produce Vitamin D by action of sunlight on skin. The pigment melanin develops if over-exposure occurs. *Supplement* Fish liver oils	(1) Aids absorption of calcium and phosphorus (2) Works with calcium and phosphorus to develop bones and teeth	*Mild* Lowered resistance to infection *Severe* Rickets (in children): bending of soft bones in legs due to increasing weight of body Osteomalacia (in adults): fragile bones, rheumatoid pains	Excess is toxic causing nausea; vomiting; headache Calcium can be deposited in soft tissue in the form of stones	(1) *Deficiency* found in housebound particularly the elderly and children not exposed to sunlight. Consecutive poor summers in the UK have led to recent reports of subclinical deficiency in the north (usually associated with a calcium deficient diet) (2) *Overdoses* caused by over-use of supplements, particularly in children	(1) Caterers involved with elderly and long stay hospital patients must monitor vitamin D levels in diet. Regularly include vitamin D rich foods, particularly in winter months. (2) Store maintained in body. (3) Not lost from foods during cooking
Vitamin E *Tocopherol*	Found mostly in plants, especially grains and pulses. *Supplement* Wheatgrain oil	Essential for a range of activities in other animals including reproduction, but its function or deficiency in man not clear. It is a powerful anti-oxidant and has been used to reduce scar tissue and in the treatment of muscular dystrophy, heart disease, sterility, etc.		General effect includes malaise and fatigue. May affect hormonal system	Rare	
Vitamin K *naphthoquinone*	*Food* Widespread *Body* Bacteria in gut produce adequate quantity of Vitamin K	Maintain blood circulation system in good order	Haemorrhaging and poor blood clotting	May cause jaundice in infants	(1) Antibiotics destroy the bacteria required for the synthesis of this vitamin. (2) Digestive disorders may affect the absorption of this vitamin	

	Sources	Function	Deficiency	Excess	Notes / at risk	Recommendations
Minerals						
Calcium	*Animal* Dairy products, Fish eaten with bones; *Plant* Fortified cereal products	Works with Vitamin D to produce strong bones and teeth. Essential for blood-clotting and muscle contraction	As for vitamin D	Excess calcium deposited in soft tissues	Rickets prevalent in some community groups. Osteomalacia not uncommon amongst elderly	as for Vitamin D
Iron	*Animal* Meat, offal; *Plant* Cocoa powder, spinach legumes, dried fruit	Needed for haemoglobin formation	anaemia	Liver damage (siderosis)	Deficiency common in female adolescents, pregnant/lactating mothers and the bedridden	Caterers involved in feeding groups *at risk* should incorporate foods rich in iron in the diet
Sodium (salt)	Table salt, Processed and preserved foods	Needed for all cell activities and muscle action	Muscular cramps.	Young children have immature kidneys which cannot cope with excess salt	Linked with high blood pressure in adults	(1) Do not add salt to infant foods. (2) restrict use of salt in all meals.

13.3 MALNUTRITION

This is a term used to describe the effects of *bad nutrition*, although commonly associated with starvation. Throughout the world people are *under-* or *over-*nourished through lack of food, poverty, or poor food choices. It is a common misconception that malnutrition is a condition which afflicts only underdeveloped countries and therefore this text concentrates on diet-related diseases commonplace in the UK.

Primitive man had no knowledge of the nutrients but he survived. This is because the body has an inborn mechanism for selecting foods to maintain health. Modern malnutrition, except in the cases of extreme food shortages, stems from a wide range of socio-economic factors which have almost destroyed our ability to feed ourselves properly. This is why nutrition education is so important, at all levels, in the community. The most powerful medicine in the treatment of malnutrition is food itself – eat properly and, other things being equal, you will be healthy.

A healthy diet

The model of a balanced diet, with foods from each food group outlined in Figure 13.1, is a well-established method of teaching nutrition. The fact that for some community groups certain types of food are best restricted, does not detract from the worldwide use and success of this model. *Inclusive* rather than *exclusive* nutritional models are more likely to produce successful dietary changes.

13.4 NUTRITIONAL STATUS IN THE UK

This country, like many others, has seen an increase in diet-related diseases such as heart disease and diabetes. The government has responded by issuing dietary guidelines which are discussed in Chapter 3 and in later sections in this chapter. These recommendations, however, do little for the members of the community who fail to obtain their dietary needs because of isolation, lack of finance, inadequate education, illness, or long stints in institutions with poor feeding patterns.

Nutritional problems experienced in this country are often *long term*, they build up slowly and have effects years later. Just as people cannot give up smoking because they *may* be ill in the future, so do they not feel immediately threatened by poor diets. A mild state of malnutrition, for example, might allow a person to catch an infection more easily than if he were well-fed. Even if this results in his death, no one is likely to know that malnutrition was to blame.

Figure 13.1 A balanced diet

Use this food guide to make sure that you are eating all the right foods your body needs.
Include a variety of foods from each group every day.

FRUIT AND VEGETABLES

Aim to have a variety of these for vitamins, minerals and fibre.
* Have some raw fruit or raw vegetables daily
* Cook vegetables quickly in a small amount of water to save vitamins

MILK, CHEESE AND YOGHURT

Have daily to provide protein and calcium for strong bones.

FILL UP ON THESE

Have at least
4 servings daily
A serving could be:
1 fresh fruit   1 potato
1 portion vegetables

For a balanced meal have foods from at least 3 different groups

Have 2 servings daily
A serving could be:
1 glass milk
1 carton yoghurt
1 slice cheese

Have at least
4 servings daily
A serving could be:
1 slice of bread
1 bowl of cereal
4 tbs rice or pasta

Have 2-3 servings daily
A serving could be:
2 slices meat
1 fish portion
½ tin beans

BREAD AND CEREALS

Eat these for energy, B-Vitamins and iron, they also provide fibre for healthy bowels.
* Go for wholemeal bread and wholegrain cereals
* Try brown rice and pasta

MEAT, FISH, EGGS, BEANS AND NUTS

Include daily to provide protein for strength, iron and B-Vitamins for healthy blood.
* Use poultry, offal and fish
* Add beans to casseroles and stews

Nutrient supplements

As already mentioned, the cure for malnutrition is the development of correct eating patterns. Gross overeating, and diet-related diseases, may involve special diets to remedy this particular problem but the use of supplements is unnecessary. An alarming modern trend – for mothers to prescribe vitamins and minerals for their children – is at best a waste of money and at worst a health hazard. Nutrient deficiencies should be remedied by adding rich food sources into normal meals.

Nutritional analysis

One of the best ways of assessing dietary adequacy is to check nutrient intake against standards for similar individuals. Computer software has made such analysis and interpretation a manageable task for all concerned with menu planning. An example of the information obtained from such software within minutes, can be seen in Figure 13.2.

It is important that information obtained from such analysis is used in conjunction with sound cookery principles described elsewhere in this book. Cooked potatoes, for example, will have no Vitamin C in them if they have been peeled the previous day and soaked all night, no matter what the computer printout says!

13.5 THE ROLE OF THE CATERER

Supplying meals of high nutritional quality for people on an *occasional* basis, in hotels and restaurants, has traditionally been of little concern to customer or caterer. However, recent interest by consumers in healthy eating, has made this an area of increasing priority. If customers can clearly see the contents of food they are buying in shops, which current legislation is encouraging, they may well soon demand the same information of food eaten out. Indeed, some caterers already offer nutritional information on menus and this trend is likely to continue (see Plate 13.1).

Caterers preparing meals for people who eat *regularly* in institutions such as schools, prisons, hospitals or work canteens must accept a high level of nutritional responsibility. Ideally, the caterers should have access to computer analysis, and carefully monitor the standard of nutrition which they offer. Whilst they cannot dictate to clients exactly what they are to eat, they should make every effort to provide acceptable, safe and balanced meals.

The future

Undoubtedly the catering industry will have to pay more attention to nutrition than it does at present. It will need (i) to employ people who can competently plan balanced menus for all nutritional groups (see

Figure 13.2 *Computer nutritional analysis*

```
ANALYSIS RESULTS - middle school                06-20-1988/20:55:59   Page   1

Average of all days/weeks
------------------------------------------------------------------------------
NAME        - ssm
AGE         - 008         ACTIVITY    - Slight
SEX         - Male        HEIGHT      - 130.00
PREGNANT    -             WEIGHT      -  20.00
LACTATING   -             BMI FACTOR  -  11.83
RDA GROUP   - 7 to 8 years old
------------------------------------------------------------------------------
                    NUTRIENT  RELATIONSHIPS
    Energy Derivation                  Important Ratios
% energy FAT........     38.15         Na/K ratio..........   667.02
    % energy MUFA...     11.30         Poly/Sat Fat Ratio..     0.27
    % energy PUFA...      3.40         Na as SALT in......g     1.69
    % energy SFA....     12.47
% energy CHO........     47.43
    % energy S & D..     24.01
    % energy Sugar..     16.20
% energy PROTEIN....     14.42
------------------------------------------------------------------------------
                      amount              percentage
Nutrient              consumed     RDA     of RDA    Nutrient
ENERGY..........Kcal     557       1980      28%     ENERGY..........Kcal
FAT.................g     23.62                       FAT.................g
Total PUFA.........g      2.10  *                     Total PUFA.........g
Total MUFA.........g      6.99  *                     Total MUFA.........g
Total SFA..........g      7.72  *                     Total SFA..........g
CARBOHYDRATE.......g     70.46                        CARBOHYDRATE.......g
SUGAR..............g     24.06  *                     SUGAR..............g
STARCH & DEXTRIN...g     35.67  *                     STARCH & DEXTRIN...g
DIETARY FIBRE......g      6.38  *   15.00   42.52%    DIETARY FIBRE......g
PROTEIN............g     20.08  *   49.00   40.99%    PROTEIN............g
CALCIUM..........mg      272     *   600      45%     CALCIUM..........mg
SODIUM...........mg      667     *  1350      49%     SODIUM...........mg
IRON.............mg      3.00    *  10.00   29.99%    IRON.............mg
VIT A (Ret.eq.)..mcg     255     *   400      64%     VIT A (Ret.eq.)..mcg
VITAMIN D........mcg     0.830   *                    VITAMIN D........mcg
THIAMIN (B1)......mg     0.34    *   0.80   42.87%    THIAMIN (B1)......mg
RIBOFLAVIN (B2)...mg     0.41    *   1.00   41.05%    RIBOFLAVIN (B2)...mg
NIC. AC. eq.......mg     8.13    *  11.00   73.94%    NIC. AC. eq.......mg
VITAMIN C.........mg      17     *    20      85%     VITAMIN C.........mg
FOLIC ACID(Total)mcg     52      *   200      26%     FOLIC ACID(Total)mcg
```

13.2); (ii) to instruct catering staff on how to prepare nutritious food; (iii) to advise customers on dietary matters and, (iv) to provide nutritional information and accept nutritional responsibility for meals consumed on the premises and therefore, the health of their clientele.

13.6 COMMUNITY NUTRITION

Whilst everyone needs the nutrients discussed in 13.2 the requirements of individuals differ widely. Unfortunately, the emphasis in catering education has been placed more on memorising the details of the

340

Plate 13.1 *Menu with nutritional data*

nutrients (a mind-boggling task!) rather than *how*, *when* and in what *quantity* they need to be supplied. The following detail aims to give an insight into the adjustments necessary to successfully nourish a few, of the many, nutritional distinct groups within our community.

Young children

Children have a rapid rate of growth and need large quantities of food in relation to their size. A 7-year-old child, for example, needs nearly as much energy, proteins and vitamins as an adult! It must be remembered that children come in all shapes and sizes and that if they are offered, regularly, a range of well-balanced meals they will eat sensibly and grow healthily. Caterers should not restrict a child's diet without instruction from the family doctor.

Number of meals

A child's stomach is small in comparison with the amount of food to be consumed. Four or five meals per day may be necessary to obtain the nutrients required.

Energy source

The importance of fat, as a concentrated source of energy, is often not appreciated. Many children in the Third World are malnourished because their only energy source is bulky carbohydrate. They simply cannot, physically, eat enough (over 3kg) to maintain requirements. Many parents in affluent countries relate their own dietary problems to their children and over-restrict fat intake.

Sugar

Sweet foods are appetite-depressants and can disrupt a child's feeding pattern. For example: a biscuit snack is given to a 2-year-old at mid-morning. This prevents an adequate intake of food at lunch-time. Within a short time the child feels hungry and is given another sweet snack whilst waiting for the next meal – a cycle of poor feeding is established. Sweets have the same effect on older children.

School meals

Hunger to a child, is disruptive both mentally and physically. Children do not have the body reserves that adults have and it is unreasonable to expect them to follow adult patterns of eating which often involve little breakfast, a snack lunch and a main meal in the evening. To overcome this difficulty most countries have a school meal service but, because of high running costs, many are inadequate. A British survey (D. P. Richardson and H. Lawson (1972) *British Medical Journal* 4, p. 697) concluded that 'the school lunch provides more energy and other nutrients than children obtain from sandwiches, snacks or going home to eat'. Of great importance in this situation, but one which is often overlooked, is the fact that hot food stimulates the appetite. It is more difficult to obtain the large quantity of necessary energy, for example, from cold bread than from hot potatoes.

Quality

The quality of meals for children, provided by caterers in this country, is constantly criticised. School meals in particular have come under attack but even in restaurants, many parents tuck into steak and fresh vegetables whilst their children are given small portions of food from a separate menu featuring fast food, high on calories, but often very low in other essential nutrients.

Many foods contain a variety of *additives* whose combined effect on the growing body is not known (see 13.7). Fresh foods should be used wherever possible and highly processed items avoided.

Education for life

Eating habits are established in childhood, and long-term health problems, associated with diet, may be avoided with this form of positive education. If children are offered, regularly, a range of balanced meals, they will grow healthily.

Rickets

This is prevalent amongst Muslim children of Asian origin living in the UK. The Save the Children organisation is working to promote better health education for this community. Rickets, in this context, is caused by a combination of factors:

(a) melanin pigmentation prevents dosage of vitamin D from the low levels of sunshine experienced in this country;
(b) traditional clothing allowing very little exposure to the sun;
(c) the social habit of small children staying indoors with their mothers for most of the day;
(d) often a vegetarian diet with very little milk.

Adolescents

The nutritional requirements of adolescents are determined by the *spurt* in growth which occurs at puberty. This is responsible, in boys, for an approximately 20cm gain in height and 18kg in weight. It is usually a little less in girls. This growth produces an increase in appetite which should be satisfied with more and/or larger meals. It is important that snacks – usually high in energy and low on other nutrients – do *not* replace meals. Unfortunately this is very common amongst adolescents in this country and a direct cause of imbalanced diets and tooth decay.

Two important conditions affect many of today's affluent youth: anorexia and obesity.

Anorexia

Cases of voluntary starvation, or *anorexia nervosa*, are increasing in number. It is a condition which dramatically affects the size of the body. It is psychological in nature and features a distorted body image and a state of permanent self-dissatisfaction. It is often associated with another disease, *bulimia*, where self-induced vomiting is used to control food intake. Whilst the cause for this irrational behaviour pattern, affecting one in every 500–700 British girls, is unclear, the severity of the problem is apparent. A reversal to health is not easy and many anorexics die – 'asking an anorexic to eat is like telling a man with pneumonia to stop coughing'.

Obesity

Obesity is becoming a common problem amongst many adolescents, both male and female. Anyone working with this age group knows well that the most significant feature of many adolescent diets is that it is imbalanced by the consumption of sweets, snacks and soft drinks. An American study clearly implicated the following features in the dietary patterns of the obese teenager:

(a) energy intake low;
(b) meals eaten less frequently than normal;
(c) meals missed frequently;
(d) physical output low;
(e) diet critically low in iron/calcium and B group vitamins.

The caterer involved in feeding this age group should take care to monitor nutritional standards with these points in mind.

Adults and diet-related diseases

In affluent societies blood cholesterol, blood pressure and body weight rise with age. These changes have been linked with later development of conditions such as obesity, diabetes, heart disease, bowel disorders and hypertension. The dietary factors implicated can be seen in Tables 13.1 and 13.2. Caterers need to be aware of these trends and to plan menus offering low-salt, low-fat, low-saturated fat, low-cholesterol, low-calorie dishes. Requests for such meals are likely to increase, rather than decrease, as we move into the next century. Heart disease, for example, is increasing rapidly and kills three in ten men and two in ten women in the UK.

Obesity

At the centre of the debate concerning diet-related diseases is the question of obesity. When maturity is reached (at approximately 22 years) growth-rate slows and food requirements are reduced. For many people the necessary dietary adjustments are difficult to make and *over-consumption* of food begins. Many modern life-styles, with little physical activity, reduce requirements further. Greater time and money for the purchase and consumption of food combine to aggravate this very common practice of overeating still further. In 1986 it was estimated that one in ten Britons were dieting to lose weight and that they spent £839m on slimming foods. (All this in a world where millions of people suffer from starvation!) Many new styles of cooking have emerged to promote a healthier image for food eaten out of the home (see Chapter 2) and there is certainly a profit to be made in catering for such customers!

Reducing diets

If weight-loss is advised by a doctor then the most effective diet is one that reduces the energy level below what is actually required. The body will then have to use some stored energy (fat!) to support normal activity. The level of *other nutrients must be maintained* to maintain health. It is ironic that the imbalance of nutrients, caused by simply cutting out certain foods, is likely to cause more problems than it solves. The reducing diet should be fully analysed for all nutrients – a tedious job without a computer – preferably with the help of a dietician.

Vegetarians

Vegetarians (see Chapter 3) account for approximately 3 per cent of the UK population, and many others prefer non-meat dishes. People from other parts of the world, where vegetarianism is traditional, have skills of blending and cooking a range of plant food to produce nutritionally balanced meals. These skills, together with imaginative Western cooking, are beginning to emerge within the catering industry. Similarly it is necessary for teachers and examining bodies to update, to ensure that these and other minorities are well catered for, particularly in the non-commercial sector.

Protein requirements

The protein content of food needs careful study if vegetarians are to be adequately fed. Proteins are composed of amino-acids, eight of which cannot be made by the body, and these must be supplied by the diet. These *essential amino-acids* are needed in different amounts. Breast-milk is the only food which contains the *correct proportions* of each essential amino-acid – all other foods containing not quite enough of some of them. Proteins from animal sources are nearer the correct balance than plants. Whole grains, nuts and beans are barely adequate on their own but if mixed together can supply all the essential amino-acids in the correct proportions. A mixture of plant foods can thereby be of an equal *quality* to foods from animal sources. *Lacto-vegetarians*, who do not object to milk and milk products, can obtain the essential amino-acids, in the correct quantities, from this source. For *vegans*, who limit themselves solely to foods of plant origin, this is more difficult without guidance on the combinations of vegetables which produce the correct balance of amino-acids.

Other nutrients

Vegans have difficulty obtaining *calcium, iron* and *Vitamin B12*. Even with the most careful dietary analysis and adjustment, supplements may be needed. Lacto-vegetarians often have poor intakes of *iron*.

Minority ethnic groups

The minority ethnic community varies between 9 and 14 per cent in the UK population and this cultural diversity has led to the introduction of many ethnic restaurants in the commercial sector of the industry. It is apparent however that within institutional catering, ethnic meals are grossly underrepresented. The Chinese, Indian or Jewish child, for example, might rarely be offered culturally acceptable food whilst at school or in hospital. Efforts to correct this imbalance must be taken up by catering colleges and examining boards. *Catering* for cultural diversity means *training* for cultural diversity!

The elderly

There is a well known saying 'man is as old as his arteries' and as heart disease and cancer are the two main causes of death there is probably some truth in it. Despite years of study however, the key to long life has not been established, but through better sanitation, medicine, shelter and food many more people are reaching the age of 65. The dietary care of such individuals is often within institutions and the nutritional knowledge of the caterer is critical. The requirements of some nutrients of importance are listed below.

1. *Energy* intake may be slightly lower due to a less active life-style. The level of other nutrients must be maintained, (see above).
2. *Iron* supplies are often depleted in bedridden, elderly people and supplements may be needed. Blood analysis is the only method of detection.
3. *Calcium* may be low if energy intake is restricted. Osteoporosis (wasting of bones with age) may not be caused by lack of calcium,but

osteomalacia (see Table 13.2, calcium) is certainly connected to calcium levels in the diet and a glass of milk a day is advisable.
4. *Vitamin D* may be low because of limited exposure to sunshine. Foods rich in this vitamin should be included regularly in the diet.
5. *Vitamin C* is a difficult vitamin to obtain if fresh fruits and vegetables are not eaten. Many elderly people – because of immobility, lack of finance, digestive disorders, false teeth, etc. – do not obtain enough Vitamin C and cases of mild scurvy are not uncommon.
6. *Folic acid* found in green vegetables, is often low for the same reasons.

Meals for the elderly, especially those living alone or in hospital, should also be stimulating both in flavour and appearance as appetite may be subdued.

13.7 FOOD QUALITY: READING THE LABEL

Customers may be presented with hygienic, nutritionally balanced meals but still be unhappy! The soup on the menu, for example, may provide nutrients for the body but *also* any number of additives that the food manufacturer may *legally* have added to the powder from which it was made. These additives are used mainly to improve flavour, colour, texture and keeping quality. Developments in food technology, labour costs and many other factors have led to caterers using more and more partially or fully processed products. There are 3700 additives currently available for use in the manufacture of food. This compares with about fifty at the beginning of this century. The recent, successful consumer lobbies, aimed at manufacturers, may well have implications for caterers. The public do not want unnecessary additives in their food – they have enough from animal feed, pesticides and fertilisers!

Types of additives

Many additives, both natural and synthetic, have a number which relates to their main function in the foods to which they are added. The prefix E is used for those additives which have been approved for use by the European Community (see Table 13.3).

The detail of the function of these additives is outside the scope of this book but some discussion has already been made of some of them as part of catering theory. Further detail can be obtained from food manufacturers and the book *E for Additives* by Maurice Hanssen.

Table 13.3 *Types of additives*

Numbers	Function
100–180	Colours
200–297	Preservatives
300–321	Anti-oxidants
322–495	Emulsifiers, stabilisers, etc.
500–578	Processing aids
620–637	Flavour enhancers
920–927	Bleaches
No numbers	Flavours
No numbers	Enzymes
No numbers	Solvents
No numbers	Modified starches
No numbers	Sweeteners

The problems with additives

1. *The profit to be made*

Additives are often added to bulk-out commodities.
Examples: (a) Brands of mayonnaise sometimes have thickening
agents to reduce the quantity of oil needed. The price is
not adjusted accordingly.
(b) Meat products often have polyphosphates added to
absorb water. Water is cheaper than meat!

2. *Allergies*

Many people suffer from intolerances to food additives. Customers need
more information, or a total ban, to be able to protect themselves.

3. *Safety*

Many additives have never been adequately screened for safety. Long-
term effects on humans, in the combinations in which they are consumed, is unknown. This is especially important for growing children
who are really the guinea-pigs for modern food.

4. *Labelling*

Regulations are not adequate.

Example: A bottle of lemon *essence* may be the essential oil, one of the natural components synthesised artificially, or a totally different substance not present in the natural oil. The word *flavouring* has a similarly obscure meaning.

5. *Necessity*

Additives make convenience foods, which can sit on the shelf until we need them, a reality. Whilst this has been a major contribution to certain aspects of life, the use of additives has extended beyond necessity. The fact that supermarkets are now reducing additives in many foods must prove this!

Some of the safety and other details are summarised in Figure 13.3, with permission from the London Food Commission.

Figure 13.3 *Additive safety details from London Food Commission*

Additives List

Many of the most common additives cause health problems. Most in this list are known to cause allergic or intolerant responses – such as asthma, rashes, hay-fever, blurred vision and tummy upsets – in some people. Some are also irritant or corrosive and are known to cause problems like skin rashes, burns, and breathlessness in food workers (they probably cause problems to some consumers too).

At a Glance	Additive	foodstuffs	Comments
COLOURS			
Azo Dyes			
E102	Tartrazine (Yellow)	There are a total of 17 azo dyes used in every kind of processed food in Great Britain.	All the azo dyes are banned in Norway and highly restricted in Sweden, Finland, Austria, Greece and Japan.
E110	Sunset Yellow (yellow)		
E123	Amaranth (red)		E123 and E124 are also banned in the USA
E124	Ponceau 4R (red)		
133	Brilliant Blue FCF (blue)		
155	Chocolate Brown HT (brown)		
Other Colours			
E141	Chlorophyllins (green)	Used in oil and processed vegetables	Banned in the USA
E160(b)	Annatto (yellow/orange)	Used in dairy products and oil	
PRESERVATIVES			
Sorbic Acid and Sorbates E200-E203		Used in yoghurt, soft drinks, cheese, packed cakes and frozen pizzas	
Benzoic Acid and Benzoates E210-E219		Used in jams, fruit juice, desserts, tinned fruit, salad cream, yoghurt and sauces.	
Sulphur Dioxide and Sulphites E220-227		Used in jam, fruit juice, beer, wine, dried vegetables, sausage meat and dried fruit.	The use of sulphites is being reviewed in the USA
Nitrates and Nitrites E249-E252		Used in smoked sausages, bacon, ham, cooked meats, tinned meats and cheese	Restricted in most European countries. Not permitted in baby food in the UK
Propionic Acid and Propionates E280-E283		Used in cakes, biscuits, pizza and bread	Banned in West Germany and Switzerland. Not permitted in baby food in the UK. The Baker's Union (BAFTU) has advised its members not to handle Calcium Propionate (E282)
ANTI-OXIDANTS			
BHA and BHT E320 E321		Used widely in foods containing fats, such as butter, margarine, oils; crisps	Not permitted in baby food in the UK. BHA is banned in Japan and restricted in Austria
Gallates E310-E312		Used in breakfast cereals, margarine, oils, crisps, dried potato mash etc.	Not permitted in baby food in the UK
EMULSIFIERS			
MDGs E471-E472		Widely used in food including margarine, chocolate drinks, desserts, custard, crisps, aerosol cream and cheese-cake.	
Polyoxethylene Sorbates 432-436		Used in cakes, biscuits and packet cake mix	Banned by the EEC in 1984
E407	Carrageenan	Used in ice-cream, cakes, desserts, frozen meals, and cheese.	
Vegetable gums E410-416		Used in ice-cream, fruit pie fillings, sauces, scotch eggs and cheese.	Karaya gum (416) banned by the EEC
FLAVOUR ENHANCERS			
621-623	Monosodium Glutamate + Glutamates	Used in soup, snacks, sausages and frozen meals	Not permitted in baby food in the UK
SWEETENERS			
Saccharin		Used widely in soft and fizzy drinks, desserts, yoghurts and low calorie foods.	At one time banned in the USA – it now carries a health warning.

SUSPECTED CARCINOGENS

Over 55 of approved food additives are suspected of causing or contributing to cancer. Some of the more common ones are listed below:

Colours
E123 Amaranth
E127 Erythrosine
128 Red 2G
133 Brilliant Blue FCF
E150 Caramels
154 Brown FK

Preservatives
E230 Dephenyl
E249-E252 Nitrates and nitrites

Anti-oxidants
E320-E321 BHA and BHT
Emulsifiers & stabilisers
E407 Carrageenan
 430 & 435 Polyoxyethylene compounds
E466 Sodium carboxymethyl cellulose

Processing aids
553 Silicates
907 Mineral oils and waxes
Sweeteners
Saccharin
Solvents
Isopropyl alcohol
Ethyl acetate

HYGIENE AT WORK

14.1   INTRODUCTION

Food hygiene is concerned with the study of the causes and prevention of illness associated with eating contaminated food. Good food hygiene also results in the control of food spoilage and this will be discussed briefly in this chapter.

Food handlers may find it easy to keep food visibly clean but food which looks, smells and tastes good may still be poisonous! It is this 'hidden danger' which makes the study of hygiene so important for catering students. Poisoning customers is not only bad for business but it may lead to prosecution, fines or even imprisonment for caterers.

In 1985 the *reported cases* of food poisoning totalled over 20 000 and this represents only about 10 per cent of the total number! Experts agree that the country is suffering an increase in food poisoning of epidemic proportions and that commercial catering is partially to blame.

It is important for food-handlers to recognise the special dangers of catering for large numbers. Catering practice often bears no resemblance to the procedures used in the home. The large quantities of food involved in catering take longer to defrost, prepare, cook, cool down and reheat. Storage space is increased and fluctuations in trade often result in the utilisation of more left-overs. It is hoped that this chapter will lead caterers to put food safety, and its implementation, high on their list of priorities. It is important however for them to see for themselves how easily micro-organisms grow, what kind of practices contaminate food and how food can be kept safe. This section is intended to be a framework on which to base the practical laboratory work necessary to understand the principles on which good food-hygiene standards are based.

14.2   FOOD-POISONING: SYMPTOMS AND CAUSES

Definition

Food-poisoning is a term used to describe gastro-intestinal illness produced as a result of eating foods that contain sufficient quantities of poisonous substances or harmful organisms.

Symptoms

Food poisoning is *usually: sudden* – often occurs within 1 to 36 hrs of eating the contaminated food; *severe* – diarrhoea, abdominal pain, nausea or vomiting, and sometimes fever; and is *often short* – complete recovery within days.

Causes

Food-poisoning symptoms can be caused by:

1. *Chemicals – cleaning agents* and *pesticides* can be consumed accidentally. Precautions must be taken to prevent this type of poisoning:

   (a) Label all chemicals clearly.
   (b) Store in room where food is not handled.
   (c) Keep storage area locked.

   Metals can also cause poisoning. Cooking in pans made from copper presents a risk of copper poisoning. Do not use untinned pans or those where the tin is wearing away.
2. *Allergies* – some people are sensitive to certain foods, e.g. chocolate, dairy foods. Reaction is usually sudden with symptoms such as indigestion, rashes and headache. Eczema and asthma are thought by some people to be allergic reactions to food.
3. *Poisonous plants and animals* – many species are found to be harmful to the human body, e.g. red kidney beans are only safe to eat if properly soaked before cooking; the white flesh of the puffer fish is a Japanese delicacy, but the rest of the fish is very poisonous and every year deaths occur from incorrectly prepared fish.
4. *Parasites* – worms from infected animals can produce diarrhoea and sickness and are certainly caused by the consumption of contaminated meat. They are, however, not normally classed as food poisoning because of the long-term and generalised illness they cause.
5. *Micro-organisms* – Microscopic organisms can contaminate food and drink invisibly and cause illness and even death.

MICRO-ORGANISMS ARE THE MOST COMMON CAUSE OF FOOD-POISONING and it is to them that we devote the rest of this chapter on food hygiene.

14.3 MICROBIAL FOOD-POISONING

Micro-organisms in historical perspective

Visual limitations of the pitiably restricted eye of man stood like an impenetrable curtain, between man and the fantastic and gittering cosmos of the microscopic world. Martin Frobisher *Fundamentals of Microbiology*(W. B. Sanders & Company) 1970.

By definition microbes are invisible to the naked eye and it was not until the discovery of the microscope that they were seen and studied. Although magnifying glasses were available in the thirteenth century it was the work of Antonj van Leeuwenhoek (1632–1723) with his home-made, yet powerful, lenses and vivid accounts of 'animalcules' in such substances as saliva, teeth scrapings and vinegar which began the study of microbiology. He examined and drew small animals, small plants, fungi and an even smaller form of life – *bacteria* (see Plate 14.1).

Louis Pasteur (1822–95) realised the link between micro-organisms and food spoilage and disease and pioneered work on the use of heat to destroy harmful microbes and the term 'pasteurisation' was first used. Alexander Fleming in 1929 added a milestone in the study of disease when he discovered, named and described a substance which could stop the growth of many microbes. This substance was penicillin, the first of many antibiotics, obtained from mould.

The picture was not complete, however, as even when the smallest bacteria were removed from fluids extracted from diseased cells 'something' was often still present and capable of transmitting disease. This was not a 'living poison' as first thought, but organisms invisible under the light microscope (maximum magnification 2000 times) but clearly visible under powerful new electron microscopes (magnification greater than 300 000 times). A clear study of *viruses* had begun. Antibiotics have little effect on viruses and the control of viral diseases is presenting an urgent challenge to the twentieth century.

Micro-organisms which contaminate food

All groups of micro-organisms (see Figure 14.1) have members which can contaminate food and cause illness in man. Sewage-polluted water, for example, can transfer dangerous small animals onto food, and diseases such as amoebic dysentery were at one time common in this country. At the present time it is bacteria which pose the greatest

Plate 14.1 *Salmonella enteritidis, the bacterium associated with food poisoning related to eggs*

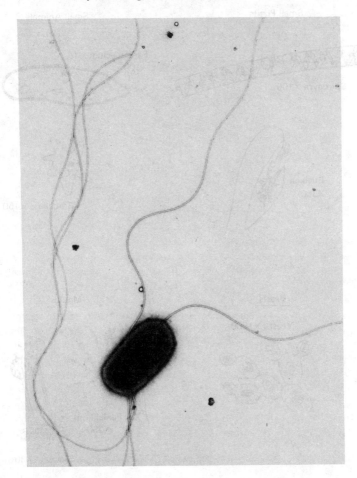

problem in terms of food hygiene in the UK. In the next century it may well be viruses that hit the headlines as they already have in other realms of medicine. It is therefore essential that students have a thorough knowledge of all groups of micro-organisms – not merely an abstract idea of 'germs'. This text offers only an introduction to food hygiene and therefore restricts itself to bacteria.

354

Figure 14.1 *Main types of micro-organisms*

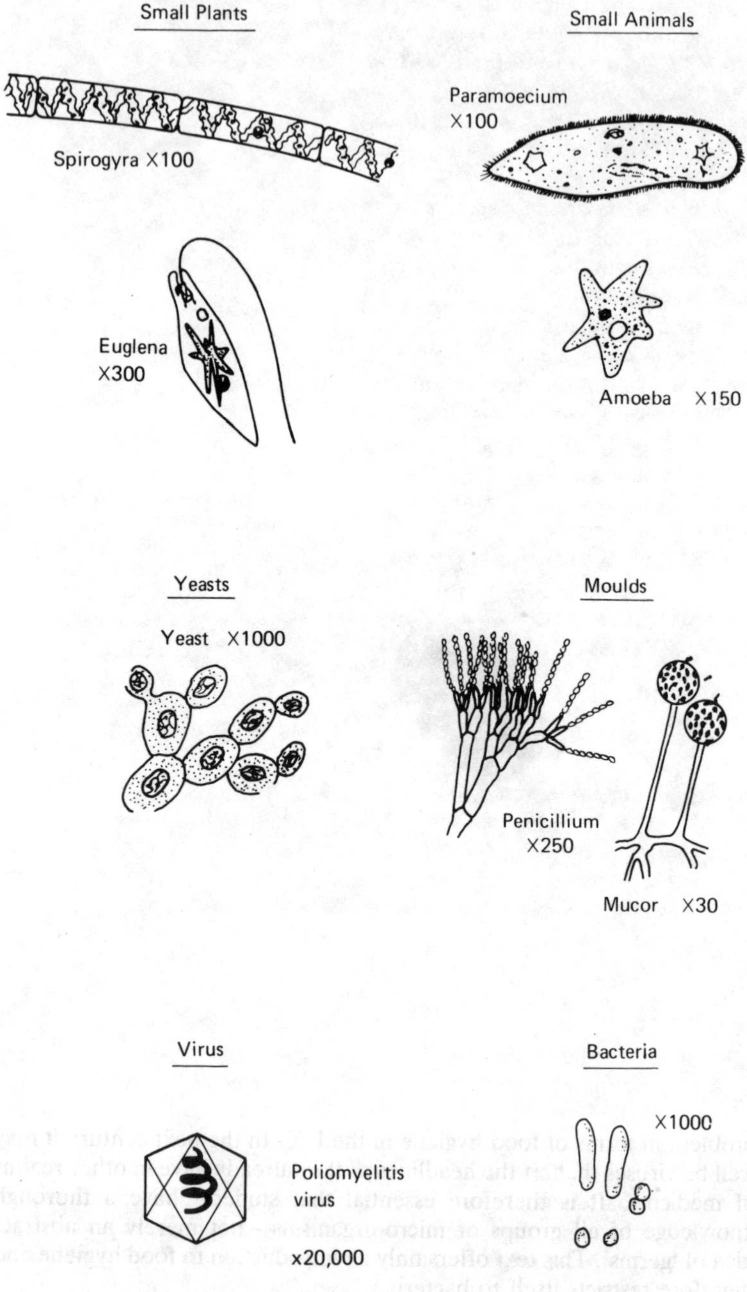

14.4   BACTERIA

Bacteria are the cause of most food-poisoning outbreaks in the 1980s. There are thousands of different types of bacteria – all with long Latin names! If we magnify food 1000 times we might just see some of the larger bacteria. They are usually round-, rod- or spiral-shaped.

Important points

1. *Most bacteria are harmless.* Bacteria are present in large numbers on our body, the food we eat and throughout the environment. It has been estimated that one small sausage, for example, contains 200 million bacteria!
2. *Some bacteria will cause food to spoil.* Some bacteria will grow on food and cause the food to become smelly/slimy/discoloured. If you do eat such food(!) you will probably come to no harm.
3. *Some bacteria can be used to produce food.* Some bacteria are used to produce food such as vinegar, bread, cheese and yogurt.
4. *Some pathogenic bacteria are found in food.* A few types of bacteria can produce disease in man. Disease-causing bacteria are called pathogenic bacteria. In the study of food hygiene it is these bacteria with which we are most concerned.

14.5   CONTAMINATION OF FOOD WITH BACTERIA

Food can be contaminated in one or more ways either *before it reaches the catering premises* or *inside the premises*.

Sources of contamination

1. *Soil/dust*   Some food-poisoning bacteria are commonly found in soil and dust. Vegetables and outdoor shoes are the most common routes for these organisms to get into the kitchen.
2. *Pests/pets*   Animals excrete food-poisoning bacteria and must be kept out of food premises. Pest-control involves regular inspection, good housekeeping and physical exclusion. Infestations should be dealt with by professionals who will use both physical and chemical means to eradicate the problem.
3. *Water*   Drinking water within the UK is chlorinated to kill pathogens but water from the hot tap can be contaminated and should not be used in food preparation.
4. *Food handler*   The human body is a source of many pathogens. The nose, throat, hands and faeces are the most important areas and personal hygiene plays an important role in preventing disease.
5. *Raw food*   Most meat is contaminated before it reaches the kitchen and must be treated with care to avoid cross-contamination. Veget-

ables are also frequently contaminated with soil as mentioned in (1) above.

6. *Refuse* Kitchen waste must not be allowed to accumulate in food-rooms because of the danger of cross-contamination. It will also serve to attract pests and should be stored in suitable bins and be removed regularly.

As mentioned earlier, pathogens are an invisible threat. If the contamination could be seen, few people would eat the food, and the risk to health would be minimal. The source or amount of contamination, however, is impossible to gauge and therefore all food should be treated as suspect.

We cannot see if food is contaminated with pathogens

14.6 CROSS-CONTAMINATION

Bacteria have no legs or wings! Once in the kitchen, however, they are spread around in no time.

Contamination spreads throughout the kitchen

CROSS-CONTAMINATION IS THE TRANSFER OF BACTERIA FROM ONE OBJECT TO ANOTHER

Example 1.   Chef's tea-towel (see Figure 14.2)

Tucked under the apron strings behind him, is the chef's one piece of equipment, carried everywhere:

- it trails across the toilet seat;
- it picks up soil when lying in the sun during tea-break;
- it dries the hands after they get blood on from raw meat;
- it is used for moulding omelettes into shape;
- it cleans the edges of flats before services;
- it wipes the work-surface clean;
- and if he sneezes . . .

Breaking this chain of cross-contamination involves changing tradition. It will not happen by education alone.

Do not use tea towels – replace with disposable paper

A word of warning. If tea-towels are suddenly removed the oven cloth would be used as an alternative!

Restrict the use of oven cloths – keep beside the oven

357

Figure 14.2 *Examples of cross-contamination: chef's tea-towel*

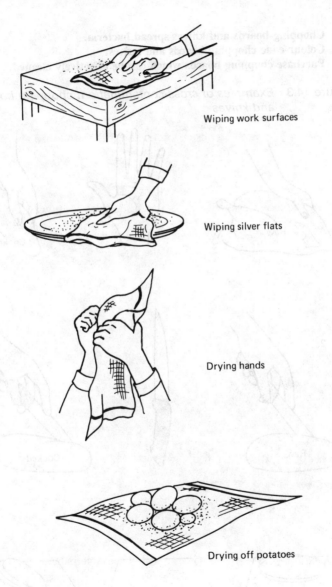

Wiping work surfaces

Wiping silver flats

Drying hands

Drying off potatoes

358

Example 2. Chopping boards and knives

Figure 14.3 shows the contamination which commonly occurs through the food-handler not washing thoroughly his knife, board and hands after use.

Chopping-boards and knives spread bacteria.
Colour-code chopping boards and knives.
Purchase chopping boards which can be effectively cleaned.

Figure 14.3 *Examples of cross-contamination: chopping boards and knives*

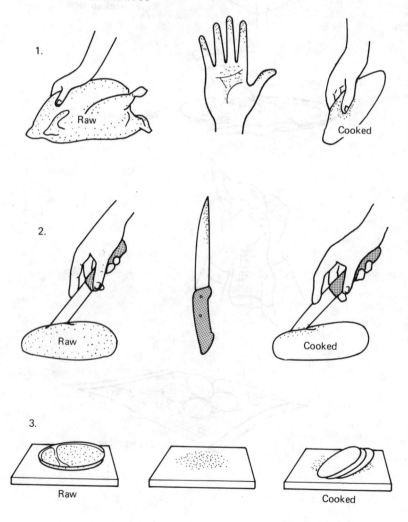

14.7 THE MULTIPLICATION OF BACTERIA

When we grow we get bigger and bigger . . . ! Bacteria grow so quickly we cannot see them increasing in size. We can only see them multiplying at a very rapid date. One bacterium 'splits' into two by a simple process called *binary fission* (see Figure 14.4).

Figure 14.14 *Example of binary fission*

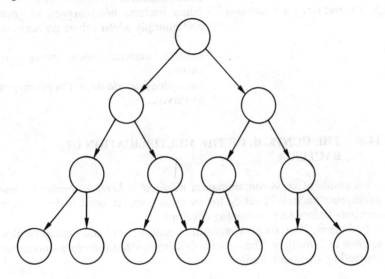

If conditions are suitable ONE bacterium can divide every 10–20 minutes to produce 70 000 million more in one working day!

Bacteria are versatile and can grow and adapt to almost any environment. For example, some types can feed off concrete or petrol whilst others can grow in the freezer or in a volcano! In the context of hygiene we are concerned only with those bacteria likely to cause disease.

Pathogenic bacteria will grow on food if they have:

1. *Warmth*   Temperatures around human body temperature 37°C; range 5–63°C are the usual limits for human pathogens.

2. *Moisture*   Dehydrated foods (water content of less than 5 per cent) will not allow growth of bacteria. Once mixed with milk or water any bacteria present will start growing and such foods should be used as quickly as possible.

3. *Food*	Most foodstuffs suitable for man to eat are also popular with bacteria. High-protein foods such as meat, poultry and dairy produce are preferred. These are termed *high-risk foods*.
4. *Time to multiply*	Under ideal conditions bacteria multiply every 10–20 minutes. Within a few hours large numbers may have been produced.
5. *Correct oxygen conditions*	Some bacteria need oxygen to grow and multiply whilst others do not. *aerobic bacteria* need oxygen to survive. *anaerobic bacteria* do not need oxygen to survive.

14.8 THE CONTROL OF THE MULTIPLICATION OF BACTERIA

As a result of cross-contamination *all food is likely to harbour some pathogenic bacteria*. Luckily for us most bacteria need to be in large numbers before food-poisoning develops.

Pathogenic bacteria need warmth, moisture, food and time to be able to grow and multiply. The control of their growth is therefore a matter of controlling these conditions.

Methods of control:

1. *Temperature* – cooking/drying/cooling/freezing
2. *Others* – acid/sugar/salt/packaging/irradiation/additives.

These methods have a combined effect which:

(a) helps to prevent the growth of all pathogens, especially known bacterial types;
(b) effectively slows down chemical and enzymic changes associated with spoilage;
(c) minimises the growth of moulds, bacteria and other spoilage organisms.

For this reason they are often termed *preservation techniques*. These are defined as operations applied to food to extend shelf-life and keep it safe from harmful organisms. Table 14.1 summarises the main preservation techniques and the discussion below is restricted to the effect of cold storage and cooking on bacterial growth.

The use of temperature to control the multiplication of pathogenic bacteria

Pathogenic bacteria grow best at body temperature 37°C. As the temperature is reduced their growth slows and eventually stops. As the temperature increases their growth slows and eventually they are killed. *Multiplication* is *stopped* by keeping food *hot* or *cold*.

KEEP FOOD COLD	below 5°C pathogens multiply very slowly and this temperature is considered safe
KEEP FOOD HOT	above 63°C is hot enough to stop multiplying and is considered safe
THE DANGER ZONE	food should be cooled or heated quickly so that it is 'warm' for the minimum of time. Remember that the kitchen is usually at temperatures of between 20°C and 40°C—the danger zone! (see Figure 14.5).

Cold temperature storage of food

The growth rate of bacterial pathogens slows as the temperature is lowered below 10°C. As outlined in Chapters 5 and 11 spoilage changes will also diminish as the temperature is reduced and at −18°C food can be kept for 6 months or more if properly packaged (see Table 14.2).

It must be stressed that at low temperatures pathogens are dormant and as soon as the temperature is raised they will continue to grow and multiply. The following general rules should be followed to obtain maximum efficiency and safety of cold storage equipment.

1. *Maintain temperature* by checking and recording at least daily.
2. *Package effectively* to avoid cross-contamination and drying-out of food.
3. *Avoid overloading* as this overloads the motor and causes fluctuations in temperature.
4. *Rotate stock* to avoid spoilage and waste.
5. *Cool hot food* before placing in cold-storage equipment. The steam produced will cause ice build up, condensation may cause cross-contamination and the temperature of the unit will rise. A cool, well-ventilated room or blast-chiller should be used for cooling hot food.
6. *Defrost frozen food at 5°C* to ensure no area of the food reaches danger zone temperatures before total defrosting has taken place.
7. *Keep clean and defrost regularly.*

Table 14.1 Preservation techniques

Technique	Shelf life	Methods	Effect on pathogens	Example
Heat treatment	Short term Long term	Pasteurisation Cooking Commercial sterilisation	Mild heat treatment to destroy pathogens Severe heat treatment to destroy all microbes and *most* bacterial spores	Cooked food, milk Canned food, UHT packaged cream
Cold storage	Short term Long term	Cold room (10°C) Refrigerator (4°C) Chiller (0–3°C) Freezer (−18°C)	Pathogens do not multiply in cold conditions Pathogens/spoilage organisms/enzymes inactive	Perishable commodities
Dehydration	Long term	Sun-drying Roller-drying Hot-air drying Accelerated freeze-drying	Removes 95 per cent of water from food, preventing growth of pathogens	Fruit Milk Peas Whole mushrooms
Chemicals	Long term	Salt Sugar Curing Vinegar Smoke Chemical additives: Preservatives Anti-oxidants	High concentration of salt/sugar in food causes microbes to dehydrate and die combined to effect of above and specific action to prevent bacterial growth* (ref. p.273) Conditions unsuitable for growth of pathogens and most spoilage organisms Specifically added to prevent growth of pathogens Prevents fat rancidity and oxidative changes	Jams, chutneys, Hams Bacon, salami Onions, beetroot, Kippers, mackerel Sulphites in sausages Nitrates/nitrites in meat products Vit C in fruit juices etc

	Variable			
Irradiation			Effects depend on dose. Can be use to kill pathogens/pests/parasites. Adverse flavour effect on some foods	Not yet legal in UK (1989)
Sterilisation Pasteurisation				
Packaging	Short term	Vacuum-packing	Without oxygen and with low temperature (4°C) storage will prevent oxidative deterioration and growth of some pathogens. Anaerobic organisms (Clostridium/Bacillus) will grow if temperatures are allowed to rise, therefore limited shelf-life	Bacon

• Sterilisation is a process which destroys *all* bacterial spores. No present heat treatment of foods can guarantee this, but enough spores are destroyed to make the foods as safe as is commercially possible.

364

Figure 14.5 *Temperature and microbial growth*

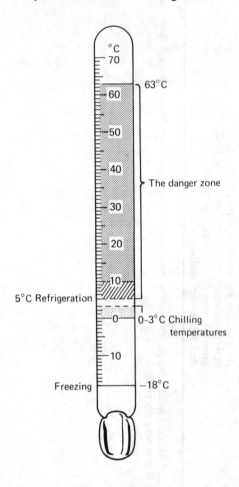

Table 14.2 *The effect of reduced temperature on microbial growth*

Area	Temp	Effect on most pathogens	Shelf life (e.g. fresh fish)
Cold room	10°C	slow multiplication	approx 1 day
Refrigerator	5°C	growth stops	approx 2 days
Chiller	0–3°C	growth stops	approx 3 days
Freezer	– 18°C	Pathogens dormant	approx 6 months

Cooking to destroy pathogenic bacteria

Cooking temperatures vary, depending on the process used, but all involve temperatures of above 63°C. At this temperature most bacteria will not grow and as the temperature rises most pathogens will die rapidly. This does not mean however that the food is always safe. Some bacteria may have produced heat resistant *spores* or *toxins*.

Bacterial spores Some pathogenic bacteria can survive the cooking process.

What would happen to the human race if there was a nuclear explosion? The lucky ones would survive in a nuclear bunker – its thick lead walls and survival rations would sustain life. If conditions were ever safe outside normal life could continue again.

Some bacteria have a similar survival mechanism. If conditions become unfavourable they produce a thick, resistant wall around all the important parts of the cell and can then survive as a *bacterial spore* (see Figure 14.6). In this form they can survive cooking processes. After the food is cooked they can grow and multiply again if warm conditions prevail.

Bacteria which produce spores can survive cooking temperatures

Figure 14.6 *Bacterial spore formation*

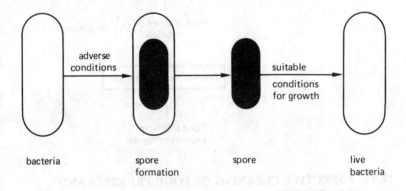

bacteria   spore   spore   live
formation   bacteria

Bacterial toxins Many food-poisoning bacteria produce chemicals which are poisonous to the body. These toxins may be excreted onto the food on which the bacteria grow. Some are heat-resistant and may not be destroyed by normal cooking temperatures.

Toxins may poison the body even if the bacteria are dead

It is a common misconception amongst food-handlers that cooked food is safe food! Three important species of food-poisoning bacteria can produce spores and some can produce heat resistant toxins. It is therefore imperative that food is handled correctly (see Figure 14.7).

Figure 14.7 *Safe handling procedures*

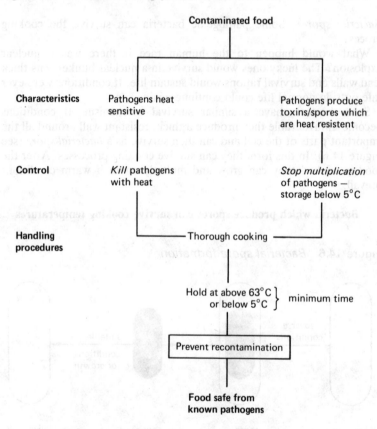

14.9 EFFECTIVE CLEANING OF FOOD PREMISES AND EQUIPMENT

Contamination of food is perhaps impossible to prevent, but the problem can be scaled down by effective cleaning. This process of *decontamination of the environment* presents a constant challenge to caterers in terms of efficiency and cost. The benefits include not only safer food and a better working environment but also customers' appreciation of aesthetically appealing surroundings.

Cleaning agents

There are three types:

Detergents   are chemicals which remove dirt and grease from surfaces. They also wash off most bacteria. e.g. soap, liquid and powdered detergents, abrasive creams.

Disinfectants   are chemicals which are used to destroy micro-organisms e.g. bleaches, household disinfectants. These substances do not kill all microbes/bacterial spores and therefore do not sterilise! They do, however, reduce micro-organisms to "a level which is neither harmful to health or to the quality of perishable foods" (British Standard BS 5283: 1976)

Sanitisers   are chemicals which have a combined detergent/disinfectantant action, (BS 5283:1976). Despite the apparent advantages of such cleansing agents is is generally considered to be more efficient and cost effective to use detergents and disinfectants separately. This is because disinfectants work more efficiently if surfaces are already clean. It is also only necessary to disinfect certain surfaces.

The use of cleaning agents

All cleaning agents should be used according to manufacturers' instructions to maintain safety and hygiene.

Disinfectants formulated specifically for food operations should be used, to avoid chemical poisoning and tainted food. Many chlorine-based compounds do not need rinsing as long as time is allowed for air-drying.

Caution: cleaning agents are toxic chemicals. Dilute as required, use protective clothing and store in a locked cupboard away from food.

The use of hot water and steam

Water above 80°C can be used to disinfect utensils after hand-washing. The utensils should be left in the hot water for at least 2 minutes. Similarly items can be boiled in water, after washing, for 5 minutes if chemical disinfectants are not available.

High-pressure steam is often used in deep-cleaning procedures because it is very effective at killing micro-organisms and even some bacterial spores. A pressure-cooker using steam will *sterilise* if sufficient contact time is allowed. This equipment forms the basis of commercial canning and the sterilisation of laboratory equipment.

The cleaning process

The cleaning of surfaces and equipment can be conveniently divided into high-risk and low-risk categories (see Table 14.3). Surfaces which are likely to contaminate food are termed high-risk and need to be treated with disinfectants to reduce this risk to a minimum. Others are adequately cleaned by thorough washing with hot water and detergent.

Table 14.3 *Cleaning methods*

Surfaces	e.g. Cleaning method
High-risk	
Food preparation equipment Work surfaces e.g. chopping boards and knives	1. Remove food scraps, etc. 2. Wash with hot water/detergent 3. Mix disinfectant in water 4. Apply to surfaces for recommended time (often 30 minutes) 5. Air-dry
Low-risk	
Surfaces not in direct contact with food e.g. walls, shelves	1. Remove food scraps, etc. 2. Wash with hot water/detergent 3. Air-dry

Cleaning routines

Cleaning is a front-line defence against food-poisoning and food-spoilage and must feature in the regular training of all staff. It is ironic that staff engaged to clean food premises are rarely trained in food hygiene. It is necessary for *detailed cleaning schedules* to be worked out to ensure

(a) the frequency of cleaning for each item;
(b) the person responsible for the cleaning/supervision;
(c) the monitoring of cleaning.

Cross-contamination

It is often forgotten that the process of cleaning can spread more poisoning than it prevents! Cloths used to wipe up blood seepage from defrosting chicken, for example, will spread contamination throughout the kitchen. It is unlikely that busy food-handlers will have time to disinfect cloths between use and the logical solution is for disposable alternatives to be used. Floor-cleaning also presents a problem in food rooms. A two-bucket method should be used to ensure bacteria are not transferred from one area of the kitchen to another. Ideally mop heads should be removed, washed, disinfected and dried between use!

In the report on the infamous Stanley Royd Hospital food-poisoning outbreak, which is detailed later, a classic example of 'cleaning' is quoted:

> Up to the day it was described to us it was the practice for the metal-topped kitchen tables to be cleaned with a high pressure disinfectant jet, to be scrubbed, on occasion with a pan wire, to be washed down with clean water, and then *wiped off with the same sqeegees as were used on the floors*.

14.10 THE FOOD-POISONING BACTERIA

Six of the currently important food-poisoning bacteria are used in this section to outline the principles of prevention. The main characteristics of these bacteria are summarised in Table 14.4. It is certainly not our intention to over-emphasise the memorising of such facts because (a) they are quickly forgotten and (b) do not serve as a cure for food-poisoning statistics. It is essential, however, to gain an understanding of the different types of food-poisoning, so that correct handling procedures can be established. Figure 14.7 summarises these.

1. Bacterial intoxications

(a) *Toxins produced as bacteria multiply in food*

Some pathogenic organisms will multiply on food to produce chemicals (called toxins) which will poison the human body if a sufficiently large dose is swallowed. The toxins may be secreted out of the bacterial cell onto the food (exotoxins) or remain inside the cell until the bacteria are destroyed in the gut (endoxins). The body reacts just as it would if it had swallowed a spoonful of arsenic – vomiting and/or diarrhoea, to remove the toxins as quickly as possible. This type of food-poisoning develops within hours of eating the contaminated food and symptoms subside rapidly in most cases.

It is important to realise that most of these toxins will poison the body whether the bacteria are *alive or dead*. Cooking the food may kill the bacteria but often will not destroy heat-resistant toxins, e.g. *Staphylococcus aureus*, *Bacillus cereus* (some types). *Clostridium botulinum* is unusual in this respect as its toxin, despite being extremely lethal, is

Table 14.4 Characteristics of bacteria commonly causing food-poisoning

Bacteria	Contamination		Characteristics			Illness			Storage/cooking and other details
	Source	Control	Multiply in gut	Toxin	Spores	Incubation period	Duration	Symptoms	
Salmonella e.g. *S.typhimurium*	Raw meat Human carriers Animals	Avoid cross-contamination Strict personal hygiene Keep pests/pets out	yes	no	no	24 hrs +	3 days +	Diarrhoea Abdominal pain Vomiting Fever	Organisms need to be swallowed *live* to produce infection, therefore food can be made safe by thorough cooking and immediate consumption
Campylobacter (e.g. *C. jejuni*)	Raw poultry Animals Human carriers Raw milk	Avoid cross-contamination Keep pest/pets out Strict personal hygiene Drink only pasteurised milk	yes	no	no	2–4 hrs +	3 days +	Diarrhoea Abdominal pain	
Clostridium perfringens	soil Animals Human carriers Raw meat	Avoid cross-contamination from raw vegetables. Keep food off the floor. Keep pests/pets out Strict personal hygiene Avoid cross-contamination	yes	yes	yes	9–12 hrs	12–48 hrs	Diarrhoea Abdominal pain Nausea	Toxins released from organisms in the gut giving the symptoms of food-poisoning. Avoid cooking in large quantities to prevent anaerobic conditions needed by this organism. Keep food hot or cool quickly

Staphylococcus aureus	Nose, throat, cuts, boils	Strict personal hygiene (50% of population are carriers)	no	yes	2–6 hrs	6–24 hrs	Vomiting Diarrhoea Abdominal pain	Heat resistant toxin produced in food as organism multiplies. Keep food hot or cool quickly to safe temperature
Clostridium botulinum	Soil/sea	Avoid home-preserved food. Avoid commercially preserved food with signs of defects (e.g. blown cans)	no	yes*	24–72 hrs	death or slow recovery (3 months+)	Double vision Difficulty in swallowing, speaking. Paralysis. Respiratory failure.	Anaerobic conditions in canned/bottled foods ideal for growth
Bacillus cereus	Vegetables and cereals	Avoid cross-contamination with raw vegetables Careful handling of cooked cereals	yes / no	[TYPE I] no [TYPE II] yes	8–16 hrs / 1–5 hrs	1–2 days / 12–24	Diarrhoea main symptoms Vomiting main symptoms	Avoid cooking in large quantities to prevent anaerobic conditions needed by the organism. Keep food hot or cool quickly

* extremely lethal

easily destroyed by heat. It is ironic that the canned food (e.g. salmon) in which it is often found is eaten cold!

(b) *Toxins produced in the intestine*

Clostridium perfringens is a bacterium which is found throughout the environment and which commonly causes food-poisoning. When contaminated food is eaten the *live* bacteria multiply in the gut, many of them producing spores and releasing them inside the intestine. There is a toxin on the outside of these spores which irritates the gut and causes symptoms of food-poisoning. The bacteria must be *live* and *present in large numbers* to produce these symptoms. *Thorough heating of food* and *correct storage* will eliminate this hazard.

2. Bacterial infections

(a) *Infection causing food-poisoning*

Food can be contaminated with certain bacteria which, if swallowed *live*, can find a place inside the digestive system to grow and multiply. This produces inflammation of the gut wall producing diarrhoea/vomiting and sometimes symptoms of an infection such as headache and fever. These infections are slower to develop than the intoxications mentioned in (a) above, and often take more than a week for the body's normal defence-mechanisms to eliminate them. Such infections are also infectious, through the faeces, and food-handlers are not allowed to work with these symptoms. Problems arise with *symptomless carriers* who are not aware that they carry infection. It is common practice in good catering operations to have regular screening of staff for the main bacterial food-poisoning infections.

The main feature of this type of food-poisoning is that (in theory) relatively small numbers of bacteria can cause the illness. Because of the acidity of the stomach it is rare, however, for small numbers to survive the route to the intestine and in most cases they have *multiplied significantly* in the food, to produce symptoms, e.g. *Salmonella typhimurium*.

(b) *Infection causing other diseases*

Food and water can transmit bacterial diseases which produce symptoms not normally associated with food-poisoning. The bacteria are carried in *water* or on *food*, into the body of humans, where they multiply very rapidly to produce serious infections. Many of these infections are characterised by fevers caused by the organisms invading the bloodstream. Medical treatment in the form of antibiotics and rehydration is necessary. These bacteria *do not multiply on food* or in water, and a small number, when ingested, can produce symptoms. *They are not usually studied in the context of food poisoning but as part of food- and water-borne diseases.* Preventive treatment in the form of vaccination and chlorination of water have led to the control of many of these bacteria in the UK, e.g. *cholera, Salmonella typhi (typhoid), tuberculosis.*

Case studies of food-poisoning outbreaks

There are few rules to follow in modern catering to ensure safe food. A degree in microbiology or even a retentive memory is not necessary. The following case studies aim to enlighten caterers about bad practice so that good practice might be appreciated. Relevant facts about individual organisms can be pin-pointed within these case-studies to aid understanding further.

Case 1   Salmonella food-poisoning at the Stanley Royd Hospital, Wakefield, 1984

The outbreak which occurred at this hospital began in the morning of Sunday, 26 August 1984 and was 'frightening in its scale and the rapidity of its onset'. A total of 355 patients and staff became ill with suspected salmonellosis with 19 deaths. As a direct result of the subsequent inquiry, Crown Immunity was lifted from hospital kitchens in an effort to curb the many outbreaks recorded in these establishments. It is important to recognise that hospital catering is not necessarily worse than other branches of the industry. The customers in hospitals are resident and the full effects of poisonous food are not diluted. They are also more susceptible because of the state of their health.

This particular outbreak is extremely complicated and some aspects have never been proved conclusively. The main features identified below are related as an indication of the typical conditions in which food is prepared – even in the twentieth century!

Chronological details

21 August   Frozen beef joints (10–20lb) were received at the hospital and transferred immediately to the freezer.
23 August   Removed from freezer at mid-day and allowed to defrost overnight at room temperature in the meat department.
24 August   Transferred to kitchen and at 11 a.m. they were unwrapped, jointed and cooked for approximately 3 hrs when they were removed from oven and left to cool. There were frozen chicken in the kitchen at this time. They had been left to defrost on a table, which was also used for food preparation, and the juices allowed to drain onto floor and into the open gulleys. *Contamination with Salmonella typhimurium from the raw chicken probably occurred during this time.* The meat was stored for the night in an uncooled room.

25 August   Between 9.15 and 11.00 a.m. the meat was sliced on a slicing machine, which was probably not clean, placed by hand on trays and covered. *The slicing machine probably contaminated any meat not at this stage contaminated.* It was at room temperature for at least 3 and perhaps 6 hours prior to being sent to the wards for tea at 5.30 p.m. *Multiplication of the infecting organism during this time (and probably the previous night) would have produced sufficient contamination to cause food poisoning.*

26 August   The first of 355 patients and staff, nineteen of whom died, developed symptoms of diarrhoea and vomiting. Investigations began. The outbreak was to last many weeks.

14 September   An Official Inquiry was instigated   The Secretary of State for Social Services announced that a Public Local Inquiry would be held amidst serious allegations of mismanagement at the hospital and criticism of the way in which the outbreak was controlled and contained.

Conclusions

Cooked meat served to patients at the hospital was contaminated with *Salmonella typhimurium* which was thought to have originated from raw poultry handled in the same kitchens. This was assumed to be caused by simple error on the part of a food-handler, probably by the use of a dirty knife or unwashed hand. The inquiry pointed out that it would *not* have occurred *if*:

(a) the meat had been refrigerated soon after cooking;
(b) it had been sliced using a clean machine;
(c) it had been returned to a refrigerator after slicing and had remained there until service time.

The role of management was also investigated and many criticisms were made of kitchen supervisors and hospital administrators alike. The standard of the food premises, equipment and food handling were all implicated in the Inquiry and some of the most important points are listed below. How many of these are still common situations in the catering industry today?

(a) *unclean conditions*   floors were found to be worn with cracked tiles, infestation with cockroaches and open gulleys impossible to clean;
(b) *lack of ventilation*   fans/ventilators not used because they were noisy; working temperatures of above 22°C;
(c) *shortage of refrigerated space*   particularly for the safe storage of cooked and uncooked food. There was also no provision for the cooling of food;
(d) *mincers/slicers*   these were not adequately cleaned after use even between using raw and cooked meats;

(e) *cloths* disposable cleaning cloths were issued once a week and when supplies ran out used ones were rinsed or left to soak in soapy water;

(f) *cleaning duties* as part of a bonus deal for kitchen staff no cleaners were employed in the kitchens; there were no detailed cleaning rotas or manuals;

(g) *food prepared over long periods* 'food was cooked as and when convenient to the staff, and not as and when appropriate for the consumers'. It was common practice for food to be cooked the day before and to be stored for periods of over an hour in heated trolleys. *The preparation of the meat for cottage pie had, on occasion, taken three days.*

Case 2 Staphylococcus food-poisoning aboard a Boeing 747

This was one of the largest outbreaks aboard an aircraft and occurred as a result of food eaten on a flight from Tokyo to Paris. The plane stopped at Anchorage, Alaska, to change crew and collect snacks and breakfast prepared by a local catering company. On arrival at Copenhagen 8 hours later, 344 passengers and 1 member of the crew were developing symptoms of food-poisoning.

Chronological details

Day 1

a.m. Chefs cracked, mixed and strained 1440 eggs. Omelettes were then cooked. Chefs removed slices of ham, by hand, from a plastic bucket and placed one in each of the omelettes. One chef had lesions (septic cuts) on his hands and contaminated the ham he handled, and other ham in the bucket, with *Staphylococcus aureus*.

p.m. *The food was left in the kitchen for 6 hours which would have been ideal conditions for the growth of contaminating bacteria.* The food was then placed in a cold room overnight (10°C).

Day 2

a.m. The omelettes were taken out of the cold room, transported to the plane, and stored in unrefrigerated conditions. This involved a total of 8 hours at ambient temperatures. *Multiplication of the organism would have been rapid under these conditions.*

p.m. Seven hours after the plane set off, the meals were heated to 154°C for 15 minutes and served immediately. *This may well have killed the bacteria but heat-resistant toxins would have survived.* One and a half hours later, as the plane landed at Copenhagen, the first of

345 passengers and crew began to become ill. Their symptoms were diarrhoea, vomiting and cramps. The flight could not continue. All patients were hospitalised and an investigation began.

Day 3

As patients began to recover, swabs taken from the infected chef implicated him as the source of the infection.

Conclusions

(a) This outbreak emphasises that people with septic cuts/boils should not handle food.

(b) Food should be stored at low enough temperatures to inhibit bacterial growth.

(c) To make sure a common food-borne illness does not incapacitate an entire flight crew, cockpit-crew members should eat different meals prepared by different chefs. (This has since been recommended by the World Health Organisation).

Case 3   Botulism in Birmingham

Four elderly people developed botulism following ingestion of tinned Alaskan salmon contaminated with *Clostridium botulinum* in 1978. In the UK botulism is infrequent, the most notorious outbreak having occurred in 1923 when all eight members of a fishing party died after eating duck paste. Before the case in question 21 cases had occurred with 12 deaths.

Chronological details

Day 1

5.00 p.m.	Two couples ate a meal of canned salmon salad.
2.00 a.m.	All began to develop nausea, vomiting, dry mouth, dizziness and blurred vision.
7.00 a.m.	Admitted to hospital with paralysis giving rise to difficulty speaking, swallowing and breathing.
11.00 a.m.	Paralysis progressed and ventilators were needed to facilitate breathing. Clinical diagnosis of botulism (mice died after being injected with patients' serum). Anti-toxin administered.
Days 2–7	Progression of paralysis halted but severe medical problems, associated with initial effect of toxin, remained. Muscular recovery slowly started.
Day 17	First patient died
Day 23	Second patient died

Day 28   Third patient resumed unaided breathing.
Day 35   Fourth patient resumed unaided breathing.
Day 75   Two survivors left hospital.

The cause of the outbreak

Remnants of salmon, obtained from the tin thought to be responsible, showed contamination with *Clostridium botulinum* type E. Available circumstantial evidence suggests that contamination of the contents had occurred during processing, probably through a defect in the can at the time of cooling. Multiplication of the bacteria with the production of toxin must have occurred in the subsequent year, before the can was opened. A tiny hole found in the can would have allowed the gases, which this particular type is known to produce, to escape, therefore giving no clue to the victims that the salmon was not safe to eat.

Conclusions

Commercially canned food is heated to very high temperatures to eliminate the extremely heat-resistant spores of *Clostridium botulinum*. If not destroyed they would subsequently flourish in the anaerobic conditions in the sealed can. This was therefore a very unusual case and no other cans were found to be contaminated. Outbreaks are more common in countries where home-processing is popular (e.g. America) or where fish (often found to be contaminated from the sea) or fish products are consumed uncooked.

Case 4 Bacillus cereus food poisoning in an industrial canteen

There are many different strains of *Bacillus cereus*, some producing mainly vomiting, others diarrhoea. They both produce heat-resistant spores and some also produce extremely heat-resistant toxins. The spores of the organism are found on most cereals originating from the soil in which they are grown.

Chronological details

7.00 a.m.   Rice was cooked for the mid-day meal of 36 workers at a factory. *Spores of Bacillus cereus would not be destroyed by this process.*
The cooked rice was left at temperatures of between 15 and 25°C until lunch time.
This is an ideal temperature for the spores to germinate and then multiply rapidly.

1.30 p.m.   A meal of meat, rice and vegetables was eaten by 18 of the 36 employees.

| 2.00 p.m. | The first victim developed nausea, vomiting and abdominal pain. During the next four hours 18 workers were taken ill. |

Conclusions

Investigations showed the cooked rice to be heavily contaminated with *Bacillus cereus* organisms and its toxins.

It was concluded that the *outbreak would have been prevented if*:

(a) the rice had been cooked immediately prior to service, *or,*
(b) the rice had been cooled down and refrigerated between cooking and lunchtime.

Case 5   Clostridium perfringens food poisoning from contaminated meat

This organism cannot grow if it is in contact with air and is therefore found in pies, pâtés, sausages and in the interior of large quantities of stews and stocks. It is commonly found in soil, on animals/meat and in the gut of humans. This organism is a common cause of food-poisoning and is usually associated with meat which has been inadequately stored after cooking. A well-documented case, reflecting typical situations leading up to outbreaks of *clostridium perfringens*, is outlined below

Chronological details

Day 1

| 10 a.m. | Hams were boned, rolled and cooked. *Meat which is rolled spreads surface contamination to interior where anaerobic conditions favour growth of Clostridium perfringens.* After cooking they were left to *cool* in a centrally heated room. *Surviving spores would germinate and multiply in these conditions.* |
| 4 p.m. | The meat was minced, in equipment contaminated with raw meat, and placed in a refrigerator. *Cross-contamination would allow transfer of bacteria to all joints.* |

Day 2

| 6 a.m. | The meat was mixed with water and soup-powder and heated in steam-heated cauldrons. *This heat treatment was not monitored and proved insufficient to kill the large numbers of organisms which had grown the day before.* |
| 12 p.m. | Lunch was served. |

6 p.m.	The first patients began to develop symptoms of diarrhoea, abdominal pain and vomiting. An investigation began.
Day 5	A total of 379 patients were affected in the four days after eating the contaminated food. One patient died.

Conclusions

The investigation confirmed that this had been an attack of *Clostridium perfringens* food poisoning and it *could have been prevented if*:

(a) the cuts of meat had been smaller to allow rapid cooling;
(b) they had been refrigerated within the recommended time after cooking;
(c) the mincers had been cleaned properly between use;
(d) the reheated mince had attained boiling temperatures throughout its bulk.

Recommendations were made by specialists after the outbreak regarding the above points and in addition they suggested that mince should only be made from raw meat and that cooked and raw processes should be separated. It should also be noted that an Environmental Health Officer had visited the hospital two months earlier and 'found widespread disrepair, obsolescence, and poor hygiene'. He had recommended 'urgent upgrading of hospital facilities'.

Case 6 Campylobacter infections in raw milk

Campylobacter species are now recognised as the commonest cause of bacterial gastro-enteritis in the country. The infection is linked to poultry, meat, milk and pets. Most food-borne outbreaks in England and Wales have been caused by the sale of untreated milk. Although strongly discouraged by the Milk Marketing Board some farmers legally bottle milk which has not been pasteurised. In England and Wales in 1985/86 202 people suffered milk-borne *Campylobacter* infection in nine separate outbreaks.

14.11 HYGIENE RULES FOR CATERERS

Standards of hygiene in a catering establishment are affected by

1. the condition of the *premises* – e.g. infestation, cleanliness, facilities;
2. the *equipment* available – e.g. separate equipment for raw and cooked food;

3. the standards of *personal hygiene* of staff;
4. *food-handling* practices.

It must be accepted that the food handlers have some control over (4), total responsibility for (3), but very little to do with (1) and (2). It is therefore not appropriate to put the onus of food hygiene only on food-handlers. They do have their part to play, but so too have managers! The thrust of training now underway should be aimed at management – many of whom are untrained – as well as the shop-floor caterer. The proof of this can be read in the case histories described above. How often were there inadequate cold-storage facilities and lack of supervision?

Tables 14.5 and 14.6 give simple guidelines for the food-handler in terms of his everyday work; the next section gives an overall view of the catering operation with respect to legislation. Unfortunately, it is this which will probably have to be extended, to bring the present situation under control. At the present time (1989) the Institution of Environmental Health Officers is pressing the government to call for *registration of all food premises* (provision of minimum facilities compulsory) and at a later stage all food-handlers may also have to be registered (by hygiene qualification) to do their job.

14.12 FOOD HYGIENE LEGISLATION

The preparation and sale of food (including non-profit-making activities) is controlled by the Food Hygiene Regulations (General) 1970. The regulations are applicable to (a) any staff involved in handling food and (b) cleaners of equipment in food rooms. The responsibility for implementing this legislation is carried by Environmental Health Officers (EHOs) who regularly visit food businesses to monitor standards and offer advice. Failure to comply with the regulations may lead to fines (maximum £2000 for each offence) or imprisonment (maximum 2 years), but legal action is used only if advice has persistently been ignored.

Detail of the legislation, which in some cases is specific and in others very general, is outlined in Table 14.7.

Table 14.5   *Effective personal hygiene for food handlers*

	Action	Explanation
Protective clothing	Clean washable over clothes worn only on food premises	To prevent contamination from outdoor clothing spreading to food, surfaces and equipment. (To avoid faecal contamination – remove apron from whites before visiting toilet).
Shoes	Kichen shoes – to be worn *exclusively for food duties* and not worn outside	Outdoor shoes carry contamination into the kitchen; spores of pathogenic species of *Bacillus* and *Clostridium* are found commonly in soil.
Hair	Hair should be entirely *enclosed*. The traditional chef's hat is totally unsuitable except for short hair styles	(1) Physical contamination with hairs. (2) Hair contains many microbes, including pathogens. Hats prevent contact with hands and transfer to food, etc.
Hands	*Decontaminate* hands frequently; wash with hot water, soap, scrubbing brush; dry with hot air or disposable towel. Wash after: visiting toilet; handling raw food/refuse; touching neck/face/nose; and on entering food room.	Direct *skin contact* can contaminate food with pathogens from body, raw food etc. e.g. *Staphylococcus aureus* – nose; Salmonella – faeces.
Cuts, boils	Cover all cuts/abrasions with waterproof dressings. Food-handlers with septic boils on the hands should not handle food	Infected skin contains large doses of *Staphylococcus aureus*.
	Treat with antiseptic cream	Will make conditions unsuitable for further growth of microbes

	Action	*Explanation*
Nails	Keep *short* and *clean*	Avoids direct exposure of food to microbes trapped under nails.
	No nail varnish	Obscures cleanliness of nails.
Jewellery	Rings, watches, bracelets, earrings, necklaces, *should not be worn*	Jewellery traps grease, dirt, bacteria and (with the exception of wedding rings) should be removed; jewellery also encourages touching of the hands/arms/neck and contamination from *Staphylococcus*
Habits	*No smoking*, tasting of food using fingers or other activities which bring hands and mouth directly in contact with food	Contamination of food, equipment and surfaces with pathogens from the body
Illness	Sickness, diarrhoea, sore throat, fever or skin infections should be *reported* to management. Investigations should be made by GP or EHO. If *Salmonella* is detected three clear stool samples are required before returning to work	*Salmonella, Staphyloccus aureus* or other pathogens could be transferred to food or other food-handlers. Even if symptoms are gone *Salmonella* can be excreted in the faeces for some time and may be transferred, via the toilet, to other workers.

Table 14.6 *Safe food-handling procedures*

Action	Explanation
Store high-risk foods below 10°C	This temperature will stop the multiplication of most pathogens
Defrost completely at 5°C	To ensure that entire area of food is kept at a safe temperature
Raw and cooked foods should be kept separate	To prevent cross-contamination of live pathogens onto food which will not be reheated
Cook in small batches	1. Quicker to cool and heat 2. Avoids anaerobic conditions necessary for some pathogens to grow
Cook thoroughly	To ensure pathogens are killed. Refrigeration space is usually limited therefore it is better to cook food on the day it is to be consumed
Serve hot food immediately or hold at a temperature above 63°C	To prevent germination/multiplication of bacterial spores surviving the cooking process
Cool cooked food to below 10°C in less than 90 minutes	Prevents multiplication of surviving spores and other bacteria. 1. Use a blast-chiller or 2. Use a well-ventilated cool room
Reheating should be *avoided*	'Warmed up' food may not reach the internal temperature required to kill pathogens

Table 14.7 *Summary of Food Hygiene Regulations (General) 1970*

Section	Detail
Premises	No *food business* shall be carried on at any insanitary premises the *situation, design* and *construction* of which is such that food is exposed to risk of contamination. *Important points*: 1. Premises should be clean 2. Premises should be suitably lit 3. Premises should be suitably ventilated 4. Premises should be kept in good repair 5. Sanitary conveniences should be provided 6. Food-production areas should not be used for sleeping 7. Adequate provision should be made for refuse
Facilities	*Must provide*: 1. First Aid materials 2. Clean, wholesome water 3. Accommodation for outdoor clothes and shoes 4. Separate facilities for washing hands, raw food and equipment
Equipment	*Should be*: 1. Clean 2. Kept in good repair 3. Constructed of non-absorbent materials
Food-handlers	*Must*: 1. Not smoke/spit 2. Cover abrasions with waterproof dressings 3. Wear clean, washable over-clothing 4. Inform management of diarrhoea, vomiting, septic cuts, boils, throat/nose infections
Food-handling	Food handlers must *protect food from risk of contamination*: 1. Food should not be placed where it can be contaminated 2. Food kept for animals must be kept away from other food 3. Food for sale must be covered or screened
Catering practice	High-risk foods for immediate consumption should be kept at above 63°C or below 10°C; e.g. gravy, meat, poultry, cream

HEALTH AND SAFETY AT WORK

15.1 LEGISLATION

Health and Safety at Work Act (1974) (HASAWA)

This act is the main legislation concerned with health and safety at work and it covers both employees and members of the public. All employers (and the self-employed) have a legal obligation to ensure, so far as is reasonably practicable, the health and safety and welfare of all employees. Safe systems of working must be provided and supervised, and training in safe practices must be given to staff. Employers must also ensure that their acts or omissions do not endanger anyone else (non-employees) affected by their work.

Duties of employers

The general duties of employers to employees are set out in section 2 of the Act. The overall requirement is as follows:

> It shall be the duty of every employer to ensure, so far as is reasonably practicable, the health, safety and welfare at work of all his employees (HASAWA, Section 2(1)).

A brief summary of the more specific requirements are given as follows:

1. To provide and maintain premises, machinery, equipment and systems of work that are safe and without risk to health.
2. To ensure safety in connection with the use, handling, storage and transport of anything.
3. To provide information, instructions, training and supervision.
4. To provide a written statement of health and safety policy to employees. (Employers with fewer than five staff are exempt from this requirement). This written statement must include:

(a) the general policy;
(b) the organisation to back it up;
(c) arrangements for carrying it out.
5. To provide a safety committee and consult with employees' representatives.

Duties to persons other than employees

Employers also have duties, under the Act, for people who are not employees but who are affected by the way the organisation is run. This will include contractors who are working on the premises and members of the public such as guests.

Duties of employees

1. To take reasonable care for the health and safety of themselves and others.
2. To cooperate with the employer and relevant others in complying with the Act.
3. Not to misuse anything relevant to the encouragement of health and safety.

Enforcement of the Health and Safety at Work Act

Government and local authority inspectors are empowered to enter a premises at any reasonable time to ensure that the health and safety standards comply with the Act.

The various procedures that inspectors can use to secure compliance fall under two headings:

1. *Informal* verbal, letters, information leaflets
2. *Formal* improvement notices, prohibition notices, prosecution.

15.2 REPORTING ACCIDENTS

Notification

After attending to the urgent priority of arranging suitable treatment for the injured, any accident which occurs on the premises, whether to employees or members of the public, must be reported. The employer will, in due course, have to report certain categories of accidents to the local Department of Environmental Health.

Employees' responsibilities for reporting

Employees must report any accident to their employer. There should be an accident book in which will be entered the details of the accident including, date, time, name, nature of injury, action taken.

Employer's responsibilities for reporting

Any employer or self-employed person must report in writing, within seven days, any accident resulting in death or major injury, or any dangerous occurrences (whether accidents resulted or not), to their local Department of Environmental Health. Dangerous occurrences include such situations as explosions, collapse of parts of building, food-poisoning.

15.3 ACCIDENT PREVENTION

Introduction

Up to 1500 people have been killed and 300 000 injured with three or more days absence from work, per year, as a result of inadequate provision for health and safety at work in British industry. These tragic figures represent considerable pain and suffering by victims and their families and emphasise the practical importance of this subject. The catering industry is a very large employer, not only because it is a large industrial sector, but as a service industry, it is labour-intensive.

Preventive factors

It is obviously essential to prevent accidents as far as possible and the Health and Safety at Work Act has increased the range of measures to assist this. Following is a range of points that help to promote a positive approach to Health and Safety at work:

1. Employees have a right in law to appoint their own union safety representative and require their employers to set up a safety committee.
2. The workplace is inspected regularly by work representatives and inspectors.
3. Complaints about lack of safety and potential hazards must be followed up when reported.
4. Conditions of the working environment that may cause ill-health over a period of time are also recognised as significant and must be put right.
5. Employees have a right to information from their employer and inspectors.

6. Safety representatives have a right to time off with pay for the purpose of attending safety courses, also for carrying out their duties in connection with safety.
7. The availability of publications on all aspects of the Act (see 15.4).
8. The availability of courses, both college and industry based, as well as training packs.
9. The availability of posters to encourage good practice.

15.4 PUBLICATIONS

Sources

A considerable range of publications and other materials on health and safety is available. Many of these have been produced as a result of the Act where responsible agents have taken initiatives to inform the public. Some of the publications are free whilst others have to be either purchased or borrowed from an employer or library.

Materials available

It is not possible within this book to catalogue the full extent of health and safety publications and materials. The following list, however, gives an indication of availability.

1. *Her Majesty's Stationery Office* (HMSO) There is a considerable range of booklets on all aspects of the Act as well as health and safety generally, e.g. *A guide to the Safety Signs Regulations; Cloakroom Accommodation and Washing Facilities; Hours of Employment of Women and Young Persons; Canteens, Messrooms and Refreshment Services.*
2. *Health and Safety Commission (HSC)* A considerable range of leaflets and booklets on all aspects of Health and Safety, e.g. *Some Legal Aspects and How they will Affect You* (HSC 1); *The Act Outlined* (HSC 2); *Statements for Health and Safety at Work.*
3. *Department of Employment (Department of Enterprise)* A wide range of technical guidance notes on specific situations and machines, e.g. *The Ventilation of Buildings: Fresh Air Requirements; Dough dividers, Safety in the Use of Rotating-table Pie and Tart Machines; Safe Operation of Automatically Controlled Steam and Hot-water Boilers; The Safe Use of Food-slicing Machines.*
4. *Trade Union Congress (TUC)* Various publications including those aimed at self-instruction and short-course instruction, e.g. *Health and Safety at Work: A short Course for Union Safety Representatives; TUC Handbook on Safety and Health at Work.*

15.5 WORKING METHODS

The most essential factor in maintaining a safe working environment is the positive attitude of all staff towards safe working methods. There are a large number of accepted rules of procedure which assist health and safety in the kitchen where the pace of work itself would pose a danger. It is these practices that are learned as a part of becoming a *caterer*.

15.6 FIRE PREVENTION

The Fire Precaution Act (1971)

All catering premises (some small establishments excepted) are required by law to obtain a *fire certificate* from the local fire authority (Fire Brigade). This will involve an appointed fire officer carrying out an inspection of the premises. The basis of this will be to look at

1. the means of escape in the case of fire;
2. the facilities for fire fighting;
3. the preventive measures against fires starting.

A *fire certificate* will specify the following:

- the various uses made of the premises
- the fire fighting equipment for the use of people in the building
- the means of escape in the case of fire
- the means of raising the alarm in the case of fire
- staff training and the keeping of records
- the maximum number of people who may be in the building at any one time

The consequences of fires can be horrific and may be caused simply by carelessness. A number of initiatives operate in all establishments to assist the prevention and control of fire through training staff to be alert to danger of fire, to know how to raise alarm and how to locate and operate fire extinguishers.

Raising the alarm

Instructions must be laid down for the procedure to be taken in the case of fire. This will involve:

- how to raise the alarm
- how to contact the fire brigade
- who to contact internally
- how to evacuate the building and assembly points

Table 15.1 *Safe working methods*

Rule	Notes
Never carry knives or other tools with the points protruding	You may walk into somebody or they may bump into you
Do not attempt to catch a falling knife	Let it drop to the ground, then pick it up
Knives must never be left in sinks of water	Bad cuts would be likely to occur to unsuspecting people putting their hands in the water
When using a knife cut away from you; when cleaning a knife wipe with the edge away from you	Knives are sharp so be aware of how they will cut you with misuse
Keep work-benches clear of unnecessary tools, especially knives	One of the signs of a competent craftsperson; correct working method; a safer situation
Keep oven cloths dry	Avoid scalding hands on hot items
Never use your hand where it is unsafe, e.g. mincing machine, bowl chopper, liquidiser, etc.	If this operation is necessary there will be utensils to do it, e.g. plastic plungers
When using an electric mixer ensure that it is in the first gear before switching on	Often left in top gear and will splash if mixing bowl is full
Where pans are removed from the oven do not leave hot handles unmarked	Unsuspecting people will burn their hands when attempting to pick the pan up particularly as a firm grip is used
Combining extremes of temperature in cooking must be done slowly	Examples in deep-frying wet items, adding stock to roux, etc.
Do not leave saucepan handles protruding from the stove top	These could easily be knocked off
Avoid the use of excess fat when grilling, frying, roasting, etc.	To avoid splashing and reduce fire risk

Never put cans (e.g. fruit) in a bain-marie to heat up	These may explode when opening or before
Unsealed containers with liquids should not be shelved above shoulder height	Avoid spillage from a height
Spillages of water and grease on the floor must be cleared up immediately	Otherwise potentially very dangerous
Breakages of glass and china must be cleared away and checked immediately	If splinters thought to be in food this must be thrown away
When lifting heavy objects from the floor do so with a straight back	Use leg and thigh muscles, not back muscles, otherwise back may easily be strained
Be particularly attentive when using electric mechanical equipment	Mechanical equipment will not stop automatically in the case of accidents
Avoid distractions when carrying out tasks, particularly when doing so at speed	This is when many accidents happen

Additionally, some special provisions will need to be included according to the type of business undertaken. In the case of hotels there will be a number, possibly very large, of guests unfamiliar with the building. People with disabilities such as immobility and deafness, will need special attention.

Fire extinguishers

Small fires may be dealt with by members of staff and there will be equipment available to do this. Occasionally people panic and/or do not have the confidence to use fire-fighting equipment. This may be based, in part, on the fear that extinguishers are difficult to control as indeed the old types were. Most fires can be put out with water although there are a number of exceptions. Adequate training is the key to providing staff with the necessary confidence and the local fire brigade may assist with this. Figure 15.1 sets out details of some of the types of fire extinguishers that are available.

392

Figure 15.1 *Fire extinguishers*

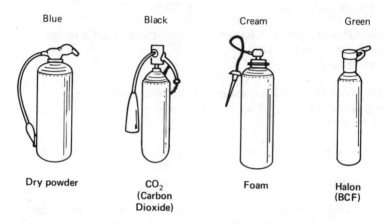

Blue   Black   Cream   Green

Dry powder CO_2 (Carbon Dioxide)   Foam   Halon (BCF)

15.7 FIRST AID

The Health and Safety (First Aid) Regulations, 1981

These regulations place a duty on employers to:

- make an adequate provision of First Aid facilities
- have sufficient First Aiders (the employer is still responsible)
- make First Aid provisions where special hazards are concerned
- inform all staff of the provisions.

Definition

The object of First Aid is to provide immediate medical treatment in the case of accidents or other sudden illness. First Aid is not medically qualified treatment but a means of saving life and/or preventing the condition getting worse, until a doctor is involved.

First-aiders

First Aiders are trained by means of a short course (four days or equivalent) which will be conducted by either the St John Ambulance, the British Red Cross, or St Andrew's Ambulance Association. A certificate is issued to successful First Aiders and this has to be updated every three years. Many large companies will employ a full-time nursing staff and in some cases, a doctor. In other situations any immediate medical assistance required will be available from a member of the workforce who is a First Aider.

First Aid boxes

First Aid boxes will be available in work-rooms and these will be periodically checked and contents replenished as required. The minimum contents requirements for First Aid boxes are shown in Table 15.2.

Table 15.2 *First Aid box contents*

| Items | Number of employees | | | | |
	1–5	6–10	11–50	50–100	101–150
Guidance card	1	1	1	1	1
* Individually wrapped sterile adhesive dressing	10	20	40	40	40
Sterile eye pad with attachment	1	2	4	6	8
Triangular bandage	1	2	4	6	8
Sterile covering for serious wounds	6	6	6	12	12
Safety pins	6	6	12	12	12
Medium-sized sterile unmedicated dressing	3	6	8	10	12
Large sterile unmedicated dressing	1	2	4	6	10
Extra large sterile unmedicated dressing	1	2	4	6	8

* Plasters are of blue colour for food handlers.

Basic First Aid treatment

There is no real substitute for proper training. Below are some brief notes on the treatment of quite common accidents for initial guidance.
General points
1. Anything likely to cause death such as, stoppage of breathing (asphyxia) or severe bleeding, must be attended to first.

2. Avoid moving a patient, especially if further injury may be caused by doing so, e.g. back injury.
3. Ensure that the patient is comfortable and as calm as possible. Try to keep calm yourself, and do not panic.
4. If the patient is unconscious s/he should be turned on his/her side; the top leg bent at the knee and the underneath arm gently pulled out behind (recovery position); false teeth should be removed.
5. Loosen any tight clothing around neck, chest, waist.

Shock   After an accident shock may be delayed. The symptoms are pale face; blueness of lips and cheeks; cold and clammy skin; quick but fairly weak pulse. Cover the patient with coat or blanket but do not allow to get too warm. Raise the legs if possible and lower head.

Cuts   Cleanliness is essential to prevent infection. Clean the cut and cover with a waterproof dressing. In the case of severe bleeding this must be stopped immediately by applying pressure. If this is not possible indirect pressure must be applied with fingers over the artery between the heart and the wound. This is done while the dressing is being prepared and should not continue beyond 15 minutes. If possible raise the wound to reduce pressure.

Electric shock   The electric current must be turned off. If this is not possible the patient must be pushed away from the electric current. On no account must the patient be touched directly while in contact with live current. Push the patient away with the aid of a wooden pole, rubber gloves, rubber mat, rubber boots. Treat according to condition. If breathing has stopped mouth-to-mouth respiration will be necessary.

Fractures   A fracture is a broken bone which must be secured before the patient is moved. On no account should a lay person attempt to set a fracture.

Burns   Cool in water until the pain subsides. If likely to blister cover with a clean dry dressing. In the case of severe burns treat for shock and contact hospital.

Fainting   Fainting is caused by a short stoppage of blood to the brain. If someone feels *faint* they should sit down with the head lowered to the knees.

Poisoning   People may be poisoned in a number of ways. Infected wounds, dangerous gases, eating contaminated foods, and overdose of medicines are some situations which can cause poisoning. Send for the doctor or ambulance.

15.8 ROLE OF THE ENVIRONMENTAL HEALTH OFFICER

EHOs are based in Local Authority Health Departments and have the same powers as Health and Safety Inspectors to enforce the Health and Safety at Work Act. To do this, Environmental Health Officers may enter a catering premises at any reasonable time to inspect. They do not require the permission of anybody for entry and may recruit police support if necessary. If a breach of the Act is discovered, the EHO will take action according to its severity. The types of actions that the EHO may take are as follows:

- issue a prohibition notice   This is to stop any activity continuing that the EHO considers may give rise to serious risk or personal injury.
- issue an improvement notice   This is a notice issued to remedy a situation in a specified time.
- advise   This may be given in verbal or written form. It will be based upon putting a potentially unsafe situation right and preventing a future problem.
- sieze, render harmless or destroy items   This would be necessary where anything could cause imminent danger.
- prosecute   This may be done instead of, or in addition to, a notice.

APPENDIX: GLOSSARY OF TECHNICAL TERMS

à la [a-la]	in the style of
à l'anglaise [a-l-ahn-gle]	a dish prepared in English style
à la française [a-la-frahn-sheez]	a dish prepared in French style
à la carte [a-la-kart]	dishes which are individually priced on a menu and prepared to order
à la minute [a-la-mee-noo]	cooked to order, as on an à la carte menu
abricot [a-bree-koh]	apricot
aigrefin [e-gre-fen]	haddock
ail [a-y]	garlic
aile [el]	wing of poultry or game
ailerons [el-ron]	winglets of poultry or game
allumette [a-lu-met]	matchstick size and shape, e.g. Pommes allumette
aloyau [al-wa-oh]	sirloin of beef on the bone
amande [a-mand]	almond
ananas [a-na-nah]	pineapple
anchoise [ahn-shwa]	anchovy
anguille [ahn-gee-y]	eel

appareil [a-pa-re-y]	prepared mixtures which are the basis of some dishes
aromates [arrow-mah]	indicating culinary herbs and spices
artichaut [ar-tee-shoh]	globe artichoke
aspic [as-pic]	savoury jelly
assorti [a-sawr-tee]	an assortment, e.g. Fromages assortis
au beurre [oh-burr]	cooked in, or served with melted butter
au bleu [oh-ble]	(a) steak cooked very underdone (b) trout poached from very fresh e.g. Truite au bleu
au four [oh-foor]	cooked in the oven, e.g. Pommes au four
au gratin [oh-gra-ten]	sprinkled with cheese and browned under a salamander grill
au jus [oh-zhu]	dishes served with a gravy
au vin blanc [oh-ven-blahn]	cooked or finished with white wine
bain-marie [ben-ma-ree]	a container of water into which foods are placed for holding or cooking
banane [ba-nan]	banana
barbue [bar-bu]	brill
bécasse [bay-kas]	woodcock
bécassine [bay-kas-seen]	snipe
betterave [be-trav]	beetroot
beurre manié [ber-man-yeh]	butter and flour kneaded together and used for thickening
beurre noisette [ber-nwa-zet]	nut-brown butter
blanc [blahn]	A cooking liquor made of water, salt, lemon juice and flour for cooking certain types of vegetables, preserving or enhancing their natural colour
blanchaille [blahnsh-ay]	whitebait
blanquette [blahn-ket]	a white stew (sauce made from cooking liquor)

blond [blohn]	refers to a blond or second-stage roux
bombe [bohnb]	an iced sweet made from various ice creams and garnished in a bombe (shaped) mould
bordure [bawr-dur]	border of rice, potato, etc. surrounding a dish
bouchée [boo-shay]	small puff-pastry case (mouthful size)
bouillon [boo-yohn]	a flavoured cooking liquor or soup
bouquet garni [boo-ke-gar-nee]	parsley stalks, bay and thyme
braiser [bre-zay]	to braise
brider [bree-day]	to truss poultry or game
brioche [bree-awsh]	a small or large rich yeast cake
broche [brawsh]	roasting spit
brochette [braw-shet]	skewer
brouillé [broo-yay]	scrambled as in Oeufs Brouillé
brun [brun]	brown
brunoise [bru-n-wa-z]	very small even dice, e.g. vegetables
buffet [bu-fe]	table set out with hot and/or cold foods for self-service
cabillaud [ka-bee-yoh]	cod
café [ka-fay]	coffee
caille [kah-y]	quail
canapé [ka-na-pay]	small savouries or hors d'oeuvre which have small shapes usually of bread (toasted or fried) as the base.
canard [ka-nar]	duck
canard sauvage [ka-nar-soh-vazh]	wild duck
caneton [kan-tohn]	duckling
caramel [ka-ra-mel]	sugar cooked to amber colour and used for various sweet preparations such as Crême Caramel

carotte [ka-rawt]	carrot
carré [kar-ray]	best end, e.g. Carré d'Agneau
carte du jour [kart-du-zhoor]	menu of the day (either table d'hôte or à la carte)
casserole [kas-rawl]	(a) a heatproof dish with lid (b) name given to dish cooked in a casserole
cerise [ser-reez]	cherry
Champignons [shahn-peen-yohn]	mushrooms
Chantilly [shan-tee-ee]	stiff sweetened whipped cream
chapelure [shap-lur]	dried breadcrumbs
charlotte [shar-lot]	certain sweet dishes made in moulds lined with bread or sponge biscuits
Chateaubriand [shah-ton-bre-on]	the thick-end sector of a fillet of beef cooked as a joint
chaud [shoh]	hot
chaud-froid [shoh-fraw]	a setting savoury sauce used for coating cold buffet dishes prior to decoration
chemise [shmeez]	line a mould with jelly, e.g. aspic
chinois [sheen-wa]	a conical strainer
chou [shoo]	cabbage
chou-fleur [shoo-fler]	cauliflower
choux de Bruxelle [shoo-de-brux-el]	brussel spouts
citron [see-trohn]	lemon
civet [see-vay]	a brown stew, e.g. Civet de lièvre
clair(e) [kl-air]	clear, e.g. Consommé (no garnish)
cloche [klawsh]	a fireproof glass cover used in cooking and presenting certain dishes, e.g. Champignons sous cloche
clouté [kloo-tay]	studded, e.g. onion studded with cloves and used in making béchamel sauce
cocotte [kaw-kawt]	fireproof dish used for various dishes, e.g. Oeufs en cocotte

colin [kaw-len]	hake
compote [kohn-pawt]	a combination of stewed fruits served, for example, as a breakfast dish, e.g. compote of fruits
concassé [kohn-cas-ay]	coarsely chopped, e.g. tomato concassé
concombre [kon-kohnbr]	cucumber
confiture [kohn-fee-tur]	jam
consommé [kohn-saw-may]	crystal-clear soup served hot or cold
contrefilet [kohntr-fee-le]	sirloin of beef off the bone
coquille St Jacques [kaw-kee-sen-zhak]	scallops
cordon [kawr-dohn]	thin thread of sauce encircling a dish
côte [kawt]	rib, e.g. Côte de boeuf roti
côtelette [koht-let]	cutlet
coupe [koop]	various garnished ice-cream-based dishes
courge [koorzh]	marrow
court bouillon [koor-boo-yohn]	cooking liquor flavoured with vegetables, herbs and vinegar used for cooking certain fish, offals, etc.
crêpe [krep]	pancake
crevette [kre-vet]	prawns
croquette [kraw-ket]	cylinder-shaped cooked food preparations coated with flour, eggwashed, and breadcrumbed and deep-fried, e.g. Pommes croquette, Croquette de volaille
croûte [kroot]	cushion of shaped fried bread on which are served various hot food preparations such as stuffing
croûton [kroo-ton]	(a) small dice of bread fried in butter and served with soups, etc. (b) shaped pieces of fried bread served as part of a garnish, e.g. heart-shaped croûtons

cuisine [kwee-zeen]	kitchen
cuisse [kwees]	leg, e.g. poultry legs
cuit [kwee]	cooked, e.g. 'bien cuit' means well-cooked
culotte [ku-lawt]	rump
dariole [dar-ee-awl]	a small mould shaped like a flower-pot
darne [dar-n]	a cut of round fish through the centre bone
déglace [day-glas]	to swill out a pan in which food has been cooked and use the liquor in the accompanying sauce
dégraisser [day-gras-ay]	to skim off the fat floating on the top of liquids such as stock
demi-glace [de-mee-glas]	brown sauce enriched by reduction
déjeuner [day-jer-nay]	luncheon
dinde [dend]	turkey
diner [dee-nay]	diner
doré [daw-ray]	golden
du jour [du-zhoor]	speciality of the day
duxelle [duck-sell]	a basic preparation of finely chopped mushroom and shallots
Ecossaise [ay-kaw-se]	Scotch style, e.g. Scotch eggs (oeufs ecossaise)
émincer [ay-manse-ay]	to slice
en croûte [ahn-kroot]	wrapped in pastry
en papillote [ahn-pa-pee-yawt]	a method of cooking and presenting food cooked in a tightly sealed envelope of greaseproof paper
en tasse [ahn-tahs]	served in cups, e.g. Consommé en tasse
entrecôte [ahn-tre-koht]	a steak cut from the sirloin of beef
épaule [ay-pohl]	shoulder

épinard [ay-pee-nar]	spinach
escalope [es-ka-lawp]	thin slice of meat usually battened out
escargot [es-kar-goh]	snail
espagnole [es-too-fard]	traditional basic brown sauce
estouffade [es-pan-yaw]	brown stock
étuver [ay-tu-vay]	cooked in own juice
faisan [fe-zahn]	pheasant
farce [fars]	stuffing
farine [fa-reen]	flour
feuilletage [fe-y-et-tazh]	puff-pastry
fines herbes [fee-ns-erb]	a mixture of parsley, tarragon and chervil being fine delicate herbs
flambé [flahn-bay]	flamed
flan [flahn]	open tart, usually sweet but also savoury
flank	a cut of meat between the breast and leg, usually used for stewing
flétan [flay-tan]	halibut
fleuron [fle-r-on]	small crescent shapes of puff-pastry used for garnishing fish and vegetable dishes
foie [faw]	liver
foie gras [fwa-grah]	goose liver pâté (full title: Pâté de foie gras)
fondant [fohn-dahn]	a textured icing
fondu [fohn-du]	melted
frappé [frap-pay]	chilled, e.g. Melon frappé
friandises [free-ahn-deez]	sugar-based petits fours
fricassé [free-ka-say]	a white stew where the meat is cooked in the sauce

fromage [fraw-mazh]	cheese
frosting	icing which gives dishes the appearance of frosting
fumée [fu-may]	smoked
fumet [fu-me]	a stock of essence, e.g. fumet de poisson (fish)
galantine [gal-an-teen]	dish made from white meat, rolled, glazed, decorated and served cold
garniture [gar-nee-tur]	foods used to decorate a dish
gâteau [gah-toh]	cake
gelée [zhe-lay]	jelly
ghee	Indian clarified butter
gibier [zhee-byay]	game
gigot [zhee-goh]	leg, e.g. Gigot d'Agneau
glace [glas]	ice cream
glacé [gla-say]	iced
glacer [gla-say]	to glaze under a salamander grill
gnocchi	a light savoury dumpling made from either choux paste, potato or semolina
gratiner [gra-tee-nay]	to brown a dish under the salamander grill using cheese and breadcrumbs
grillé [gree-y]	grilled, e.g. Entrecôte grillé
grouse	grouse
hache [ash]	chop finely or mince
haggis	Scottish dish made from finely chopped sheep's liver, lights and heart mixed with oatmeal and seasoning and cooked in the stomach-bag of a sheep
hanche [ahnsh]	leg or loin of venison
hareng [a-rahn]	herring
huile [weel]	oil

huître	oyster
[weetr]	
jalousie	a gâteau made from puff-pastry
[zha-loo-zee]	
jambon	ham
[zhahn-bohn]	
jardinière	vegetables, etc. cut in batten-shapes
[zhar-dee-nyer]	
julienne	vegetables, etc. cut in very thin strips
[zhu-lee-en]	
jugged	a brown stew of game, e.g. Jugged Hare
junket	Devonshire sweet dish made from milk and rennet
jus lié	thickened gravy
[zhu-lyay]	
jus de rôti	roast gravy
[zhu-de-roh-tee]	
kari	curry
lait	milk
[le]	
laitance	soft roe of fish
[le-tohn-s]	
laitue	lettuce
[le-tu]	
lard	bacon
[lar]	
langue	tongue
[lahng]	
larder	to insert strips of fat into lean meat such as
[lar-day]	beef with a larding needle, i.e. to lard
lardon	small pieces of bacon used for garnish
[lar-don]	
laurier	bay
[law-ryay]	
légumes	vegetables
[lay-gum]	
liaison	egg-yolk and cream mixed and used to
[lye-zohn]	enrich and thicken certain soups and sauces
lier	to thicken
[lyay]	
longe	loin
[lohnzh]	
losange	cut diamond shape, e.g. runner bean
[law-zahnzh]	
macédoine	(a) a dice-shape, approx 6mm each way

[ma-say-dwan]	(b) mixture of fruits or vegetables, e.g. macédoine de fruits, macédoine de légumes
maquereau [ma-kroh]	mackerel
marinade [ma-ree-nad]	to soak in prepared flavoured liquor, e.g. brine
marmite [mar-meet]	stock pot
marron [ma-rohn]	chestnut
médaillon [may-da-yohn]	foods prepared in a round shape, e.g. Médaillon de veau
melon [me-lohn]	melon
menthe [mahnt]	mint
merlan [mer-lahn]	whiting
mie de pain [mee-de-pen]	fresh breadcrumbs
mignonnette [meen-yaw-net]	crushed fresh peppercorns
mille-feuilles [meel-fe-y]	a gâteau made from puff-pastry, i.e. 'thousand leaves'
mirepoix [meer-pwa]	a preparation of root vegetables for certain soups and sauces
mise en place [meez-ahn-plas]	everything in place, i.e. preparation
monter [mohn-tay]	to finish a sauce by adding unmelted butter
mousse [moos]	sweet or savoury light textured dish
moutard [moo-tard]	mustard
napper [nap-ay]	mask with a sauce
navarin [na-va-ren]	brown lamb stew
navet [na-ve]	turnip
noisette [nwa-zet]	pear-shaped cut of lamb from the loin
nouille [noo-y]	noodles

oeuf [e-r-f]	egg
oignon [aw-nyohn]	onion
oseille [aw-ze-y]	sorrel
paille [pah-y]	straws as in Pommes pailles
pain [pen]	bread, e.g. Petits pain (bread rolls)
pamplemousse [pahn-ple-moos]	grapefruit
panaché [pa-na-shay]	mixed, e.g. Salad panaché
panade [pan-ar-d]	a basic preparation used for binding, e.g. flour panade used for chou paste
panais [pa-ne]	parsnip
pané [pa-nay]	coated, e.g. with breadcrumbs
paupiette [poh-pe-yet]	a strip of fish, poultry or meat stuffed and rolled, e.g. Paupiette de sole
paysanne [pay-ee-zahn]	cut of small vegetable slices
pêche [pesh]	peach
perdreau [per-droh]	partridge
persil [per-see]	parsley
petits pois [per-tee-pwa]	peas
pilaw [peel-aw]	braised rice
piquant(e) [pee-kahn]	sharp, e.g. sauce piquante
piqué [pee-kay]	(a) studded as in Oignon piqué (b) larded
plie [plee]	plaice
pluvier [plu-vyay]	plover
poêle [pwal]	a moist method of roasting under cover
poire [pwar]	pear

poireau [pwa-roh]	leek
poivre [pwavr]	pepper
pomme [pawm]	apple
pomme de terre [pawm-de-ter]	potato; this is usually abbreviated to pommes and the distinction between potatoes and apples is usually clear by the context
praline [pra-leen]	crushed brittle nut toffee
printanière [pren-ta-nyay]	use of Spring vegetables
profiteroles [praw-fee-tur-al]	large or small choux paste buns used for garnish or sweet dishes
purée [pu-ray]	foods passed through sieve or liquidised
quenelle [ke-nel]	forcemeat, shaped and poached, e.g. Quenelle of sole
ragôut [ra-goo]	stew, e.g. Ragôut de boeuf
raie [re]	skate
réchauffer [ray-shoh-fay]	to reheat
risotto	Italian rice dish
rognon [rawn-yohn]	kidney
rôtir [roh-teer]	to roast
roux [roo]	fat and flour cooked together for thickening: white roux, blond roux, brown roux
rutabaga [ru-ta-ba-ga]	swede (rooty baker)
sabayon [sab-ay-on]	egg-yolk and a liquid whisked over heat and used as a basis for sauces and sweets
salamander [sal-a-man-der	a grill with the heat radiated from the top
saumon fumé [sau-mohn-fu-may]	smoked salmon
sauter [soh-tay]	to toss in shallow fat using a sauté pan
selle [sel]	saddle

soubise [soo-beez]	a purée of onion
soufflé [soo-flay]	a sweet or savoury dish where air has been incorporated to give a light texture
sucre [sukr]	sugar
suprême [su-prem]	the best part, e.g. breast of chicken (Suprême de volaille)
tamis [ta-mee]	a fine sieve of hair, cloth or wire
terrine [te-reen]	an earthenware container for cooking
topinambour [taw-pee-nahn-boor]	Jerusalem artichoke
tortue [tawr-tu]	turtle
tourné [toor-nay]	turned, i.e. shape as barrel, olive, etc.
tranche [trahnsh]	slice
tronçon [trohn-sohn]	cut of large flat fish with bone, e.g. Tronçon de turbot
truite [trweet]	trout
turbot [tur-bow]	turbot
velouté [ve-loo-tay]	a soup or sauce with velvety consistency
vert [ver]	green
viande [vyahnd]	meat
vinaigrette [vee-ne-gret]	a dressing of oil, vinegar and seasoning
vol-au-vent [vawl-oh-vahn]	puff-pastry case larger than bouchée
volaille [vaw-la-y]	poultry

QUESTIONS

CHAPTER 1

1. Match the developments in the left-hand column to the historical period in the right-hand column.

   1. Seaside bathing   (a) Middle Ages
   2. Pilgrimages   (b) Sixteenth century
   3. Coffee houses   (c) Seventeenth century
   4. The commercial inn   (d) Eighteenth century
   5. Taverns   (e) Nineteenth century
   6. Clubs

2. Which are the three main factors that account for the emergence of industrial canteens in the early twentieth century? (a) the shortage of other catering outlets; (b) the shortage of food supplies; (c) longer hours of work not allowing people to return home so often to eat; (d) concern for the health of the nation; (e) a shortage of fuel for home cooking; (f) a limit on wages resulting in other benefits to compensate.

3. Consider the principal needs of the various client groups in the left-hand column below and match these to the appropriate catering outlet in the right-hand column below. In some cases more than one catering outlet will be appropriate.

   (a) Wedding reception for 100   1. Speciality restaurant (Indian)
       people   2. Medium-size hotel
   (b) A birthday luncheon for two   3. Meals-on-wheels
   (c) Quick economical lunch for   4. Pizza House
       shoppers with children   5. Public house
   (d) Housebound Senior Citizens
   (e) Fast high class luncheon for
       business executives
   (f) Economical lunch for students
   (g) Healthy eating conscious group
       of office workers

4. Which of the following statements are true in relation to *tourism*?
(a) The words *catering* and *tourism* have the same meaning;
(b) British rail is a part of the tourist industry; (c) Tourism is an export industry; (d) Entertainment is a part of the tourist industry.

5. According to the British Hotels, Restaurants and Caterers Association analysis 1987, which of the following statements are correct?
(a) Educational catering is a larger sector than clubs; (b) Restaurants and cafes are a smaller sector than hotels and other tourist accommodation; (c) Contract catering is a smaller sector than educational catering; (d) Industrial and office catering is a larger sector than medical and other health service catering; (e) Public houses are a larger sector than hotels and other tourist accommodation.

6. (a) Which pieces of cooking equipment have been used throughout the centuries and are still in use today?
   (b) State whether the following statements are true (T) or false (F). Labour-saving devices used in a kitchen contribute to:
   (i) Cutting down on the number of staff required.   T/F
   (ii) Increasing the kitchen output.   T/F
   (iii) Better portion control.   T/F
   (iv) Smaller kitchens.   T/F

7. Which two of the following factors have been most influential in the evolution of cookery? (a) availability of spices; (b) discovery of fire; (c) food fashions; (d) availability of meat.

8. Which one of the following is the main purpose of the chef's uniform: (a) identity; (b) promotion of pride in craft; (c) to protect food while it is being prepared; (d) protect the cook's outside clothes.

9. State whether the following statements are true (T) or false (F):
   (a) Gastronomy is confined to French cookery only.   T/F
   (b) Gastronomy requires the very best food and wine.   T/F
   (c) There are professional associations that promote gastronomy   T/F
   (d) Gastronomy is concerned with healthy eating.   T/F
   (e) Gastronomy should be studied by all chefs.   T/F

CHAPTER 2

1. Popular catering may involve the use of the following:
   (a) Restricted menus   T/F
   (b) Classical French cuisine   T/F
   (c) Cook–chill   T/F
   (d) Standard restaurant decor   T/F

2. Function catering may involve the use of:
   (a) Large numbers of casual staff   T/F
   (b) A cook–chill system   T/F
   (c) à la carte menus   T/F
   (d) Mobile kitchen facilities   T/F

CHAPTER 3

1. Identify the TEN principles of Nouvelle Cuisine discussed in this chapter. The first and last letter of key words are set out below to assist memory.

   M—U
   A————C
   T—E
   T————Y
   I————E
   N————N
   S————Y
   F————S
   I————E
   L—T

2. Which of the following ingredients would not be used or would be restricted in Cuisine Minceur? (a) powdered milk; (b) skimmed milk; (c) fats; (d) sugar substitute; (e) oils; (f) flour; (g) egg yolk; (h) sugar.

3. Which of the following religious groups do not eat beef? (a) Jew; (b) Buddhist; (c) Muslim; (d) Roman Catholic; (e) Mormon.

4. Which of the following religious groups do not drink alcohol? (a) Roman Catholic; (b) Jew; (c) Mormon; (d) Muslim; (e) Hindu.

5. In relation to the principles of nouvelle cuisine, decide whether the following statements are true or false:
   (a) The best method of service for nouvelle cuisine is silver service   T/F
   (b) With shorter cooking times and simpler dishes, menus are usually extended with nouvelle cuisine.   T/F
   (c) One of the most important principles in nouvelle cuisine is adhering strictly to the recipe provided.   T/F
   (d) Traditional stock is acceptable as a base for nouvelle cuisine dishes   T/F
   (e) Dishes should be served on highly decorated crockery to enhance the presentation.   T/F

6. The Government's recommendations for healthy eating are that we should eat less:

S——
S——
F——

We should eat more:

F——

CHAPTER 4

1. Which two of the following are most influential in determining the size of a kitchen? (a) style of operation; (b) number of customers catered for; (c) type of equipment used; (d) type of menu used.
2. Match the right and left-hand columns

(a) Chef Communard	(1) Pastry
(b) Sous Chef	(2) Vegetables
(c) Chef Garde Manger	(3) Plain roast joints
(d) Chef Entremettier	(4) Cold food preparation
(e) Chef Potager	(5) Relief
(f) Chef Saucier	(6) Poêlés
(g) Chef Tournant	(7) Administration
(h) Chef Pâtissier	(8) Staff meals
(i) Chef Rôtissier	(9) Soup

3. Identify from the left-hand column in Question 2 the chef or chefs involved in the preparation and service of the following dishes in the partie system: Consommé Royale; Consommé en gelée; Roast Beef and Yorkshire Pudding; Beef Stroganoff; Pommes Croquette; Pommes Duchesse; Courgette Provençale; Soufflé au Fromage; Bread and Butter Pudding.
4. Which are the three most important features of the partie system: (a) status; (b) specialisation; (c) speed; (d) economy; (e) quality.
5. A Which of the catering operations below may be organised as either *in house* or *contract*?
   B Which of the catering operations below will have strictly defined job titles with matching salary structure?
   C Which of the catering operations below are profit-making?
   D Which of the catering operations below are subsidised?
   (tick appropriate box or boxes)

	A	B	C	D

1 Army catering
2 Educational institution catering
3 Holiday camp catering
4 Hospital catering
5 Industrial canteen catering
6 Inflight catering
7 Leisure centre catering
8 Motorway catering
9 Mobile contract catering
10 Royal Air Force catering
11 Royal Navy Catering
12 Schools Meals Service

6. Which three of the following are the main advantages of kitchen routine in food preparation? (a) working-pace regulation; (b) staff morale; (c) hygiene regulation enforcement; (d) consistent quality.

7. To be prepared for a possible sudden increase in chance customers on any one day the following **two** techniques should be used: (Tick the best two) (a) menus to combine a mix of fresh and convenience foods; (b) restrict menu choices; (c) feature only 'cooked to order' items on the menu; (d) ensure microwave cooker available; (e) adequate mise en place.

8. Which of the following specialists are legally required to hold qualifications in order to carry out work? (a) electrician; (b) plumber; (c) gardener; (d) carpenter.

CHAPTER 5

1. Match the following storage items with suitable temperatures:
   bread   (a)
   lettuce   (b)
   meat   (c)
   ice cream   (d)
   cooked chicken   (e)
   (1) −18°C (2) 4°C (3) 20°C (4) 0–3°C

2. (i) Place the following list in order of perishability starting with the most perishable first.
   (ii) Which two commodities in the list would be given separate storage from most other goods?
   (iii) Which commodities from this list preferably require dark storage?
   (iv) Which commodities from the list would be ordered on a daily basis?

414

(a) tinned pineapple rings
(b) potato crisps
(c) fresh plaice
(d) bananas
(e) dried apricots
(f) fresh, grade 1 tomatoes
(g) fresh lobsters
(h) lettuce
3. (a) Opening and closing stock value totals are both necessary in the calculation of trading profit. T/F
(b) Stock taking is only necessary in large catering operations. T/F
(c) What would be the effect on the trading profit figure if closing stock was overvalued when stocktaking?
(d) Which of the following details will a bin card contain? reference number; issue unit; goods in; portion sizes.
4. Which one of the following can best prevent cross-contamination in the storage area: (a) separate storage areas for cooked and uncooked food; (b) correct temperature in the refrigerator; (c) regular hygiene checks; (d) stock rotation.
5. You are required to make 64 portions of the sweet known as Bavarois. The recipe indicates that you need 8 pints of cream. Cream is supplied from the dairy in litres. How much would you order for this dish?
6. Indicate the best portion size for each of the following.

Smoked salmon	6ozs	100g	50g
Consommé	150cm³	100cm³	250cm³
Spaghetti (main course)	60g	30g	250g
Darne of salmon	180g	250g	300g

CHAPTER 6

1. To calculate the value of materials sold for a trading period the formula is:
(a) Opening stock − purchases = closing stock   T/F
(b) Closing stock + purchases = opening stock   T/F
(c) Opening stock + purchases = closing stock   T/F

2. Which of the following costs would normally change as a result of increased business?

	unchanged	change in proportion to trade	change partially
(a) Materials	[]	[]	[]
(b) Labour costs	[]	[]	[]
(c) Rates	[]	[]	[]
(d) Depreciation on premises	[]	[]	[]
(e) Fuel	[]	[]	[]
(f) Insurance	[]	[]	[]
(g) Replacements	[]	[]	[]
(h) Laundry	[]	[]	[]

3. If an establishment is working on the basis of marking up dishes at 40 per cent food cost what is the selling price of the following?

	Food cost	à la carte menu selling-price		
(a)	96p	£2.00	£2.40	£1.20
(b)	£1	£2.00	£2.50	£1.50
(c)	80p	£2.50	£1.60	£2.00
(d)	£2.33	£4.00	£5.00	£6.00
(e)	15	38p	40p	55p

4. Which is the best procedure for estimating the selling-price per head of a set function menu? (a) to round up the cost of each individual dish before adding them all together to price the function menu per head; (b) to work out the exact cost of the total menu before rounding up the price per head.

5. Which of the following statements are true of standard recipes? (a) they may contain photographs; (b) they always show the costings; (c) they always show the yield of portions; (d) they may be built into a computerised control system.

6. Which three from the following list best aid portion control? (a) purchase specifications; (b) standard-sized crockery; (c) multiple service-points; (d) staff training; (e) scales; (f) standard recipes.

CHAPTER 7

Choose from the list a–c, the letter indicating the correct answer to questions 1–5: (a) Table d'hôte; (b) à la carte; (c) Special function

1. On which type of menu would you not normally feature 'Mixed Grill'?
2. On which type of menu would the price not normally appear on the menu?
3. Which type of menu is the most difficult to control for costs?
4. On which type of menu would you not normally feature 'Steak and Kidney Pudding'?
5. Which menu has a choice and a fixed price?

6. Which one of the following dishes (a)(b)(c)(d), would fit best into the menu below? (a) Suprême de Volaille Princesse; (b) Poulet Sauté Chasseur; (c) Carbonnade de Boeuf Flamande; (d) Vol-au-Vent de Volaille.

Menu
Consommé Julienne

————————?
Pommes Fondante
Asperge Polonaise

Mille-Feuilles

7. In menu balance the term repetition refers to: (a) words; (b) ingredients; (c) cooking process; (d) nutrients.

8. Which of the following dishes have the same colour? (a) Blanquette d'Agneau; (b) Pommes Nouvelle; (c) Chouxfleur Mornay; (d) Pommes Marquise.

9. Which of the following are functions of any type of menu? (a) advance information; (b) communication; (c) production schedule; (d) cost per head.

10. Which of the following are à la carte menu items? (a) Ragoût de boeuf; (b) Escalope de veau Holstein; (c) Contrefilet de boeuf rôti; (d) Omelette Arnold Bennett.

11. If the food cost of an à la carte dish is £1.50 what would be the selling price to yield 60 per cent gross profit?
(a) £3.75; (b) £3.00; (c) £4.50; (d) £3.90

12. Match the following

(a) Doria	(1) Green peas
(b) Argenteuil	(2) Spinach
(c) Conti	(3) Cucumber
(d) Clamart	(4) Cauliflower
(e) Florentine	(5) Asparagus
(f) Vichy	(6) Cherries
(g) Washington	(7) Lentils
(h) Montmorency	(8) Carrots
(i) Dubarry	(9) Green peas
(j) St Germain	(10) Sweetcorn

CHAPTER 8

1. Which of the following best describes *mise en place*? (a) the skills required to perform a task; (b) the principle of day-to-day kitchen routine preparation; (c) the classification of basic food preparations; (d) a series of recipes which comprise a menu.
2. Fonds de cuisine refer to: (a) all cookery processes used to prepare for a function; (b) all dishes prepared on a particular day; (c) the basic preparations from which dishes are prepared; (d) basic garnishes used for more than one dish.
3. Which is the most important rule in the routine care of stocks? (a) maintenance of rapid boiling; (b) skimming to remove grease and scum; (c) adding ingredients in stages; (d) stirring periodically.
4. Match the commodity in column two to the basic sauce in column one.

1. Béchamel	(a) egg yolks and oil
2. Velouté	(b) 3rd stage roux and estouffade
3. Espagnole	(c) egg-yolk sabayon and melted butter
4. Hollandaise	(d) 2nd stage roux and white stock
5. Mayonnaise	(e) 1st stage roux and infused milk

5. Identify *true* (T) or *false* (F) to the following statements:

(a) Soups are always served hot.	T/F
(b) Basic sauces may be used as a basis for some soups.	T/F
(c) A purée soup may be thickened with béchamel.	T/F
(d) Cream soups may be made from a velouté base.	T/F
(e) Consommé soups are always clarified.	T/F

6. Write down two examples of the appropriate hors-d'oeuvre in the categories below:
   (a) Hot simple
   (b) Hot compound
   (c) Cold simple
   (d) Cold compound
7. Which one of the following egg preparations can be cooked the day before and reheated? (a) omelette; (b) poached; (c) scrambled; (d) fried.
8. Match the two lists below:

1. Gnocchi Romaine	(a) choux paste base
2. Gnocchi Parisienne	(b) semolina base
3. Gnocchi Piédmontaise	(c) potato base

9. Which of the following preparations are obtainable from a small flat fish:

goujon	fillet
colbert	en tresse
tronçon	paupiette
suprême	délice
darne	en colère

10. Which of the following are usually hung before cooking: (a) duck; (b) turkey; (c) pheasant; (d) grouse; (e) venison; (f) chicken.

CHAPTER 9

1. The efficiency of a high-pressure steamer is improved by: a. air being excluded before the steam is introduced; b. dry steam is used; c. pressure always lower than 34 kPa; d. food items being covered.

2. The following types of radiation can be used to process food: a. gamma rays; b. microwaves; c. infra-red rays; d. ultra-violet rays.

3. The term *blanching* is used to describe: a. easier removal of tomato skin; b. removal of excess salt from meat; c. cooking vegetables slightly underdone to be reheated; d. immersing food for a short time in boiling water.

4. Heat is transferred to food in a general purpose oven by: a. forced air currents; b. radiation and convection; c. conduction and convection; d. natural convection.

5. Meat should be cooked to an internal temperature of 80°C to: a. prevent bacterial and parasitic infection; b. satisfy customer's expectations; c. reach an acceptable texture; d. improve keep qualities.

6. The main problem(s) with using a pressure deep-fryer is/are: a. not as economical as traditional deep-frying; b. increased fat absorption; c. not suitable for a crisp finish; d. food is not seen during cooking.

7. Which of the following items could not be cooked in a microwave oven: a. beefburgers; b. raw fish in a cooked sauce; c. croissants; d. trout.

8. The braising of food usually involves: a. a bed of root vegetables; b. steaming inside a lidded pan; c. stock; d. fat as the main ingredient of the cooking liquor.

CHAPTER 10

1. Gastronorm and Euronorm involve the same measurements. T/F
2. Modular equipment is used only in large establishments T/F
3. Gastronorm measurements refer to the outside of the container only T/F
4. The temperature at which hot food is held for service in a hotplate is 70°C. T/F
5. Microwave ovens have a cookery temperature. T/F
6. When in operation, the oil in cool zone deep fryers is cooler at the bottom than the top. T/F
7. Tilting kettles, because of their movement, cannot be heated by direct steam supply. T/F
8. The temperature in a forced air convection oven is hotter at the top than the bottom. T/F
9. A salamander grill heats from above and is suitable for glazing dishes and making toast. T/F
10. The storage period of blast chilled food should not exceed five days. T/F
11. Mayonnaise must never be stored in a refrigerator. T/F
12. In a restricted space a Pass Through Dish Washer would be preferable to a Conveyor Dish Washer. T/F
13. Aluminium saucepans may discolour white sauces. T/F
14. Jelly bags are used for both sweet and savoury preparations. T/F
15. All copper equipment is tin-lined. T/F
16. The most effective way of cleaning earthenware is to plunge straight into hot water and detergent immediately after use. T/F
17. Iron cooking implements must be kept lightly greased. T/F
18. Paper hand-towels are always disposable. T/F
19. Plastic containers are best suited for storing hot foods. T/F
20. Colour-coding can be used for chopping boards and knives and is to ensure that raw and cooked foods are prepared with different tools. T/F
21. A blunt knife is less likely to cause injury than a sharp one. T/F
22. Knives made of stainless steel have many advantages over steel ones. T/F
23. The three most important points to consider when planning the requirements of kitchen space are: (a) length of meal times; (b) number of people employed in the kitchen; (c) type of equipment used; (d) size of the menu featured; (e) type of food service system; (f) requirements of the Health and Safety at Work Act. T/F
24. Sinks should be fitted along external walls. T/F
25. Which are the two most important factors: kitchen floors should be selected on the basis of: (a) ease of cleaning; (b) not showing dirt; (c) non-slip.

26. Which are the two most important factors: kitchen wall surfaces should be selected on the basis of: (a) ease of cleaning; (b) attractive and hygienic appearance; (c) light-reflecting.

CHAPTER 11

1. In what ways does a Central Production Unit differ from a traditional kitchen?
   (a) fewer food handlers;
   (b) more hygienic;
   (c) production line operation;
   (d) high technology based.
2. Which of the following are the advantages of using Gastronorm equipment? (a) fuller utilisation of space; (b) improved hygiene because there is less movement of food; (c) portion-control easier; (d) more even cooking of larger quantities.
3. Which is the best cooking method for the regeneration of cook–chill dishes?: (a) baking; (b) roasting; (c) grilling; (d) steaming.
4. Which is the maximum period of time that unsealed cook–chill dishes may be kept before regeneration? (a) 5 days; (b) 10 days; (c) 12 days; (d) 14 days.
5. Which one of the following is the main difference between cook–chill and sous vide? (a) storage temperature; (b) regeneration method; (c) use of vacuum; (d) combination of raw and cooked ingredients.
6. Which one of the following is the correct minimum temperature to which cook–chill foods must be heated throughout before service? (a) 100°C; (b) 200°C; (c) 50°C; (d) 70°C.

CHAPTER 12

1. Match each item in list one with the appropriate definition in list two:

   List one   *List two*
   (a) rye   (1) starch derived from potato
   (b) gluten   (2) starch used in thickening
   (c) fécule   (3) protein in some cereals
   (d) maize   (4) used to make bread

2. Match the meat item in list one to the most appropriate description in list two:

   List one   *List two*
   (a) Flank   (1) suitable for grilling steak
   (b) Kidney   (2) poor quality of meat
   (c) Bobby veal   (3) used for barbecued spareribs
   (d) Bacon   (4) offal with a high % of iron
   (e) Breast of lamb   (5) coarse meat with a lot of connective tissue
   (f) Topside   (6) poor quality meat

3. Match the fish specified in list one to an appropriate cooking method in list two. (In some cases more than one cooking method could be used. However, once you have selected a cooking method, do not use it again for any other fish given in the question.)

List one	List two
(a) whitebait	(1) grilling
(b) lemon sole	(2) deep-frying
(c) trout	(3) boiling
(d) skate	(4) poaching
(e) herring	(5) meuniére

CHAPTER 13

1. Match the substances in list one with the description in list two:

List one	List two
(a) ascorbic acid	(1) flavour enhancer
(b) annatto	(2) natural food colour
(c) nitrate	(3) anti-oxidant
(d) monosodium glutamate	(4) used for curing meats

2. Which of the following nutrients is most likely to be deficient in the diets of lacto- and vegan vegetarians: (a) B12; (b) iron; (c) calcium; (d) B6.
3. Which of the following principles apply to the feeding of adolescents: (a) limit snacks between meals; (b) reduce energy content of foods; (c) offer 3–4 meals per day; (d) offer mineral supplements.
4. The term malnutrition is used to describe: (a) over-eating; (b) starvation; (c) inbalanced diets; (d) incorrect nutrition.
5. Match the following:

(a) requirements increase whilst taking oral contraceptives	(1) Vitamin D
(b) bedridden may need extra supplement	(2) Vitamin A
(c) overdoses cause yellowing of the skin	(3) iron
(d) Asian children may be at risk from deficiency	(4) pyridoxine

CHAPTER 14

1. Match the appropriate bacteria in list one to situation in list two:

List one
(a) *Salmonella typhimurium*
(b) *Campylobacter jejuni*

(c) *Staphylococcus aureus*
(d) *Clostridium botulinum*
(e) *Bacillus cereus*
(f) *Clostridium perfringens*

List two
(1) Frequently contaminating rice
(2) Possible cause of a *blown* can of food
(3) Contracted from raw milk
(4) Found in skin lesions
(5) Excreted in the faeces
(6) Produces toxins in the gut

2. 'On Saturday 10 January, 280 people at a factory ate a buffet supper. Two to three days later, 80 became ill with diarrhoea and stomach pains. Within one week they had all recovered.' Was the outbreak likely to have been caused by: (a) a bacterial food-poisoning intoxication; (b) a bacterial food-poisoning infection.

3. Match the following:
(a) Sterilant
(b) Detergent

(c) Sanitiser
(d) Antiseptic

(1) Kills all microbes and bacterial spores.
(2) Produces conditions unsuitable for bacterial growth.
(3) Kills some micro-organisms.
(4) Removes dirt and grease.

4. Which of the following is true? (a) Bacterial toxins always survive cooking temperatures; (b) Freezing temperatures immobilise pathogens; (c) Bacterial spores are not destroyed by cooking; (d) Vacuum-packaging might not inhibit the growth of anerobes.

5. High-risk foods should be kept: (a) below 5°C; (b) below 63°C; (c) between 5°C–63°C; (d) above 63°C.

6. Which of the following are high-risk foods? (a) gravy; (b) cooked meat; (c) synthetic cream; (d) raw vegetables.

7. Match the bacteria with one probable source of contamination:
(a) Salmonella
(b) Bacillus cereus
(c) Staphylococcus aureus
(d) Clostridium perfringens

1. Cockroaches
2. Food handler with flu
3. Soil
4. Raw meat

8. Which of the following are *typical* characteristics of the condition known as food-poisoning? (a) occurs within hours of eating contaminated food; (b) the body recovers from the illness usually without medication; (c) severe symptoms which subside in a short time; (d) long-term illness caused by consumption of contaminated food.

9. *Typical* food-poisoning symptoms could be caused by which of the following? (a) an allergy to strawberries; (b) eating mouldy cheese; (c) consumption of foods with chemical preservatives; (d) food which has been in contact with raw chicken.

10. Which of the following practices are likely to be the direct cause of a food poisoning outbreak? (a) the separation of raw and cooked food processes; (b) leaving food within the *danger zone* for long periods; (c) rapid chilling of cooked foods; (d) defrosting raw meat at 20°C.

CHAPTER 15

1. The Health and Safety at Work Act covers: (a) just the employees of the company; (b) both employees and customers; (c) all persons who may be affected by the business; (d) employees and contract-workers.
2. Which of the following are true statements relating to the Health and Safety at Work Act? (a) an employer is required to organise training for staff; (b) the formation of a safety committee is optional; (c) all establishments that serve food to the public are included; (d) all responsibility for health and safety rests with the employer; (e) all accidents must be reported to an employer.
3. Which one of the following fire extinguishers could be used for a fire where electricity was involved? (a) dry powder; (b) carbon dioxide; (c) foam; (d) water.
4. In the first-aid treatment of shock you would: (a) give hot sweet tea; (b) lay the patient down; (c) get the patient to an open window; (d) loosen the clothing.
5. An Environmental Health Officer is empowered to: (a) advise only on health and safety matters; (b) enter a premises at anytime to inspect; (c) immediately stop activities which infringe the Act; (d) enter every commercial premises that serves food.

ANSWERS

CHAPTER 1

Q1 (1) e (2) a (3) c (4) c (5) a (6) d
Q2 b d e
Q3 (a) 2 (b) 124 (c) 4 (d) 3 (e) 123 (f) 145 (g) 1
Q4 (a) F (b) T (c) T (d) T
Q5 (a) T (b) T (c) F (d) F (e) T
Q6 (a) ovens, grills, (b) (i) T (ii) T (iii) T (iv) T
Q7 a b
Q8 c
Q9 (a) F (b) T (c) T (d) F (e) F

CHAPTER 2

Q1 (a) T (b) F (c) T (d) T
Q2 (a) T (b) T (c) F (d) T

CHAPTER 3

Q1 menu
artistic
time
technology
influence
nutrition
simplicity
freshness
inventive
light

Q2 c e f g h
Q3 b c
Q4 c d e
Q5 (a) F (b) F (c) F (d) F (e) F
Q6 sugar   salt   fat   fibre

CHAPTER 4

Q1 a c
Q2 (a) 8 (b) 7 (c) 4 (d) 2 (e) 9 (f) 6 (g) 5 (h) 1 (i) 3
Q3 (1) e (2) c (3) i (4) f (5) i (6) d (7) d (8) h (9) h
Q4 b c e
Q5 (1) A B   D
    (2) A B   D
    (3) A   C
    (4) A B   D
    (5) A   D
    (6) A B C
    (7) A   C
    (8) A   C
    (9) A   C
    (10) A B   D
    (11) A B   D
    (12) A B   D
Q6 a c d
Q7 d e
Q8 a

CHAPTER 5

Q1 (a) 3 (b) 2 (c) 4 (d) 1 (e) 2
Q2 (i) c g h f d b e a
    (ii) c g
    (iii) h f a
    (iv) c f d h
Q3 (a) T (b) F (c) increase (d) first three
Q4 a
Q5 5
Q6 50g 250cm³ 60g 180g

CHAPTER 6

Q1 (a) F (b) F (c) F
Q2 (a) change in proportion
    (b) change partially
    (c) unchanged
    (d) unchanged
    (e) change partially
    (f) unchanged
    (g) change partially
    (h) change partially
Q3 (a) £2.40 (b) £2.50 (c) £2 (d) £6 (e) 38p
Q4 b
Q5 a c d
Q6 a d f

CHAPTER 7

Q1 c
Q2 c
Q3 b
Q4 b
Q5 a
Q6 b
Q7 a
Q8 a b c
Q9 a b c
Q10 b d
Q11 c
Q12 (a) 3 (b) 5 (c) 7 (d) 1 or 9 (e) 2 (f) 8 (g) 10 (h) 6 (i) 4 (j) 1 or 9

CHAPTER 8

Q1 b
Q2 c
Q3 b
Q4 (1) e (2) d (3) b (4) c (5) ab
Q5 (a) F (b) T (c) F (d) T (e) T
Q7 b
Q8 (1) b (2) a (3) c
Q9 goujon, colbert, filet, en tresse, paupiette, délice
Q10 c d e

CHAPTER 9

Q1 b
Q2 a, b, c
Q3 a, b, c, d
Q4 b
Q5 a
Q6 c
Q7 c
Q8 a, b, c

CHAPTER 10

Q1 F
Q2 F
Q3 F
Q4 F
Q5 T
Q6 T
Q7 F
Q8 F
Q9 T
Q10 T
Q11 F
Q12 T
Q13 T
Q14 T
Q15 F
Q16 F
Q17 T
Q18 T
Q19 F
Q20 T
Q21 F
Q22 T
Q23 ace
Q24 T
Q25 ac
Q26 a c

CHAPTER 11

Q1 c d
Q2 a b c d

Q3 d
Q4 a
Q5 c
Q6 d

CHAPTER 12

Q1 (a) 4 (b) 3 (c) 1 (d) 2
Q2 (a) 6 (b) 4 (c) 2 (d) 6 (e) 3 (f) 1
Q3 (a) 2 (b) 4 (c) 5 (d) 3 (e) 1

CHAPTER 13

Q1 (a) 3 (b) 2 (c) 4 (d) 1
Q2 a
Q3 a
Q4 d
Q5 (a) 4 (b) 3 (c) 2 (d) 1

CHAPTER 14

Q1 (a) 5 (b) 3 (c) 4 (d) 2 (e) b (f) 1
Q2 b
Q3 (a) 1 (b) 4 (c) 3 (d) 2
Q4 b c d
Q5 a
Q6 a b c
Q7 (a) 1 (b) 3 (c) 2 (d) 4
Q8 a b c
Q9 a d
Q10 b d

CHAPTER 15

Q1 C
Q2 ace
Q3 b
Q4 b
Q5 b c d

INDEX